BEST OF THE PERL JOURNAL

Web, Graphics, and Perl/Tk

Related titles from O'Reilly

The Best of the Perl Journal Series

Volume 1: Computer Science and Perl Programming

Volume 2: Web, Graphics, and Perl/Tk

Volume 3: Games, Diversions, and Perl Culture

Other Perl titles

Advanced Perl Programming	Perl Cookbook
Beginning Perl for Bioinformatics	Perl for System Administration
CGI Programming with Perl	Perl for Web Site Management
Embedding Perl in HTML with Mason	Perl Graphics Programming
Learning Perl on Win32 Systems	Perl in a Nutshell
Learning Perl	Perl Pocket Reference
Mastering Algorithms with Perl	Perl/Tk Pocket Reference
Mastering Perl/Tk	Programming Perl, 3rd Edition
Mastering Regular Expressions	Programming the Perl DBI
Perl & LWP	Programming Web Services with Perl
Perl & XML	Writing Apache Modules with Perl and C

Also available

The Perl CD Bookshelf

BEST OF THE PERL JOURNAL

Web, Graphics, and Perl/Tk

Edited by Jon Orwant

O'REILLY®

Beijing · Cambridge · Farnham · Köln · Paris · Sebastopol · Taipei · Tokyo

Web, Graphics, and Perl/Tk: Best of the Perl Journal
compiled and edited by Jon Orwant

Published by O'Reilly & Associates, Inc., 1005 Gravenstein Highway North, Sebastopol, CA 95472.

O'Reilly & Associates books may be purchased for educational, business, or sales promotional use. Online editions are also available for most titles (*safari.oreilly.com*). For more information, contact our corporate/institutional sales department: (800) 998-9938 or *corporate@oreilly.com*.

Editor:	Jon Orwant
Production Editor:	Colleen Gorman
Cover Designers:	Hanna Dyer and Ellie Volckhausen
Interior Designer:	David Futato

Printing History:

March 2003:	First Edition.

ISBN: 0-596-00311-0
[C]

Table of Contents

Part I.   Web

Part II. Graphics

Part III. Perl/Tk

Preface

Jon Orwant

This is the second of three "Best of the Perl Journal" O'Reilly books, containing the crème de la crème of the 247 articles published during the Perl Journal's 5-year existence as a standalone magazine. This particular book contains 39 articles covering the web, graphics, and Perl/Tk.

This book is divided into three sections:

Part I, *Web*

> This section contains 22 articles on how Perl can make the web do your bidding: CGI scripting, Apache/mod_perl programming, content management, the LWP library, securing and bulletproofing your web server, automating deductions about web page content, and even transmitting web pages wirelessly.

Part II, *Graphics*

> The nine articles in this section cover graphics, from the simple (generating charts and logos) to the advanced (OpenGL programming, ray tracing, evolving images, digitzing video) to the practical (generating images with the Gimp, and creating graphical applications with Glade and Gnome on Linux).

Part III, *Perl/Tk*

> Perl/Tk is Perl's most popular GUI toolkit, letting you create Perl-controlled graphical applications in minutes. This final section contains eight articles, six written by Perl/Tk guru Steve Lidie. Steve is also a co-author of *Mastering Perl/Tk* (O'Reilly); if the material here whets your appetite, look there for the full meal.

Be aware that this book has 23 different authors. Each section, and the articles within them, are loosely ordered from general to specific, and also from easiest to hardest where possible. (It wasn't always possible.) The book may be read straight through, or sampled at random. (In deference to the Perl motto, There's More Than One Way To Read It.)

Normally, O'Reilly likes their books to be written by one author, or just a few. Books that are collections of many independently-written chapters may get to press more quickly, but discordant tones, styles, and levels of exposition are jarring to the reader;

worse, authors writing in parallel and under deadline rarely know what other contributors have covered, and therefore can't provide the appropriate context to the reader.

That would indeed be a problem for this book had it been written in two months by 23 authors writing simultaneously. But in a sense, this book was written very carefully and methodically over six years.

Here's why. As editor of *The Perl Journal*, I had a difficult decision to make with every issue. TPJ was a grassroots publication with no professional publishing experience behind it; I couldn't afford to take out full color ads or launch huge direct-mail campaigns. So word of the magazine spread slowly, and instead of a steady circulation, it started tiny (400 subscribers for issue #1) and grew by several hundred each issue until EarthWeb began producing the magazine with issue #13.

Every issue, there were a lot of new subscribers, many of whom were new to Perl. Common sense dictated that I should include beginner articles in every issue. But I didn't like where that line of reasoning led. If I catered to the novices in every issue, far too many articles would be about beginner topics, crowding out the advanced material. And I'd have to find a way to cover the important material over and over, imparting a fresh spin every time. Steve Lidie's Perl/Tk column was a good example: it started with the basics and delved deeper with every article. Readers new to Perl/Tk who began with TPJ #15 didn't need to know about the intricacies of Perl/Tk menus covered in that issue; they wanted to know how to create a basic Perl/Tk application—covered way back in TPJ #1. But if I periodically "reset" topics and ran material already covered in past issues, I might alienate long-time subscribers.

So I did something very unusual for a magazine: I made it easy (and cheap) for subscribers to get every single back issue when they subscribed, so they'd always have the introductory material. As a result, I had to keep reprinting back issues as I ran out. This is what business calls a Supply Chain Management problem. The solution: my basement.

A side-effect of this approach was that the articles hold well together: they tell a consistent "story" in a steady progression from TPJ #1 through TPJ #20, with little redundancy between them. TPJ was always a book—it just happened to be published in 20 quarterly installments.

There is another advantage to having a book with programs by 23 Perl experts: collectively, they constitute a good sampling of Perl "in the wild." Every author has his own preferences—whether it's use of the English pragma, prototyping subroutines, embracing or eschewing object-oriented programming, or any of the other myriad ways in which Perl's expressivity is enjoyed. When you read a book by one author, you experience a single coherent (and hopefully good) style; when you read a book by dozens of experienced authors, you benefit from the diversity. It's an Olympic-size meme pool.

Naturally, there's some TPJ material that doesn't hold up well over age: modules become obsolete, features change, and news becomes history. Those articles didn't make the cut; the rest are in this book and its two companions, *Computer Science & Perl Programming: Best of the Perl Journal* and *Games, Diversions, and Perl Culture: Best of the Perl Journal*.

Enjoy!

Finding Perl Resources

Beginning with TPJ #10, I placed boxes at the top of most articles telling readers where they could find resources mentioned in the article. Often, it ended up looking like this, because nearly everything in Perl is available on CPAN:

```
Perl 5.004 or later.................CPAN
Class::ISA..........................CPAN
Memoize.............................CPAN
Class::Multimethods.................CPAN
```

The CPAN (Comprehensive Perl Archive Network) is a worldwide distributed repository of Perl modules, scripts, documentation, and Perl itself. You can find the CPAN site nearest you at *http://cpan.org*, and you can search CPAN at *http://search.cpan.org*. To find, say, the Class::Multimethods module, you could either search for "Multimethods" at *http://search.cpan.org*, or visit *http://cpan.org* and click on "Modules" and then "All Modules". Either way, you'll find a link for a *Class-Multimethods.tar.gz* file (which will include a version number in the filename). Download, unpack, build, and install the module as I describe in *http://cpan.org/modules/INSTALL.html*.

For information and code that isn't available on CPAN, there are Reference sections at the ends of articles.

Conventions Used in This Book

The following conventions are used in this book:

Italic
> Used for filenames, directory names, URLs, emphasis, and for the first use of a technical term.

Constant width
> Used for code, command output, program names, and email addresses.

Constant width bold
> Used for user input and code emphasis.

Constant width italic
> Used for code placeholders, e.g., open(*ARGUMENTS*).

Comments and Questions

Please address comments and questions concerning this book to the publisher:

O'Reilly & Associates, Inc.
1005 Gravenstein Highway North
Sebastopol, CA 95472
(800) 998-9938 (in the United States or Canada)
(707) 829-0515 (international/local)
(707) 829-0104 (fax)

There is a web page for this book, which lists errata, examples, or any additional information. You can access this page at:

http://www.oreilly.com/catalog/tpj2

To comment or ask technical questions about this book, send email to:

bookquestions@oreilly.com

For information about books, conferences, Resource Centers, and the O'Reilly Network, see the O'Reilly web site at:

http://www.oreilly.com

Acknowledgments

First, an obvious thanks to the 120 contributors, and a special shout-out to the most prolific: Lincoln D. Stein, Mark-Jason Dominus, Felix Gallo, Steve Lidie, Chris Nandor, Nathan Torkington, Sean M. Burke, and Jeffrey Friedl.

Next up are the people who helped with particular aspects of TPJ production. TPJ was mostly a one-man show, but I couldn't have done it without the help of Nathan Torkington, Alan Blount, David Blank-Edelman, Lisa Traffie, Ellen Klempner-Beguin, Mike Stok, Sara Ontiveros, and Eri Izawa.

Sitting in the third row are people whose actions at particular junctures in TPJ's existence helped increase the quality of the magazine and further its reach: Tim O'Reilly, Linda Walsh, Mark Brokering, Tom Christiansen, Jeff Dearth, the staff of Quantum Books in Cambridge, Lisa Sloan, Neil Bauman, Monica Lee, Cammie Hufnagel, and Sandy Aronson. Best wishes to the folks at CMP: Amber Ankerholz, Edwin Rothrock, Jon Erickson, and Peter Westerman.

Next, the folks at O'Reilly who helped this book happen: Claire Cloutier, Tom Dinse, Hanna Dyer, Paula Ferguson, Colleen Gorman, Sarmonica Jones, Linda Mui, Erik Ray, Betsy Waliszewski, Ellie Volckhausen, Neil Walls, Sue Willing, Joe Wizda, and the late great Frank Willison.

People who helped out in small but crucial ways: David H. Adler, Tim Allwine, Elaine Ashton, Sheryl Avruch, Walter Bender, Pascal Chesnais, Damian Conway, Eamon Daly, Liza Daly, Chris DiBona, Diego Garcia, Carolyn Grantham, Jarkko Hietaniemi, Doug Koen, Uri Guttman, Dick Hardt, Phil Hughes, Mark Jacobsen, Lorrie LeJeune, Kevin Lenzo, LUCA, Tuomas J. Lukka, Paul Lussier, John Macdonald, Kate McDonnell, Chris Metcalfe, Andy Oram, Curtis Pew, Madeline Schnapp, Alex Shah, Adam Turoff, Sunil Vemuri, and Larry Wall.

Finally, a very special thanks to my wife, Robin, and my parents, Jack and Carol.

## CHAPTER 1

Introduction

Jon Orwant

This book is a collection of 39 articles about Perl programs that create things to look at: web pages, Perl/Tk applications, and for lack of a better word, pictures. Much of Perl's success is due to its capabilities for developing web sites; the Web section covers popular topics such as CGI programs, mod_perl, spidering, HTML parsing, security, and content management. The Graphics section is a grab bag of techniques, ranging from simple graph generation to ray tracing and real time video digitizing. The final third of the book shows you how to use the popular Perl/Tk toolkit for developing graphical applications. Perl/Tk programming is different from conventional Perl programming, and learning it takes a little effort, but it pays off: once you've got the basics down, you can create standalone graphical applications in minutes—and they'll work on both Unix/Linux and Windows without a single change.

There are still some people who think of Perl as a language tailored for text processing or system administration, simply because it's so good at those duties. But Perl has emerged as a compelling choice for visual tasks as well—not because of any intrinsic support for graphics, but because it allows you to program quickly regardless of the problem domain.

Never underestimate the utility of rapid prototyping. Many programmers enjoy programming because, when you get right down to it, they're impatient. We hate the delayed gratification inherent in other endeavors. A biological experiment might take months before revealing success or failure; a mistake in March might not be discernible until July. If you write an article or a book, it'll be months before you can see it in print. Programming, in contrast, is kinder. You can run a program and know immediately whether it works. Programmers receive little bits of gratification all along the way, especially if the programs are built in parts and snapped together (as all serious programs should be).

That goes double for Perl; its expressivity, speed, and interpreted nature give its users near-instant gratification. Perl programmers spend less time waiting.

It goes triple for visual problem domains. Pictures are the most effective way we know to convey large amounts of information. You can tell at a glance whether your web page or data visualization worked, far faster than linearly scanning a ranked list or otherwise examining textual data. The best way to interpret complex phenomena is by exploiting the inherent parallelism of the human visual system, whether the domain is protein folding, financial planning, or (more generally) finding patterns in data with many dimensions. In fact, one of the quickest ways to find patterns in data with more than three dimensions is to map each dimension onto a feature of a human face—noses, eyes, and so forth—and then view all the faces at once. These are called *Chernoff faces* after their inventor, the statistician Herman Chernoff.

First up: the Web articles, introduced by one of the seminal figures in web development: Lincoln Stein, the inventor of the Perl CGI module.

PART I

Web

Much of Perl's fame is due to the Web. The CGI module, mod_perl, and easy HTML manipulation make Perl the language of choice for many web developers, and the 22 articles in this section provide a tour of the myriad ways in which Perl can be applied to the web.

We start off with three articles from Lincoln Stein, the TPJ web columnist. He begins with *CGI Programming*, an article from the premier issue that introduced his most famous contribution to Perl: the CGI module. He follows up with *Saving CGI State* and *Cookies*, which show you how user information can be maintained across all the pages in your site, either indefinitely or just for the duration of a browsing session.

Lincoln's first three articles rely on the CGI module, which allows your web server to serve web pages made from the HTML your Perl programs print. This requires the web server to launch Perl every time someone visits your web page. An obvious shortcut is to keep the Perl interpreter around in memory, and that's exactly what the Apache web server can do by using mod_perl, introduced by Lincoln and mod_perl creator Doug MacEachern in *mod_perl*. mod_perl also gives Perl sweeping access to many of the tasks that web servers can perform, such as proxying, authentication, and authorization; these are discussed in Lincoln and Doug's article, and elaborated upon in Mike Fletcher's *Creating mod_perl Applications*, Lincoln's *Proxying with mod_perl*, and Michael Parker's *Authentication with mod_perl*. Lincoln concludes the section by showing how to use mod_perl to add navigation bars to each page on a web site.

We then turn from web servers to web clients, with seven articles about downloading and manipulating web pages. This is nearly always done using the modules supplied in Gisle Aas's LWP bundle (also known as *libwww-perl*) available on CPAN. Lincoln introduces LWP in *Scripting the Web with LWP*, and Dan Gruhl and myself continue with *Five Quick Hacks: Downloading Web Pages*, demonstrating how LWP can turn web pages (for news, weather, U.S. street addresses, stock quotes, and currency exchange rates) into makeshift web services. Rob Svirskas follows up with an article showing how those programs can be made to work through proxy servers in *Downloading Web Pages Through a Proxy Server*, and then Ken MacFarlane and Sean M. Burke show how to parse the resulting HTML in *HTML::Parser* and *Scanning HTML*. Finally, the mysterious Tkil shows how to write a web spider in one line of Perl (*A Web Spider in One Line*), and Ed Hill describes using LWP to create a personalized newspaper in *webpluck*.

Returning to web servers, two articles by Lincoln show how to ensure that your server is up to the demands of the always populous and occasionally malicious public in *Torture-Testing Web Servers and CGI Scripts* and *Securing Your CGI Scripts*. Joe Johnston then demonstrates Perl's most popular content management system in *Building Web Sites with Mason*.

Lincoln follows with two articles on the lighthearted side, but with nonetheless valuable techniques: *Surreal HTML* turns web page content into a parody of itself (demonstrating HTML filters along the way), and *Web Page Tastefulness* rates the tastefulness of web pages, which can be used to rank web pages by how vacuous they seem. If a web page turns out to have real content, your Perl program can create an automatic summary using the system described by computer scientists Ave Wrigley and Tony Rose in *Summarizing Web Pages with HTML::Summary*. Finally, Dan Brian describes how to make your web site's content available to mobile phones in *Wireless Surfing with WAP and WML*.

## CHAPTER 2

CGI Programming

Lincoln D. Stein

In this first article, I introduce you to the elements of CGI scripting using the basic CGI module, CGI.pm. In subsequent articles, I cover the more advanced CGI::* library, a collection of modules providing an object-oriented class hierarchy which gives you more control over the behavior of CGI scripts.

CGI stands for Common Gateway Interface; it's the standard way to attach a piece of software to a World Wide Web URL. The majority of URLs refer to static files. When a remote user requests the file's URL, the web server translates the request into a physical file path and returns it. However, URLs can also refer to executable files known as *CGI scripts*. When the server accesses this type of URL, it executes the script, sending the script's output to the browser. This mechanism lets you create dynamic pages, questionnaires, database query screens, order forms, and other interactive documents. It's not limited to text: CGI scripts can generate on-the-fly pictures, sounds, animations, applets, or anything else.

CGI Programming Without CGI.pm

Basic CGI scripts are very simple:

```
#!/usr/bin/perl

print "Content-type: text/html\015\012";
print "\015\012";

chomp($time = `date`);

print <<EOF;
<HTML><HEAD>
<TITLE>Virtual Clock</TITLE>
</HEAD>
<BODY>
<H1>Virtual Clock</H1>
At the tone, the time will be
<STRONG>$time</STRONG>.
</BODY></HTML>
EOF
```

This script begins by printing out an *HTTP header*, which consists of a series of email style header fields separated by carriage-return/newline pairs. In Perl, this is normally represented as \r\n, but the actual ASCII values of those characters can vary from platform to platform. The HTTP standard requires the specific octal values 15 and 12, so we send those instead of \r\n.

After the last field, the header is terminated by a blank line—another \015\012 sequence. Although HTTP recognizes many different field names, the only one you usually need is Content-type, which tells the browser the document's MIME (Multipurpose Internet Mail Extension) type, determining how it will be displayed. You'll usually want to specify text/html for the value of this field, but any MIME type, including graphics and audio, is acceptable.

Next, the script uses the Unix date command to place the current time in the Perl variable $time. It then proceeds to print a short HTML document, incorporating the timestamp directly into the text. The output will look like Figure 2-1.

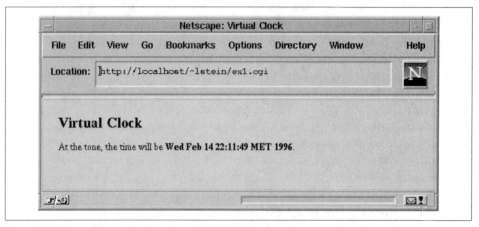

Figure 2-1. The web page displayed by a simple CGI script

Each time you reload this script you'll see a different time and date.

Things get trickier when you need to process information passed to your script from the remote user. If you've spent any time on the Web, URLs invoking CGI scripts will look familiar. CGI scripts can be invoked without any parameters:

```
http://some.site/cgi-bin/hello_world.pl
```

To send parameters to a script, add a question mark to the script name, followed by whatever parameters you want to send. Here, we send the two keywords CGI and perl to the *index_search.pl* program:

```
http://some.site/cgi-bin/index_search.pl?CGI+perl
```

This illustrates the *keyword list* style, in which the parameters are a series of keywords separated by + signs. This style is traditionally used for various types of index searches.

In the following URL, the `cat_no` parameter is set to 3921 and the `quantity` parameter is set to 2:

```
http://some.site/cgi-bin/order.pl?cat_no=3921&quantity=2
```

This shows a *named parameter list*: a series of "parameter=value" pairs with & characters in between. This style is used internally by browsers to transmit the contents of a fill-out form.

Both the script's URL and its parameters are subject to URL escaping rules. Whitespace, control characters, and most punctuation characters are replaced by a percent sign and the hexadecimal code for the character. For example, the space between the words "John Doe" is passed to a CGI script like this, since spaces are 32 in ASCII, and 32 in hexadecimal is 20:

```
http://some.site/cgi-bin/find_address.pl?name=John%20Doe
```

The CGI.pm Module

The problem with processing script parameters is that, for various historical reasons, the rules for fetching and translating the parameters are annoyingly complex. Sometimes the script parameters are found in an environment variable. But they can also be accessed via the command-line (`@ARGV`) array. Or, they can be passed via standard input. Usually you'll have to recognize the URL escape sequences and translate them, but in some circumstances the server will do that for you. Which rules apply depend on whether your script was generated by a GET or POST request (the former is usually generated when a user selects a hypertext link; the latter when a browser submits the contents of a fill-out form), whether the parameters are formatted using the keyword list or named parameter styles, and whether the browser takes advantage of the Netscape 2.0 file upload feature.

Fortunately, the CGI.pm module (and the CGI::* modules discussed in subsequent articles) knows the rules. It takes care of the details so that you can concentrate on your application. CGI.pm is distributed with Perl and is also available on CPAN.

CGI.pm includes several functions:

- It parses and decodes CGI parameter lists.
- It provides access to HTTP header information provided by the browser and server.
- It provides an easy way of generating HTTP header responses.
- It acts as a shortcut HTML generator for creating fill-out forms, and produces HTML that helps maintain the state of a form from page to page.

Using CGI.pm, we can enhance the simple virtual clock script to allow the remote user some control over the time format. This script allows the user to control whether the time, day, month, and year are displayed, and toggle between displaying the time in 12-hour or 24-hour format.

```perl
#!/usr/bin/perl

use CGI;

$q = new CGI;
if ($q->param) {
    if ($q->param('time')) {
        $format = ($q->param('type') eq '12-hour') ? '%r ' : '%T ';
    }
    $format .= '%A ' if $q->param('day');
    $format .= '%B ' if $q->param('month');
    $format .= '%d ' if $q->param('day-of-month');
    $format .= '%Y ' if $q->param('year');
} else { $format = '%r %A %B %d %Y' }

chomp($time = `date '+$format'`);

# print the HTTP header and the HTML document
print $q->header;
print $q->start_html('Virtual Clock');

print "<H1>Virtual Clock</H1>At the tone, the time will be <STRONG>$time</STRONG>.";

print "<HR><H2>Set Clock Format</H2>";

# create the clock settings form
print $q->start_form, "Show: ";
print $q->checkbox(-name=>'time', -checked=>1),
      $q->checkbox(-name=>'day', -checked=>1);

print $q->checkbox(-name=>'month', -checked=>1),
      $q->checkbox(-name=>'day-of-month', -checked=>1);

print $q->checkbox(-name=>'year', -checked=>1), "<P>";
print "Time style: ",
      $q->radio_group(-name=>'type', -values=>['12-hour','24-hour']), "<P>";

print $q->reset(-name => 'Reset'), $q->submit(-name => 'Set');
print $q->end_form;
print $q->end_html;
```

Before I explain how this program works, you can see the web page it generates in Figure 2-2.

Let's walk through this script step by step:

1. We load the CGI module and invoke the new method of the CGI class. This creates a new CGI object, which we store in the Perl variable $q. Parameter parsing takes place during the new call, so you don't have do it explicitly.

2. Next, using specifications determined by the script parameters, we create a format string to pass to the Unix date command. The key to accessing script parameters is the CGI param call, which is designed for the named parameter list style of script argument. (Another method call, keywords, is used to access keyword lists.)

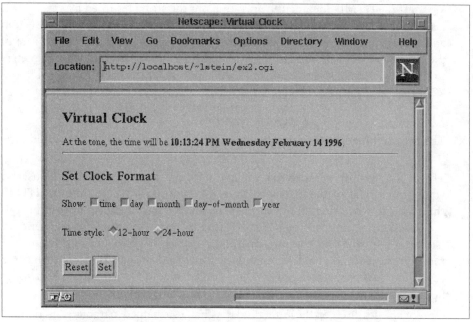

Figure 2-2. The web page generated by the CGI.pm script

Called without arguments, param returns an array of all the named parameters. Called with the name of a parameter, param returns its value, or an array of values if the parameter appears more than once in the script parameter list. In this case, we look for parameters named time, day, month, day-of-month, year, and style. Using their values, we build up a time format specifier to pass to the date command (see its manual page for details). If no parameters are present—for instance, if the script is being called for the very first time—we create a default format specifier. Then we call the date command and save its value in $time as before.

3. We create the HTTP header using the CGI header method. This method returns a string containing a fully-formed HTTP header, which the program immediately prints out. Called without any parameters, header returns a string declaring that the document is of the content type text/html. To create documents of other MIME types, you can call header with the MIME type of your choice. For example:

```
print $q->header('image/gif');
```

You can also use the named-parameter style of calling to produce headers containing any of the fields defined in the HTTP protocol:

```
print $q->header(       -Status => 200,
                        -Type => 'image/gif',
                        -Pragma => 'no cache',
            '-Content-length' => 8457);
```

You don't have to remember to write that blank line after the HTTP header; header does it for you.

4. We start the HTML document by printing out the string returned by start_html. Called with just one argument, this method returns an HTML <HEAD> section and the opening tag for the HTML <BODY>. The argument becomes the title of the document. As with header, you can call start_html with named parameters to specify such things as the author's email address, or the background color:

```
print $q->start_html(  -Title => 'Virtual Document',
                       -Author => 'andy@putamen.com',
                       -BGCOLOR => '#00A0A0');
```

5. The program then spits out a few lines of HTML, including the formatted time string.

6. This is followed by a horizontal line and a fill-out form that allows the user to adjust the format of the displayed time. CGI.pm has a whole series of HTML shortcuts for generating fill-out form elements. We start the form by printing out the <FORM> string returned by the start_form method, and then create a series of checkboxes (using the checkbox method), a pair of radio buttons (using the radio_group method), and the standard Reset and Submit buttons (using the reset and submit methods). There are similar methods for creating text input fields, popup menus, scrolling lists, and clickable image maps.

One of the features of these methods is that if a named parameter is defined from an earlier invocation of the script, its value is "sticky": a checkbox that was previously turned on will remain on. This feature makes it possible to keep track of a series of user interactions in order to create multipart questionnaires, shopping-cart scripts, and progressively more complex database queries. Each of these methods accepts optional arguments that adjust the appearance and behavior; for example, you can adjust the height of a scrolling list with the -size parameter. After we finish the form, we close it with a call to end_form.

7. We end the virtual document by printing the string returned by end_html, which returns the </BODY> and </HTML> tags.

In addition to its basic parameter-parsing, HTTP header-creating, and HTML shortcut-generating abilities, CGI.pm contains functions for saving and restoring the script's state to files and pipes, generating browser redirection instructions, and accessing useful information about the transaction, such as the type of browser, the machine it's running on, and the list of MIME types it can accept.

The next article will discuss how to handle errors generated by CGI scripts, and additional techniques for maintaining state in CGI transactions.

## CHAPTER 3

Saving CGI State

Lincoln D. Stein

We live in a stateful world. Just to be certain, I collected a few examples this morning:

1. Today I'm in a certain frantic state of mind because this article is due. I'll be this way for at least the rest of the afternoon, or until the article is done, whichever comes first. This is an example of a short-term state.

2. The federal budget is in a dreadful state of affairs that won't clear up until the last state has voted in the general election. This is an example of a long-term state.

3. The weather is truly lovely today with balmy spring weather and bright sunshine. Because this New England, however, it'll stay nice only until sometime tonight, when the weather report predicts a snowstorm followed by an iron frost. This is typical of an unstable state.

If the world has state, why doesn't the Web? It would seem reasonable for the Web to have some memory. After all, people do tend to hang around a site for a while, exploring here and there. It would seem only polite for a web site to remember the user who's been rattling around inside it for the past hour. But the HTTP protocol is stateless. Each request for a document is a new transaction; after the document is delivered, the web server wipes its hands of the whole affair and starts fresh.

The HTTP protocol was designed that way because a stateless model is appropriate for the bulk of a web server's job: to listen for requests for HTML documents and deliver them without fuss, frills, or idle chitchat. That the implementors of the protocol saw fit to build this stateless protocol on top of the connection-oriented TCP network communications protocol, ensuring the Web is hobbled by the performance limitations of TCP without reaping any of its benefits, is a small irony we won't discuss further.

State in CGI Scripts

CGI scripts in particular fit the stateless model poorly. Many CGI scripts are search engines of some sort. People pose a question, the CGI script does a search, and returns an answer. The user looks at the results, refines or modifies his question, and asks again. Unfortunately, by the time the user has refined his query and wants to build on previous results, the original CGI script has terminated, and the search has to start all over again. Or consider CGI shopping carts. A user browses around an online catalog for a while, and whenever something takes his fancy, he presses a button that adds it to his shopping cart. When he's ready, he reviews the contents of the cart and (the vendor hopes) presses a button that performs an online order.

In the absence of any stateful behavior in HTTP itself, CGI script writers have to keep track of state themselves. There are several techniques for doing this: most of them rely on tricking or cajoling the browser into keeping track of the state for you.

- Maintain state variables in the CGI parameters. The simplest trick is to store all the data you want to keep track of in the query string passed from the browser to the CGI script. You can store the data directly in the URL used in a GET request, or as settings in a fill-out form. As the previous column showed, this is relatively easy to do with CGI.pm, because it was designed to create "sticky" state-maintaining forms. This paradigm breaks down, however, when there's a lot of data to keep track of or when it's important to maintain a chronologically accurate record of the user's actions even when the user hits the Back and Forward buttons.

- Maintain the state on the server side with a specially-spawned HTTP server. You can defeat the limitation on HTTP by creating a state-aware web server. When a remote user starts a session, you spawn a new HTTP server dedicated to maintaining the state of that session, and you redirect the user to the new server's URL. This is how the state-maintaining MiniSvr module works, available on CPAN.

- Save the session's state to a disk file and use a session key to keep track of the files. This technique works even when there's large amounts of state data, and requires minimal data to be stored on the browser side of the connection. This is the technique that I'll focus on in this article.

A Sample State-Maintaining CGI Script

Example 3-1 shows a state-maintaining CGI script called remember.cgi. When invoked, it displays a form containing a single text input field and two buttons labeled ADD and CLEAR (see Figure 3-1). The user may type a short phrase into the text field and press ADD. This adds the phrase to the bottom of a growing list of phrases displayed at the bottom of the page. When the user presses CLEAR, the list is emptied.

Example 3-1. A state-maintaining CGI script

```
01 #!/usr/bin/perl
02 # Collect the user's responses in a file and echo them back when requested.
03
04 $STATE_DIR = "./STATES"; # must be writable by 'nobody'
05
06 use CGI;
07
08 $q = new CGI;
09 $session_key = $q->path_info( );
10 $session_key =~ s|^/||; # get rid of the initial slash
11
```

Example 3-1. A state-maintaining CGI script (continued)

```
     # If no valid session key was provided, we generate one, and append it
     # to the URL as additional path information, and redirect the user to
     # this new location.

12 unless (&valid($session_key)) {
13     $session_key = &generate_session_key($q);
14     print $q->redirect($q->url( ) . "/$session_key");
15     exit 0;
16 }
17
18 $old_state = &fetch_old_state($session_key);
19
20 if ($q->param('action') eq 'ADD') { # Add any new items to the old list
21     @new_items = $q->param('item');
22     @old_items = $old_state->param('item');
23     $old_state->param('item', @old_items, @new_items);
24 } elsif ($q->param('action') eq 'CLEAR') {
25     $old_state->delete('item');
26 }
27
28 &save_state($old_state, $session_key); # Save the new list to disk
29
30 print $q->header;        # At last, generate something for the user to see.
31 print $q->start_html("The growing list");
32 print <<END;
33 <h1>The Growing List</h1>
34 Type a short phrase into the text field below. When you press <I>AD</I>, it
35 will be added to a history of the phrases that you've typed. The list is
36 maintained on disk at the server end, so it won't get out of order if you
37 press the "back" button. Press <I>CLEAR</I> to clear the list and start fresh.
38 END
39 print $q->start_form;
40 print $q->textfield(-name=>'item',-default=>'',-size=>50,-override=>1),"<p>";
41 print $q->submit(-name=>'action', -value=>'CLEAR');
42 print $q->submit(-name=>'action', -value=>'ADD');
43 print $q->end_form;
44 print "<hr><h2>Current list</h2>";
45
46 if ($old_state->param('item')) {
47     print "<ol>";
48     foreach $item ($old_state->param('item')) {
49         print "<li>",$q->escapeHTML($item);
50     }
51     print "</ol>";
52 } else { print "<i>Empty</i>" }
53
54 print <<END;
55 <hr><address>Lincoln D. Stein, lstein\@genome.wi.mit.edu<br>
56 <a href="/">Whitehead Institute/MIT Center for Genome Research</a></address>
57 END
58 print $q->end_html;
59
```

Example 3-1. A state-maintaining CGI script (continued)

```
   # Silly technique: we generate a session key from the remote IP address
   # plus our PID. More sophisticated scripts should use a better technique.
60 sub generate_session_key {
61     my $q = shift;
62     my ($remote) = $q->remote_addr;
63     return "$remote.$$";
64 }
65
66 sub valid {          # Make sure the session ID passed to us is valid
67     my $key = shift; # by looking for pattern ##.##.##.##.##
68     return $key =~ /^\d+\.\d+\.\d+\.\d+\.\d+$/;
69 }
70


   # Open the existing file, if any, and read the current state.
   # We use the CGI object here, because it's straightforward to do.
   # We don't check for success of the open(  ), because if there is
   # no file yet, the new CGI(FILEHANDLE) call will return an empty
   # parameter list, which is exactly what we want.

71 sub fetch_old_state {
72     my $session_key = shift;
73     open(SAVEDSTATE, "$STATE_DIR/$session_key");
74     my $state = new CGI(SAVEDSTATE);
75     close SAVEDSTATE;
76     return $state;
77 }
78
79 sub save_state {
80     my($state,$session_key) = @_;
81     open(SAVEDSTATE, ">$STATE_DIR/$session_key") ||
82     die "Failed opening session state file: $!";
83     $state->save(SAVEDSTATE);
84     close SAVEDSTATE;
85 }
```

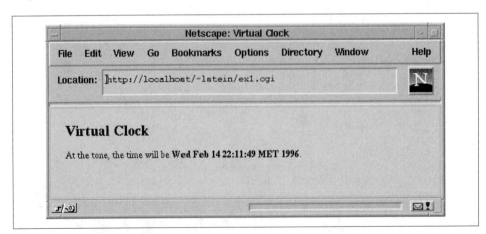

Figure 3-1. A state-maintaining form

The script works by maintaining each session's state in a separate file. The files are kept in a subdirectory that is readable and writable by the web server daemon. We keep track of the correspondence between files and browser sessions by generating a unique session key when the remote user first accesses the script. After the session key is generated, we arrange for the browser to pass the key back to us on each subsequent access to the script.

The technique this script uses to maintain the session key is to store it in the "additional path information" part of the URL. This is the part of the URL between the name of the script and the beginning of the query string. For example, in the URL:

```
http://toto.com/cgi-bin/remember.cgi/202.2.13.1.117?item=hi%20there
```

the text /202.2.13.1.117 is the additional path information. Although the additional path information syntax was designed for passing file information to CGI scripts, there's no reason it can't be used for other purposes, and it's often easier to keep the session key here than mixing it up with the other script parameters.

Lines 8 to 16 are responsible for generating a unique session key. After creating a new CGI object, the script fetches the additional path information and strips off the initial slash (lines 9–10). The session key is next passed to the subroutine valid (lines 66–69). This subroutine performs a pattern match on the session key to ensure that it is a key generated by our program rather than something that the user happened to type in. Importantly, the valid subroutine also returns false if the session key is an empty string, which happens the first time our script is called.

If the session key is blank or invalid we generate a new key (lines 12–16) using the subroutine generate_session_key. This subroutine, located at lines 60–64, is responsible for generating something that won't conflict with other concurrent sessions. In this example we use the simple but imperfect expedient of concatenating the remote machine's IP address with the CGI script's process ID.

After creating a new session key we generate a redirect directive to the browser, incorporating the session key into the new URL. If our script's URL is *http://toto.com/cgi-bin/remember.cgi* and the newly-generated session key is 202.2.13.1.117, we redirect the browser to *http://toto.com/cgi-bin/remember.cgi/202.2.13.1.117*.

The scripts exists after printing the redirect. It will be reinvoked almost immediately by the browser when it retrieves the new URL/session key combination.

The remainder of the script, from line 18 onward, contains the code that is invoked when the browser provides a valid session key. Line 18 calls fetch_old_state to retrieve the current list of text lines. This subroutine, defined in lines 71–77, opens up a file that contains the saved state by using the session key directly as the name of the file. More sophisticated scripts will want to use the session key in more clever ways, such as the key to a record in a DBM file or a handle into a relational database session.

fetch_old_state opens the file indicated by the session key, ignoring any "file not found" errors, and passes the filehandle to the CGI new method. This creates a new CGI object with parameters initialized from data stored in the file. We create a new CGI object here solely because its param method offers a convenient way to store multiple named parameters and because of its ability to save and restore these named parameters to a file. We don't check first whether the file exists. If the file doesn't exist already, the CGI new method returns an empty parameter list, which is exactly what we want. We close the file and return the new CGI object.

We now have two CGI objects. The first object, stored in the variable $q, was initialized from the current query and contains the contents of the text field and information about which button the user pressed when he submitted the fill-out form. The second object, stored in the variable $old_state, is the CGI object initialized from the saved file, and contains cumulative information about the user's previous actions.

Lines 20 to 26 manipulate the saved state depending on the user's request. We find out which button the user pressed by examining the CGI query's action parameter (line 20). If equal to ADD, we recover the contents of the text field from the query parameter item and add it to the cumulative list (line 23). If the action parameter is CLEAR, then we clear the list completely (line 25). Otherwise, no button was pressed and we continue onward.

Next, we save the updated list back to disk with save_state, which reverses the process by opening up the file indicated by the session key and using the CGI save method to dump out the contents of $old_state.

So far no text at all has been transmitted to the browser. It's a good idea to do all the back end work first, because network delays can make your CGI script hang during output. If the user presses the "stop" button during this period your CGI script will be terminated, potentially leaving things in an inconsistent state.

Lines 30 through 58 generate the HTML document. The script generates the HTTP header followed by the HTML preliminaries and some explanatory text (lines 30–38). Next it creates the fill-out form, using the start_form, end_form, and form element generating subroutines discussed in the previous column. The only trick in this section is the use of the -override parameter in the call to textfield. We want the contents of this field to be blank each time the page is displayed. For this purpose we set the contents to an empty string and use -override to have CGI.pm suppress the usual sticky behavior of fields.

After closing the form, we print out the current list of phrases in lines 44–52. Because there's no control over what the user types into the text field, it's important to escape any special HTML characters (such as angle brackets and ampersands) before incorporating it into our own document. Otherwise the script might create a page that doesn't display properly. The escapeHTML method accomplishes this.

Last, we end the page with end_html and exit.

This script doesn't save a vast amount of state information: only one parameter, and a short one at that. However, the same techniques can be used to store and manipulate the contents of hundreds of parameters. In order to turn this from an example into a real world script, you'll need to make a few refinements.

You might want to change the way session keys are chosen. Although this script chooses its keys in a way that minimizes the chances of conflict between two sessions, it isn't suitable for security-sensitive applications. Such scripts should make sure that the remote user is entitled to use the provided session key in order to prevent one user from "stealing" another user's state. Checking the IP address for consistency is a one way to do this; password-protecting the script and incorporating the encrypted password into the session key would be an even better technique.

In order to make this script useful in the real world you'll also need to remove state files when they've gone out of date. Otherwise the scripts' PIDs will eventually roll over and start using ancient state files that are no longer valid. (There's also the risk of proliferating state files filling up your disk!) The easiest way to handle this on a Unix system is with a cron job that runs at regular intervals looking for old state files and deleting them.

Another thing you might want to change is the way the session key is maintained. Most browsers support a "magic cookie" field that is guaranteed to be maintained for the entire length of a browser/server session. You can set the browser's magic cookie when the script first accesses the script, using CGI.pm's set_cookie method, and retrieve it on subsequent invocations of the script using get_cookie.

In the next article I discuss cookies, a flexible and powerful way for a server to store state information inside a user's browser.

CHAPTER 4
Cookies

Lincoln D. Stein

A *cookie* is just a name=value pair, much like the named parameters used in the CGI query string and discussed in *CGI Programming*. When a web server or CGI script wants to save some state information, it creates a cookie or two and sends them to the browser inside the HTTP header. The browser keeps track of all the cookies sent to it by a particular server, and stores them in an on-disk database so that the cookies persist even when the browser is closed and reopened later. The next time the browser connects to a web site, it searches its database for all cookies that belong to that server and transmits them back to the server inside the HTTP header.

Cookies can be permanent or set to expire after a number of hours or days. They can be made site-wide, so that the cookie is available to every URL on your site, or restricted to a partial URL path. You can also set a flag in the cookie so that it's only transmitted when the browser and server are communicating via a secure protocol such as SSL. You can even create promiscuous cookies that are sent to every server in a particular Internet domain.

The idea is simple but powerful. If a CGI script needs to save a small amount of state information, such as the user's preferred background color, it can be stored directly in a cookie. If lots of information needs to be stored, you can keep the information in a database on the server's side and use the cookie to record a session key or user ID. Cookies now have their own standard (RFC 2109) and are accepted by all major browsers.

Creating Cookies

So how do you create a cookie? If you use the CGI.pm library, it's a piece of cake:

```
0 #!/usr/bin/perl
1
2 use CGI qw(:standard);
3
4 $cookie1 = cookie( -name => 'regular',
5                    -value => 'chocolate chip');
6 $cookie2 = cookie( -name => 'high fiber',
```

```
7                 -value => 'oatmeal raisin');
8 print header(-cookie => [$cookie1, $cookie2]);
```

Line 2 loads the CGI library and imports the :standard set of function calls. This allows you to call all of the CGI object's methods without explicitly creating a CGI instance—a default CGI object is created for you behind the scenes. Lines 4 through 7 create two new cookies using the CGI cookie method. The last step is to incorporate the cookies into the document's HTTP header. We do this in line 8 by printing out the results of the header method, passing it the -cookie parameter along with an array reference containing the two cookies.

When we run this script from the command line, the result is:

```
Set-cookie: regular=chocolate%20chip
Set-cookie: high%20fiber=oatmeal%20raisin
Content-type: text/html
```

As you can see, CGI.pm translates each space into %20, as the HTTP cookie specification prohibits whitespace and certain other characters such as the semicolon. (It also places an upper limit of a few kilobytes on the size of a cookie, so don't try to store the text of Hamlet in one.) When the browser sees these two cookies it squirrels them away and returns them to your script the next time it needs a document from your server.

Retrieving Cookies

To retrieve the value of a cookie sent to you by the browser, use cookie without a -value parameter:

```
0 #!/usr/bin/perl
1
2 use CGI qw(:standard);
3
4 $regular    = cookie('regular');
5 $high_fiber = cookie('high fiber');
6
7 print header(-type => 'text/plain'),
8 "The regular cookie is $regular.\n",
9 "The high fiber cookie is $high_fiber.";
```

In this example, lines 4 and 5 retrieve the two cookies by name. Lines 7 through 9 print out an HTTP header (containing no cookie this time), and two lines of text. The output of this script, when viewed in a browser, would be:

```
The regular cookie is chocolate chip.
The high fiber cookie is oatmeal raisin.
```

The cookie method is fairly flexible. You can save entire arrays as cookies by giving the -value parameter an array reference:

```
$c = cookie( -name => 'specials',
             -value => ['oatmeal', 'chocolate chip','alfalfa']);
```

Or you can save and restore entire hashes:

```
$c = cookie(-name => 'prices', -value => {          'oatmeal' => '$0.50',
                                           'chocolate_chip' => '$1.25',
                                                   'alfalfa' => 'free'   });
```

Later you can recover the two cookies this way:

```
@specials = cookie('specials');
%prices   = cookie('prices');
```

By default, browsers will remember cookies only until they exit, and will only send the cookie out to scripts with a URL path that's similar to the script that generated it. If you want them to remember the cookie for a longer period of time, you can pass an -expires parameter containing the cookie's shelf life to the cookie function. To change the URL path over which the cookie is valid, pass its value in -path:

```
$c = cookie(-name => 'regular',            -value => 'oatmeal raisin',
            -path => '/cgi-bin/bakery', -expires => '+3d');
```

This cookie will expire in three days' time (+3d). Other cookie parameters allow you to adjust the domain names and URL paths that trigger the browser to send a cookie, and to turn on cookie secure mode. The -path parameter shown here tells the browser to send the cookie to every program in /cgi-bin/bakery.

A Sample Cookie Program

Example 4-1 is a CGI script called configure.cgi that generates pages such as Figure 4-1. When you call this script's URL, you are presented with the fill-out form shown above. You can change the page's background color, the text size and color, and even customize it with your name. The next time you visit this page (even if you've closed the browser and come back to the page weeks later), it remembers all of these values and builds a page based on them.

Example 4-1. The configure.cgi script

```
00 #!/usr/bin/perl
01
02 use CGI qw(:standard :html3);
03
04 # Some constants to use in our form.
05 @colors = qw/aqua black blue fuchsia gray green lime maroon navy olive
               purple red silver teal white yellow/;
06 @sizes = ("<default>", 1..7);
07
08 # Recover the "preferences" cookie.
09 %preferences = cookie('preferences');
10
11 # If the user wants to change the name or background color, they can
12 foreach ('text', 'background', 'name', 'size') {
13     $preferences{$_} = param($_) || $preferences{$_};
14 }
15
```

Example 4-1. The configure.cgi script (continued)

```
16 # Set some defaults
17 $preferences{background} = $preferences{background} || 'silver';
18 $preferences{text}       = $preferences{text} || 'black';
19
20 # Refresh the cookie so that it doesn't expire.
21 $the_cookie = cookie( -name => 'preferences',
22                       -value => \%preferences,
23                        -path => '/',
24                     -expires => '+30d');
25 print header(-cookie => $the_cookie);
26
27 # Adjust the title to incorporate the user's name, if provided.
28 $title = $preferences{name} ? "Welcome back, $preferences{name}!"
                                : "Customizable Page";
29
30 # Create the HTML page, controlling the background color and font size.
31 #
32 print start_html(  -title => $title,
33                  -bgcolor => $preferences{background},
34                    -text => $preferences{text});
35
36 print basefont({SIZE=>$preferences{size}}) if $preferences{size} > 0;
37
38 print h1($title),<<END;
39 You can change the appearance of this page by submitting
40 the fill-out form below. If you return to this page any time
41 within 30 days, your preferences will be restored.
42 END
43 ;
44 # Create the form.
45 print hr,
46       start_form,
47
48       "Your first name: ",
49       textfield(   -name => 'name',
50                 -default => $preferences{name},
51                    -size => 30), br,
52       table(
53           TR(
54              td("Preferred"),
55              td("Page color:"),
56              td(popup_menu(   -name => 'background',
57                             -values => \@colors,
58                            -default => $preferences{background})
59              )
60           ),
61           TR(
62              td(''),
63              td("Text color:"),
64              td(popup_menu(   -name => 'text',
65                             -values => \@colors,
66                            -default => $preferences{text})
```

Example 4-1. The configure.cgi script (continued)

```
67                  )
68               ),
69            TR(
70              td(''),
71              td("Font size:"),
72              td(popup_menu(    -name => 'size',
73                              -values => \@sizes,
74                             -default => $preferences{size})
75              )
76            )
77         ),
78      submit(-label => 'Set preferences'),
79      end_form,
80      hr;
81
82 print a({HREF => "/"}, 'Go to the home page');
```

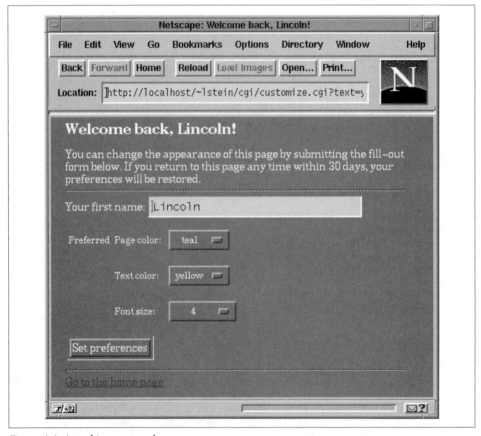

Figure 4-1. A cookie-aware web page

This script recognizes four CGI parameters used to change the configuration:

background
> Set the background color.

text
> Set the text color.

size
> Set the size to the indicated value (1–7).

name
> Set the username.

Usually these parameters are sent to the script via the fill out form that it generates, but you could set them from within a URL this way:

```
/cgi-bin/configure.pl?background=silver&text=blue&name=Stein
```

Let's walk through the code. Line 2 imports the CGI library, bringing in both the standard method calls and a number of methods that generate HTML3-specific tags. Next we define a set of background colors and sizes. The choice of colors may seem capricious, but it's not: These are the background colors defined by the HTML 3.2 standard, and they're based on the original colors used by the IBM VGA graphics display.

Line 9 is where we recover the user's previous preferences, if any. We use the cookie method to fetch a cookie named "preferences", and store its value in a like-named hash.

In lines 12 through 14, we fetch the CGI parameters named text, background, name, and size. If any of them are set, it indicates that the user wants to change the corresponding value saved in the browser's cookie. We store changed parameters in the %preferences hash, replacing the original values.

Line 17 and 18 set the text and background colors to reasonable defaults if they can't be found in either the cookie or the CGI script parameters.

Lines 21 through 25 generate the page's HTTP header. First, we use the cookie method to create the cookie containing the user's preferences. We set the expiration date for the cookie for 30 days in the future so that the cookie will be removed from the browser's database if the user doesn't return to this page within that time. We also set the optional -path parameter to /. This makes the cookie valid over our entire site so that it's available to every URL the browser fetches. Although we don't take advantage of this yet, it's useful if we later decide that these preferences should have a site-wide effect. Lastly, we emit the HTTP header with the -cookie parameter set.

In lines 30 to 36 we begin the HTML page. To make it personalizable, we base the page title on the user's name. If it's set, the title and level 1 header both become "Welcome back <name>!" Otherwise, the title becomes an impersonal "Customizable page." Line 32 calls the start_html method to create the top part of the HTML page. It sets the title, the background color and the text color based on the values in the %preferences array. Line 36 sets the text size by calling the basefont method. This simply generates a <BASEFONT> HTML tag with an appropriate SIZE attribute.

Lines 38 and up generate the content of the page. There's a brief introduction to the page, followed by the fill-out form used to change the settings. All the HTML is generated using CGI.pm "shortcuts," in which tags are generated by like-named method calls. For example, the hr method generates the HTML tag <HR>. As shown in the first column in this series, we start the fill-out form with a call to start_form, create the various form elements with calls to textfield, popup_menu, and submit, and close the form with end_form.

When I first wrote this script, the popup menus and popup menus in the form didn't line up well. Because all the elements were slightly different widths, everything was crooked. To fix this problem, I used the common trick of placing the form elements inside an invisible HTML3 table. Assigning each element to its own cell forces the fields to line up. You can see how I did this in lines 52 through 77, where I define a table using a set of CGI.pm shortcuts. An outer call to table generates the surrounding <TABLE> and </TABLE> tags. Within this are a series of TR methods, each of which generates a <TR> tag. (In order to avoid conflict with Perl's built-in tr/// operator, this is one instance where CGI.pm uses uppercase rather than lowercase shortcut names.) Within each TR call, in turn, there are several td calls that generate the <TD> (table data) cells of the HTML table.

Fortunately, my text editor auto-indents nicely, making it easy to see the HTML structure.

On a real site, of course, you'd want the user's preferences to affect all pages, not just one. This isn't a major undertaking; many modern web servers now allow you to designate a script that preprocesses all files of a certain type. You can create a variation on the script shown here that takes an HTML document and inserts the appropriate <BASEFONT> and <BODY> tags based on the cookie preferences. Now, just configure the server to pass all HTML documents through this script, and you're set.

In the next article, Doug MacEachern and I introduce mod_perl, a Perl interpreter embedded inside the Apache web server.

mod_perl

Lincoln D. Stein and Doug MacEachern

One of the minor miracles of the World Wide Web is that it makes client/server network programming easy. With the Common Gateway Interface (CGI), anyone can create dynamic web pages, frontends for databases, and even complex intranet applications with ease. If you're like many web programmers, you started out writing CGI scripts in Perl. With its powerful text-processing facilities, forgiving syntax, and tool-oriented design, Perl lends itself to the small programs for which CGI was designed.

Unfortunately, the love affair between Perl and CGI doesn't last forever. As your scripts get larger and your server more heavily loaded, you inevitably run into a performance barrier. A thousand-line Perl CGI script that runs fine on a lightly loaded web site becomes unacceptably slow when it increases to 10,000 lines and the hit rate triples. You might even have tried switching to a different programming language—and been disappointed. Because CGI relaunches the script every time it's requested, even compiled C won't give you the performance boost you expect.

If your applications go beyond simple dynamic pages, you might have run into the limitations of the CGI protocol itself. Many interesting things happen deep inside web servers, such as the smart remapping of URLs, access control and authentication, and the assignment of MIME types to documents. The CGI protocol doesn't give you access to these internals. You can neither find out what's going on nor intervene in any meaningful way.

To go beyond simple CGI scripting, you must use some protocol that doesn't rely on launching and relaunching an external program each time a script runs. Alternatives include NSAPI on Netscape servers, ISAPI on Windows servers, Java servlets, server-side includes, Active Server Pages (ASP), FastCGI, Dynamic HTML, ActiveX, JavaScript, and Java applets.

Sadly, choosing among these technologies is a no-win situation. Some choices lock you into a server platform for life. Others limit the browsers you can support. Many offer proprietary solutions that aren't available in other vendors' products. Nearly all of them require you to throw out your existing investment in Perl CGI scripts and reimplement everything from scratch.

The Apache server offers you a way out. Apache is a freely distributed, full-featured web server that runs on Unix and Windows NT systems. Derived from the popular NCSA *httpd* server, Apache dominates the Web; over half of the servers reachable from the Internet are Apache. Like its commercial cousins from Microsoft and Netscape, Apache has a programmer's API, allowing you to extend the server with modules of your own design. Apache modules can behave like CGI scripts, creating interactive pages on the fly. Or, they can make fundamental changes in the operation of the server, such as logging web accesses to a relational database or replacing standard HTTP authentication with a system integrated with Kerberos, DCE, or one-time passwords. Regardless of whether they're simple or complex, Apache modules perform much better than even the fastest conventional CGI scripts.

The best thing about Apache modules, however, is mod_perl. mod_perl is a fully-functional Perl interpreter embedded inside Apache. With mod_perl, you simply take your existing scripts and plug them in to the server, usually without any source code changes whatsoever. Your scripts run exactly as before, but many times faster—nearly as fast as fetching static HTML pages in many cases. Better yet, mod_perl offers a Perl interface to the Apache API, allowing complete access to Apache internals. Instead of writing Perl scripts, you can write Perl modules that control every aspect of the Apache server's operations. Move your existing Perl scripts over to mod_perl to get an immediate and dramatic performance boost. As you need to, you can add new features to your scripts that take advantage of the Apache API.

This article introduces mod_perl and shows how its unique features speed up web sites. Instructions for installing mod_perl are in the following sidebar, "Installing mod_perl."

Installing mod_perl

The mod_perl distribution is available from a CPAN site near you. Look in *modules/ by-module/Apache/* or visit the mod_perl home page at *http://perl.apache.org/* and *http://apache.perl.org/*. In addition to mod_perl, you'll need Perl 5.004 or higher, and Apache 1.2.0 or higher. Just like any other Perl module, you can build mod_perl and Apache from source code with these three commands:

```
perl Makefile.PL
make test
make install
```

To run mod_perl on the Windows version of Apache, you'll need Apache 1.3b3 or higher. A binary release of mod_perl for Windows is available.

mod_perl has been running strong on a great many Unix systems serving busy web sites, including the Denver Broncos site. (We can only speculate whether mod_perl contributed to their 1998 Superbowl win.)

Like most Perl utilities, mod_perl is free. It is distributed under the same terms as the Apache server license.

Transaction Handlers

mod_perl code is organized quite differently than conventional CGI scripts. Instead of writing standalone scripts, you create *handlers*, snippets of code that handle one or more of the phases of the Apache server's operation. "The Phases of mod_perl" shows the phases in chronological order.

To install handlers for any of these phases, you create a *.pm* file and add the appropriate mod_perl directive (shown in parentheses) to the server's *httpd.conf* or *.htaccess* file. You use a different directive for each phase. For example, you install a log phase handler with the directive PerlLogHandler, and a content phase handler with the directive PerlHandler (since the content handler is the one installed most frequently, it has the most generic name). So to install logging and URI translation handlers for all URIs below the virtual directory /magic, you could enter something like this in access.conf:

```
<Location /magic>
    PerlTransHandler    Apache::Magic
    PerlLogHandler      Apache::MyLog
</Location>
```

By convention, mod_perl modules are members of the Apache:: namespace. They don't inherit from Apache.pm; don't follow the convention if you don't care to.

Because Apache often associates content handlers with real files on the basis of their MIME types, you need a slightly different incantation when installing a content handler:

```
<Location /virtual>
    SetHandler      perl-script
    PerlHandler     Apache::Virtual
</Location>
```

All URIs that begin with /virtual will be passed through the module Apache::Virtual, regardless of whether they correspond to physical files on the server. The module will be passed the remainder of the URI to do with as it pleases. You can turn the remaining components of the URI path into a database query, treat them as verbs in a command language, or just plain ignore them.

A Typical Content Handler

Content handlers are straightforward. A minimal handler looks like this:

```
package Apache::Simple;
use Apache::Constants qw(OK DECLINED);

sub handler {
    my $r = shift;
    my $host = $r->get_remote_host;
    $r->content_type('text/plain');
    $r->send_http_header;
    $r->print("Good morning, $host!");
    return OK;
}

1;
```

The Phases of mod_perl

1. Module initialization (`PerlModule`, `PerlRequire`). Called once in the parent server, during startup and restarts. This is where the interpreter object is constructed.

2. Reading the configuration file (`<Perl> ... </Perl>`). Called by the parent server during startup and restarts to read the server configuration files. Also called when *.htaccess* files are found at request time.

3. Child initialization (`PerlChildInitHandler`). Called when a new Apache process has been launched.

4. Post read request (`PerlPostReadRequestHandler`). Called after the client request has been read, but before any other processing has been performed. Here's where you can examine HTTP headers and change them before Apache gets a crack at them.

5. URI translation (`PerlTransHandler`). Called to perform the translation between the virtual URI and the physical filename. For example, you can use this to override the way that Apache translates URIs into paths in the document root, or to perform fancy string mappings.

6. Header parsing (`PerlHeaderParserHandler`). Now that the URI has been mapped to a resource, the module is given another chance to look at the request. Here it can decide if the request structure needs to be modified in some way or terminated altogether before the server performs resource-intensive tasks.

7. Access control (`PerlAccessHandler`). When a URL is under access control (access restriction that doesn't require user authentication such as a password), `PerlAccessHandler` is called. This lets you specify your own restrictions for a directory, such as restricting access based on the day of the week or phase of the moon.

8. Authentication (`PerlAuthenHandler`). When invoked, this phase determines whether the user is who he says he is (by username and password).

9. Authorization (`PerlAuthzHandler`). This phase decides whether the user is permitted access to this particular URI.

10. MIME type mapping (`PerlTypeHandler`). This phase maps URIs to MIME types. You can use this to override Apache's default file extension to MIME type mappings. For example, you could look the MIME type up in a database, or infer it from the file's "magic number."

11. Miscellaneous fixups (`PerlFixupHandler`). This phase is invoked just before content generation so that modules can "fixup" the request now that it knows exactly who will handle the response. For example, this is where Apache's mod_env environment-handling module processes the `SetEnv` and `PassEnv` directives before passing the environment to CGI scripts.

12. Content generation (`PerlHandler`). This is where you create HTML pages, redirections, or any other type of HTTP response. This is the most frequently handled phase of the transaction.

—continued—

---

13. Logging (`PerlLogHandler`). Called after all the other phases to log the results. You can use this to customize Apache's log format, or to change logging completely. For example, you can compute summary statistics and store them in a relational database.
14. Registered cleanups (`PerlCleanupHandler`). Modules may register functions to be called after the client connection has been closed and just before the various request resources are cleaned up.
15. Child exit (`PerlChildExitHandler`). Called just before an Apache process terminates.

We first declare a unique package name: Apache::Simple. This step is very important. Because all mod_perl modules live in the same Perl process, namespace conflicts became a very real possibility. Next, we import two constants, OK and DECLINED, from the Apache::Constants module, bundled with the mod_perl distribution. Last, we declare a subroutine named `handler`. By default, mod_perl looks for a subroutine by this name when processing a handler directive.

When `handler` is called, it is passed an Apache request object as its single argument. This object contains information about the current request, and serves as an interface to the Apache server. You can use it to modify the request, to send information to the browser, and to request services from Apache such as filename translation. In this script, we first have the request object retrieve the name of the remote host. Then we create the response, first setting the HTTP header to MIME type text/plain with a call to content_type, and then sending the HTTP header with send_http_header. Next, we create the content with a call to the print method and send a friendly message to the browser. Finally, we return a result code of OK, telling Apache that we successfully handled the request. We could also have returned DECLINED, signalling Apache to try a different handler.

Here's how a content handler can redirect the browser to a different URI using an HTTP REDIRECT instruction:

```
package Apache::Redirect;

use Apache::Constants qw(OK DECLINED REDIRECT);

sub handler {
    my $r = shift;
    my $remote_url = 'http://www.somewhere.else/go/away.html';

    $r->header_out(Location=>$remote_url);
    return REDIRECT;
}

1;
```

In this case, we call the header_out method to set the outgoing HTTP Location header for the redirection. There's no need to invoke send_http_header or send a document body. Apache takes care of this for us when the return code is anything other than DECLINED or OK. In this case, returning REDIRECT makes Apache generate a 302 Moved Temporarily status code and send the HTTP headers. Normally, there's no need to send a document body because most clients will follow the Location header. However, to be HTTP-compliant, Apache generates a tiny document with a link to the new Location. If you're using a decent browser, you'll never know.

Apache::Registry

Although you can do everything you want with the content handlers just described, there are some drawbacks. First, during the development and debugging phase, Perl modules are not automatically recompiled when you change the source code—unless you configure the Apache::StatINC module. Second, as you can see, these handlers look nothing like CGI scripts. CGI scripts read from STDIN and write to STDOUT, and obtain configuration information from environment variables. Code written for CGI won't run as a content handler without radical alterations.

Enter Apache::Registry. Apache::Registry is a content handler that wraps around other Perl scripts. It emulates the CGI environment using a variety of tricks (such as tied filehandles). Most CGI scripts written as standalone applications will run unmodified under Apache::Registry, while those that know about mod_perl can take advantage of its special features. The best aspect of Apache::Registry is that it caches the compiled script inside a subroutine and executes it when a request comes in. Code is recompiled automatically when the source file is updated on disk. The handler acts as a registry for subroutines, hence its name.

A Typical Non-Content Handler

To demonstrate a handler that doesn't create content, consider the log handler. It gets called relatively late in the process—stage 13—after the response has been generated. We can create a LogMail handler to place watchpoints on particular files and directories. Whenever someone accesses a watchpointed directory, the server sends mail to some designated address. Here's an entry in *access.conf* that places a watchpoint on all the files in Lincoln's public directory:

```
<Location /~lstein>
   PerlLogHandler       Apache::LogMail
   PerlSetVar           mailto lstein@w3.org
</Location>
```

Note the PerlSetVar directive, which allows us to send configuration information to the handler. It expects two arguments: a key name and a value. In this case, the key name is mailto and the value is lstein@w3.org. Here's what LogMail.pm looks like:

```
package Apache::LogMail;
use Apache::Constants ':common';
```

```perl
sub handler {
    my $r       = shift;
    my $mailto  = $r->dir_config('mailto');
    my $request = $r->the_request;
    my $uri     = $r->uri;
    my $agent   = $r->header_in("User-agent");
    my $bytes   = $r->bytes_sent;
    my $remote  = $r->get_remote_host;
    my $status  = $r->status_line;
    my $date    = localtime;

    unless (open (MAIL, "|/usr/lib/sendmail -oi -t")) {
        $r->log_error("Couldn't open mail: $!");
        return DECLINED;
    }

    print MAIL <<END;
To: $mailto
From: Mod Perl <webmaster>
Subject: Somebody looked at $uri

At $date, a user at $remote looked at $uri using the $agent
browser. The request was $request, which resulted returned a code of
$status.

$bytes bytes were transferred.
END

    close MAIL;

    return OK;
}

1;
```

This script calls a bunch of Apache request methods to fetch the URI of the request, the remote host, the user agent (browser vendor information), the number of bytes transmitted, and the status of the response. It bundles everything up into a mail message that it sends with the trusty sendmail program. Note how we retrieve the value of the "mailto" configuration variable with a call to dir_config. The resulting mail looks something like this:

```
From: Mod Perl <webmaster@w3.org>
To: lstein@w3.org
Subject: Somebody looked at /~lstein/innocent.html
Date: Fri, 20 Feb 1998 21:42:04 -0500

At Fri Jan 20 21:42:02 1998, a user at www.readable.com
looked at /~lstein/innocent.html using the Mozilla/3.01Gold
(X11; I; Linux 2.0.30 i586) browser.

The request was GET /~lstein/innocent.html HTTP/1.0, which resulted
returned a code of 200 OK.

635 bytes were transferred.
```

In addition to sending out the message, Apache creates its usual log entry.

Getting Fancy: A Stately Script

In *Saving CGI State*, Lincoln bemoaned the difficulties in maintaining state across CGI scripting sessions. Because each CGI process exits after processing its request, you must resort to awkward workarounds in order to maintain the page's state. For example, you can hide state information in hidden fields of fill-out forms, or stash the data in HTTP cookies (*Cookies*).

Another difference between mod_perl and conventional CGI scripting is that mod_perl scripts are *persistent*. After initial compilation, they remain in memory and are executed by the server each time they're needed. This means that scripts can stash state information in their own global variables, to be accessed later.

To see how useful this can be, we'll consider a longer example, stately.cgi, shown later in Example 5-2. This script implements file paging: when the user first accesses the script's URI, it displays a screen like the one shown in Figure 5-1. A textfield prompts the user to type his name, and a popup menu allows him to select from a fixed menu of interesting articles. When he presses the Select Article button, a screen like the one in Figure 5-2 appears. The top of the page displays the user's name and the selected article. Beneath it is a shaded block of text containing one page of the article (in this case, a page is defined as a fixed number of lines). Above and below the text are a row of buttons for navigating through the article. You can page backward and forward, or jump directly to an arbitrary page.

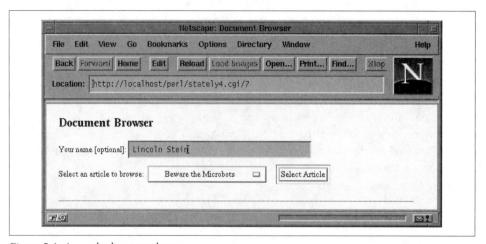

Figure 5-1. A stately document browser

If this script reminds you of paging through a search engine's results, it ought to. The only difference is that search engines sometimes use small inline images rather than standard HTML buttons. This script could be modified easily to use graphical buttons—just replace the appropriate calls to submit with calls to image_button. You'll have to provide your own artwork, of course.

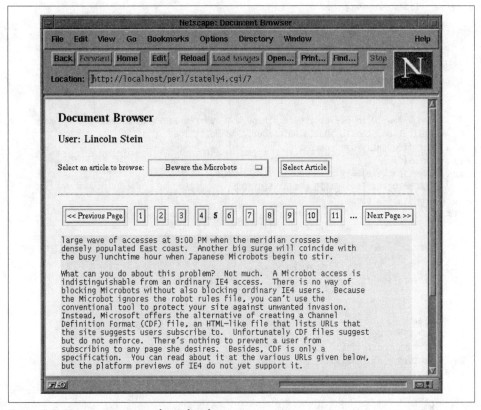

Figure 5-2. Using state to page through a document

This script has to store a lot of state between accesses. The user's name, the article being read, and the page being displayed all need to be remembered between accesses. While this could be achieved by cleverly using hidden fields, stately.cgi uses the simpler method of storing all the state information in memory. This has the important advantage of *long-term persistence*. If the user bookmarks the page and returns later, the page will be displayed exactly as he left it, even if he shut down and restarted his browser in the interim! Furthermore, the server can be shut down as well; you can kill the web server, have some pasta and a glass of wine, and when you restart the server all the session information will be magically restored.

Before we examine stately.cgi, have a look at Example 5-1, which implements the primary state-saving features. This defines a small utility package called PageSession that holds all the state information of a particular session. Each session has a unique ID, and fields for the user name, the article, and the current page. The new method (line 10) creates a new PageSession object with empty fields, the fetch method (line 22) fetches an existing PageSession given its ID, and a save method (line 28) saves the modified PageSession object to a memory structure for future accesses. Methods named id, name, article, and page allow you to get and set the object's fields.

Example 5-1. State-saving features

```
 0   package PageSession;
 1
 2   use vars qw($NEXTID $MAX_SESSIONS %SESSIONS);
 3   $MAX_SESSIONS = 100;
 4
 5   $NEXTID = 0 if $NEXTID eq '';
 6
 7   # Find a new ID to use by cycling through a numeric list. In a real
 8   # application, the ID should be unique, and maintained in a
 9   # most-frequently-used cache.
10   sub new {
11       my ($package) = @_;
12       $NEXTID = 0 if $NEXTID > $MAX_SESSIONS;
13       my $self = bless {
14                           name => '',
15                        article => '',
16                           page => 0,
17                             id => $NEXTID++
18                       }, $package;
19       return $self;
20   }
21
22   sub fetch {
23       my ($package, $id) = @_;
24       return undef if $id eq '';
25       return $SESSIONS{$id};
26   }
27
28   sub save {
29       my $self = shift;
30       $SESSIONS{$self->{id}} = $self;
31   }
32
33   sub id { $_[0]->{id} }
34   sub name { $_[0]->{name} = $_[1] if defined($_[1]); $_[0]->{name}; }
35   sub article { $_[0]->{article} = $_[1] if defined($_[1]); $_[0]->{article}; }
36   sub page {
37       $_[0]->{page} = $_[1] if defined($_[1]);
38       $_[0]->{page} = 0 if $_[0]->{page} < 0;
39       $_[0]->{page};
40   }
41
42   1;
```

Internally, PageSession objects are stored in %SESSIONS, a package-wide global hash indexed by the PageSession ID. The IDs are simple integers maintained in a global named $NEXTID, which is incremented whenever a new PageSession is requested. In order to keep the demands on memory reasonable, the number of stored PageSessions is restricted. After the maximum number is reached, $NEXTID is reset to zero and old session IDs are reused, deleting the older sessions to make way for newer ones. This isn't the most sophisticated way of maintaining session IDs; a more sophisticated scheme would prioritize sessions on the basis of how recently they were last used, rather than how recently they were created. Also, a real application would choose IDs that are a little harder to predict than small numbers, perhaps by hashing the ID with the user's IP address. This scheme makes it easy for one user to peek at another's session just by guessing a valid session ID.

Now let's look at the primary focus of this article, stately.cgi, shown in Example 5-2. It represents an interesting hybrid of straight mod_perl scripting and CGI scripting. Because it is run under Apache::Registry, it can take advantage of routines that depend on the CGI environment, such as CGI.pm's parameter parsing routines.

Example 5-2. stately.cgi

```
0    #!/usr/bin/perl
1    # File: stately.cgi
2
3    use strict vars;
4    use CGI qw(:html2 :html3 start_form end_form
5             center textfield submit param popup_menu);
6    use Apache::Constants qw(:response_codes :common);
7    use PageSession;
8
9    my %ARTICLES = (
10                        'emr.txt' => 'The Electronic Medical Record',
11                  'microbot.txt' => 'Beware the Microbots',
12                      'sbox.txt' => 'Box and Wrapped',
13                  'servlets.txt' => 'Back to the Future'
14                   );
15   my $ARTICLE_ROOT   = "/articles";
16   my $LINES_PER_PAGE = 20;
17   my $MAX_BUTTONS    = 10;     # How many page buttons
18
19   my $r       = Apache->request;
20   my $id      = get_session_id($r);
21   my $session = PageSession->fetch($id);
22
23   unless ($session) {
24       $session = PageSession->new();
25       # Remove any path info already there
26       my $uri = $r->path_info ?
27               substr($r->uri, 0, -length($r->path_info)) : $r->uri;
28       my $new_uri = "$uri/" . $session->id;
29       $r->header_out(Location => $new_uri);
30       $r->send_http_header;
31       $session->save;
32       return REDIRECT;
33   }
34
35   # If we get here, we have a session object in hand and
36   # can proceed.
```

Example 5-2. stately.cgi (continued)

```
37  $r->content_type('text/html');
38  $r->send_http_header;
39  $r->print(start_html(-bgcolor => 'white',
40                               -Title => 'Document Browser'),
41          h1('Document Browser'),
42          start_form()
43          );
44
45  # Set the user's name to whatever is specified in the
46  # CGI parameter.
47  $session->name(param('name'));
48
49  # If there's no name in the session, then prompt the
50  # user to enter it.
51  unless ($session->name) {
52      $r->print("Your name [optional]: ",
53              textfield(-name => 'name', -size => 40), br);
54  } else {
55      $r->print( h2("User: ",$session->name) );
56  }
57
58  # Here's where we do something based on the action
59  my $action = param('action');
60  CASE: {
61   $session->page($session->page+1),last CASE if $action eq 'Next Page >>';
62   $session->page($session->page-1),last CASE
63                                        if $action eq '<< Previous Page';
64   $session->page($action-1),last CASE if $action =~ /^\d+$/;
65   do_select($session,param('article'))
66                              if $action eq 'Select Article' || param('name');
67  }
68  # Popup menu to select article to view
69  $r->print('Select an article to browse: ',
70          popup_menu(   -name => 'article', -values => \%ARTICLES,
71                      -default => $session->article),
72          submit( -name => 'action',
73                  -value => 'Select Article'), p(),
74          );
75
76  # Fetch the article and divide it into pages
77  my @pages = fetch_article($r,$session);
78  if (@pages) {
79
80      # truncate page counter if it's off.
81      $session->page($#pages) if $session->page > $#pages;
82
83      # List of page buttons.  (Note the one-based indexing.)
84      my @buttons = map { $_ == $session->page+1 ?
85                              strong($_) :
86                              submit(-name=>'action',-value=>"$_") } (1..@pages);
87      # Trim the buttons to the left and right of the page.
```

Example 5-2. stately.cgi (continued)

```
88      # Want <= MAX_BUTTONS shown at any time.
89      splice(@buttons, 0, $session->page - $MAX_BUTTONS/2, strong('...'))
90        if @buttons > $MAX_BUTTONS && $session->page > $MAX_BUTTONS/2;
91      splice(@buttons, $MAX_BUTTONS+1, @buttons-6, strong('...'))
92        if @buttons > $MAX_BUTTONS;
93      unshift(@buttons,submit(-name=>'action',-value=>'<< Previous Page'))
94        if $session->page > 0;
95      push(@buttons, submit(-name=>'action', -value=>'Next Page >>'))
96        if $session->page < $#pages;
97
98      $r->print(hr,
99              table({-width=>'100%'}, TR(td(\@buttons))),
100             table({-width=>'100%'},
101             TR(
102                td({-bgcolor=>'yellow'},
103                   $session->page == 0 ? center(strong("-start-")) : '',
104                   pre($pages[$session->page]),
105                $session->page == $#pages ? center(strong("-end-")) : ''
106                     ))
107               ),
108             table({-width=>'100%'}, TR(td(\@buttons)))
109             );
110 } # end if (@pages)
111
112 $r->print(
113         end_form( ),
114         hr( ),end_html( ) );
115 $session->save;
116
117 sub get_session_id {
118     my $r = shift;
119     my ($session) = $r->path_info( ) =~ m!^/(\d+)!;
120     return $session;
121 }
122
123 sub do_select {
124     my ($session, $article) = @_;
125     $session->page(0);
126     $session->article($article);
127 }
128
129 sub fetch_article {
130     my ($r, $session) = @_;
131     return ( ) unless $ARTICLES{$session->article};
132     my $path = $r->lookup_uri("$ARTICLE_ROOT/" .
133                                     $session->article)->filename( );
134     return ( ) unless $path;
135
136     my (@lines, @pages);
137     open (FILE,$path) || return ( );
138     @lines = <FILE>;       # Slurp in all the lines
```

Example 5-2. stately.cgi (continued)

```
139      close FILE;
140      push(@pages,
141          join('',splice(@lines,0,$LINES_PER_PAGE)))
142        while @lines;
143      return @pages;
144 }
```

The script starts out by bringing in the modules that it needs. It imports some functions from CGI.pm, Apache::Constants, and the PageSession package. Because all modules are compiled into one Perl interpreter object, chances are that these modules are already compiled and ready to be launched, so the use statements will execute quickly. (You can even have mod_perl compile modules at startup time if you wish.)

Next, we define some packagewide global variables, including the names of the articles, their location, and the page length (lines 9–17).

The fun part begins in lines 19–21. The goal here is to deduce whether the request is coming from a new user or an old one. If the user is new, we need to generate a unique session ID and trick his browser into passing it back to us on subsequent requests. If it's an old user, we need to recover his session object. We accomplish this task with one of the older tricks of the web trade: storing the session ID in the script's URI. URIs used to access this script should look something like this:

    http://your.site/perl/stately.cgi/42

The script's URI is followed by additional path information containing the session ID, in this case 42. If a user tries to access the script without a session ID, the script assumes that it is a new session, generates a new empty session object for the user, and redirects the browser to the URI with the session ID tacked onto the end. Otherwise it recovers the session ID from the additional path information and recovers the corresponding PageSession object from memory.

First, we fetch the current request object (line 19). Unlike the standard handlers shown before, Apache::Registry scripts don't define a handler subroutine. Instead, they ask the Apache package for their request object. After recovering this object, we use it to recover the session ID by calling the subroutine defined in lines 117–121: get_session_id. We now call the PageSession::fetch subroutine to recover the corresponding PageSession (which might be undefined).

If no PageSession object is found, then the script's URI either provided no session number at all, or provided an unused one. In this case, we generate a new session object and redirect the user's browser to our URI with the ID of the new object tacked onto the end. This happens in lines 23 through 33, where we call PageSession::new to make a new object, synthesize a new URI from the base URI concatenated with the session ID, and generate a redirect directive as shown earlier. The mess beginning on line 26 handles users who access the script with a URI already containing additional path information. This strips the URI down to its base before appending the session ID.

When the user's browser sees the redirect, it immediately bounces back to our script with a valid session ID. We can then generate an HTML document. Lines 37 through 43 create the HTTP header and the constant section at the top of the document. To emphasize that this is mod_perl rather than CGI, we use Apache's content_type, send_http_header, and print methods; but since we're running under Apache::Registry, we could just as easily have called Perl's regular print function and used CGI::header.

The next step is to update the session object to reflect commands issued by the user. This script recognizes six different parameters, each of which affects the state of the page. They are shown in Table 5-1.

Table 5-1. stately.cgi parameters

Parameter	Value	Comment
name	(textfield contents)	The user name
article	(popup menu contents)	The article name
action	Select Article	Start reading a new article
action	<< Previous Page	Decrement page number
action	Next Page>>	Increment page number
action	numeric value	Go to the indicated page

Notice that the action parameter is used for four different commands. That's okay, because only one command can be issued at a time. We use the CGI.pm param subroutine to recover the CGI parameters, something possible only with Apache::Registry. First, if a parameter named name is present, we update the session object to contain it (line 47). If the parameter is missing and the session object doesn't already contain the user's name, we generate a textfield to request it from the user.

Next, we process the action parameter (lines 60–67). action can be generated by any of the page navigation buttons, or by the "Select Article" button. This code detects which button was pressed and takes the appropriate action, either by changing the value of the session's page field or by changing the contents of the article field.

We now begin to lay out the rest of the page. In lines 68–73 we create a popup menu to display the list of articles. This example uses a deliberately small list; a real application might generate the list from directory contents, a database, or a keyword search.

Line 77 calls the fetch_article routine, which fetches the article given by the session and divides it into pages. The pages are stored in the @pages array.

The complicated code in lines 78 through 110 displays the navigation bar and the current page from the selected article. To generate the navigation bar, we first create a list of HTML pushbuttons in @buttons. We then trim the list so they'll all be visible simultaneously. After centering the list so that the entry for the current page is always displayed, we replace the part of the list that's too far to the left or the right with "...". After trimming, we add the Previous and Next buttons.

In lines 98 through 110, we print out this list of buttons with the current page of text. To make everything line up nicely, both the list of buttons and the text itself are placed in HTML 3.2 tables. By embedding the article in a table cell, we gain the benefit of being able to change its background color. Another way to accomplish the same effect would be to use a cascading style sheet—but that's a subject for another article!

Although it isn't visible in the screenshot, the script actually prints the navigation bar twice: once at the top of the article, and once at the bottom. Most users hate to scroll.

The last bit of work is to print out the end of the HTML page and save the session (lines 112–115).

Let's look at the subroutines now. get_session_id (lines 117–121) is responsible for retrieving the session ID from the browser's request. It extracts the additional URI path information from the Apache request object, and looks for a numeral, returning the match, if any. do_select sets the session article field and zeroes out the page number. This displays the new article starting with the first page.

More interesting is the fetch_article subroutine spanning lines 129 through 144. It turns an article name into a physical file path. First, it checks whether the indicated article is listed in %ARTICLES. If so, it calls the Apache request object's lookup_uri function to turn the article path (expressed as a virtual URI) into a physical path. lookup_uri is actually a callback into the current Apache URI translation handler, and illustrates how smoothly mod_perl integrates into Apache. If this step is successful, we open the file, read it into an array, and divide it into bite-size pieces of $LINES_PER_PAGE size.

To run this script, you need to make it executable and place it in an appropriate directory, such as a /perl subdirectory below the server root. You'll also need to include a section like this in your *access.conf* file:

```
<Location /perl>
  SetHandler Perl-script
  PerlHandler Apache::Registry
  Options +ExecCGI
</Location>
```

The SetHandler and PerlHandler directives, as we've seen before, tell Apache to use Apache::Registry as its content handler for all files inside /perl. The ExecCGI option is turned on in order to satisfy one of Apache::Registry's safety checks. It requires that ExecCGI be enabled for any directory under its purview, and that all programs in those directories be executable, just like mod_cgi. Although the scripts are never run as standalone applications, this constraint prevents you from introducing security holes from files inadvertently left in the directory, such as from a text editor's autosaves.

You can now test the script with a mod_perl-enabled Apache launched in single-process mode. Here's how you do that:

```
# httpd -X -d /home/www
```

Impaled by the Fork

What is single-process mode? Normally, Apache preforks itself several times, so that there are a half-dozen or so processes hanging around to handle incoming requests. This tactic distributes the load on the web server and makes the response time of heavily-loaded sites noticeably better. The -X command-line switch suppresses this behavior, forcing Apache to run as a single process. The reason we use single-process mode is because the script as written *will not work correctly* in prefork mode. The reason becomes clear on reflection. After forking, each Apache process has its own independent copy of %SESSION and $NEXTID. When one server process assigns a new user an ID and PageSession object, there's no guarantee that the user will connect to the same process the next time he fetches the page. The user might well contact a new process, starting things over from scratch.

This is unacceptable—it precludes the benefits of persistent storage. Fortunately, there's a simple, almost-transparent solution. Benjamin Sugars' IPC::Shareable module allows several processes to share Perl variables using System V shared memory. You simply tie the variables you wish to share, specifying a unique four-letter identifier for each variable. After this, each process can share data simply by reading and storing to the tied variable.

Example 5-3 shows the PageSession module modified to use IPC::Shareable. The main addition is on lines 6 and 7, where we tie $NEXTID and %SESSIONS. The other changes are strategically-placed calls to IPC::Shareable's shlock and shunlock methods. To avoid the risk of two processes trying to update the same variable simultaneously, we lock the variable before writing to it, and unlock it when we're through. Now the session objects are shared across all Apache processes and we can safely run the server in normal mode. An added benefit is that the persistent information remains in shared memory space even after the Apache process terminates. The result: we can stop the server, restart it, and all previous user sessions will still be available!

Example 5-3. The PageSession module

```
0   package PageSession;
1
2   use IPC::Shareable;
3   use vars qw($NEXTID $MAX_SESSIONS %SESSIONS);
4   $MAX_SESSIONS = 100;
5
```

Example 5-3. The PageSession module (continued)

```
 6  tie $NEXTID,   IPC::Shareable, 'S000', { create => 1, mode => 0600};
 7  tie %SESSIONS, IPC::Shareable, 'S001', { create => 1, mode => 0600};
 8
 9  $NEXTID = 0 if $NEXTID eq '';
10
11  # Find a new ID to use by cycling through a
12  # a list. In a real application, the ID should
13  # be unique and kept in a most-frequently-used cache.
14  sub new {
15      my ($package) = @_;
16      tied($NEXTID)->shlock;
17      $NEXTID = 0 if $NEXTID > $MAX_SESSIONS;
18      my $self = bless {
19                          name => '',
20                       article => '',
21                          page => 0,
22                            id => $NEXTID++
23                      }, $package;
24      tied($NEXTID)->shunlock;
25      return $self;
26  }
27
28  sub fetch {
29      my ($package, $id) = @_;
30      return undef if $id eq '';
31      # Storeable makes this a PageSession object
32      return $SESSIONS{$id};
33  }
34
35  sub save {
36      my $self = shift;
37      # Store the object
38      tied(%SESSIONS)->shlock;
39      $SESSIONS{$self->{id}} = $self;
40      tied(%SESSIONS)->shunlock;
41  }
42
43  sub id      { $_[0]->{id}; }
44  sub name    { $_[0]->{name} = $_[1] if defined($_[1]); $_[0]->{name}; }
45  sub article {
46      $_[0]->{article} = $_[1] if defined($_[1]);
47      $_[0]->{article};
48  }
49  sub page {
50      $_[0]->{page} = $_[1] if defined($_[1]);
51      $_[0]->{page} = 0 if $_[0]->{page} < 0;
52      $_[0]->{page};
53  }
54
55  1;
```

Other mod_perl Features

To wrap up, we'll discuss a few of the other reasons to use mod_perl.

Startup scripts

You can designate a script to run when the Apache server first starts up. It might adjust the library search path, set global variables, or compile commonly-used modules, avoiding the overhead when individual handlers are first called.

Server-side includes

The standard Apache mod_include module has been integrated with mod_perl, so you can embed snippets of Perl code in your HTML pages like this:

```
Perl is

<!--#perl sub="sub {for (0..10) {print "very "}}"-->

fun to use!
```

Two sophisticated server-side packages, Apache::Embperl and Apache::ePerl, are built on top of mod_perl.

Perl-based server configuration

With mod_perl you can dynamically configure Apache with <Perl> sections inside its configuration files. These sections can contain Perl code to inspect and change Apache's configuration in every way conceivable. You can write a configuration file that senses its environment and autoconfigures itself!

Stacked handlers

One Perl handler can chain to another, allowing you, for instance, to build up a chain of filters that progressively modify an HTML document.

Persistent database connections

mod_perl persistence allows you to open a single database handle when a child server starts and use it for all subsequent requests. This avoids the overhead of constantly opening and closing connections that CGI scripts suffer. The Perl DBI and Apache::DBI modules have been integrated to make persistent connections transparent; just add this to your server configuration file:

```
PerlModule Apache::DBI
```

On top of these features, dozens of mod_perl fans have contributed a growing list of useful modules, including a traffic analyzer, a module that blocks unwanted robots, a module that chooses from multiple documents based on the user's language preference, a module to compress response data on the fly, and a slew of user authentication packages. See *http://perl.apache.org* for a full list of available modules.

## CHAPTER 6

Creating mod_perl Applications

Mike Fletcher

*Because mod_perl is, frankly, scarier
than a typical Apache module.*
—Jon Udell, *Byte*, March 1998

While it may be scarier than most Apache modules, mod_perl (*http://perl.apache.org*)
is also one of the most powerful additions available. In *mod_perl*, Doug MacEachern
(author of mod_perl) and Lincoln Stein (of CGI.pm fame) presented an introduction
to mod_perl. This article builds on their foundation and demonstrates a full-fledged
mod_perl application that lets users provide feedback on web documentation. I'll
also describe some of the performance concerns and how your Apache configuration
should be modified to make the most of mod_perl.

So, What Is This mod_perl Thing, Anyhow?

Most people are familiar with CGI scripts written in Perl that add dynamic content
generation to a web server. In addition to CGI, most web servers provide some sort
of interface that allows code to be run inside the server, such as Microsoft's ISAPI.

Apache lets you create a chunk of code, called a *handler*, that is invoked when the
server fulfills a browser's request. That might happen when a URL is translated into
a local pathname, or when a child process terminates. mod_perl embeds a Perl interpreter within each Apache httpd process, giving you the ability to write handlers in
Perl instead of C.

Aside from exposing the Apache module API, mod_perl also provides other benefits,
such as running existing CGI scripts inside the persistent interpreter, and letting you
configure Apache with Perl code enclosed in <Perl>...</Perl> tags and placed in
your server configuration files. You can do anything—from setting the port Apache
listens on for requests, to configuring virtual hosts based on the contents of a database. For more information on <Perl> configuration, see the *mod_perl.pod* document bundled with the mod_perl distribution.

Developing with mod_perl

There are several ways to use mod_perl to speed up web applications, including:

- Using Apache::Registry to run existing CGI scripts
- Using Embperl to embed code in HTML pages
- Using Apache.pm directly

Each has its own particular strengths and weaknesses.

Apache::Registry

If you already have existing CGI scripts written in Perl, the Apache::Registry module lets you run them with little (if any) changes—but much more quickly because the Perl interpreter is already resident in memory. The first time a URI is requested, Apache::Registry compiles the CGI script and stores a reference to the compiled code. Forever after, the program is run within the child httpd process, rather than launching a new Perl process each time.

In essence, Apache::Registry wraps up your entire existing script as a subroutine named handler inside a package named after the script's name. It then calls this pre-compiled handler whenever the corresponding URL is accessed. If the file containing the script changes on disk, Apache::Registry notices and recompiles the code.

This example, modeled after a slide from Doug's O'Reilly Perl Conference presentation, shows the code that Apache::Registry wraps around a CGI script. The contents of the script are read into a string. Everything up until the local $^W = 1; is prepended by Apache::Registry, and it appends the last }. The entire string is then passed to Perl's eval function and compiled.

```
package Apache::Root::mp::example_2epl;

use Apache qw(exit);

sub handler {
    #line 1 /usr/local/apache/mp/example.pl
    local $^W = 1; #!/usr/bin/perl

    use CGI;

    my $q = CGI->new;
    my $them = $q->remote_host;

    print $q->header('text/html' ),
                    $q->start_html(-title => 'My Apache::Registry Example');
    print <<EOT;
<h1>My Apache::Registry Example</h1>
<p>Hello browser at $them.</p>
EOT

    print $q->end_html;
}
```

There's a caveat: not all CGI scripts run without modifications (for example, those with __DATA__ or __END__ tokens won't run at all). Also, by the time Apache::Registry kicks in, several stages of the request (such as user authentication and authorization) have already finished. So just as with regular CGI scripts, you don't have any way to authenticate or authorize users.

On the positive side, most web servers have some sort of capability to run CGI scripts, making it easy to port to and from non-Apache web servers. And since CGI is widespread, programmers can easily leverage their existing web scripting knowledge while enjoying the reduced overhead. For more information on Apache::Registry, see the file *cgi_to_mod_perl.pod* which comes with mod_perl, or read it on the web at *http://perl.apache.org/dist/cgi_to_mod_perl.html*. In this book, see the article *mod_perl*.

Embperl

In addition to faster CGI service, another popular reason to use mod_perl is for fast Embperl processing. This module allows Perl code to be embedded within HTML documents, just like the standard Apache SSI (Server Side Include) module mod_include. The Perl code should appear between one of four delimiters; the delimiter you use determines what Embperl does with your code:

[+ *PERL_CODE* +]
> Replaces the code with what it evaluates to.

[- *PERL_CODE* -]
> Executes the Perl code invisibly.

[! *PERL_CODE* !]
> Same as [- *PERL_CODE* -], but the code is only executed the first time it's encountered. This is used to define subroutines and perform one-time initialization.

[$ *COMMAND_ARG* $]
> Executes an Embperl metacommand. The commands (e.g., if and while) are listed in the Embperl documentation.

Embperl also understands HTML and is capable of dynamically generating tables, lists, and form selection buttons. Here's an example taken from the Embperl manual page that prints the contents of the environment:

```
[- @k = keys %ENV -]
<TABLE>
  <TR>
    <TD>[+ $i=$row +]</TD>
    <TD>[+ $k[$row] +]</TD>
    <TD>[+ $ENV{$k[$i]} +]</TD>
  </TR>
</TABLE>
```

The first line sets @k to the names of the environment variables and produces no output; that's why the minus signs are used as delimiters. Embperl then parses the table and looks for use of any of three special variables: $row, $col, or $cnt. If none are found in the table it is passed through with no modification. If they are used, Emb-perl repeats the text between `<tr>` and `</tr>` as many times as there are elements in @k.

As with Apache::Registry, Embperl processes pages only after many other stages of the request have finished. Code is compiled once and cached, giving much better performance over other similar embedded constructs such as mod_include.

Writing Your Own Handler

The last alternative is writing your own request handler directly, using Apache.pm to access the Apache API. Under the hood, this is exactly what Apache::Registry and Embperl do. You can create handlers for each step that Apache takes to respond to a request. Handlers can be used to provide access control, to rewrite incoming URLs, or to implement custom logging, such as logging to a database system instead of a log file. Apache.pm lets you do everything in Perl that you can do in C.

```perl
package MyHandler;

use Apache::Constants qw(:common);

sub handler {
    # $r contains Apache request object
    my $r = shift;
    # $them is the client's hostname or IP address
    my $them = $r->get_remote_host;

    $r->content_type( "text/html" );
    $r->send_http_header;
    print qq{
            <html>
            <head>
            <title>My First Handler</title>
            </head>
            <body bgcolor="#ffffff">
            <h1>My First Apache Handler</h1>
            <p>Hello to the browser at $them.</p>
            <p>Here are the headers your browser sent me:</p>
            <pre>
            };

    my %headers = $r->headers_in;
    foreach ( sort keys %headers ) {
        $r->print( "$_: $headers{$_}\n" );
    }

    print qq{
            </pre>
            </body>
            </html>
            };
    return OK;
}

1;
```

You have direct access to the entire Apache API. In contrast, CGI and HTML::Emb-perl pages are limited to executing during the content generation phase, while handler routines can run at any of the 14 different stages. However, if you aren't familiar with the Apache API, you might find writing your own handlers a bit daunting since it requires detailed knowledge of how Apache handles requests. For generating simple dynamic pages, Apache::Registry/CGI and Embperl perform admirably.

Performance

While mod_perl is a great improvement over vanilla CGI, you should be aware of some of the issues involved in squeezing the most efficiency from it. If you're just running a small web application on its own dedicated machine, used inside your company by 20 people, you might not be that concerned. But if your site is intended for a large audience, you need to be aware of these issues.

Preload Your Modules

One of the biggest items to be aware of is the fact that each Apache process with mod_perl requires more memory than one without mod_perl. This can cause performance to suffer if your system runs out of physical memory and needs to swap out to disk. This `PerlModule` configuration directive can help; it causes mod_perl to load the named module (or modules) at server startup:

```
PerlModule CGI Apache::Registry MyFavoriteModule
```

Preloading modules that will be used by your scripts improves the performance of requests and reduces the amount of memory needed, since the memory can be shared between all the processes. (Whether this actually buys you anything depends on how your operating system handles shared memory between spawned processes.) While modifying Perl modules used by your application, you might want to set `PerlFreshRestart On` in one of your server configuration files (e.g., *httpd.conf*). Otherwise, Apache won't know to reload your Perl modules when it next restarts, and you won't see any changes you have made.

Use Multiple Servers

Another performance enhancement is to run multiple servers. You can run servers on different ports on the same machine, or on different machines entirely. One server can have mod_perl installed for the content requiring it, and another server will be without mod_perl, for static content such as images. With the Apache mod_proxy module or Squid (an HTTP cache/proxy program) you can make the multiple servers appear as one.

For a more thorough discussion of tweaking mod_perl to get the most performance from it, see the *mod_perl_tuning.pod* document bundled with the mod_perl distribution. Information on configuration directives such as `PerlModule` can be found in the *mod_perl.pod* documentation.

Our Sample Application

To demonstrate how to use mod_perl to create applications, we'll develop a site that provides documentation (such as FAQs, tech notes, and white papers) to customers, and accept feedback on which documents are the most helpful and most used. The idea comes from a paper presented at last year's O'Reilly Perl Conference by Dav Amann of Netscape on the customer support site they developed using Perl. The site (*http://help.netscape.com/*) allows customers quick access to the most frequently requested tech notes, and allows customers to give feedback on the documents to Netscape (both a simple yes-or-no "This document answered my question" as well as a more detailed questionnaire). A sample is shown in Figure 6-1.

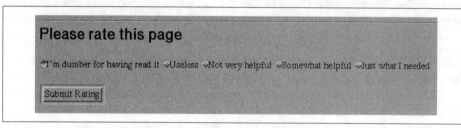

Please rate this page

○I'm dumber for having read it ○Useless ○Not very helpful ○Somewhat helpful ○Just what I needed

Submit Rating

Figure 6-1. A footer added to every document by Apache::Sandwich

Our sample application will manage a document tree, provide a count of the number of hits for each document within the tree, and allow readers to rate each document from 1 to 5. Our application will use a little bit of all three approaches: CGI scripts, Embperl pages, and Apache handlers.

A handler routine will be used during the PerlTransHandler stage so that we can map URIs to filenames based on a database. This *translation handler* will also arrange for another handler to be called during the log phase to update the hit counts in the database for each file. An Embperl document will be used to dynamically generate an index of the most frequently accessed documents, based on the contents of the database shown in Figure 6-2. Finally, two CGI scripts will be used to record user feedback and manage adding and removing files. In addition to the modules we develop, we'll use several existing Perl modules to handle access control and adding footers to pages.

Bookmarks 🔖 Go To: `http://lemur/topten/`
Internet Lookup New&Cool

Top Ten Tracked Documents

#	Title	Hits	Rating
1	Unclogging pipes with $|	22	4.80
2	Sandblasting your Lemur	837	3.21
3	HTTP POST with LWP	12	3.21
4	Creating Applications with mod_perl and Apache	2	1.50
5	Teach Yourself Quantum Physics in 21 Attofortnights	51047	1.21

All Tracked Documents

Figure 6-2. An Embperl-generated table

Components

There are many Perl modules available for use with mod_perl and Apache; a complete list of Apache-specific modules is at *http://perl.apache.org/src/apache-modlist.html*. All modules should also be available from your favorite CPAN mirror. A quick introduction to the modules used in the sample application follows. Here, we use four modules: DBI, Apache::DBI, Apache::AuthDBI, and Apache::Sandwich.

DBI and Apache::DBI

DBI is a Perl module that provides a consistent method of accessing almost any relational database system from Perl. You use the same Perl methods regardless of which database you're using. Different database driver modules (DBDs) handle the database specifics so you don't have to.

Apache::DBI improves the performance of DBI by caching database connections. Opening a connection to a database often takes a lot of time, so Apache::DBI maintains a cache of open database handles. As long as Apache::DBI is loaded before the DBI module, all connect requests will be handled by Apache::DBI. One limitation of the cache: you cannot create database connections in the parent Apache process and have them shared by child processes.

For developing the sample application, I used the freely available PostgreSQL (*http://www.postgresql.org/*) and its driver, DBD::Pg. However, any database for which you have the proper DBD:: module installed should work.

Apache::AuthDBI

This module provides two handlers, Apache::AuthDBI::authen and Apache::AuthDBI::authz, which allow you to store authentication (i.e., usernames and passwords) and authorization information (e.g., group membership) in a database accessed via DBI. To use these modules, you must have enabled the appropriate Perl handlers when you built mod_perl. See the Apache::AuthDBI documentation for the required handlers, and the INSTALL file in the mod_perl distribution to learn how to enable handlers at build time.

Apache::Sandwich

This module allows you to "sandwich" a page's contents between a header and footer without modifying the page's source. Apache sends the headers, then the contents of the requested URI, and finally the footers. We'll use this module to append an HTML form that lets users provide feedback on the usefulness of the documents. Thanks to Apache::Sandwich, we won't have to modify any of our documents to add these footers.

Writing the Application Code

In this section, we'll step through the tasks involved in creating our application—setting up the database and creating three programs: index.epl, rateit, and ttadmin.

Database Setup

The first task is to create the tables in our database. The documents table keeps track of the title and number of hits for each file being tracked. The rating and raters fields are used to calculate the average rating given to the document by readers. Several indices are created to maintain unique entries and to speed up queries. The other table, users, maintains username and password information for Apache::AuthDBI. In this case, Apache::AuthDBI is probably overkill for the minuscule number of users we'll be concerned with, but we'll stick with it for instructional purposes.

In addition to creating the tables, you'll probably want to create a user account for use by Apache; we'll use ap_auth in the examples that follow. The SQL code to create the tables can be found on the web page for this book.

TopTenTrans.pm

Our application uses a PerlTransHandler to customize the mapping of URIs to filenames. A translation handler can change the default mapping of URIs to filenames. Similar to Apache's Alias configuration directive, the TopTenTrans::handler subroutine modifies the filename to which URIs with a specified prefix resolve.

The translation handler also allows us to map URIs based on the database contents. For example, the fifth most useful document is accessible as *http://server/topten/5*. The handler connects to the database, retrieves the corresponding record, and sets the filename accordingly. Later stages use this information to return the contents of the request.

The translation handler requests that Apache let mod_perl handle the content generation phase of the request, and that mod_perl should use Apache::Sandwich as the PerlHandler to generate the content. This is the runtime equivalent of placing these lines in *access.conf*:

```
SetHandler perl-script
PerlHandler Apache::Sandwich
```

Lastly, the handler arranges for a subroutine to be called during the logging phase of the request (after the page has been sent) using Apache::push_handlers, which allows a Perl handler to specify which handlers should be called during later phases. The TopTenTrans::log_hit subroutine increments the hits field in the database record for the corresponding file.

This facility is useful if you have a long-running task but don't want to delay sending a response back to the client until it is complete. On a busy site, the overhead of updating the hit count for each file immediately might be too much of a load; one possible solution is to keep the statistics in memory using the IPC::Shareable module and then periodically send the statistics to the database using a log handler subroutine. The TopTenTrans module can be found on the web page for this book at *http://www.oreilly.com/catalog/tpj2*.

index.epl

The next component is the *document index*, which can list all tracked documents or just the top ten. This is implemented using Embperl to generate the listing on the fly. Why use Embperl? Because the index page is just a table, which is a snap to create with Embperl's dynamic table generation facilities. The Embperl code is in `index.epl`, shown in Example 6-1.

Example 6-1. index.epl

```
<html> <head> <title>Top Ten Documents</title> </head>
<body bgcolor="#ffffff">
<h1>
[$ if $ENV{QUERY_STRING} eq 'all' $]
All
[$ else $]
Top Ten
[$ endif $]
Tracked Documents
</h1>

[!
    sub colorsub { return shift() % 2 ? '#ffffff' : '#cccccc'; }
!]

[-
    ## Connect to database
    use DBI;
    my $dbh = DBI->connect( "dbi:Pg:dbname=tpj", "ap_auth" )
      or die "Can't connect: $DBI::errstr\n";
    my $sth = $dbh->prepare( qq{
                            select title, path, hits, rating from documents
                            order by rating desc, hits desc;
                            });
        $sth->execute or die "Can't execute: $DBI::errstr";

    ## Slurp first 10 results (or all results if
    ## $ENV{QUERY_STRING} is 'all') into arrayref and
    ## store that into $indexdata
    $indexdata = $ENV{QUERY_STRING} eq 'all' ?
                $sth->fetchall_arrayref :
                [@{$sth->fetchall_arrayref}[0..9]];
    $sth->finish;
    $dbh->disconnect;
-]

<table border="0" width="75%">
  <tr><th>#</th><th>Title</th><th>Hits</th><th>Rating</th></tr>
  <tr bgcolor="[+ colorsub( $row ) +]">
    <td>
```

Example 6-1. index.epl (continued)

```
      <a href="[+ $row + 1 +]">[+ $row + 1 +]</a>
    </td>
    <td width="50%">
      [- $escmode = 0; -]
      <a href="[+ "$indexdata->[$row]->[1]" +]">
      [- $escmode = 1; -]
      [+ $indexdata->[$row]->[0] +]</a>
    </td>
    <td>[+ $indexdata->[$row]->[2] +]</td>
    <td>[+ sprintf "%-0.2f", $indexdata->[$row]->[3] +]</td>
  </tr>
</table>

[$ if $ENV{QUERY_STRING} eq 'all' $]
<a href="/[+ $req_rec->dir_config( 'TopTenPrefix')||'topten' +]/">
Top Ten Documents</a>
[$ else $]
<a href="/[+ ($req_rec->dir_config( 'TopTenPrefix')||'topten') . '/?all' +]">
All Tracked Documents</a>
[$ endif $]
</body>
</html>
```

Depending on whether it is called with a query string of all (that is, *http://server/ topten?all* versus *http://server/topten*), the embedded code pulls the appropriate information from the database and stores it in an array reference. Embperl's dynamic table generation creates an HTML table listing the rank, title, hits, and rating for each document.

rateit

The Apache::Sandwich routine appends a file, *rate.html*, to each document that contains a form users can use to rate how useful they found the document. The results will be processed by a CGI script called rateit that computes the new rating.

There isn't anything mod_perl specific about rateit, so we won't go into much detail about it. If the user didn't select a rating, the script asks them to use the back button and select one. If they did check one of the boxes, the script retrieves the current rating and the number of people who have submitted ratings from the database, uses these values to calculate the new rating, and updates the database with the new information. The script then prints a message with the user's choice, the new rating, and links back to the document and Top Ten index.

ttadmin

The last component we need is some method of administering documents. The ttadmin script provides a means of adding new files to the repository, zeroing the hit count for a file, and deleting a file from the repository. When called with no parameters, it returns a page (Figure 6-3) with three forms on it: one to let the user specify a file to upload;

another form get a page from which to choose a file to zero the hit counter for; and one to retrieve a listing so that the files can be deleted from the repository.

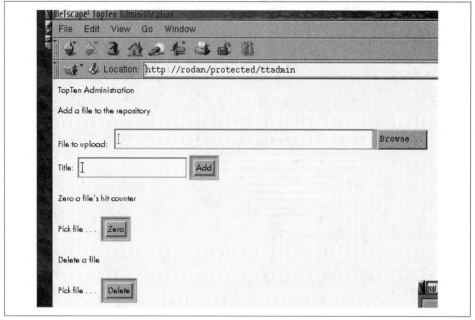

Figure 6-3. The web page generated by ttadmin

Like `rateit`, `ttadmin` is pretty much a vanilla CGI script. The section that adds a file simply copies the uploaded file into the Top Ten root directory and adds the appropriate information to the database. The counter zeroing and deletion routines use the `list_all_files` subroutine to generate a table listing all of the entries from the database if called without the `victimfile` query parameter being set. If the parameter is set, the appropriate changes are made to the database.

Keep in mind that in order to add files to the repository, the repository directory needs to be writeable by the user ID the apache processes are running as (usually the *nobody* account; look for a `User` directive in your *httpd.conf* file if you're not sure). `index.epl`, `rate.html`, `rateit`, and `ttadmin` can all be found at *http://www.oreilly.com/catalog/tpj2*.

Putting It All Together

Now that the code has been written, you'll need to place all of the components in the correct locations and let Apache and mod_perl know where to find them. In Example 6-1, I have Apache installed in */usr/local/apache* and the Top Ten root directory is located in */home/fletch/topten*. The Top Ten repository appears under the URI *http://servername/topten/*. Your copy of mod_perl should have been compiled with at least `PERL_TRANS`, `PERL_AUTHEN`, `PERL_CLEANUP`, `PERL_STACKED_HANDLERS`, `PERL_SECTIONS`, and `PERL_SSI` enabled. See the mod_perl *INSTALL* file for more information.

httpd.conf

The following directives should go in your server configuration (*httpd.conf*) file. The first line tells mod_perl to force a reload of modules when Apache is restarted. The `<Perl>...</Perl>` section is Perl code to be executed by Apache at server startup. In this case, all it does is add the directory containing the handler modules to Perl's library search path. The *TopTenTrans.pm* file should be located in this directory. The last line instructs mod_perl that the three modules listed should be loaded by the server at startup time. (A complete *httpd.conf* file is available on the web page for this book.)

```
PerlFreshRestart on

<Perl>
  use lib qw(/usr/local/apache/lib);
</Perl>

PerlModule Apache::DBI Apache::AuthDBI HTML::Embperl
```

The next set of directives tells Apache how we want our directories to appear in the server's URL namespace. The first two lines below create aliases in the server's document tree to the directories where our Apache::Registry CGI scripts reside (one which will not be password protected, the other which is). The third line tells the server that the output generated by Embperl files should be given a MIME content type of `text/html`.

The next group of lines (in between the `<Files>` directives) tells Apache to allow mod_perl to handle any files which end in *.epl*. The actual Perl handler which will be called is the `HTML::Embperl::handler` subroutine, defined by Embperl.

```
Alias /perl/ /usr/local/apache/perl/
Alias /protected/ /usr/local/apache/protected/
AddType text/html .epl

<Files *.epl>
  SetHandler perl-script
  PerlHandler HTML::Embperl
</Files>
```

Next comes the configuration of the two locations that were aliased above. The `<Location /perl>` section arranges for scripts in */usr/local/apache/perl* to be run under Apache::Registry. It also specifies several environment variables that should be set in `%ENV` for the scripts.

The next set of directives sets up the authentication for any URLs, beginning with /protected. The first lines in this section make Apache call Apache::Registry to handle requests. The various `PerlSetVar` commands set configuration data for the Auth-DBI handler, such as the DBI data source and table containing user/password information, and what field names to use from that table.

The last variable controls whether AuthDBI uses the `crypt` routine to encrypt the password before comparing it against the value from the database. For development, it is easier to leave this turned off to facilitate adding users by hand, but in most cases you should never store the plaintext of passwords. It's just asking for trouble.

```
<Location /perl>
  SetHandler perl-script
  PerlHandler Apache::Registry

  Options ExecCGI

  PerlSetEnv TopTenDB     tpj
  PerlSetEnv TopTenPrefix topten
  PerlSetEnv TopTenRoot   /home/fletch/topten
</Location>

<Location /protected>
  SetHandler perl-script
  PerlHandler Apache::Registry
  PerlAuthenHandler Apache::AuthDBI::authen

  Options ExecCGI

  AuthName "My Protected Area"
  AuthType Basic

  PerlSetVar Auth_DBI_data_source dbi:Pg:dbname=tpj
  PerlSetVar Auth_DBI_username ap_auth

  ##
  ## SELECT pwd_field FROM pwd_table WHERE uid_field=$user
  ##
  PerlSetVar Auth_DBI_pwd_table users
  PerlSetVar Auth_DBI_uid_field username
  PerlSetVar Auth_DBI_pwd_field password

  PerlSetVar Auth_DBI_encrypted off

  PerlSetEnv TopTenDB     tpj
  PerlSetEnv TopTenPrefix topten
  PerlSetEnv TopTenRoot   /home/fletch/topten
  <Limit GET>
    require valid-user
  </Limit>
</Location>
```

The final set of directives set up the TopTenTrans and Apache::Sandwich modules. The PerlSetVar lines specify the location of our feedback footer, what database to connect to, where the tracked documents reside in the filesystem, and what document to use for the index page.

```
PerlTransHandler TopTenTrans
<Location /topten>
  PerlSetVar FOOTER /topten/rate.html

  PerlSetVar TopTenDB     tpj
  PerlSetVar TopTenPrefix topten
  PerlSetVar TopTenRoot   /home/fletch/topten
  PerlSetVar TopTenIndex  /home/fletch/topten/index.epl
</Location>
```

## CHAPTER 7

Proxying with mod_perl

Lincoln D. Stein

One of the darker secrets of the web protocols is how proxy servers work. In this article we plunge into the depths and show you how to write a proxy module for the Apache web server. This module will handle the proxy's basic job of fetching web documents on your behalf and forwarding them to you, but with a twist: it acts as an advertisement filtering service.

An ordinary web server returns local documents in response to incoming requests. In contrast, a proxying server has elements of both server and client. Instead of sending the proxy server a request for a local document, the client requests the URL of a document located somewhere else on the Internet. The proxy then acts as a client itself by fetching the document and forwarding it to the waiting client.

Why Proxy?

What's the purpose of this? Proxy servers have several uses. Historically the most important use for proxies was to allow web requests to cross firewalls. Many firewall systems are configured to prohibit port 80 traffic. In order to circumvent this restriction, administrators installed web server proxies on the firewall system. Users then configured their browsers to connect to the firewall machine for web access, and the proxy did the rest. Nowadays all commercial firewall systems come with built-in web proxies and it is no longer necessary to run a general purpose web server on the firewall (which was never much of a good idea for security reasons).

A second reason to proxy is that some proxying servers, Apache included, can cache the contents of the remote documents by saving them to disk files. If they later receive a request for a previously-cached document, they return the cached document instead of fetching it remotely. This cuts down on network bandwidth and improves performance, particularly if the server is connected to the Internet by a slow connection. America Online uses caching proxies to improve response time for its large and content-hungry membership. Unfortunately, caching introduces a lot of complexity. When is a cached document no longer fresh, requiring another fetch again from its source? Given the web's eclectic mixture of static pages, CGI scripts, dynamic HTML, and server-side includes, not even the best caching proxies answer this question correctly 100% of the time.

A third use for proxy servers is to filter the request. A proxy server can change the outgoing request or modify the document on its way back to the user. This allows for many useful applications. One popular use of this technique is to create an anonymizing proxy. Such a proxy sits on the Internet somewhere and is used by people who want to protect their identities. As the anonymizer receives incoming requests, it strips out all potentially identifying information from the outgoing request, including the User-Agent field, which identifies the browser make and model, HTTP cookies, and the Referer field, which contains the URL of the last document the user viewed.

Like an anonymizer, the example proxy in this article filters the data that passes through it. However, instead of modifying the outgoing request, it modifies the document that is returned to the user. Each proxied document is examined to see whether it might be an advertising banner image. If so, the proxy replaces the banner with a transparent GIF generated on the fly, preserving the size and shape of the original image. The result is shown in Figure 7-1 (before) and Figure 7-2 (after).

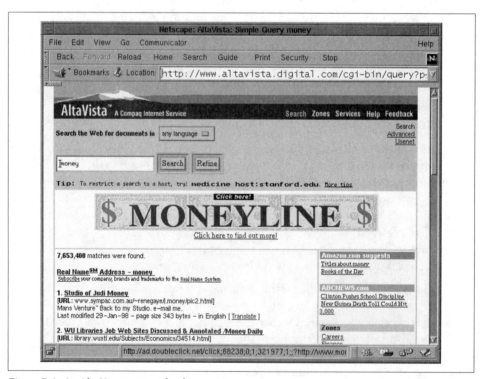

Figure 7-1. An AltaVista page with ads

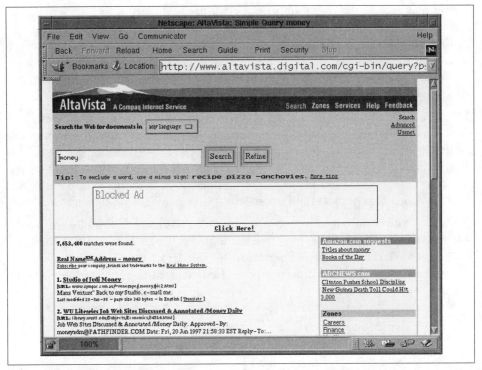

Figure 7-2. An AltaVista page viewed through Apache::AdBlocker

You might use this proxy if you are offended by the web's crass commercialism, or just easily distracted by the blinking, brightly colored ads on your favorite search page.

The proxy is written as an add-in module for the Apache server running mod_perl, the embedded Perl interpreter that Doug MacEachern and I wrote about in *mod_perl*. The code itself was written by Doug MacEachern, and is used with his permission.

How the Proxy Protocol Works

Despite its aura of the arcane, the basic proxy protocol is ridiculously simple. A normal web request begins with the browser sending a server a line of ASCII text, like this:

```
GET /path/to/document HTTP/1.0
```

The server responds by returning the document located at the indicated path.

In contrast, to make a proxy request, the browser modifies the first line of the request to look like this:

```
GET http://some.site/path/to/document HTTP/1.0
```

If the server is proxy-capable, it sees that the requested URL contains the protocol and hostname, and forwards the request to the indicated remote host. Some proxies can only handle requests for HTTP URLs, while others can also handle FTP, Gopher, and (occasionally) WAIS.

As you may recall from the *mod_perl* article, Apache divides each browser transaction into ten different phases responsible for handling everything from translating a URI into a physical pathname, to generating the page content, to writing information about the completed transaction into a log file. To extend the server's abilities, you write "handlers" to intercept one or more of the phases, supplementing Apache's built-in handlers or replacing them entirely.

The easiest way to intercept and handle proxy requests is to write two different handlers. The first handler operates during the URI translation phase and is responsible for distinguishing a proxy request from an ordinary one. When the URI translation handler detects a proxy request, it installs the second handler, whose job is to service the content-generation phase of the transaction. It is the content handler that does the actual proxy request and returns the (possibly modified) document.

Example 7-1 gives the complete code for a module called Apache::AdBlocker. To use this module, you'll need the LWP bundle and the Image::Size and GD modules. LWP is needed to fetch the remote page, Image::Size is used to determine the size of retrieved GIF and JPEG advertisements, and GD is used to generate a transparent GIF of the same size and shape as the blocked ad. You'll also need Apache 1.3.0 or higher, and a recent version of mod_perl.

Example 7-1. Apache::AdBlocker

```
0   package Apache::AdBlocker;
1
2   use strict;
3   use vars qw(@ISA $VERSION);
4   use Apache::Constants qw(:common);
5   use GD ();
6   use Image::Size qw(imgsize);
7   use LWP::UserAgent ();
8
9   @ISA = qw(LWP::UserAgent);
10  $VERSION = '1.00';
11
12  my $UA = __PACKAGE__->new;
13  $UA->agent(join "/", __PACKAGE__, $VERSION);
14  my $Ad = join "|", qw{ads? advertisements? banners? adv promotions?};
15
16  sub handler {
17      my($r) = @_;
18      return DECLINED unless $r->proxyreq;
19      $r->handler("perl-script");                # Okay, let's do it
20      $r->push_handlers(PerlHandler => \&proxy_handler);
21      return OK;
22  }
23
24  sub proxy_handler {
25      my ($r) = @_;
26
```

Example 7-1. Apache::AdBlocker (continued)

```perl
27    my $request = HTTP::Request->new($r->method => $r->uri);
28    my %headers_in = $r->headers_in;
29
30    while (my($key, $val) = each %headers_in) {
31        $request->header($key,$val);
32    }
33
34    if ($r->method eq 'POST') {
35        my $len = $r->header_in('Content-length');
36        my $buf;
37        $r->read($buf, $len);
38        $request->content($buf);
39    }
40
41    my $response = $UA->request($request);
42    $r->content_type($response->header('Content-type'));
43
44    # Feed response back into our request
45    $r->status($response->code);
46    $r->status_line(join " ", $response->code, $response->message);
47    $response->scan(sub {
48        $r->header_out(@_);
49    });
50
51    $r->send_http_header();
52    my $content = \$response->content;
53
54    if ($r->content_type =~ /^image/ && $r->uri =~ /\b($Ad)\b/i) {
55        $r->content_type("image/gif");
56        block_ad($content);
57    }
58
59    $r->print($$content);
60
61    return OK;
62 }
63
64 sub block_ad {
65    my $data = shift;
66    my ($x, $y) = imgsize($data);
67
68    my $im = GD::Image->new($x,$y);
69
70    my $white = $im->colorAllocate(255, 255, 255);
71    my $black = $im->colorAllocate(0,     0,   0);
72    my $red   = $im->colorAllocate(255,   0,   0);
73
74    $im->transparent($white);
75    $im->string(GD::gdLargeFont(), 5, 5, "Blocked Ad", $red);
76    $im->rectangle(0, 0, $x-1, $y-1, $black);
77
78    $$data = $im->gif;
```

Example 7-1. Apache::AdBlocker (continued)

```
79 }
80
81 1;
82
83 __END__
```

The module starts by declaring its package name. By convention, Apache modules are placed in the Apache:: namespace. We then turn on strict syntax checking, and bring in code from GD, Image::Size, and LWP::UserAgent. We also bring in commonly used constants from the Apache::Constants package.

Lines 9 and 10 inherit from the LWP::UserAgent class. LWP::UserAgent is used by the LWP library for all objects that are capable of making web client requests, such as robots and browsers. Although we don't actually override any of LWP::User-Agent's methods, declaring the module as a subclass of LWP::UserAgent allows us to cleanly customize these methods at a later date should we need to. We then define a version number, as every module intended for reusability should.

In lines 11 to 14, we create two package globals. $UA is the LWP::UserAgent that we use for our proxy requests. It's created using the special token __PACKAGE__, which evaluates at runtime to the name of the current package. Here, __PACKAGE__->new is equivalent to Apache::AdBlocker->new (or new Apache::AdBlocker if you prefer Perl's indirect object style of method call). Immediately afterward we call the object's agent method with a string composed of the package name and version number. This is the calling card LWP sends to the remote hosts' web servers as the HTTP User-Agent field. Provided that the remote server records this information, the string that will show up in the access log will be Apache::AdBlocker/1.00.

Line 14 defines a regular expression that detects many (but not all) banner ads. It's a simple expression that matches the words "ads," "banners," "promotion," and so on. If you use this service regularly, you'll probably want to broaden this expression to catch more ads.

Lines 16 through 22 define the *translation handler*, a subroutine which, by convention, is named handler. This subroutine is simple enough. It begins by copying the Apache request object from the argument stack to a lexical variable, $r. The request object is the interface between user-written modules and Apache, and can be used both to learn about the current transaction and to send commands back to the server.

In this case, we call the request object's proxyreq method to learn whether the current request is an ordinary one for a local document, or a proxy request for a URL on another system. If this is just an ordinary request, we decline to handle it, returning the DECLINED status code. This tells Apache to handle the translation phase using its default mechanism. Otherwise, we set the stage for a custom content-phase handler.

There are now two things that need to be done. First, we need to tell Apache that the Perl interpreter will be handling the content phase. We do this with a call to the request object's `handler` method, giving it an argument of `perl-script`, which is the internal name that mod_perl uses for the Perl interpreter. Next, we need to tell Perl what user-written subroutine to call when the time comes. We do this with a call to `push_handlers`. This routine takes two arguments: the name of the phase to handle, and a reference to the subroutine to call. `PerlHandler` is the name used for the content phase (the others are more descriptive, such as `PerlTransHandler` or `PerlLogHandler`), and `proxy_handler` is the subroutine that we want to run. As its name implies, you can call `push_handlers` multiple times in order to set up a chain of handlers that will be called in order. (We don't take advantage of this facility in this example.) The last thing we do is to return an `OK` status code, telling Apache that we handled the request ourselves and no more needs to be done.

Apache now takes over very briefly until it reaches the content-handling phase of the transaction, at which point we find ourselves inside the `proxy_handler` routine (lines 24 through 62). As a content handler, this subroutine is responsible for producing the document that is eventually transmitted back to the browser. When a proxied document is requested, this routine will be called once for the main document, and once for each image, sound, or other inline content.

As before, the routine starts by copying the request object into lexical variable `$r`. It now uses the LWP library to construct an HTTP::Request, an object that contains the various and sundry headers in an HTTP request. We need all the header fields that were passed to Apache to be passed through to the LWP library. This is so that cookies, authorization information, and the list of acceptable MIME types continue to work as expected. First, we create a generic HTTP::Request object by calling its `new` method with the request method and the request URI (derived from the request object's `method` and `uri` methods respectively). Next, we copy all the incoming header fields to the new HTTP::Request object. The Apache request object's `headers_in` method returns a hash of field name-value pairs. We iterate over this hash, inserting each header into the HTTP::Request object.

If the current request uses the `POST` method, there's also content data to copy over—typically the contents of fill-out forms. In lines 34 through 39 we retrieve the request's content length by calling the request object's `header_in` method with an argument of `Content-length`. This call is similar to `headers_in`, but returns the value of a single field, rather than a hash containing them all.

We actually send out the request in line 41. We pass the fully prepared `HTTP::Request` object to the user agent object's `request` method. After a brief delay for the network fetch, the call returns an HTTP::Response object, which we copy into the lexical variable `$response`.

And now the process of copying the headers is reversed. Every header in the LWP HTTP::Response object must be copied to the Apache request object. First, we handle a few special cases. The Apache API has a call named `content_type` to get and set the document's MIME type. In line 42, we call the HTTP::Response object's header method to fetch the content type, and immediately pass the result to the Apache request object's content_type method. Next, we set the numeric HTTP status code and the human-readable HTTP status line (this is the text like 200 OK or 404 Not Found that begins each response from a web server). We call the HTTP::Response object's code and message methods to return the numeric code and human readable messages respectively, and copy them to the Apache request object, using the status and status_line methods to set the values.

When the special case headers are done, we copy all the other header fields, using the HTTP::Response object's scan method to rapidly loop through each of the header name-value pairs (lines 47 through 49). For each header field, scan invokes an anonymous callback routine that sets the appropriate field in the Apache request object with the header_out method. header_out works just like header_in, but accepts the name-value pair of a outgoing header field to set.

At this point, the outgoing header is ready to be sent to the waiting browser. We call the request object's send_http_header method (line 51) to have Apache send a correctly-formatted HTTP header.

Identifying Ads

The time has now come to deal with potential banner ads. To identify something as an ad, we require that the document be an image and that its URI satisfy a regular expression match that detects words like "advertisement" and "promotion." On line 52, we invoke the HTTP::Response object's content method to return the data contained within the response, and store a reference to it in the lexical variable $content. Next, in lines 54–57, we use the information stored in the Apache request object to check whether the MIME type corresponds to an image, and if so, whether the URL matches the ad scanner pattern. If both these conditions are true, we set the content type to image/gif and call an internal subroutine named block_ad to replace the original image with a custom GIF. On line 59, we send the possibly modified content on to the browser by passing it to the Apache request object's print method. Lastly, we return a status code of OK to inform Apache that we handled the transaction successfully.

The block_ad subroutine, beginning on line 64, is short and sweet. Its job is to take an image in any of several possible formats and replace it with a custom GIF of exactly the same dimensions. The GIF will be transparent, allowing the page background color to show through, and will have the words "Blocked Ad" printed in large friendly letters in the upper left-hand corner.

To get the width and height of the image we call imgsize, a function imported from the Image::Size module. imgsize recognizes most web image formats, including GIF, JPEG, XBM, and PNG. Using these values, we create a new blank GD::Image object and store it in a variable named $im. We call the image object's colorAllocate method three times to allocate color table entries for white, black, and red, and declare that the white color is transparent, using the transparent method. The routine calls the string method to draw the message starting at coordinates (5,5), and finally frames the whole image with a black rectangle. The custom image is now converted into GIF format with the gif method, and copied into $$data, overwriting whatever was there before.

This ends the module. The only remaining step is to tell Apache about it. You do this by placing the following directive in one of Apache's configuration files:

```
PerlTransHandler Apache::AdBlocker
```

Apache::AdBlocker's handler subroutine will now be invoked to inspect all incoming requests.

## CHAPTER 8

Authentication with mod_perl

Michael Parker

Soon after I learned about mod_perl, I wanted to know how I could use it to secure my web site. Apache has a number of phases it progresses through as it serves web pages. Three of those phases are *access control*, *authentication*, and *authorization*. In this article, I'll discuss each phase and demonstrate five examples of what they can do.

Access Control

The *access control* phase is the first of the three authentication phases available in Apache. This phase allows you to restrict access to specific URLs based on criteria other than who the visitor is. This has traditionally been used to allow or deny access for certain hosts. However, with mod_perl you can restrict access to specific directories for any reason you like: time of day or week, phase of the moon, user agent, the referring page, and just about anything else you can envision.

The Apache::HostLimit module (Example 8-1) is a simple access control handler you can use to exclude particular hosts. For a more detailed explanation of handlers, read the *mod_perl* article in this book, or get Lincoln Stein and Doug MacEachern's book *Writing Apache Modules in Perl and C* (O'Reilly).

To activate the access control handler, you need the following in your configuration file:

```
PerlAccessHandler Apache::HostLimit
```

This tells Apache to invoke the Apache::HostLimit module during access control.

Example 8-1. Excluding particular hosts with Apache::HostLimit

```
1   package Apache::HostLimit;
2
3   use strict;
4   use Apache::Constants ':common';
5
6   sub handler {
7       my $r = shift;
8
9       my $host = $r->get_remote_host;
10
```

```
11      if ($host eq "somebadhost.com") {
12          $r->log_error("Apache::HostLimit - Denied access for $host");
13          return FORBIDDEN;
14      }
15      elsif ($host eq "127.0.0.1") {
16          $r->log_error("Apache::HostLimit - Denied access for $host");
17          return FORBIDDEN;
18      }
19      else {
20          return DECLINED;
21      }
22  }
23
24  1;
```

The module is simple. It determines what computer the visitor is coming from, and then it either returns FORBIDDEN, indicating that the user is not to be granted access, or DECLINED, indicating that the module has no opinion one way or the other. Line 1 contains the package declaration common to all Perl modules. Line 3 contains the use strict pragma. All mod_perl modules should employ the strict pragma to help overcome some of the traps associated with mod_perl (see *mod_perl_traps.pod*, bundled with the mod_perl distribution). Line 4 pulls in the common Apache return codes for use later. Line 6 begins handler, the standard handler routine. Whenever mod_perl executes a handler, it looks for a subroutine by that name. All mod_perl handlers are called with one argument, the request object. (The one exception is when the handler has a $$ prototype. Then it's treated as an object-oriented method call.)

Line 9 makes use of the request object, $r, to obtain the name of the browser's computer. Lines 11 to 21 determine the request's fate. If the host variable matches, the module notes this in the error log, (line 12 and 16) and returns FORBIDDEN. If the host does not match, the request falls through, returning DECLINED to indicate that all is well and the request can move on to the next handler.

This example is very simple, but it shows how much can be accomplished in this phase. For instance, you might have handler read the information from a file so that it could be updated without restarting the server. (If you want to stop an annoying person or robot from accessing your website, you would be better off using the URI translation handler. The translation handler is the first phase after the request has been read; by denying access there, you avoid the extra processing for a request that is destined to fail anyway.)

Authentication

In the second access-checking phase, *authentication*, the server uses a technique like username/password verification to determine if the visitor is welcome. You can invoke a variety of resources at this point, including:

- Authentication from more then one *htpasswd* file
- The Unix password database
- Oracle grant tables
- Authentication on a Windows domain server

Windows Domain Server Authentication

Example 8-2 demonstrates the Apache::AuthenSmb module, which authenticates users against a Windows domain server—a nice feature for Unix web servers in a Windows environment. This is a stripped down example, lacking the authorization phase; you can obtain the complete module from CPAN or create your own.

Example 8-2. The Apache::AuthenSmb module

```
1   package Apache::AuthenSmb;
2
3   use strict;
4   use Apache::Constants ':common';
5   use Authen::Smb;
6
7   sub handler {
8       my $r = shift;
9       my($res, $sent_pwd) = $r->get_basic_auth_pw;
10      return $res if $res;     # Decline if not Basic
11
12      my $name = $r->connection->user;
13
14      my $pdc    = $r->dir_config('myPDC');
15      my $bdc    = $r->dir_config('myBDC')    || $pdc;
16      my $domain = $r->dir_config('myDOMAIN') || "WORKGROUP";
17
18      if ($name eq "") {
19          $r->note_basic_auth_failure;
20          $r->log_reason("No Username Given", $r->uri);
21          return AUTH_REQUIRED;
22      }
23
24      if (!$pdc) {
25          $r->note_basic_auth_failure;
26          $r->log_reason("Configuration error, no PDC", $r->uri);
27          return AUTH_REQUIRED;
28      }
29
30      my $return = Authen::Smb::authen($name,
31                                       $sent_pwd,
32                                       $pdc,
33                                       $bdc,
34                                       $domain);
35
36      if ($return) {
37          $r->note_basic_auth_failure;
```

Example 8-2. The Apache::AuthenSmb module (continued)

```
38          $r->log_reason("user $name: password mismatch", $r->uri);
39          return AUTH_REQUIRED;
40      }
41
42      return OK;
43 }
44
45 1
```

The configuration directives for this module make use of `PerlSetVar` to avoid hard-coding configuration details. (`PerlSetVar` allows you to set variables that will be accessible in your Apache modules.) In addition to some mod_perl directives, you must use the `AuthName`, `AuthType`, and `require` directives for Apache to invoke the authentication handlers. Documentation on these is bundled with Apache.

```
AuthName "Authentication Realm"
AuthType Basic
PerlSetVar myPDC PDCSERVER
PerlSetVar myBDC BDCSERVER
PerlSetVar myDOMAIN DOMAIN
PerlAuthenHandler Apache::AuthenSmb
require valid-user
```

In addition to the PerlSetVar directives, which in this case provide several configuration details for the module, a handler directive is required. This directive behaves just like the access control module directive that we used for Apache::HostLimit.

The interesting part begins on line 9, where a call into the Apache API obtains the type of authentication and the password sent. Line 10 checks to make sure the authentication type is basic. Line 12 makes another call into the request object to get the username entered by the client. Lines 14 to 16 pull in the configuration information set by `PerlSetVar`.

The downside of basic password authentication is that it sends the username and password to the server in the clear. Apache also supports *digest authentication*, a more secure method, but some browsers don't support it.

Until this point, this listing shows a standard setup for an authentication module. Now we start getting into the heart of the module. The first step is to check that the user actually entered a username. If not, the module calls note_basic_auth_failure on line 19, logs the error, and returns AUTH_REQUIRED, which indicates that authentication was unsuccessful. The next lines, 24 to 28, check to make sure a PDC (Primary Domain Controller) was configured. If not, the module again notes and logs the failure and returns AUTH_REQUIRED. Line 30 makes a call into the Authen::Smb module (on CPAN) using the username and password sent, along with the configuration details. Line 36 checks the return value of the Authen::Smb call. If the call fails, it notes and logs the failure, returning AUTH_REQUIRED. If the request makes it this far, line 42 returns OK indicating success and allows Apache to continue with the request.

More NT Authentication

The Apache::AuthenOverrideSmb module builds on Apache::AuthenSmb. It allows you to override or supplement the users available in your NT domain with an external password file. This can be convenient if you need to grant access to individuals or groups that might not have an NT account.

This module is configured in much the same way as Apache::AuthenSmb, adding only the definition of the external password file:

```
AuthName "Authentication Realm"
AuthType Basic
PerlSetVar myPDC PDCSERVER
PerlSetVar myBDC BDCSERVER
PerlSetVar myDOMAIN DOMAIN
PerlSetVar password_file /your/.htpasswd
PerlAuthenHandler
Apache::AuthenOverrideSmb
require valid-user
```

The Apache::AuthenOverrideSmb module (Example 8-3) is similar to the previous two. However, it adds line 11, which pulls in the path to the password file. Lines 18 to 22 create an HTTPD::UserAdmin object using the path to our password file. Lines 24 to 32 check to see if an entry exists in the password file. If so, the module checks to make sure the password is correct. In that case, the module returns OK; otherwise, the module notes and logs the failure and returns AUTH_REQUIRED. From this point the module is the same as Apache::AuthenSmb, making a call to Authen::Smb to determine if the user should be granted access.

Example 8-3. Adding an external password file with Apache::AuthenOverrideSmb

```
1   package Apache::AuthenOverrideSmb;
2
3   use strict;
4   use HTTPD::UserAdmin ( );
5   use Apache::Constants qw(OK AUTH_REQUIRED);
6   use Authen::Smb;
7
8   sub handler {
9       my $r = shift;
10
11      my $PASSWD_FILE = $r->dir_config("password_file") || "";
12
13      my ($res, $sent_pwd) = $r->get_basic_auth_pw;
14      return $res if $res; #decline if not Basic
15
16      my $user = $r->connection->user;
17
18      my $u = HTTPD::UserAdmin->new(
19                                    DB => $PASSWD_FILE,
20                                    DBType => "Text",
21                                    Server => "apache",
22                                    Locking => 0);
23
```

```
24      if (my $passwd = $u->password($user)) {
25          if (crypt($sent_pwd, $passwd) eq $passwd) {
26              return OK;
27          }
28          else {
29              $r->note_basic_auth_failure;
30              $r->log_reason("user $user: password mismatch", $r->uri);
31              return AUTH_REQUIRED;
32          }
33      }
34      else {
35          my $pdc = $r->dir_config('myPDC');
36          my $bdc = $r->dir_config('myBDC') || $pdc;
37          my $domain = $r->dir_config('myDOMAIN) || "WORKGROUP";
38
39          if ($name eq "") {
40              $r->note_basic_auth_failure;
41              $r->log_reason("No Username Given", $r->uri);
42              return AUTH_REQUIRED;
43          }
44
45          if (!$pdc) {
46              $r->note_basic_auth_failure;
47              $r->log_reason("Configuration error, no PDC", $r->uri);
48              return AUTH_REQUIRED;
49          }
40
51          my $return = Authen::Smb::authen($user,
52                                           $sent_pwd,
53                                           $pdc,
54                                           $bdc,
55                                           $domain);
56
57          if ($return) {
58              $r->note_basic_auth_failure;
59              $r->log_reason("user $user: password mismatch", $r->uri);
60              return AUTH_REQUIRED;
61          }
62          return OK;
63      }
64  }
65
66  1;
```

Authorization

Once a user has been authenticated, we're ready for the final stage: *authorization*. This stage determines whether an authenticated user possesses the proper credentials to access the protected URL. This is where you can use the Apache require directive in most any Apache module, allowing you to specify whether access should be granted to a valid user, a list of users, or to a Unix group.

Basic Authorization

Example 8-4 shows the Apache::AuthzExample module, which demonstrates a very basic authorization handler that handles the require user <username> and require valid-user directives. The configuration details for authorization handlers are similar to other handlers. However, in addition to the require directive, you have to add a mod_perl directive like the one below:

```
PerlAuthzHandler Apache::AuthzExample
require valid-user
```

Example 8-4. Authorizing particular users with Apache::AuthzExample

```
1   package Apache::AuthzExample;
2
3   use strict;
4   use Apache::Constants ':common';
5
6   sub handler {
7       my $r = shift;
8       my $requires = $r->requires;
9       return OK unless $requires;
10
11      my $name = $r->connection->user;
12
13      for my $req (@$requires) {
14          my ($require, @rest) = split /\s+/, $req->{requirement};
15          if ($require eq "user") {
16              return OK if grep $name eq $_, @rest;
17          }
18          elsif ($require eq "valid-user") {
19              return OK;
20          }
21      }
22
23      $r->note_basic_auth_failure;
24      $r->log_reason("user $name: not authorized", $r->uri);
25      return AUTH_REQUIRED;
26  }
27
28  1;
```

This module begins much like the others, pulling in the required modules and getting the request object. Line 8 makes an API call to get the array of require directives. If no directives have been defined, line 9 returns OK. Line 11 obtains the username entered in the authentication phase. (Remember that this user has already passed the authentication phase by this point.)

Lines 13 to 21 iterate over the require directives. Line 14 splits off the type of require from the rest of the information for that directive. Line 15 checks to see if the type is user, and if so, line 16 checks to see if the username is present. If so, it returns OK. Line 18 checks whether the type is valid-user, returning OK if so because the user has already been authenticated. If any of these checks fail, the module drops through to the final statements, which logs the failure and returns AUTH_REQUIRED to the client.

More Sophisticated Authorization

The Apache::AuthzManager module (Example 8-5) is similar to Apache::AuthzExample, but it shows how easily you can add a type to the require directive. Assume that you want to limit access based on the user's manager, a good tool for department-level web pages. I'll assume the existence of a function named CheckManager that takes care of the work behind the scenes.

Example 8-5. More sophisticated authorization with Apache::AuthzManager

```
1   package Apache::AuthzManager;
2
3   use strict;
4   use CheckManager;
5   use Apache::Constants ':common';
6
7   sub handler {
8       my $r = shift;
9       my $requires = $r->requires;
10      return OK unless $requires;
11
12      my $name = $r->connection->user;
13
14      for my $req (@$requires) {
15          my ($require, @rest) = split /\s+/, $req->{requirement};
16          if ($require eq "manager") {
17              for my $manname (@rest) {
18                  if (checkManager($manname, $name)) {
19                      return OK;
20                  }
21              }
22          }
23      }
24
25      $r->note_basic_auth_failure;
26      $r->log_reason("user $name: not authorized", $r->uri);
27      return AUTH_REQUIRED;
28
29  }
```

This module is exactly the same as Apache::AuthzExample, except for how the require type is handled in lines 16 to 22. Here, the module looks for the manager keyword and calls the checkManager function for each keyword found. It returns OK if the user is allowed access; it falls through to the failure state and returns AUTH_REQUIRED if the user is not authorized.

Conclusion

These examples illustrate some of the simplest mechanisms for access checking. You can customize them in as sophisticated a manner as you wish; for instance, you could limit access to URLs during business hours, exclude hosts from a continuously-updated blacklist, or authenticate against a company LDAP database. For more information on mod_perl, see *http://www.modperl.com* and *http://perl.apache.org*. Questions about mod_perl can be sent to the mod_perl mailing list; to join, send a message to *modperl-subscribe@perl.apache.org*.

## CHAPTER 9

Navigation Bars with mod_perl

Lincoln D. Stein

I admit it. I love navigation bars. I go completely green with envy whenever I browse one of those fancy web sites with navigation bars that change color as you move the mouse over them or expand and contract a table of contents with one click.

Sometimes I think, "Okay, that's it. I'm going to install a navigation bar like this one *right now*." So I download the HTML source code for the page and have a peek. What I see always diminishes my enthusiasm substantially. Navigation bars are a lot of work! Either they're done by hand using individually crafted HTML pages, or they require a slow-loading Java applet, or most frequently, they consume several pages of JavaScript code filled with convoluted workarounds for various makes and models of browser.

One of the cardinal virtues of programming is laziness, and as a Perl programmer I have this virtue in spades. I don't want to do any hard work to create my navigation bar. I just want it to appear, automatically, when I write an HTML page and save it into my web site's document directory. When I finally bit the bullet and got down to writing a site-wide navigation bar, I used mod_perl, the nifty embedded Perl module for Apache, to create a system that automatically adds a navigation bar to all my pages without my having to lift a finger. You need the Apache web server, Version 1.3.3 or higher, mod_perl Version 1.16 or higher, and Perl 5.004_03 or higher to use this system.

Figure 9-1 shows a page from my laboratory's web site with the navigation bar at the top. The bar is a single row of links, embedded inside an HTML table, running along the top and bottom of the page. Each link represents a major subdivision of the site. In this case, the subdivisions are groups of software products that I maintain, namely "Jade", "AcePerl", "Boulder", and "WWW." There's also a "Home" link for the top level page of the site. When the user selects a link, it takes him directly to the chosen section. The link then changes to red to indicate that the selected section is currently active. The link remains red for as long as the user is browsing pages contained within or beneath the section (as determined by the URL path). When the user jumps out of the section, either by selecting a link from the navigation bar or by some other means, the navigation bar updates to reflect his new position.

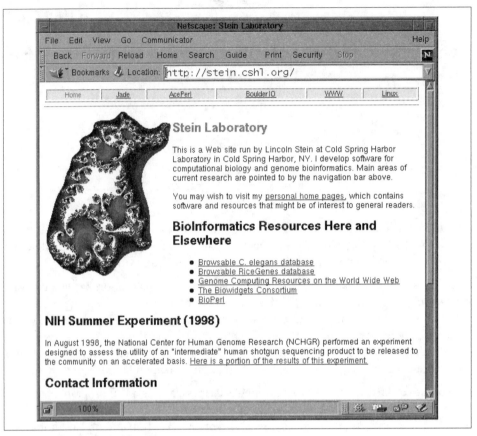

Figure 9-1. http://stein.cshl.org/

The Configuration File

The nice feature about this system is that there's no hardcoded information any-where: neither the HTML pages themselves about the organization of the site nor the appearance of the navigation bar. The navigation bar is added to the page using con-figuration information contained in a site-wide configuration file. The bar's appear-ance is determined by Perl code. I favor a visually simple horizontal navigation bar with text links with a few adjustments to the code; however, you could change the bar so that it displays vertically, or uses inline images as its links. It's also possible to associate different sections of the site with different navigation bars, or hide the navi-gation bar completely.

The configuration file is usually stored with Apache's other configuration files inside the server root directory's *etc* subdirectory. Below you can see the configuration I use at my site. It's a simple text file consisting of tab-delimited text. The first column contains the URLs to link to for each of the site's major sections. The second column contains the text to display for each link. Blank lines and lines beginning with the comment character are ignored.

```
# stein.cshl.org navigation bar
# file etc/navigation.conf
/index.html          Home
/jade/               Jade
/AcePerl/            AcePerl
/software/boulder/   BoulderIO
/software/WWW/       WWW
/linux/              Linux
```

Notice that you can link to either a filename, e.g., *index.html*, or to a directory name, e.g., /jade/. The navigation bar systems treats the two cases slightly differently when deciding whether to consider a certain section "active." The system uses prefix mapping to determine whether a page lies within a section. In the example above, any page that starts with the URL /jade will be considered to be part of the "Jade" area, and the corresponding label will be highlighted in red. However, since /index.html refers to a file rather than a partial path, only the home page itself is ever considered to be within the "Home" area.

Major sections do not have to correspond to a top level directory. For example, the "Boulder" and "WWW" sections are both subdirectories beneath "software", which doesn't have an explicit entry. The navigational system will also work with user-supported directories. For example:

```
/~lstein/      Lincoln's Pages
```

Activating the Navigation Bar

Apache itself needs to be configured to use the navigation bar system. This is done by adding the <Location> directive section shown below to one of Apache's configuration files. There are three directives in this section. The SetHandler directive tells Apache that every URL on the site is to be passed to the embedded Perl interpreter. The PerlHandler directive tells the Perl interpreter what to do with the URL when it gets it. In this case, we're telling Perl to pass the URL through the Apache::NavBar module. The last directive, PerlSetVar, sets a configuration variable named NavConf to the relative configuration file path *etc/navigation.conf*. The Apache::NavBar module will use NavConf to find its configuration file.

```
<Location />
  SetHandler   perl-script
  PerlHandler  Apache::NavBar
  PerlSetVar   NavConf etc/navigation.conf
</Location>
```

In this example, the <Location> directive's path argument is /, indicating that the navigation bar system is to be applied to each and every URL served by the web site. To apply the navigation bar to a portion of the site only, you would just modify the path accordingly. You can even apply different navigation bar configuration files to different parts of your web site!

Generating the Navigation Bar

Example 9-1 shows the code for the navigation bar module. The file should be named NavBar.pm and stored in the Apache subdirectory of the Perl library directory. This is a slightly longer code example than you've seen in previous columns, so we'll walk through it in chunks.

Example 9-1. NavBar.pm

```perl
package Apache::NavBar;
# file Apache/NavBar.pm

use strict;
use Apache::Constants qw(:common);
use Apache::File ();

my %BARS = ();
my $TABLEATTS   = 'WIDTH="100%" BORDER=1';
my $TABLECOLOR  = '#C8FFFF';
my $ACTIVECOLOR = '#FF0000';

sub handler {
    my $r = shift;

    $r->content_type eq 'text/html'   || return DECLINED;
    my $bar   = read_configuration($r) || return DECLINED;
    my $table = make_bar($r, $bar);

    $r->update_mtime;
    $r->set_last_modified($bar->modified);
    my $rc = $r->meets_conditions;
    return $rc unless $rc == OK;

    my $fh = Apache::File->new($r->filename) || return DECLINED;

    $r->send_http_header;
    return OK if $r->header_only;

    local $/ = "";
    while (<$fh>) {
        s:(<BODY.*?>):$1$table:soi;
        s:(</BODY>):$table$1:oi;
    } continue {
        $r->print($_);
    }
    return OK;
}

sub make_bar {
    my ($r, $bar) = @_;

    # Create the navigation bar
    my $current_url = $r->uri;
```

Example 9-1. NavBar.pm (continued)

```perl
    my @cells;
    foreach my $url ($bar->urls) {
        my $label = $bar->label($url);
        my $is_current = $current_url =~ /^$url/;
        my $cell = $is_current ?
            qq(<FONT COLOR="$ACTIVECOLOR" CLASS="active">$label</FONT>) :
            qq(<A HREF="$url" CLASS="inactive">$label</A>);
        push @cells,
           qq(<TD CLASS="navbar" ALIGN=CENTER BGCOLOR="$TABLECOLOR">$cell</TD>\n);
    }
    return qq(<TABLE CLASS="navbar" $TABLEATTS><TR>@cells</TR></TABLE>\n);
}

# Read the navigation bar configuration file and return it as a hash.
sub read_configuration {
    my $r = shift;
    return unless my $conf_file = $r->dir_config('NavConf');
    return unless -e ($conf_file = $r->server_root_relative($conf_file));
    my $mod_time = (stat _)[9];
    return $BARS{$conf_file} if $BARS{$conf_file}
            && $BARS{$conf_file}->modified >= $mod_time;
    return $BARS{$conf_file} = NavBar->new($conf_file);
}

package NavBar;

sub new {                          # Create a new NavBar object
    my ($class, $conf_file) = @_;
    my (@c, %c);
    my $fh = Apache::File->new($conf_file) || return;
    while (<$fh>) {
        chomp;
        next if /^\s*\#/;  # skip comments
        my($url, $label) = /^(\S+)\s+(.+)/;
        push @c, $url;      # keep the url in an ordered array
        $c{$url} = $label; # keep its label in a hash
    }
    return bless {    'urls' => \@c,
                    'labels' => \%c,
                  'modified' => (stat $conf_file)[9]}, $class;
}

# Return ordered list of all the URLs in the navigation bar
sub urls { return @{shift->{'urls'}}; }

# Return the label for a particular URL in the navigation bar
sub label { return $_[0]->{'labels'}->{$_[1]} || $_[1]; }

# Return the modification date of the configuration file
sub modified { return $_[0]->{'modified'}; }

1;
```

After declaring the package, the module turns on the strict pragma, thus avoiding the use of barewords, undeclared globals, and other sloppy programming practices. The module then brings in two helper packages.

```
package Apache::NavBar;
# file Apache/NavBar.pm

use strict;
use Apache::Constants qw(:common);
use Apache::File ();
```

As its name implies, Apache::Constants provides various constant values that are meaningful to the Apache server. We bring in the "common" constants, and then Apache::File, which contains routines useful for manipulating files.

```
my %BARS = ();
my $TABLEATTS   = 'WIDTH="100%" BORDER=1';
my $TABLECOLOR  = '#C8FFFF';
my $ACTIVECOLOR = '#FF0000';
```

These lines define several file-wide lexical variables. %BARS is a hash that will be used to hold a set of "NavBar" navigation bar objects. The NavBar class, which we'll examine later, defines methods for reading and parsing navigation bar configuration files, and for returning information about a particular navigation bar. Because a site is free to define several different navigation bars, the %BARS hash is necessary to keep track of them. The hash's keys are the paths to each navigation bar's configuration file, and its values are the NavBar objects themselves.

The $TABLEATTS, $TABLECOLOR, and $ACTIVECOLOR globals control various aspects of the navigation bar's appearance. $TABLEATTS controls the table's width and border attributes, $TABLECOLOR sets the background color of each cell, and $ACTIVECOLOR sets the color of the active links.

```
sub handler {
    my $r = shift;
```

This begins the definition of the handler subroutine, which Apache calls to fetch a requested document. The subroutine begins by shifting the request object off the subroutine stack. The request object will be used subsequently for all communication between the subroutine and Apache.

```
$r->content_type eq 'text/html'  || return DECLINED;
my $bar = read_configuration($r) || return DECLINED;
my $table = make_bar($r, $bar);
```

In this section we attempt to read the configuration file and create or retrieve the appropriate navigation bar object. The first thing we do is test the requested document's MIME type by calling the content_type method. If the MIME type is anything other than text/html, it doesn't make any sense to add a navigation bar, so we return a result code of DECLINED. This tells Apache to pass the request on to the next module that has expressed interest in processing requests. Usually this will be Apache's default document handler, which simply sends the file through unmodified.

Otherwise, we try to read the currently configured navigation bar definition file, using an internal routine named read_configuration. If this routine succeeds, it will return the navigation bar object. Otherwise, it returns undef. Again, we exit with a DECLINED error code in case of failure.

In the fourth line, we call an internal routine named make_bar, which turns the NavBar object into a properly formatted HTML table.

```
$r->update_mtime;
$r->set_last_modified($bar->modified);
my $rc = $r->meets_conditions;
return $rc unless $rc == OK;
```

This bit of code represents a useful optimization. In order to reduce network usage, most modern browsers temporarily cache the files they retrieve on the user's hard disk. Then, in the request header, the browser sends the server an HTTP header called If-Modified-Since, which contains the modification time and date of the cached file. In order to avoid an unnecessary file transmission, the server should compare the modification time specified in the If-Modified-Since header to the modification time of the file on disk. If the modification time of the server's copy is the same as the time specified by the browser, then there's no reason to retransmit the document, and the server can return an HTTP_NOT_MODIFIED status code. Otherwise, the server should send the updated file.

In this case, the logic is more complicated, because the contents of the requested document depend on two factors: the modification time of the file, and the modification time of the navigation bar configuration file. Fortunately, Apache has a general mechanism for dealing with these situations. We begin calling the request object's update_mtime method to copy the requested file's modification time into Apache's internal table of outgoing HTTP header fields. Next, we call set_last_modified with the modification date of the navigation bar configuration file. This updates the modification time that is sent to the browser, but only if it's more recent than the modification time of the requested file. The navigation bar's modification date is, conveniently enough, returned by the NavBar object's modified method.

The next line calls the request object's meets_conditions method. This checks whether the browser made a conditional request using the If-Modified-Since header field (or any of the conditional fetches defined by HTTP/1.1). The method returns OK if the document satisfies all the conditions and should be sent to the browser, or another result (usually HTTP_NOT_MODIFIED) otherwise. To implement the conditional fetch, we simply check whether the result code is OK. If not, we return the status code to Apache and it forwards the news on to the browser. Otherwise, we manufacture and transmit the page.

```
my $fh = Apache::File->new($r->filename) || return DECLINED;
```

This next line attempts to open the requested file for reading, using the Apache::File class. Apache::File is an object-oriented filehandle interface. It is similar to IO::File, but has less of an impact on performance and memory footprint. The request object's filename method returns the physical path to the file. If anything fails at this point, we return DECLINED, invoking Apache's default handling of the request. Otherwise, the filehandle object returned by Apache::File->new is stored in a variable named $fh.

```
$r->send_http_header;
return OK if $r->header_only;
```

The send_http_header method makes Apache send the HTTP header off to the browser. This header includes the If-Modified-Since field set earlier, along with other header fields set automatically by Apache. The second line represents yet another optimization. If the brower sent a HEAD request, then it isn't interested in getting the document body and there's no reason for this module to send it. The header_only method returns true if the current request uses the HEAD method. If so, we return OK, telling Apache that the request was handled successfully.

```
local $/ = "";
while (<$fh>) {
    s:(<BODY.*?>):$1$table:soi;
    s:(</BODY>):$table$1:oi;
} continue {
    $r->print($_);
}
return OK;
```

These lines send the document body. We read from the HTML file paragraph by paragraph, looking for <BODY> and </BODY> tags. When we find either, we insert the HTML table containing the navigation bar adjacent to it. The bar is inserted beneath <BODY> and immediately above </BODY>. The reason for using paragraph mode and a multiline regular expression is to catch the common situation in which the <BODY> tag is spread across several lines. The regular expression isn't guaranteed to catch all possible <BODY> tags (in particular, it'll mess up on tags with an embedded > symbol), but it works for the vast majority of cases.

We then send the possibly modified text to the browser using the request object's print method. After reaching the end of the file, we return OK, completing the transaction. Note that there is no need to explicitly close the Apache::File object. The filehandle is closed automatically when the object goes out of scope.

We now turn our attention to some of the utility functions used by this module, starting with make_bar:

```
sub make_bar {
    my ($r, $bar) = @_;

    # Create the navigation bar
    my $current_url = $r->uri;
    my @cells;
    foreach my $url ($bar->urls) {
        my $label = $bar->label($url);
        my $is_current = $current_url =~ /^$url/;
```

```
            my $cell = $is_current ?
                qq(<FONT COLOR="$ACTIVECOLOR" CLASS="active">$label</FONT>) :
                qq(<A HREF="$url" CLASS="inactive">$label</A>);
            push @cells,
                qq(<TD CLASS="navbar" ALIGN=CENTER BGCOLOR="$TABLECOLOR">$cell</TD>\n);
        }
        return qq(<TABLE CLASS="navbar" $TABLEATTS><TR>@cells</TR></TABLE>\n);
    }
```

The make_bar function takes two arguments, the request object and the previously-created NavBar object. Its job is to create an HTML table that correctly reflects the current state of the navigation bar. make_bar begins by fetching the current URL, calling the request object's uri method. Next, it calls the NavBar object's urls method to fetch the list of partial URLs for the site's major areas, and iterates over them in a foreach loop.

For each URL, the function fetches its human-readable label by calling $bar->label and determines whether the current document is part of the area. What happens next depends on whether the current document is contained within the area or not. If so, the code generates a label enclosed within a <FONT> tag with the COLOR attribute set to red and enclosed in a <B> tag. In the latter case, the code generates a hypertext link. The label or link is then pushed onto a growing array of HTML table cells. At the end of the loop, the code incorporates the table cells into a one-row table, and returns the HTML to the caller.

The next bit of code defines the read_configuration function, which is responsible for parsing the navigation bar configuration file and returning a new NavBar object.

```
# Read the navigation bar configuration file and return it as a hash.
sub read_configuration {
    my $r = shift;
    return unless my $conf_file = $r->dir_config('NavConf');
    return unless -e ($conf_file=$r->server_root_relative($conf_file));

    my $mod_time = (stat _)[9];
    return $BARS{$conf_file} if $BARS{$conf_file}
        && $BARS{$conf_file}->modified >= $mod_time;
    return $BARS{$conf_file} = NavBar->new($conf_file);
}
```

The most interesting feature of read_configuration is that it caches its results so that the configuration file is not reparsed unless it has changed recently. The function begins by calling the request object's dir_config method to return the value of the directory configuration variable NavConf (this was previously set in the <Location> section with the PerlSetVar configuration directive). If no such configuration variable is defined, dir_config returns undef and we exit immediately.

Otherwise, we can call server_root_relative in order to turn a relative pathname (etc/navigation.conf) into an absolute one (/usr/local/apache/etc/navigation.conf). We test for the existence of the configuration file using Perl's -e switch, and then fetch the file's modification time using the stat call. We now test the cached version of the configuration file to see if we can still use it by comparing the modification time of the configuration file with the time returned by the cached copy's modified method. We return the cached copy of the navigation bar object if it exists and it is still fresh. Otherwise, we invoke the NavBar class's new method to create a new object from the configuration file, store the returned object in the %BARS object cache, and return the object.

The next bit of code defines the NavBar class, which is really just an object-oriented interface to the configuration file.

```perl
package NavBar;

# create a new NavBar object
sub new {
    my ($class, $conf_file) = @_;
    my (@c, %c);
    my $fh = Apache::File->new($conf_file) || return;
    while (<$fh>) {
        chomp;
        next if /^\s*#/; # skip comments
        next unless my($url, $label) = /^(\S+)\s+(.+)/;
        push @c, $url; # keep urls in an array
        $c{$url} = $label; # keep its label in a hash
    }
    return bless {    'urls' => \@c,
                    'labels' => \%c,
                  'modified' => (stat $conf_file)[9]}, $class;
}
```

Following the package declaration, we define the NavBar::new method. The method takes two arguments, the classname and the path to the configuration file. The method begins by opening the configuration file, again using the Apache::File utility class to return an open filehandle. The code reads from the filehandle line by line, skipping comments and blank lines. Otherwise, we parse out the section URL and its label and store them it into an array and a hash. Both are necessary because we need to keep track of both the mapping from URL to section label and the order in which to list the sections in the navigation bar. When the navigation bar has been completely read, the list of section URLs, the labels, and the modification time of the configuration file are all stored into a new object, which we return to the caller.

```perl
# Return ordered list of the URLs in the bar
sub urls { return @{shift->{'urls'}}; }

# Return the label for a URL in the navigation bar
sub label { return $_[0]->{'labels'} || $_[1]; }

# Return the modification date of the config file
sub modified { return $_[0]->{'modified'}; }
```

The last three subroutines defined in this module are accessors for NavBar configuration date. `urls` returns the ordered list of URLs that define the configured main sections of the site. `label` takes a section URL and returns the corresponding section label. If no label is configured, it just returns the original URL. Finally, `modified` returns the modification time of the configuration file, for use in caching.

A Foundation to Build On

The navigation bar displayed by this module is spartan in appearance because my taste runs to simplicity. However, with a little work, it can be made as snazzy as you desire. One of the simpler ways to change the appearance of the navigation bar is to take advantage of the cascading stylesheet standard. Both the navigation bar table and the individual cells are tagged with the "navbar" style, which is currently unused. Further, the links themselves contain style tags. The links for the active, current section are tagged with the style class named `active`, while the links for the other sections are tagged with `inactive`. By placing a stylesheet definition in your pages, you can adjust the appearance of the table to suit your preferences.

You might wish to enhance the navigation bar by turning it into a column of labels that runs down the left hand side of the page. To do this, you'd either have to use frames, or place both the navigation bar and the HTML page into a table in two side-by-side cells. Or you could replace the links with in-line images of buttons or tabs to create a spiffy graphical navigation bar. In this case, you'd want two sets of buttons: one for the button in unpressed inactive state, and one for its pressed active state to indicate that the user is in its corresponding section.

Finally, a nice enhancement would be to add an extra dimension to the navigation bar, creating a hierarchical list of sections and subsections that expands outward to show more detail when the user enters a particular section. That'll put an end to navigation bar envy!

In the next article, I'll explore the LWP library, which allows you to create your own spiders and otherwise automate many of the tasks that a web browser performs.

CHAPTER 10
Scripting the Web with LWP

Lincoln D. Stein

In previous articles I've focused on the Web from the server's point of view. We've talked about how the CGI protocol works, how to write server scripts, and how to maintain long-running transactions across the Web. But what about the client side of the story? Does Perl offer any support for those of us who wish to write our own web-creeping robots, remote syntax verifiers, database accessors, or even full-fledged graphical browsers? Naturally it does, and the name of this support is LWP.

LWP (Library for WWW access in Perl), is a collection of modules written by Martijn Koster and Gisle Aas and is available on CPAN. To understand what LWP can do, consider the tasks your average Web browser is called upon to perform:

- Read and parse a URL
- Connect to a remote server using the protocol appropriate for the URL (e.g., HTTP, FTP)
- Negotiate with the server for the requested document, providing authentication when necessary
- Interpret the retrieved document's headers
- Parse and display the document's HTML content

The LWP library provides support for all of the tasks listed above, and several others, including handling proxy servers. In its simplest form, you can use LWP to fetch remote URLs from within a Perl script. With more effort, you can write an entirely Perl-based web browser. In fact, the Perl/Tk library comes complete with a crude but functional graphical browser based on LWP.

The LWP modules are divided into the following categories:

URI::*
:   URL creation and parsing

HTML::*
:   HTML creation, parsing, and formatting

HTTP::*

    The HTTP protocol

LWP::UserAgent

    Object-oriented interface to the library

LWP::Simple

    Procedural interface to the library

LWP::Protocol::*

    Interfaces to various protocols

To illustrate what you can do with LWP, I've written a Perl script called get_weather (Example 10-1) that fetches and prints the current weather report.

Example 10-1. get_weather: an LWP program that fetches the current weather report

```
 1 #!/usr/bin/perl
 2
 3 use LWP::UserAgent;
 4 use HTML::TokeParser;
 5
 6 $CITY = shift || 'BOS';
 7 $URL = "http://www.wunderground.com/cgi-bin/findweather/getForecast?query=";
 8
 9 # Retrieve the content of the Web page
10 $agent = new LWP::UserAgent;
11 $request = new HTTP::Request('GET', "$URL$CITY");
12 $response = $agent->request($request);
13 die "Couldn't get URL. Status code = ", $response->code
14   unless $response->is_success;
15
16 # Parse the HTML
17 $parser = HTML::TokeParser->new(\$response->content);
18 while ($tokeref = $parser->get_token) {
19   if ($tokeref->[0] eq "T") {
20     $text .= HTML::Entities::decode($tokeref->[1]), "\n";
21   }
22 }
23
24 $text =~ s/\A.*?Forecast as of/Forecast as of/sm;
25 $text =~ s/Yesterday's.*?\Z//sm;
26 $text =~ s/\n+/\n/gm;
27 $text =~ s/[ \t]+/ /gm;
28 print $text;
```

You invoke this script from your shell with the city code as its argument (with a default of "BOS"). An example of the script's chilling output:

```
Forecast as of 11:35 am EST on February 6, 2002

This Afternoon
Partly sunny. Highs 30 to 35. West wind around 10 mph.
```

Tonight
Partly cloudy. Lows from near 20 Countryside to upper 20s Boston.
Southwest wind around 10 mph.

Thursday
Cloudy. A chance of rain or snow in the afternoon. Highs in the lower 40s.
Southwest wind 10 to 15 mph becoming southeast late. Chance of precipitation
40 percent.

Thursday Night
A chance of snow or rain early...otherwise clearing. Lows near 30. Chance
of precipitation 30 percent.

Friday
Mostly sunny. Highs in the lower 40s.

Friday Night
Partly cloudy. Lows in the mid 20s.

Saturday
Cloudy. A chance of snow or rain late. Highs in the lower 40s.

Sunday
Snow or rain likely. Lows near 30 and highs in the lower 40s.

Monday
Partly cloudy and breezy. Lows in the lower 30s and highs in the lower 40s.

Tuesday
Mostly cloudy. Lows in the upper 20s and highs near 40.

You could run this script from an hourly cron job and incorporate the result into an
HTML page, or use it to produce the text for a scrolling marquee applet (and produce a special effect that does something useful for a change!).

This script uses the weather forecasts provided by the Weather Underground. Its
servers were designed for human interactive use using fill-out forms; by changing the
form, you can choose any city for which forecasts are available. Casual inspection of
Wunderground URLs reveals that you can obtain a basic weather report for Boston
via this URL:

```
http://www.wunderground.com/cgi-bin/findweather/getForecast?query=BOS
```

Every weather report our script retrieves uses this URL, but with whatever city code
we want in place of BOS. When you fetch this URL you'll receive a page of HTML
containing the weather report plus a bunch of graphics and links.

Thanks to the LWP library, the code is very straightforward. Lines 3 and 4 load the
components of the LWP library that we need. In addition to the LWP::UserAgent
module, which provides URL-fetching functionality, we use the HTML::TokeParser
module, which will give us the ability to extract just the text from the web page, leaving tags, links, and other HTML information behind.

Lines 6 and 7 declare the two global variables. The city is read from the command line, and globals for the server URL and its CGI parameters are defined.

The interesting part begins in lines 10–14, where we connect to the NOAA server, send the query, and retrieve the result. First, we create a LWP::UserAgent object, which is essentially a virtual browser. Next, we create an HTTP::Request object to hold information about the URL we're requesting. We initialize the request object with the string GET to indicate we want to make a GET request, and with the URL we want to fetch. The actual connection and data transfer occurs in line 12, where we invoke the UserAgent's request method and receive an HTTP::Response object as the result. Lastly, we check the transaction's result code by calling the response object's is_success method and die with an informative error message if there was a problem.

We now have an HTTP::Response object in hand. It contains the HTTP status code, the various MIME headers that are transmitted along with the document, and the document itself. In lines 17–22, we extract the text from the document, using HTML::Entities::decode to turn HTML entities into human-readable versions. First, we extract the HTML document using the response object's content method, and immediately pass a reference to the result to an HTML::TokeParser object that we create on the fly and store in $parser. We then iterate through the tokens in $parser, appending all of the plain text that we find to one long string: $text.

The script isn't quite done, however, because the pretty-printed page still contains details that we're not interested in. Lines 24 and 25 narrow down $text to just the portion that interests us: the text beginning with Forecast as of and ending immediately before Yesterday's. We collapse extra newlines and spaces in lines 26 and 27, and finally print out the weather report in line 28.

This example only gives a taste of what you can do with LWP. The LWP library distribution is itself a good source for ideas. Among the sample application programs that accompany it is a web mirror application that can be used to replicate a tree of web pages, updating the local copies only if they are out of date with respect to the remote ones. Other parts of the library include the basic components required to write your own web crawling robots.

CHAPTER 11

Five Quick Hacks: Downloading Web Pages

Jon Orwant and Dan Gruhl

Sometimes it's nice to visit web sites without being in front of your computer. Maybe you'd prefer to have the text of web pages mailed to you, or be notified when a web page changes. Or maybe you'd like to download a lot of information from a huge number of web pages (as in the article *webpluck*), and you don't want to open them all one by one. Or maybe you'd like to write a robot that scours the web for information. Enter the LWP bundle (sometimes called libwww-perl), which contains two modules that can download web pages for you: LWP::Simple and LWP::UserAgent. LWP is available on CPAN and is introduced in *Scripting the Web with LWP*.

Dan Gruhl submitted five tiny but exquisite programs to TPJ, all using LWP to automatically download information from a web service. Instead of sprinkling these around various issues as one-liners, I've collected all five here with a bit of explanation for each.

The first thing to notice is that all five programs look alike. Each uses an LWP module (LWP::Simple in the first three, LWP::UserAgent in the last two) to store the HTML from a web page in Perl's default scalar variable $_. Then they use a series of s/// substitutions to discard the extraneous HTML. The remaining text—the part we're interested in—is displayed on the screen, although it could nearly as easily have been sent as email with the various Mail modules on CPAN.

Downloading Currency Exchange Rates

The currency.pl program converts money from one currency into another, using the exchange rates on *www.oanda.com*. Here's how to find out what $17.39 is worth in Euros:

```
$ currency 17.39 USD EUR
--> 17.39 US Dollar = 20.00069 Euro
```

The LWP::Simple module has a function that makes retrieving web pages easy: get. When given a URL, get returns the text of that web page as one long string. In currency.pl, get is fed a URL for *oanda.com* containing the three arguments provided to the program: $ARGV[0], $ARGV[1], and $ARGV[2], which correspond to 17.39, USD, and EUR in the sample run above. The resulting web page is stored in $_, after which four s/// substitutions discard unwanted data.

```perl
#!/usr/bin/perl -w

# Currency converter.
# Usage: currency.pl [amount] [from curr] [to curr]

use LWP::Simple;

$_= get("http://www.oanda.com/convert/
                    classic?value=$ARGV[0]&exch=$ARGV[1]&expr=$ARGV[2]");

# Remove the text we don't care about
s/^.*<!-- conversion result starts//s;
s/<!-- conversion result ends.*$//s;
s/<[^>]+>//g;
s/\s+/ /gm;

print $_, "\n";
```

The first s/// removes all text before the HTML comment <!-- conversion result starts; the tail of that comment (-->) becomes the arrow that you see in the output. The second s/// removes all text after the conversion result. The third s/// dumbly removes all tags in the text that remains, and the final s/// replaces consecutive spaces and newlines with a single space each.

Downloading Weather Information

Weather information is downloaded from *www.intellicast.com* in much the same way as currency information is downloaded from *www.oanda.com*. The URL is different, some of the s/// substitutions are different, but the basic operation is the same. As an added treat, weather.pl uses the Text::Wrap module to format the output to 76 columns. Here's the gloomy forecast for Boston in February:

```
$ weather bos
Wednesday: Overcast. High near 49F. Winds SSE 15 to 20 mph. Wednesday
night: Rain showers early becoming steady overnite. Low near
43F. Winds S 10 to 15 mph. Rainfall around a quarter of an inch.

Thursday: A steady rain in the morning. Showers continuing in the
afternoon. High near 55F. Winds SW 15 to 20 mph. Chance of precip
80%. Rainfall around a quarter of an inch. Thursday night: A few clouds
from time to time. Low around 38F. Winds W 10 to 15 mph.

Friday: More clouds than sun. Highs in the low 50s and lows in the low 30s.

Saturday: Mostly cloudy. Highs in the mid 40s and lows in the low 30s.

Sunday: More clouds than sun. Highs in the upper 40s and lows in the upper
30s.
```

Monday: Occasional showers. Highs in the upper 40s and lows in the upper 20s.

Tuesday: Showers possible. Highs in the low 40s and lows in the upper 20s.

Wednesday: Considerable cloudiness. Highs in the low 40s and lows in the upper 20s.

Thursday: Considerable cloudiness. Highs in the low 40s and lows in the upper 20s.

Friday: Partly Cloudy

Here's weather.pl:

```perl
#!/usr/bin/perl

# Prints the weather for a given airport code
#
# Examples: weather.pl bos
#           weather.pl sfo

use LWP::Simple;
use Text::Wrap;

$_ = get("http://intellicast.com/Local/USLocalStd.asp?loc=k" . $ARGV[0] .
         "&seg=LocalWeather&prodgrp=Forecasts&product=Forecast&prodnav=
         none&pid=nonens");

# Remove the text we don't care about
s/Click Here for Averages and Records/\n/gim;
s/<[^>]+>//gm;
s/Trip Ahead.*$//sim;
s/ / /gm;
s/^(?!\w+day:).*?$//gm;
s/^\s+$//gm;

print wrap('', '', $_);        # Format and print the weather report
```

Downloading News Stories

The CNN home page displays the top news story; our cnn.pl program formats and displays it using Text::Wrap. I sandwiched Dan's code in a while loop that sleeps for 5 minutes (300 seconds) and retrieves the top story again. If the new story (as usual, stored in $_) is different than the old story ($old), it's printed.

```perl
#!/usr/bin/perl
#
# cnn.pl: continuously display the top story on CNN

use LWP::Simple;
use Text::Wrap;

$| = 1;
```

```
while (1) {                          # Run forever
    $_ = get("http://www.cnn.com");
    s/FULL STORY.*\Z//sm;
    s/\A.*Updated.*?$//sm;
    s/<[^>]+>//gm;
    s/\n\n+/\n\n/gm;
    if ($old ne $_) {                # If it's a new story,
        print wrap('', '', $_);      # Format and print it
        $old = $_;                   # ...and remember it
    }
    sleep 300;                       # Sleep for five minutes
}
```

Completing U.S. Postal Addresses

Back in 1999, there was a TPJ subscriber in Cambridge who wasn't getting his issues. When each issue went to press, Jon FTP'd the TPJ mailing list to a professional mail house for presorting and bagging and labeling that the U.S. Post Office requires (an improvement over the days when Jon addressed every issue himself in a cloud of Glu-Stik vapors).

The problem was that the mail house fixed addresses that seemed incorrect. "Albequerque" became "Albuquerque," and "Somervile" became "Somerville". Which is great, as long as the rules for correcting addresses—developed by the Post Office—work. They usually do, but occasionally a correct address is "fixed" to an incorrect address. That's what happened to this subscriber, and here's how Jon found out.

The address.pl program pretends to be a user typing information into the fields of the post office's web page at *http://www.usps.com/ncsc/*. That page asks for six fields: company (left blank for residential addresses), urbanization (valid only for Puerto Rico), street, city, and zip. You need to provide the street, and either the zip *or* the city and state. Regardless of which information you provide, the site responds with a complete address and mail route:

```
$ address company "O'Really" urbanization ""
  street "90 Shirman" city "Cambridge" state "MA" zip ""

90 SHERMAN ST
CAMBRIDGE MA 02140-3233
Carrier Route : C074
County : MIDDLESEX
Delivery Point : 90
Check Digit : 3
```

Note that I deliberately inserted a spelling error: O'Really and Shirman. The post office's database is reasonably resilient.

One inconvenience of address.pl is that you have to supply placeholders for all the fields, even the ones you're leaving blank, like urbanization and zip above.

This program is trickier than the three you've seen. It doesn't use LWP::Simple, but two other modules from the LWP bundle: LWP::UserAgent and HTTP::Request::Common. That's because LWP::Simple can handle only HTTP GET queries. This web site uses a POST query, and so Dan used the more sophisticated LWP::UserAgent module, which has an object-oriented interface.

First, a LWP::UserAgent object, $ua, is created with new and its request method invoked to POST the address data to the web page. If the POST was successful, the is_success method returns true, and the page contents can then be found in the _content attribute of the response object, $resp. The address is extracted as the _content is being stored in $_, and two more s/// substitutions remove unneeded data.

```
#!/usr/bin/perl -w
# Need *either* state *or* zip

use LWP::UserAgent;
use HTTP::Request::Common;

# Create a new UserAgent object and invoke its request() method
$ua = new LWP::UserAgent;
$resp = $ua->request(POST 'http://www.usps.com/cgi-bin/zip4/zip4inq2', [@ARGV]);

exit -1 unless $resp->is_success;

# Remove the text we don't care about
($_ = $resp->{_content}) =~ s/^.*address is:<p>\n//si;
s/Version .*$//s;
s/<[^>]+>//g;

print;
```

You can use address.pl to determine the zip code given an address, or to find out your own nine-digit zip code, or even to find out who's on the same mail carrier route as you. If you type in the address of the White House, you'll learn that the First Lady has her own zip code, 20500-0002.

Downloading Stock Quotes

Salomon Smith Barney's web site is one of many with free 15-minute delayed stock quotes. To find the stock price for Yahoo, you'd provide stock with its ticker symbol, yhoo:

```
$ stock.pl YHOO
$17.30
```

Like address.pl, stock.pl needs the LWP::UserAgent module since it's making a POST query.

Just because LWP::UserAgent has an OO interface doesn't mean the program has to spend an entire line creating an object and explicitly storing it ($object = new Class), although that's undoubtedly what Gisle Aas envisioned when he wrote the interface. Here, Dan's preoccupation with brevity shows, as he invokes an object's method in the same statement that creates the object: (new LWP::UserAgent)->request(...).

```
#!/usr/bin/perl

# Pulls a stock quote from Salomon Smith Barney's web site.
#
# Usage:        stock.pl ibm
#
# or whatever stock ticker symbol you like.

use LWP::UserAgent;
use HTTP::Request::Common;

$response = (new LWP::UserAgent)->request(POST
        'http://www.salomonsmithbarney.com/cgi-bin/benchopen/sb_quote',
            [ search_type => "1",
            search_string => "$ARGV[0]" ]);

exit -1 unless $response->is_success;
$_ = $response->{_content};
m/ Price.*?(\$\d+\.?\d+)/gsm;
print $1;
```

Conclusion

These aren't robust programs. They were dashed off in a couple of minutes for one person's pleasure, and they most certainly will break as the companies in charge of these pages change the web page formats or the URLs needed to access them.

We don't care. When that happens, these scripts will break, we'll notice that, and we'll amend them accordingly. Sure, each of these programs could be made much more flexible. They could be primed to adapt to changes in the HTML, the way a human would if the information were moved around on the web page. Then the s/// expressions would fail, and the programs could expend some effort trying to understand the HTML using a more intelligent parsing scheme, perhaps using the HTML::Parse or Parse::RecDescent modules. If the URL became invalid, the scripts might start at the site home page and pretend to be a naive user looking for his weather or news or stock fix. A smart enough script could start at Yahoo and follow links until it found what it was looking for, but so far no one has written a script like that.

Of course, the time needed to create and test such programs would be much longer than making quick, brittle, and incremental changes to the code already written. No, it's not rocket science—it's not even computer science—but it gets the job done.

Afterword

All five of these programs worked as originally printed in TPJ #13, but as one would expect, all five of them broke in the two years between publication of the magazine and publication of this book. Since the template of the programs was sound, it took only a few minutes to update each, and the programs you see here all work perfectly as of December 2002.

The next article, *Downloading Web Pages Through a Proxy Server*, shows how to adapt these programs for use in computing environments with firewalls.

## CHAPTER 12

Downloading Web Pages Through a Proxy Server

Rob Svirskas

The previous article presented five simple but elegant programs that download information from various web services: stock quotes, weather predictions, currency information, U.S. postal address correction, and CNN headline news. If you're like me, your company uses a firewall to repel wily hackers, which means that we have to use a proxy server to access most URLs. A proxy server (sometimes called a "gateway") is simply an intermediary computer that sends your request to a server and returns its response to you. The bad news: if you try to use the LWP::Simple get function without first letting it know about your proxy server, it returns nothing at all.

The good news: there's a simple way around this. The LWP::Simple module checks an environment variable called http_proxy. If $ENV{http_proxy} contains the name of a computer, your calls to get use it as a proxy server. You can set environment variables in two ways: either by assigning a value to $ENV{http_proxy}, or by using whatever mechanism your shell or operating system provides. For instance, you can define your proxy server under the Unix bash shell as follows:

```
% export http_proxy=http://proxy.mycompany.com:1080
```

This makes LWP::Simple route requests through port 1080 of the proxy server proxy.mycompany.com. You may need to use the set or setenv command, depending on your shell. There are also related environment variables for non-http services: ftp_proxy, gopher_proxy, and wais_proxy. There's also a no_proxy variable; we'll talk about that in a bit. Since we are using Perl, There's More Than One Way To Do It. We can still access URLs via a proxy without mucking with environment variables if we replace LWP::Simple with LWP::UserAgent and HTTP::Request::Common. Let's look at a version of the currency converter (the first example from *Five Quick Hacks: Downloading Web Pages*) that uses LWP::UserAgent:

```
#!/usr/bin/perl -w

# Currency converter.
# Usage: currency.pl [amount] [from curr] [to curr]

use LWP::UserAgent;
use HTTP::Request::Common;
```

```
$ua = new LWP::UserAgent( );

# Set up the proxy server
$ua->proxy('http','http://proxy.mycompany.com:1080');

# Retrieve the page
$resp = $ua->request(GET
  "http://www.oanda.com/convert/classic?value=$ARGV[0]&exch=$ARGV[1]&expr=$ARGV[2]");
$_ = $resp->{_content};

# Remove the text we don't care about
s/^.*<!-- conversion result starts//s;
s/<!-- conversion result ends.*$//s;
s/<[^>]+>//g;
s/\s+/ /gm;

print $_, "\n";
```

The line beginning $ua->proxy defines our proxy server. This routes the user agent's HTTP requests through *proxy.mycompany.com*. To use a proxy server for multiple protocols, specify them in a list as below:

```
$ua->proxy(['http','ftp','wais'] => 'http://proxy.mycompany.com:1080');
```

The programs that download the weather report and the CNN top story (the second and third examples from *Five Quick Hacks: Downloading Web Pages*) are also easy to convert: replace LWP::Simple with LWP::UserAgent and HTTP::Request::Common, and the calls to get with the user agent code as described above. The U.S. Postal Address program, *address.pl*, already has the UserAgent code—all we need to do is add the single line of code after the UserAgent has been created:

```
$ua = new LWP::UserAgent( );
$ua->proxy('http','http://proxy.mycompany.com:1080');
```

Or, if you're into brevity, create the user agent and set its proxy server in one line:

```
($ua=(new LWP::UserAgent))->proxy('http', 'http://proxy.mycompany.com:1080');
```

Most proxy servers will not let you access URLs within your own domain. That's why you often need to use your browser's Preferences menu to identify exceptions, telling your browser which domains to access without using the proxy. Fortunately, we can do that in our programs as well. If you prefer using environment variables:

```
export no_proxy="mycompany.com"
```

this will bypass the proxy server for URLs ending in `mycompany.com` (including URLs like *www.itsmycompany.com*). As you might expect, this can be done in the program instead:

```
$ua->no_proxy('mycompany.com');
```

If your program only needed to access web sites inside your firewall, you wouldn't need to declare the proxy server in the first place, so the `no_proxy` would be superfluous.

Afterword

Since this article was originally published, an additional twist was added where I work: we have to authenticate ourselves to the proxy server with a username and password. If we don't, we get an error stating "Proxy Authentication Required". Fortunately, authenticating to a proxy is something that HTTP::Request has in its bag of tricks. All we need to do is add a call to the proxy_authorization_basic subroutine after the GET (or POST). Let's revisit the currency converter as an example. In the version of the program shown in this chapter, we have a single statement that sets the request and gets the response:

```
$resp = $ua->request(GET "http://www.oanda.com/convert/classic ...
```

We'll just need to split it up:

```
$request = GET "http://www.oanda.com/convert/classic?value=$ARGV[0]&exch
                =$ARGV[1]&expr=$ARGV[2]";
$request->proxy_authorization_basic(qw(username password));
$resp = $ua->request($request);
```

We first put the GET request in the variable $request. We then authenticate to the proxy with username and password. Finally, we get the response. The rest of the program remains the same.

If we're doing a POST instead of a GET, the method for authenticating is identical. To change the address.pl program as shown in *Five Quick Hacks: Downloading Web Pages*, simply replace the line that gets the response:

```
$resp = $ua->request(POST 'http://www.usps.com/cgi-bin/zip4/zip4inq2',
[@ARGV]);
```

with these four lines:

```
$ua->proxy('http','http://proxy.mycompany.com:1080');
$request = POST 'http://www.usps.com/cgi-bin/zip4/zip4inq2',[@ARGV];
$request->proxy_authorization_basic(qw(username password));
$resp = $ua->request($request);
```

We can take the same approach with the *stock.pl* program. In keeping with the brevity of the original program in *Five Quick Hacks: Downloading Web Pages*, we'll replace Dan's single statement:

```
$response = (new LWP::UserAgent)->request(POST ...
```

with these three:

```
($ua = (new LWP::UserAgent))->proxy
('http','http://proxy.mycompany.com:1080');
($request = POST
'http://www.salomonsmithbarney.com/cgi-bin/benchopen/sb_quote',
        [ search_type => 1,
        search_string => "$ARGV[0]"])->proxy_authorization_basic
        (qw(username password));
        $resp = $ua->request($request);
```

CHAPTER 13

HTML::Parser

Ken MacFarlane

 Since the original publication of this article, the HTML::Parser module has *continued to evolve (version* evolved (Version 3.25 as of this update), enabling *one* you to write develop powerful parsing tools with a minimum of coding. For those readers who are using this wonderful tool for the first time, the examples here should provide the means and feel for basic HTML parsing techniques, which can then be further extended to meet one's needs. This article may also be useful for those new to object-oriented programming (I once was myself!) as it covers the concept of subclassing.

Perl is often used to manipulate the HTML files constituting web pages. For instance, one common task is removing tags from an HTML file to extract the plain text. Many solutions for such tasks usually use regular expressions, which often end up complicated, unattractive, and incomplete (or wrong). The alternative, described here, is to use the HTML::Parser module available on CPAN. HTML::Parser is an object-oriented module, and so it requires some extra explanation for casual users.

HTML::Parser works by scanning HTML input, and breaks it up into segments by how the text would be interpreted by a browser. For instance, this input: input would be broken up into three segments: a start tag (`<A HREF="index.html">`), text (`This is a link`), and an end tag (`</A>`).

```
<A HREF="index.html">This is a link</A>
```

As each segment is detected, the parser passes it to an appropriate subroutine. There's a subroutine for start tags, one for end tags, and another for plain text. There are subroutines for comments and declarations as well.

In this article, I'll first give a simple example on how to read and print out all the information found by HTML::Parser. Next, I'll demonstrate differences in the *events* triggered by the parser. Finally, I'll show how to access specific information passed along by the parser.

As of this writing, there are two major versions of HTML::Parser available. Both version Version 2 and version Version 3 work by having you *subclass* the module. For this article, I will mostly concentrate on the subclassing method, because it will work with both major versions, and is a bit easier to understand for those not overly familiar with some of Perl's finer details. In version Version 3, there is more of an emphasis on the use of references, anonymous subroutines, and similar topics; advanced users who may be interested will see there is a brief example at the end of this articlearticle for advanced users who may be interested.

Getting Started

The first thing to be aware of when using HTML::Parser is that, unlike other modules, it appears to do absolutely nothing. When I first attempted to use this module, I used code similar to this:

```
#!/usr/bin/perl -w

use strict;
use HTML::Parser;

my $p = new HTML::Parser;
$p->parse_file("index.html");
```

No output whatsoever. If you look at the source code to the module, you'll see why:

```
sub text
{
# my($self, $text) = @_;
}

sub declaration
{
# my($self, $decl) = @_;
}

sub comment
{
# my($self, $comment) = @_;
}

sub start
{
# my($self, $tag, $attr, $attrseq, $origtext) = @_;
# $attr is reference to a HASH, $attrseq is reference to an ARRAY

}

sub end
{
# my($self, $tag, $origtext) = @_;
}
```

The whole idea of the parser is that as it chugs along through the HTML, it calls these subroutines whenever it finds an appropriate snippet (start tag, end tag, and so on). However, these subroutines do nothing. My program works, and the HTML is being parsed—but I never instructed the program to *do* anything with the parse results.

The Identity Parser

The following is an example of how HTML::Parser can be subclassed, and its methods overridden, to produce meaningful output. This example simply prints out the original HTML file, unmodified:

```
1  #!/usr/bin/perl -w
2
3  use strict;
4
5  # Define the subclass
6  package IdentityParse;
7  use base "HTML::Parser";
8
9  sub text {
10     my ($self, $text) = @_;
11     # Just print out the original text
12     print $text;
13 }
14
15 sub comment {
16     my ($self, $comment) = @_;
17     # Print out original text with comment marker
18     print "<!--", $comment, "-->";
19 }
20
21 sub start {
22     my ($self, $tag, $attr, $attrseq, $origtext) = @_;
23     # Print out original text
24     print $origtext;
25 }
26
27 sub end {
28     my ($self, $tag, $origtext) = @_;
29     # Print out original text
30     print $origtext;
31 }
32
33 my $p = new IdentityParse;
34 $p->parse_file("index.html");
```

Lines 6 and 7 declare the IdentityParse package, having it inherit from HTML::Parser. (Type `perldoc perltoot` for more information on inheritance.) We then override the text, comment, start, and end subroutines so that they print their original values. The result is a script which reads an HTML file, parses it, and prints it to standard output in its original form.

The HTML Tag Stripper

Our next example strips all the tags from the HTML file and prints just the text:

```
1   #!/usr/bin/perl -w
2
3   use strict;
4
5   package HTMLStrip;
6   use base "HTML::Parser";
7
8   sub text {
9       my ($self, $text) = @_;
10      print $text;
11  }
12
13  my $p = new HTMLStrip;
14  # Parse line-by-line, rather than the whole file at once file at once
15  while (<>) {
16      $p->parse($_);
17  }
18  # Flush and parse remaining unparsed HTML
19  $p->eof;
```

Since we're only interested in the text and HTML tags, we override only the text subroutine. Also note that in lines 13–17, we invoke the parse method instead of parse_file. This lets us read files provided on the command line. When using parse instead of parse_file, we must also call the eof method (line 19); this is done to check and clear HTML::Parser's internal buffer.

Another Example: HTML Summaries

Suppose you've hand-crafted your own search engine for your web site, and you want to be able to generate summaries for each hit. You could use the HTML::Summary module described Chapter 22in the article *Summarizing Web Pages with HTML::Summary*, but we'll describe a simpler solution here. We'll assume that some (but not all) of your site's pages use a <META> tag to describe the content:

```
<META NAME="DESCRIPTION" CONTENT="description of file">
```

When a page has a <META> tag, your search engine should use the CONTENT for the summary. Otherwise, the summary should be the first H1 tag if one exists. And if that fails, we'll use the TITLE. Our third example generates such a summary:

```
1   #!/usr/bin/perl -w
2
3   use strict;
4
5   package GetSummary;
6   use base "HTML::Parser";
7
8   my $meta_contents;
9   my $h1     = "";
```

```
10   my $title = "";
11
12   # Set state flags
13   my $h1_flag    = 0;
14   my $title_flag = 0;
15
16   sub start {
17       my ($self, $tag, $attr, $attrseq, $origtext) = @_;
18
19       if ($tag =~ /^meta$/i && $attr->{'name'} =~ /^description$/i) {
20           # Set if we find META NAME="DESCRIPTION"
21           $meta_contents = $attr->{'content'};
22       } elsif ($tag =~ /^h1$/i && ! $h1) {
23           # Set state if we find <H1> or <TITLE>
24           $h1_flag = 1;
25       } elsif ($tag =~ /^title$/i && ! $title) {
26           $title_flag = 1;
27       }
28   }
29
30   sub text {
31       my ($self, $text) = @_;
32       # If we're in <H1>...</H1> or <TITLE>...</TITLE>, save text
33       if ($h1_flag)    { $h1    .= $text; }
34       if ($title_flag) { $title .= $text; }
35   }
36
37   sub end {
38       my ($self, $tag, $origtext) = @_;
39
40       # Reset appropriate flag if we see </H1> or </TITLE>
41       if ($tag =~ /^h1$/i)    { $h1_flag = 0; }
42       if ($tag =~ /^title$/i) { $h1_flag = 0; }
43   }
44
45   my $p = new GetSummary;
46   while (<>) {
47       $p->parse($_);
48   }
49   $p->eof;
50
51   print "Summary information: ", $meta_contents ||
52       $h1 || $title || "No summary information found.", "\n";
```

The magic happens in lines 19–27. The variable $attr contains a reference to a hash where the tag attributes are represented with key/value pairs. The keys are lowercased by the module, which is a code-saver; otherwise, we'd need to check for all casing possibilities (name, NAME, Name, and so on).

Lines 19–21 check to see if the current tag is a META tag and has a field NAME set to DESCRIPTION; if so, the variable $meta_contents is set to the value of the CONTENT field. Lines 22–27 likewise check for an H1 or TITLE tag. In these cases, the information we want is in the text between the start and end tags, and not the tag itself. Furthermore, when the text subroutine is called, it has no way of knowing which tags (if any) its text is between. This is why we set a flag in start (where the tag name is known) and check the flag in text (where it isn't). Lines 22 and 25 also check whether or not $h1 and $title have been set; since we only want the first match, subsequent matches are ignored.

Another Fictional Example

Your company has been running a successful product site, *http://www.bar.com/foo/*. However, the web marketing team decides that *http://foo.bar.com/* looks better in the company's advertising materials, so a redirect is set up from the new address to the old.

Fast forward to Friday, 4:45 in the afternoon, when the phone rings. The frantic voice on the other end says, "*foo.bar.com* just crashed! We need to change all the links back to the old location!" Just when you though a simple search-and-replace would suffice, the voice adds: "And marketing says we can't change the text of the web pages, only the links."

"No problem," you respond, and quickly hack together a program that changes the links in A HREF tags, and nowhere else.

```
1  #!/usr/bin/perl -w -i.bak
2
3  use strict;
4
5  package ChangeLinks;
6  use base "HTML::Parser";
7
8  sub start {
9      my ($self, $tag, $attr, $attrseq, $origtext) = @_;
10
11     # We're only interested in changing <A ...> tags
12     unless ($tag =~ /^a$/) {
13         print $origtext;
14         return;
15     }
16
17     if (defined $attr->{'href'}) {
18         $attr->{'href'} =~ s[foo\.bar\.com][www\.bar\.com/foo];
19     }
20
21     print "<A ";
22     # Print each attribute of the <A ...> tag
23     foreach my $i (@$attrseq) {
24         print $i, qq(="$attr->{$i}" );
25     }
26     print ">";
27 }
28
29 sub text {
```

```
30      my ($self, $text) = @_;
31      print $text;
32  }
33
34  sub comment {
35      my ($self, $comment) = @_;
36      print "<!--", $comment, "-->";
37  }
38
39  sub end {
40      my ($self, $tag, $origtext) = @_;
41      print $origtext;
42  }
43
44  my $p = new ChangeLinks;
45  while (<>) {
46      $p->parse($_);
47  }
48  $p->eof;
```

Line 1 specifies that the files will be edited in place, with the original files being renamed with a *.bak* extension. The real fun is in the start subroutine, lines 8–27. First, in lines 12–15, we check for an A tag; if that's not what we have, we simply return the original tag. Lines 17–19 check for the HREF and make the desired substitution.

$attrseq appears in line 23. This variable is a reference to an array with the tag attributes in their original order of appearance. If the attribute order needs to be preserved, this array is necessary to reconstruct the original order, since the hash $attr will jumble them up. Here, we dereference $attrseq and then recreate each tag. The attribute names will appear lowercase regardless of how they originally appeared. If you'd prefer uppercase, change the first $i in line 24 to uc($i).

Using HTML::Parser Version 3

Version 3 of the module provides more flexibility in how the handlers are invoked. One big change is that you no longer have to use subclassing; rather, *event handlers* can be specified when the HTML::Parser constructor is called. The following example is equivalent to the previous program but uses some of the version Version 3 features:

```
1  #!/usr/bin/perl -w -i.bak
2
3  use strict;
4  use HTML::Parser;
5
6  # Specify events here rather than in a subclass
7  my $p = HTML::Parser->new( api_version => 3,
8                                  start_h => [\&start,
9                                                  "tagname, attr, attrseq, text"],
10                                  default_h => [sub { print shift }, "text"],
11                             );
12  sub start {
```

```
13      my ($tag, $attr, $attrseq, $origtext) = @_;
14
15      unless ($tag =~ /^a$/) {
16          print $origtext;
17          return;
18      }
19
20      if (defined $attr->{'href'}) {
21          $attr->{'href'} =~ s[foo\.bar\.com][www\.bar\.com/foo];
22      }
23
24      print "<A ";
25      foreach my $i (@$attrseq) {
26          print $i, qq(="$attr->{$i}" );
27      }
28      print ">";
29  }
30
31  while (<>) {
32      $p->parse($_);
33  }
34  $p->eof;
```

The key changes are in lines 7–10. In line 8, we specify that the start event is to be handled by the start subroutine. Another key important change is line 10; version Version 3 of HTML::Parser supports the notion of a default handler. In the previous example, we needed to specify separate handlers for text, end tags, and comments; here, we use default_h as a catch-all. This turns out to be a code saver as well.

Take a closer look at line 9, and compare it to line 9 of the previous example. Note that $self hasn't been passed. In version Version 3 of HTML::Parser, the list of attributes which that can be passed along to the handler subroutine is configurable. If our program only needed to use the tag name and text, we can change the string tagname, attr, attrseq, text to simply tagname, text and then change the start subroutine to only use two parameters. Also, handlers are not limited to subroutines. If we changed the default handler like this, the text that would have been printed is instead pushed onto @lines:

```
my $p = HTML::Parser->new( api_version => 3,
                           start_h => [\&start,
                                       "tagname, attr, attrseq, text"],
                    default_h => \@lines, "text"],
                );
```

Version 3 of HTML::Parser also adds some new features; notably, one can now set options to recognize and act upon XML constructs, such as <TAG/> and <?TAG?>. There are also multiple methods of accessing tag information, instead of the $attr hash. Rather than go into further detail, I encourage you to explore the flexibility and power of this module on your own.

Acknowledgments

The HTML::Parser module was written by Gisle Aas and Michael A. Chase. Excerpts of code and documentation from the module are used here with the authors' permission.

## CHAPTER 14

Scanning HTML

Sean M. Burke

 This article turned out to be so popular that I ended up writing a whole book, *Perl & LWP* (O'Reilly), which goes into great detail about the many ways of pulling data out of markup languages like HTML.

In the previous article, Ken MacFarlane describes how the HTML::Parser module scans HTML source as a stream of start tags, end tags, text, comments, and so on. In another issue of TPJ (and republished in *Computer Science & Perl Programming: Best of the Perl Journal*), I described tree data structures. Now I'll tie it together by discussing trees of HTML.

The CPAN module HTML::TreeBuilder takes the tags that HTML::Parser extracts, and builds a *parse tree*—a tree-shaped network of objects representing the structured content of an HTML document. Once the document is parsed as a tree, you'll find the common tasks of extracting data from that HTML document/tree to be quite straightforward.

HTML::Parser, HTML::TreeBuilder, and HTML::Element

HTML::TreeBuilder can construct a parse tree out of an HTML source file simply by saying:

```
use HTML::TreeBuilder;
my $tree = HTML::TreeBuilder->new( );
$tree->parse_file('foo.html');
```

$tree now contains a parse tree built from the HTML in foo.html. The parse tree is represented as a network of objects—$tree is the *root*, an element with tag name html. Its children typically include head and body elements, and so on. Each element in the tree is an object of the class HTML::Element.

If you take this source:

```
<html><head><title>Doc 1</title></head>
<body>
```

```
    Stuff <hr> 2000-08-17
    </body></html>
```

and feed it to HTML::TreeBuilder, it'll return a tree of objects that looks like this:

This is a pretty simple document. If it were any more complex, it'd be a bit hard to draw in that style, since it sprawls left and right. The same tree can be represented a bit more easily sideways, with indenting:

- html
  - head
    - title
      - "Doc 1"
  - body
    - "Stuff"
    - hr
    - "2000-08-17"

Both representations express the same structure. The root node is an object of the class HTML::Element (actually, of HTML::TreeBuilder, but that's just a subclass of HTML::Element) with the tag name html, and with two children: an HTML::Element object whose tag names are head and body. And each of those elements have children, and so on down. Not all elements have children—the C element doesn't, for instance. And not all nodes in the tree are elements—the text nodes (Doc 1, Stuff, and 2000-08-17) are just strings.

Objects of the class HTML::Element have three noteworthy attributes:

_tag

> Best accessed as $element->tag. The element's tag name, lowercased (e.g., em for an EM element). [*]

_parent

> Best accessed as $element->parent. The element that is the element's parent, or undef if this element is the root.

_content

> Best accessed as $element->content_list. The list of nodes (i.e., elements or text segments) that are the element's children.

---

[*] Yes, this is misnamed. In proper SGML lingo, this is instead called a GI (short for "generic identifier") and the term "tag" is used for a token of SGML source that represents either the start of an element (a start tag like <em lang='fr'>) or the end of an element (an end tag like </em>). However, since more people claim to have been abducted by aliens than to have ever seen the SGML standard, and since both encounters typically involve a feeling of "missing time," it's not surprising that the terminology of the SGML standard is not closely followed.)

Moreover, if an element has any attributes, those are readable as $element->
attr('name')—for example, with the object built from <a id='foo'>bar</a>, the
method call $element->attr('id') returns the string foo. Furthermore, $element->tag
on that object returns the string "a", $element->content_list returns a list consisting
of just the single scalar bar, and $element->parent method returns the parent of this
node—which might be, for example, a <p> element.

And that's all that there is to it: you throw HTML source at TreeBuilder, and it
returns a tree of HTML::Element objects and some text strings.

However, what do you *do* with a tree of objects? People code information into
HTML trees not for the fun of arranging elements, but to represent the structure of
specific text and images—some text is in this li element, some other text is in that
heading, some images are in this table cell with those attributes, and so on.

Now, it may happen that you're rendering that whole HTML tree into some layout
format. Or you could be trying to make some systematic change to the HTML tree
before dumping it out as HTML source again. But in my experience, the most common programming task that Perl programmers face with HTML is trying to extract
some piece of information from a larger document. Since that's so common (and also
since it involves concepts required for more complex tasks), that is what the rest of
this article will be about.

Scanning HTML Trees

Suppose you have a thousand HTML documents, each of them a press release. They
all start out:

```
[...lots of leading images and junk...]

<h1>ConGlomCo to Open New Corporate Office in Ouagadougou</h1>

BAKERSFIELD, CA, 2000-04-24 -- ConGlomCo's vice president in
charge of world conquest, Rock Feldspar, announced today the
opening of a new office in Ouagadougou, the capital city of
Burkina Faso, gateway to the bustling "Silicon Sahara" of
Africa...

[...etc...]
```

For each document, you've got to copy whatever text is in the h1 element, so that
you can make a table of its contents. There are three ways to do this:

- You can just use a regex to scan the file for a text pattern. For simple tasks, this
  will be fine. Many HTML documents are, in practice, very consistently formatted with respect to placement of linebreaks and whitespace, so you could just get
  away with scanning the file like so:

```
sub get_heading {
    my $filename = $_[0];
```

```
    local *HTML;
    open(HTML, $filename) or die "Couldn't open $filename);
    my $heading;
Line:
    while (<HTML>) {
        if( m{<h1>(.*?)</h1>}i ) {
            $heading = $1;
            last Line;
        }
    }
    close(HTML);
    warn "No heading in $filename?" unless defined $heading;
    return $heading;
}
```

This is quick, fast, and fragile—if there's a newline in the middle of a heading's text, it won't match the above regex, and you'll get an error. The regex will also fail if the h1 element's start tag has any attributes. If you have to adapt your code to fit more kinds of start tags, you'll end up basically reinventing part of HTML::Parser, at which point you should probably just stop and use HTML::Parser itself.

- You can use HTML::Parser to scan the file for an h1 start tag token and capture all the text tokens until the h1 end tag. This approach is extensively covered in the previous article. (A variant of this approach is to use HTML::TokeParser, which presents a different and handier interface to the tokens that HTML::Parser extracts.)

  Using HTML::Parser is less fragile than our first approach, since it is insensitive to the exact internal formatting of the start tag (much less whether it's split across two lines). However, when you need more information about the context of the h1 element, or if you're having to deal with tricky HTML bits like tables, you'll find that the flat list of tokens returned by HTML::Parser isn't immediately useful. To get something useful out of those tokens, you'll need to write code that knows which elements take no content (as with C elements), and that </p> end tags are optional, so a <p> ends any currently open paragraph. You're well on your way to pointlessly reinventing much of the code in HTML::TreeBuilder, and as the person who last rewrote that module, I can attest that it wasn't terribly easy to get right! Never underestimate the perversity of people creating HTML. At this point you should probably just stop and use HTML::TreeBuilder itself.

- You can use HTML::Treebuilder and scan the tree of elements it creates. This last approach is diametrically opposed to the first approach, which involves just elementary Perl and one regex. The TreeBuilder approach involves being comfortable with the concept of tree-shaped data structures and modules with object-oriented interfaces, as well as with the particular interfaces that HTML::TreeBuilder and HTML::Element provide.

However, the TreeBuilder approach is the most robust, because it involves dealing with HTML in its "native" format—the tree structure that HTML code represents, without any consideration of how the source is coded and with what tags are omitted.

To extract the text from the h1 elements of an HTML document with HTML::Tree-Builder, you'd do this:

```
sub get_heading {
    my $tree = HTML::TreeBuilder->new;
    $tree->parse_file($_[0]);
    my $heading;
    my $h1 = $tree->look_down('_tag', 'h1');
    if ($h1) {
        $heading = $h1->as_text;
    } else {
        warn "No heading in $_[0]?";
    }
    $tree->delete;      # clear memory
    return $heading;
}
```

This uses some unfamiliar methods. The parse_file method we've seen before builds a tree based on source from the file given. The delete method is for marking a tree's contents as available for garbage collection when you're done. The as_text method returns a string that contains all the text bits that are children (or otherwise descendants) of the given node; to get the text content of the $h1 object, we could just say:

```
$heading = join '', $h1->content_list;
```

but that will work only if we're sure that the h1 element's children will be only text bits. If the document contained this:

```
<h1>Local Man Sees <cite>Blade</cite> Again</h1>
```

then the subtree would be:

- h1
  - "Local Man Sees "
  - cite
    - "Blade"
  - " Again'

so join '', $h1->content_list will result in something like this:

```
Local Man Sees HTML::Element=HASH(0x15424040) Again
```

Meanwhile, $h1->as_text would yield:

```
Local Man Sees Blade Again
```

Depending on what you're doing with the heading text, you might want the as_HTML method instead. It returns the subtree represented as HTML source. $h1->as_HTML would yield:

```
<h1>Local Man Sees <cite>Blade</cite> Again</h1>
```

However, if you wanted the contents of $h1 as HTML, but not the $h1 itself, you could say:

```
join '',
  map(
    ref($_) ? $_->as_HTML : $_,
    $h1->content_list
  )
```

This map iterates over the nodes in $h1's list of children, and for each node that's only a text bit (like Local Man Sees is), it just passes through that string value, and for each node that's an actual object (causing ref to be true), as_HTML will be used instead of the string value of the object itself (which would be something quite useless, as most object values are). So for the cite element, as_HTML will be the string <cite>Blade</cite>. And then, finally, join just combines all the strings that the map returns into one string.

Finally, the most important method in our get_heading subroutine is the look_down method. This method looks down at the subtree starting at the given object (here, $h1), retrieving elements that meet criteria you provide.

The criteria are specified in the method's argument list. Each criterion consists of two scalars: a key and a value expressing an element and attribute. The key might be _tag or src, and the value might be an attribute like h1. Or, the criterion can be a reference to a subroutine that, when called on an element, returns true if it's a node you're looking for. If you specify several criteria, that means you want all the elements that satisfy *all* the criteria. (In other words, there's an implicit "and.")

And finally, there's a bit of an optimization. If you call the look_down method in a scalar context, you get just the *first* node (or undef if none)—and, in fact, once look_down finds that first matching element, it doesn't bother looking any further. So the example:

```
$h1 = $tree->look_down('_tag', 'h1');
```

returns the first element at or under $tree whose _tag attribute has the value h1.

Complex Criteria in Tree Scanning

Now, the above look_down code looks like a lot of bother, with barely more benefit than just grepping the file! But consider a situation in which your criteria are more complicated—suppose you found that some of your press releases had several h1 elements, possibly before or after the one you actually want. For example:

```
<h1><center>Visit Our Corporate Partner
        <br><a href="/dyna/clickthru">
        <img src="/dyna/vend_ad"></a>
    </center>
</h1>
<h1><center>ConGlomCo President Schreck to Visit Regional HQ
```

```
      <br><a href="/photos/Schreck_visit_large.jpg">
      <img src="/photos/Schreck_visit.jpg"></a>
   </center></h1>
```

Here, you want to ignore the first h1 element because it contains an ad, and you want the text from the second h1. The problem is how to formalize what's an ad and what's not. Since ad banners are always entreating you to "visit" the sponsoring site, you could exclude h1 elements that contain the word "visit" under them:

```
my $real_h1 = $tree->look_down( '_tag', 'h1',
                    sub { $_[0]->as_text !~ m/\bvisit/i } );
```

The first criterion looks for h1 elements, and the second criterion limits those to only the ones with text that doesn't match m/\bvisit/. Unfortunately, that won't work for our example, since the second h1 mentions "ConGlomCo President Schreck to *Visit Regional HQ*".

Instead, you could try looking for the first h1 element that doesn't contain an image:

```
my $real_h1 = $tree->look_down('_tag', 'h1',
                    sub { not $_[0]->look_down('_tag', 'img') } );
```

This criterion subroutine might seem a bit odd, since it calls look_down as part of a larger look_down operation, but that's fine. Note if there's no matching element at or under the given element, look_down returns false (specifically, undef) in a boolean context. If there are matching elements, it returns the first. So this means "return true only if this element has no img element as descendants and isn't an img element itself."

```
sub { not $_[0]->look_down('_tag', 'img') }
```

This correctly filters out the first h1 that contains the ad, but it also incorrectly filters out the second h1 that contains a non-advertisement photo near the headline text you want.

There clearly are detectable differences between the first and second h1 elements— the only second one contains the string "Schreck", and we can just test for that:

```
my $real_h1 = $tree->look_down('_tag', 'h1',
                    sub { $_[0]->as_text =~ m{Schreck} } );
```

And that works fine for this one example, but unless all thousand of your press releases have "Schreck" in the headline, it's not generic enough. However, if all the ads in h1s involve a link with a URL that includes /dyna/, you can use that:

```
my $real_h1 = $tree->look_down('_tag', 'h1',
                    sub {
                        my $link = $_[0]->look_down('_tag','a');

                        # No link means it's fine
                        return 1 unless $link;

                        # A link to there is bad
                        return 0 if $link->attr('href') =~ m{/dyna/};
                        return 1;    # Otherwise okay
                    } );
```

Or you can look at it another way, and say that you want the first h1 element that either contains no images, or else with an image that has a src attribute whose value contains /photos/:

```
my $real_h1 = $tree->look_down('_tag', 'h1',
                    sub {
                            my $img = $_[0]->look_down('_tag','img');

                            # No image means it's fine
                            return 1 unless $img;

                            # Good if a photo
                            return 1 if $img->attr('src') =~ m{/photos/};

                            return 0; # Otherwise bad
                    } );
```

Recall that this use of look_down in a scalar context returns the first element at or under $tree matching all the criteria. But if you can formulate criteria that match several possible h1 elements, with the *last* one being the one you want, you can use look_down in a list context, and ignore all but the last element of the returned list:

```
my @h1s = $tree->look_down('_tag', 'h1', ...maybe more criteria... );

die "What, no h1s here?" unless @h1s;

my $real_h1 = $h1s[-1];  # last or only element
```

A Case Study: Scanning Yahoo! News

The above (somewhat contrived) case involves extracting data from a bunch of pre-existing HTML files. In such situations, it's easy to know when your code works, since the data it handles won't change or grow, and you typically need to run the program only once.

The other kind of situation faced in many data extraction tasks is in which the program is used recurringly to handle new data, such as from ever-changing web pages. As a real-world example of this, consider a program that you could use to extract headline links from subsections of Yahoo! News (*http://dailynews.yahoo.com/*). Yahoo! News has several subsections, such as:

> *http://dailynews.yahoo.com/h/tc/* for technology news
> *http://dailynews.yahoo.com/h/sc/* for science news
> *http://dailynews.yahoo.com/h/hl/* for health news
> *http://dailynews.yahoo.com/h/wl/* for world news
> *http://dailynews.yahoo.com/h/en/* for entertainment news

All of them are built on the same basic HTML template—and a scarily complicated template it is, especially when you look at it with an eye toward identifying the real headline links and screening out the links to everything else. You'll need to puzzle over the HTML source, and scrutinize the output of $tree->dump on the parse tree of that HTML.

Sometimes the only way to pin down what you're after is by position in the tree. For example, headlines of interest may be in the third column of the second row of the second table element in a page:

```
my $table = (  $tree->look_down('_tag','table') )[1];
my $row2  = ( $table->look_down('_tag', 'tr' )  )[1];
my $col3  = (  $row2->look-down('_tag', 'td')   )[2];

...then do things with $col3...
```

Or they might be all the links in a `<p>` element with more than two `<br>` elements as children:

```
my $p = $tree->look_down('_tag', 'p',
    sub { 2 < grep { ref($_) and $_->tag eq 'br' } $_[0]->content_list } );

@links = $p->look_down('_tag', 'a');
```

But almost always, you can get away with looking for properties of the thing itself, rather than just looking for contexts. If you're lucky, the document you're looking through has clear semantic tagging, perhaps tailored for CSS (Cascading Style Sheets):

```
<a href="...long_news_url..." class="headlinelink">Elvis seen in tortilla</a>
```

If you find anything like that, you could leap right in and select links with:

```
@links = $tree->look_down('class', 'headlinelink');
```

Regrettably, your chances of observing such semantic markup principles in real-life HTML are pretty slim. (In fact, your chances of finding a page that is simply free of HTML errors are even slimmer. And surprisingly, the quality of the code at sites like Amazon or Yahoo! is typically worse than at personal sites whose entire production cycle involves simply being saved and uploaded from Netscape Composer.)

The code may be "accidentally semantic," however—for example, in a set of pages I was scanning recently, I found that looking for td elements with a width attribute value of 375 got me exactly what I wanted. No one designing that page ever conceived of width=375 as *meaning* "this is a headline," but if you take it to mean that, it works.

An approach like this happens to work for the Yahoo! News code, because the headline links are distinguished by the fact that they (and they alone) contain a b element:

```
<a href="...long_news_url..."><b>Elvis seen in tortilla</b></a>
```

Or, diagrammed as a part of the parse tree:

- a [href="...long_news_url..."]
  - b
    - "Elvis seen in tortilla"

A rule that matches these can be formalized as "look for any a element that has only one daughter node, which must be a b element." And this is what it looks like when

cooked up as a look_down expression and prefaced with a bit of code to retrieve the
Yahoo! News page and feed it to TreeBuilder:

```
use strict;
use HTML::TreeBuilder 3;
use LWP 5.64;
sub get_headlines {
    my $url = $_[0] || die "What URL?";

    my $response = LWP::UserAgent->new->get($url);

    unless ($response->is_success) {
        warn "Couldn't get $url: ", $response->status_line, "\n";
        return;
    }

    my $tree = HTML::TreeBuilder->new( );
    $tree->parse($response->content);
    $tree->eof;

    my @out;
    foreach my $link ( $tree->look_down('_tag', 'a',
                            sub {
                                    return unless $_[0]->attr('href');
                                    my @c = $_[0]->content_list;
                                    @c == 1 and ref $c[0] and $c[0]->tag eq 'b';
                            } ) ) {
        push @out, [$link->attr('href'), $link->as_text ];
    }

    warn "Odd, fewer than 6 stories in $url!" if @out < 6;
    $tree->delete;
    return @out;
}
```

And we add a bit of code to call get_headlines and display the results:

```
foreach my $section (qw[tc sc hl wl en]) {
    my @links = get_headlines( "http://dailynews.yahoo.com/h/$section/" );
    print $section, ": ", scalar(@links), " stories\n",
        map(("  ", $_->[0], " : ", $_->[1], "\n"), @links), "\n";
}
```

Now we have our own headline extractor service! By itself, it isn't amazingly useful
(since if you want to see the headlines, you can just look at the Yahoo! News pages),
but it could easily be the basis for features like filtering the headlines for particular
topics of interest.

One of these days, Yahoo! News will change its HTML template. When this happens, the above program finds no links meeting our criteria—or, less likely, dozens
of erroneous links that meet the criteria. In either case, the criteria will have to be
changed for the new template; they may just need adjustment, or you may need to
scrap them and start over.

Regardez, Duvet!

It's often a challenge to write criteria that match the desired parts of an HTML parse tree. Very often you can pull it off with a simple `$tree->look_down('_tag', 'h1')`, but sometimes you have to keep adding and refining criteria, until you end up with complex filters like I've shown in this article. The benefit of HTML parse trees is that one main search tool, the `look_down` method, can do most of the work, making simple things easy while keeping hard things possible.

CHAPTER 15

A Web Spider in One Line

Tkil

One day, someone on the IRC #perl channel was asking some confused questions. We finally managed to figure out that he was trying to write a web robot, or "spider," in Perl. Which is a grand idea, except that:

1. Perfectly good spiders have already been written and are freely available at *http://info.webcrawler.com/mak/projects/robots/robots.html*.

2. A Perl-based web spider is probably not an ideal project for novice Perl programmers. They should work their way up to it.

Having said that, I immediately pictured a one-line Perl robot. It wouldn't do much, but it would be amusing. After a few abortive attempts, I ended up with this monster, which requires Perl 5.005. I've split it onto separate lines for easier reading.

```
perl -MLWP::UserAgent -MHTML::LinkExtor -MURI::URL -lwe '
    $ua = LWP::UserAgent->new;
    while (my $link = shift @ARGV) {
        print STDERR "working on $link";
        HTML::LinkExtor->new(
          sub {
            my ($t, %a) = @_;
            my @links = map { url($_, $link)->abs() }
                        grep { defined } @a{qw/href img/};
            print STDERR "+ $_" foreach @links;
            push @ARGV, @links;
        } ) -> parse(
          do {
              my $r = $ua->simple_request
                (HTTP::Request->new("GET", $link));
              $r->content_type eq "text/html" ? $r->content : "";
          }
        )
}' http://slinky.scrye.com/~tkil/
```

I actually edited this on a single line; I use shell-mode inside of Emacs, so it wasn't that much of a terror. Here's the one-line version.

```
perl -MLWP::UserAgent -MHTML::LinkExtor -MURI::URL -lwe
'$ua = LWP::UserAgent->new; while (my $link = shift @ARGV) {
```

```
print STDERR "working on $link";HTML::LinkExtor->new( sub
{ my ($t, %a) = @_; my @links = map { url($_, $link)->abs( )
} grep { defined } @a{qw/href img/}; print STDERR "+ $_"
foreach @links; push @ARGV, @links} )->parse(do { my $r =
$ua->simple_request (HTTP::Request->new("GET", $link));
$r->content_type eq "text/html" ? $r-> content : ""; } )
}' http://slinky.scrye.com/~tkil/
```

After getting an ego-raising chorus of groans from the hapless onlookers in #perl, I thought I'd try to identify some cute things I did with this code that might actually be instructive to TPJ readers.

Callbacks and Closures

Many modules are designed to do grunt work. In this case, HTML::LinkExtor (a specialized version of HTML::Parser) knows how to look through an HTML document and find links. Once it finds them, however, it needs to know what to do with them.

This is where *callbacks* come in. They're well known in GUI circles, since interfaces need to know what to do when a button is pressed or a menu item selected. Here, HTML::LinkExtor needs to know what to do with links (all tags, actually) when it finds them.

My callback is an anonymous subroutine reference:

```
sub {
     my ($t, %a) = @_;
     my @links = map { url($_, $link)->abs( ) }
                    grep { defined } @a{qw/href img/};
     print STDERR "+ $_" foreach @links;
     push @ARGV, @links;
}
```

I didn't notice until later that $link is actually scoped just outside of this subroutine (in the while loop), making this subroutine look almost like a closure. It's not a classical closure—it doesn't define its own storage—but it does use a lexical value far away from where it is defined.

Cascading Arrows

It's amusing to note that, aside from debugging output, the while loop consists of a single statement. The arrow operator (->) only cares about the value of the left hand side. This is the heart of the Perl/Tk idiom:

```
my $button = $main->Button( ... )->pack( );
```

We use a similar approach, except we don't keep a copy of the created reference (which is stored in $button above):

```
HTML::LinkExtor->new(...)->parse(...);
```

This is a nice shortcut to use whenever you want to create an object for a single use.

Using Modules with One-Liners

When I first thought of this one-liner, I knew I'd be using modules from the libwww-perl (LWP) library. The first few iterations of this "one-liner" used LWP::Simple, which explicitly states that it should be ideal for one-liners. The -M flag is easy to use, and makes many things very easy. LWP::Simple fetched the files just fine. I used something like this:

```
HTML::LinkExtor->new(...)->parse( get $link );
```

Where get is a function provided by LWP::Simple; it returns the contents of a given URL.

Unfortunately, I needed to check the Content-Type of the returned data. The first version merrily tried to parse *.tar.gz* files and got confused:

```
working on ./dist/irchat/irchat-3.03.tar.gz
Use of uninitialized value at
    /usr/lib/perl5/site_perl/5.005/LWP/Protocol.pm line 104.
Use of uninitialized value at
    /usr/lib/perl5/site_perl/5.005/LWP/Protocol.pm line 107.
Use of uninitialized value at
    /usr/lib/perl5/site_perl/5.005/LWP/Protocol.pm line 82.
```

Oops.

Switching to the "industrial strength" LWP::UserAgent module allowed me to check the Content-Type of the fetched page. Using this information, together with the HTTP::Response module and a quick ?: construct, I could parse either the HTML content or an empty string.

The End

Whenever I write a one-liner, I find it interesting to think about it in different ways. While I was writing it, I was mostly thinking from the bottom up; some of the complex nesting is a result of this. For example, the callback routine is fairly hairy, but once I had it written, I could change the data source from LWP::Simple::get to LWP::UserAgent and HTTP::Request::content quite easily.

Obviously, this spider does nothing more than visit HTML pages and try to grab all the links off each one. It could be more polite (as the LWP::RobotUA module is) and it could be smarter about which links to visit. In particular, there's no sense of which pages have already been visited; a tied DBM of visited pages would solve that nicely.

Even with these limitations, I'm impressed at the power expressed by that "one" line. Kudos for that go to Gisle Aas (the author of LWP) and to Larry Wall, for making a language that does all the boring stuff for us. Thanks Gisle and Larry!

webpluck

Ed Hill

The promises of smart little web agents that run around the web and grab things of interest have gone unfulfilled. Like me, you probably have a handful of web pages that you check on a regular basis, and if you had the time, you'd check many more.

Listed below are a few of the bookmarks that I check on a regular basis. Each of these pages has content that changes every day, and it is, of course, the content of these pages that I am interested in—not their layout, nor the advertising that appears on the pages.

> Dilbert (of course)
> CNN U.S. News
> Astronomy Picture of the Day
> C|Net's News.com
> The local paper (The Daily Iowan)
> ESPNET Sportszone

These pages are great sources of information. My problem is that I don't have time to check each one every day to see what is there or if the page has been updated. What I want is my own personal newspaper built from the sources listed above.

Similar Tools

This is not an original idea, but after spending many hours searching for a tool to do what I wanted, I gave up. Here are the contenders I considered, and why they didn't do quite what I wanted.

First there is the "smart" agent, a little gremlin that roams the net trying to guess what you want to see using some AI technique. Firefly was an example; you indicate interest in a particular topic and it points you at a list of sites that others have ranked. When I first looked at Firefly, it suggested that since I was interested in "computers and the internet," I should check out "The Amazing Clickable Beavis" (Figure 16-1).

Figure 16-1. The Amazing Clickable Beavis

This is why I don't have much confidence in agents. Besides, I know what I want to see. I have the URLs in hand. I just don't have the time to go and check all the pages every day.

The second type of technology is the "custom newspaper." There are two basic types. CRAYON (Create Your Own Newspaper, headquartered at *http://www.crayon.net/*), is one flavor of personalized newspaper. CRAYON is little more than a page full of links to other pages that change everyday. For me, CRAYON just adds to the problem, listing tons of pages that I wish I had time to check out. I was still stuck clicking through lists of links to visit all the different pages.

Then there are sites like My Yahoo (*http://my.yahoo.com/*), a single page that content changes every day. This is very close to what I wanted—a single site with all of the information I need. My Yahoo combines resources from a variety of different sources. It shows a one-line summary of an article; if it's something that I find interesting, I can click on the link to read more about it. The only problem with My Yahoo is that it's restricted to a small set of content providers. I want resources other than what Yahoo provides.

Since these tools didn't do exactly what I wanted, I decided to write my own. I figured with Perl, the LWP library, and a weekend, I could throw together exactly what I wanted. Thus webpluck was born. My goal was to write a generic tool that would automatically grab data from any web page and create a personalized newspaper exactly like My Yahoo. I decided the best approach was to define a regular expression for each web page of interest. webpluck uses the LWP library to retrieve the web page, extracts the content with a regular expression tailored to each, and saves it to a local cache for display later. Once it has done this for all the sources, I use a template to generate my personal newspaper.

How to Use webpluck

I don't want this article to turn into a manual page (since one already exists), but here's a brief summary of how to use webpluck. You first create a configuration file containing a list of *targets* that define which pages you want to read, and the regular expression to match against the contents of that page. Here is an example of a target definition that retrieves headlines from the CNN U.S. web page.

```
name cnn-us
url http://www.cnn.com/US/
regex <h2>([^\<]+)<\/h2>.*?<a href=\"([^\"]+)\"
fields title:url
```

These definitions define the following: the name of the file to hold the data retrieved from the web page; the URL of the page (if you point at a page containing frames, you need to determine the URL of the page that actually contains the content); the Perl regular expression used to extract data from the web page; and the names of the fields matched in the regular expression that you just defined. The first pair of parentheses in the regex field matches the first field, the second pair matches the second, and so on. For the configuration shown, ([^\<]+) is tagged as the title and ([^\"]+) is tagged as the url. That url is the link to the actual content, distinct from the url definition on the second line, which is the starting point for the regex.

Running webpluck with the target definition above creates a file called *cnn-us* in a cache directory that you define. Here's the file from March 25, 1997:

```
title:Oklahoma bombing judge to let 'impact witnesses' see trial
url:http://www.cnn.com/US/9703/25/okc/index.html

title:Simpson's attorneys ask for a new trial and lower damages
url:http://www.cnn.com/US/9703/25/simpson.newtrial/index.html

title:U.S. playing low-key role in latest Mideast crisis
url:http://www.cnn.com/WORLD/9703/25/us.israel/index.html

title:George Bush parachutes -- just for fun
url:http://www.cnn.com/US/9703/25/bush.jump.ap/index.html
```

As you might expect, everything depends on the regular expression, which must be tailored for each source. Not everyone, myself included, feels comfortable with regular expressions; if you want to get the most use out of webpluck, and you feel that your regular expression skills are soft, I recommend Jeffrey Friedl's book *Mastering Regular Expressions* (O'Reilly).

The second problem with regular expressions is that as powerful as they are, they can only match data they expect to see. So if the publisher of the web page you are after changes his or her format, you'll have to update your regular expression. webpluck notifies you if it couldn't match anything, which is usually a good indication that the format of the target web page has changed.

Once all the content has been collected, webpluck takes those raw data files and a template file that you provide, and combines them to create your "dynamic" HTML document.

webpluck looks for any <clip> tags in your template file, replacing them with webplucked data. Everything else in the template file is passed through as is. Here is an example of a segment in my daily template file (again using the CNN U.S. headlines as an example):

```
<clip name="cnn-us">
<li><a href="url">title</a>
</clip>
```

This is replaced with the following HTML (the lines have been split to make them more readable):

```
<li><a href="http://www.cnn.com/US/9703/25/okc/index.html">
      Oklahoma bombing judge to let 'impact witnesses' see trial
    </a>

<li><a href="http://www.cnn.com/US/9703/25/simpson.newtrial/index.html">
      Simpson's attorneys ask for a new trial and lower damages
    </a>

<li><a href="http://www.cnn.com/WORLD/9703/25/us.israel/index.html">
      U.S. playing low-key role in latest Mideast crisis
    </a>

<li><a href="http://www.cnn.com/US/9703/25/bush.jump.ap/index.html">
      George Bush parachutes -- just for fun
    </a>
```

I personally use webpluck by running one cron job every morning and one during lunch to re-create my "daily" page. I realize webpluck could be used for a lot more than this; that's left as an exercise for the reader.

How webpluck Works

Now on to the technical goodies. For those who don't know what the LWP library is—learn! LWP is a great collection of Perl objects that allows you to fetch documents from the web. What the CGI library does for people writing web server code, LWP does for people writing web client code. You can download LWP from CPAN.

webpluck is a simple program. Most of the code takes care of processing command-line arguments, reading the configuration file, and checking for errors. The guts rely on the LWP library and Perl's powerful regular expressions. The following is part of the main loop in webpluck. I've removed some error checking to make it smaller, but the real guts are shown below.

```perl
use LWP;

$req = HTTP::Request->new( GET => $self->{'url'} );
$req->header( Accept => "text/html, */*;q=0.1" );
$res = $main::ua->request( $req );

if ($res->is_success()) {
    my (@fields) = split( ':', $self->{'fields'} );
    my $content  = $res->content();
    my $regex    = $self->{'regex'};

    while ($content =~ /$regex/isg) {
        my @values = ($1, $2, $3, $4, $5, $6, $7, $8);

        # URL's are special fields; they might be relative, so check for that

        for ($i = 0; $i <= $#fields; $i++) {
            if ($fields[$i] eq "url") {
                my $urlobj = new URI::URL($values[$i], $self->{'url'});
                $values[$i] = $urlobj->abs()->as_string();
            }
            push(@datalist, $fields[$i] . ":" . $values[$i]);
        }
        push( @{$self->{'_data'}}, \@datalist );
    }
}
```

The use LWP imports the LWP module, which takes care of all the web-related tasks (fetching documents, parsing URLs, and parsing robot rules). The next three lines are all it takes to grab a web page using LWP.

Assuming webpluck's attempt to retrieve the page is successful, it saves the document as one long string. It then iterates over the string, trying to match the regular expression defined for this target. The following statement merits some scrutiny:

```perl
while ( $content =~ /$regex/isg ) {
```

The /i modifier of the above regular expression indicates that it should be a case-insensitive match. The /s modifier treats the entire document as if it were a single line (treating newlines as whitespace), so your regular expression can span multiple lines. /g allows you to go through the entire document and grab data each time the regular expression is matched, instead of just the first.

For each match webpluck finds, it examines the fields defined by the user. If one of the fields is url, it's turned into an absolute URL—specifically, a URI::URL object. I let that object translate itself from a relative URL to an absolute URL that can be used outside of the web site from where it was retrieved. This is the only data from the target page that gets massaged.

Lastly, I take the field names and the data that corresponds to each field and save that information. Once all the data from each matched regular expression is collected, it's run through some additional error checking and saved to a local file.

The Dark Side of the Force

Like any tool, webpluck has both good and bad uses. The program is a sort of web robot, which raises some concerns for me and for users. A detailed list of the considerations can be found on the Web Robots Page at *http://www.robotstxt.org/wc/robots.html*, but a few points from the Web Robot Guide to Etiquette stand out.

Identify Yourself

webpluck identifies itself as webpluck/2.0 to the remote web server. This isn't a problem since few people use webpluck, but it could be if sites decide to block my program.

Don't Overload a Site

Since webpluck only checks a finite set of web pages that you explicitly define—that is, it doesn't tree-walk sites—this isn't a problem. Just to be safe, webpluck pauses for a small time period between retrieving documents. It should only be run once or twice a day—don't launch it every five minutes to ensure that you constantly have the latest and greatest information.

Obey Robot Exclusion Rules

This is the toughest rule to follow. Since webpluck is technically a robot, I should be following the rules set forth by a web site's */robots.txt* file. However, since the data that I am after typically changes every day, some sites have set up specific rules telling robots not to index their pages.

In my opinion, webpluck isn't a typical robot. I consider it more like an average web client. I'm not building an index, which I think is the reason that these sites tell robots not to retrieve the pages. If webpluck followed the letter of the law, it wouldn't be very useful since it wouldn't be able to access many pages that change their content. For example, CNN has this in their robot rules file:

```
User-agent: *
Disallow: /
```

If webpluck were law-abiding, it wouldn't be able to retrieve any information from CNN, one of the main sites I check for news. So what to do? After reading the Robot Exclusion Standard (*http://www.robotstxt.org/wc/norobots.html*), I believe webpluck doesn't cause any of the problems meant to be prevented by the standard. Your interpretation may differ; I encourage you to read it and decide for yourself. webpluck has two options (--naughty and --nice) that instruct it whether to obey the robot exclusion rules found on remote servers. (This is my way of deferring the decision to you.)

Just playing nice as a web robot is only part of the equation. Another consideration is what you do with the data once you get it. There are obvious copyright considerations. Copyright on the web is a broad issue. I'm just going to mention a few quandaries raised by webpluck; I don't have the answers.

1. Is it okay to extract the URL from the Cool Site of the Day home page and jump straight to the cool site? The Cool Site folks don't own the URL, but they would certainly prefer that you visit their site first.

2. Is it okay to retrieve headlines from CNN? What about URLs for the articles?

3. How about grabbing the actual articles from the CNN site and redisplaying them with your own layout?

4. And for all of these tasks, does it matter if they're for your own personal use as opposed to showing it to a friend, or redistributing it more widely?

Obviously, people have different opinions of what is right and what is wrong. I personally don't have the background, knowledge, or desire to try to tell you what to do. I merely want to raise the issues so you can think about them and make your own decisions.

For a final example of a potential problem, let's take a look at Dilbert. Here's the target I have defined for Dilbert at the time of this writing.

```
name dilbert
url http://www.unitedmedia.com/comics/dilbert/
regex SRC=\"?([^>]?\/comics\/dilbert\/archive.*?\.gif)\"?\s+
fields url
```

The cartoon on the Dilbert page changes every day, and instead of just having a link to the latest cartoon (*todays-dilbert.gif*), they generate a new URL every day and include the cartoon in their web page. They do this because they don't want people setting up links directly to the cartoon. They want people to read their main page—after all, that's where the advertising is. Every morning I find out where today's Dilbert cartoon is located, bypassing all of United Media's advertising. If enough people do this, United Media will probably initiate countermeasures. There are at least three things that would prevent webpluck (as it currently works) from allowing me to go directly to today's comic.

- A CGI program that stands between me and the comic strip. The program would then take all kinds of steps to see if I should have access to the image (e.g., checking Referer headers, or planting a cookie on me). But almost any such countermeasure can be circumvented with a clever enough webpluck.

- The advertising could be embedded in the same image as the cartoon. That'll work for Dilbert since it's a graphic, but not for pages where the content is plain HTML.

- The site could move away from HTML to another display format such as VRML or Java that takes over an entire web page with a single view. This approach makes the content far harder for robots to retrieve.

Most funding for web technology exists to solve the needs of content providers, not users. If tools like webpluck are considered a serious problem by content providers, steps will be taken to shut them down, or make them harder to operate.

It isn't my intent to distribute a tool to filter web advertising or steal information from web pages so that I can redistribute it myself, but I'm not so naïve as to think this can't be done. Obviously, anyone intent on doing these things can do so; webpluck just makes it easier. Do what you think is right.

You can find more information about webpluck at *http://www.edsgarage.com/ed/webpluck/*. The program is also on this book's web site at *http://www.oreilly.com/catalog/tpj2*.

## CHAPTER 17

Torture-Testing Web Servers and CGI Scripts

Lincoln D. Stein

It's a sad fact of life that computer programs aren't bug free. Loops overwrite array boundaries, memory is mistakenly freed twice, *if-then* statements make decisions based on random data in uninitialized variables, and while blocks go into endless loops. Perl programmers like ourselves have much to rejoice about because we don't have to worry about the memory management problems that plague C and C++ programmers. Of course, we have our own idiosyncratic problems, such as inadvertently using a string in a numeric context.

Many of the programs you use on any given day have bugs. Many of the bugs are minor, and most are invisible. You won't know a program contains a bug until a particular combination of conditions triggers it. For example, a word processing program might work fine for months, and then crash one day when memory is tight and you attempt a global search and replace on a large document.

Bugs are usually just a nuisance. The text editor eats your homework, the printer pours out reams of gibberish, the graphics program flood fills the diagram you've labored over for hours with magenta polka dots. When the bug occurs in software that's part of a web site, however, the consequences can be more frightening. A bug in a web server can cause it to crash, making the site unavailable until someone notices and reboots the server. A bug in a CGI script or server module may cause the browser to display a bewildering "Internal Error" message.

Worse, however, is the risk that a bug in the server software or one of its CGI scripts can be exploited by a malicious remote user. A bug that crashes a web server can be used deliberately to bring a site down in a denial-of-service attack. Scarier still is the possibility that the bug can be exploited to break into the host machine, steal information from it, or modify its files. If this is possible, the software bug becomes a major security hole.

In the past, there have been two major types of bugs that blast security holes in web sites. The first is the failure of the programmer to check user-provided input before passing it to a command shell. This kind of bug shows up frequently in CGI scripts, and unfortunately more often than not in Perl CGI scripts. A clever user can trick a CGI script containing this bug into executing whatever Unix or NT command he likes. Fortunately, there's an easy way to avoid this trap. Activate Perl taint checks by placing a -T flag on the top line of your script, right after #!/usr/bin/perl. (A *tainted* variable is something that contains data from the outside, like $name = <>, that might be used by nefarious people for nefarious purposes. Taint-checking ensures that $name is a name and not something suspicious like /etc/passwd.)

The second type of bug is more commonly found in CGI scripts and web servers written in a compiled language, typically C. In this type of bug, the programmer fails to check the length of data before copying it into a statically allocated buffer. Unexpectedly long data will overwrite memory, and again, a clever remote user can exploit this to gain access to both Unix and NT shells. This bug plagued the NCSA *httpd* server up to version 1.3. Remote users could exploit it to run any Unix program they cared to on the web server. More recently, this bug surfaced in Microsoft's Internet Information Server (up to Version 3.0). By sending the server a URL of a particular length, remote users could make it crash.

In this article, I present a short Perl script called torture.pl designed to catch web servers and CGI programs that suffer from memory allocation problems. It employs a technique called "random input testing" in which the web server is pummeled with a long series of requests for random URLs of varying lengths, some of which can be quite large. A well-designed server or CGI script will accept the random input gracefully and produce some sort of reasonable error message. Software with a memory allocation bug will crash or behave unpredictably. Although this type of testing is inefficient, the program does catch the problem in both the NCSA *httpd* and IIS servers.

torture.pl can be used locally to test your own server, or remotely to test other peoples' (but be sure to get their permission first!). To use it, provide torture.pl with the URL of the server or CGI script you wish to test. For example:

```
$ torture.pl http://www.foo.bar.com/cgi-bin/search
torture.pl version 1.0 starting
  Base URL: http://www.foo.bar.com/cgi-bin/search
  Max random data length: 1024
  Repetitions: 1
  Post: 0
  Append to path: 0
  Escape URLs: 0

200 OK
```

In this example, we've asked the script to test the server at *www.foo.bar.com*, using the default settings of one test repetition and a maximum URL length of 1,024 bytes. After echoing its settings, the script does a single fetch of the indicated URL and returns the HTTP result code, in this case 200 OK, indicating that the URL was fetched successfully. If we look at the server log, we'll see an entry something like this:

```
pico lstein - [22/Nov/1997:12:54:17 -0400] "GET /cgi-bin/search?%F18n%99%DB
%15_a%5E8%C2%A7)%7D%AD%196%9DZ%C1%OFX%%D9K%5D%AA%BA=%CC%C7%85%A4%93%81%A9%7F
```

```
%E3%B7%A6%B0%E1%_%FA%5B%FCV%1D%AEC%E6%F9%A0%91%B4%DE%5E%7De%04%11%85%85%BA
%05j%C3%BD%12t%9F7%D4%9A%93%D1%F1%B1%DE%A0%F4%C5%9B%96XPu%B7%CD%DB%BB%DFbB
%9Ag%AC_&%BE%D4%C6%F6%A9b%8A%7CT%3C%5C%F42 HTTP/1.0" 200 928
```

This entry shows that `torture.pl` generated a URL containing a query string consisting of 928 bytes of random data.

Fetching a URL just once isn't much of a torture test. Let's make things more challenging for the CGI script by fetching 1,000 random URLs, each containing a random query string of up to 5K in length:

```
$ torture.pl -t 1000 -l 5000 http://www.foo.bar.com/cgi-bin/search
torture.pl version 1.0 starting
  Base URL: http://www.foo.bar.com/cgi-bin/search
  Max random data length: 5000
  Repetitions: 1000
  Post: 0
  Append to path: 0
  Escape URLs: 0

200 OK
200 OK
200 OK
200 OK
...
```

This time we use the -t option to set the repetitions to 1,000, and the -l option to set the maximum length to 5,000 bytes. The script fires off the URLs and begins printing out the server responses.

By default, the torture script uses the GET method to access the server. This actually imposes a server-specific limit on the length of the URL. Many servers will truncate URLs that are larger than some reasonable length. If you'd like to blast a CGI script with large requests, use the POST command instead. To do this, pass -P to torture.pl.

If you're more interested in testing the server itself than a CGI script, you should use the -p option. That makes the script randomly generate URL paths rather than query strings. The output looks like this:

```
$ torture.pl -p -t 1000 -l 5000 http://www.foo.bar.com/
torture.pl version 1.0 starting
  Base URL: http://www.foo.bar.com/
  Max random data length: 5000
  Repetitions: 1000
  Post: 0
  Append to path: 1
  Escape URLs: 0

400 Bad Request
404 File Not Found
404 File Not Found
404 File Not Found
400 Bad Request
400 Bad Request
...
```

Now, because the script is generating random URL pathnames, the expected outcome is either 400 Bad Request for a URL that contains invalid characters, or 404 File Not Found for a valid URL that doesn't point to any particular file.

The server log shows the difference between this and the previous tests:

```
pico.foo.bar.com lstein - [22/Nov/1997:13:21:03 -0400] "GET /%F2%F1%FE%98
%8C%F5%8E0%BC%17%A0%F1%DE%DD%9D%99%D4%9C%ACb%EA%AEg%BC*%B3%D2E%8C%E39~%E3
%D1%D9%60=%97x%DE%89W%BC'%F0%91%C4%FA?(%E5%EE%90%A3%19Ew_%D1%5C%98QAj%5D
%1B%CB%9A%B3Dz%3E%9C7e%8D%C9+%88 HTTP/1.0" 500 404
```

When -p is used, the random data is appended to the URL with a / character rather than a ? character. The server treats the request as an attempt to fetch a document, rather than as an attempt to pass a query string to a CGI script.

The final option that torture.pl recognizes is -e. When this is provided, the script uses URL escape codes to generate invalid but legal URLs. Otherwise, the script generates arbitrary binary data, including nulls and control characters. This tests the server's ability to handle binary input.

In all the examples I've shown so far, the script and server have passed the test by processing the request or exiting with an error. What happens when a program fails the test? If the testing causes a CGI script to crash, you'll see something like this:

```
200 OK
200 OK
200 OK
500 Internal Server Error
200 OK
200 OK
500 Unexpected EOF
```

Every so often the random testing triggers a bug in the CGI script that causes it to abort. Depending on whether the bug occurred before or after the script printed its HTTP header you may see a 500 Internal Server Error message or 500 Unexpected EOF message. Either way, you've got a problem.

If the server itself crashes during testing, the results are even more dramatic:

```
200 OK
200 OK
200 OK
200 OK
200 OK
500 Internal Server Error
500 Could not connect to www.foo.bar.com:80
500 Could not connect to www.foo.bar.com:80
500 Could not connect to www.foo.bar.com:80
500 Could not connect to www.foo.bar.com:80
...
```

In this sequence, everything went along well until the torture script triggered a bug in the server, causing a 500 Internal Server Error message. The server then went down completely, making it unavailable for future incoming connections.

The Code

Example 17-1 shows the code for torture.pl. It makes extensive use of Martijn Koster and Gisle Aas's excellent LWP web client library, available from CPAN and discussed in web_lwp.

Example 17-1. torture.pl

```
1
2  # file: torture.pl
3  # Torture test web servers and scripts by sending them large
4  # arbitrary URLs and record the outcome.
5
6  use LWP::UserAgent;
7  use URI::Escape 'uri_escape';
8  require "getopts.pl";
9
10 $USAGE = <<USAGE;
11 Usage: $0 -[options] URL
12 Torture-test Web servers and CGI scripts
13
14 Options:
15 -l <integer> Max length of random URL to send [1024 bytes]
16 -t <integer> Number of times to run the test [1]
17 -P           Use POST method rather than GET method
18 -p           Attach random data to path instead of query string
19 -e           Escape the query string before sending it
20 USAGE
21     ;
22 $VERSION = '1.0';
23
24 # Process command line
25 &Getopts('l:t:Ppe') || die $USAGE;
26 # Seed the random number generator (not necessary in modern Perls)
27 srand();
28
29 # get parameters
30 $URL    = shift  || die $USAGE;
31 $MAXLEN = $opt_l ne '' ? $opt_l : 1024;
32 $TIMES  = $opt_t || 1;
33 $POST   = $opt_P || 0;
34 $PATH   = $opt_p || 0;
35 $ESCAPE = $opt_e || 0;
36
37 # Can't do both a post and a path at the same time
38 $POST = 0 if $PATH;
39
40 # Create an LWP agent
41 my $agent = new LWP::UserAgent;
42
43 print <<EOF;
44 torture.pl version $VERSION starting
45   Base URL: $URL
46   Max random data length: $MAXLEN
```

Example 17-1. torture.pl (continued)

```
47    Repetitions: $TIMES
48    Post: $POST
49    Append to path: $PATH
50    Escape URLs: $ESCAPE
51
52 EOF
53 ;
54
55 # Do the test $TIMES times
56 while ($TIMES--) {
57     # create a string of random stuff
58     my $garbage = random_string(rand($MAXLEN));
59     $garbage = uri_escape($garbage) if $ESCAPE;
60     my $url = $URL;
61     my $request;
62
63     if (length($garbage) == 0) { # If no garbage to add, fetch URL
64         $request = new HTTP::Request ('GET', $url);
65     }
66
67     elsif ($POST) { # handle POST request
68         my $header = new HTTP::Headers (
69                        Content_Type => 'application/x-www-form-urlencoded',
70                     Content_Length => length($garbage)
71                                      );
72         # Garbage becomes the POST content
73         $request = new HTTP::Request ('POST',$url,$header,$garbage);
74
75     } else {                              # Handle GET request
76
77         if ($PATH) {                      # Append garbage to the base URL
78             chop($url) if substr($url, -1, 1) eq '/';
79             $url .= "/$garbage";
80         } else { # Append garbage to the query string
81             $url .= "?$garbage";
82         }
83
84         $request = new HTTP::Request ('GET', $url);
85     }
86
87     # Do the request and fetch the response
88     my $response = $agent->request($request);
89
90     # Print the numeric response code and the message
91     print $response->code, ' ', $response->message, "\n";
92 }
93
94 # Return some random data of the requested length
95 sub random_string {
96     my $length = shift;
97     return unless $length >= 1;
98     return join('', map chr(rand(255)), 0..$length-1);
99 }
```

In lines 6–8, we bring in the LWP::UserAgent library, which provides all the functions we need for generating and processing HTTP requests. We next import the uri_escape function from the URI::Escape module, which implements the rules for escaping URLs. Finally, we load the *getopts* library, a handy package for parsing a script's command-line options.

 getopts.pl is obsolete; today the Getopt::Std module should be used instead.

In lines 24–38, we process the command-line options and assign defaults to any not provided. The only required argument is the base URL to fetch. If present on the command line, we assign it to $URL. Otherwise we abort with a usage statement.

We also seed the random number generator in order to avoid generating the same series of random URLs each time the script is run. This step is no longer necessary as of Perl 5.004, which seeds the random number the first time you invoke the rand function.

In lines 41–53, we create a new UserAgent object (think of it as a virtual browser) that will connect to the web server and make the URL request. We then print the test parameters so that they can be recorded.

Lines 56–92 are the meat of the program. We enter a loop that repeats as many times as requested. Each time through the loop, we create a string of random data by calling the random_string function described below, assigning the result to a variable with the inelegant but descriptive name $garbage. We also assign the base URL to a local variable named $url.

What we do now depends on the length of the random data and the script's options. If the random data happens to be of zero length, we do nothing with it. We simply generate a GET request to fetch the base URL by creating a new HTTP::Request object (line 64). The two arguments to HTTP::Request::new are the request method (GET in this case) and the URL to fetch.

Otherwise, if the user requested a POST transaction, we need to set up the HTTP headers that will be sent to the server. We do this by creating a new HTTP::Headers object in line 68, passing the new method a hash with the HTTP headers we wish to send. For a valid POST operation, we'll need two header fields: a Content-Type field with a value of application/x-www-form-urlencoded, to fool the script into thinking that the random data was generated by a bona fide fill-out form, and a Content-Length field containing the length of the random data. We now create an HTTP::Request using the four-argument form of HTTP::Request::new (line 73). As before, the first and second arguments correspond to the request method and the URL to fetch. The optional third and fourth arguments contain the HTTP::Headers object and content to be POSTed. In this case, the content is the random data that we generated earlier.

In lines 77–84, we create a GET request for non-zero–length random data. This is merely a matter of appending the random data to the requested URL and generating the appropriate HTTP::Request object. If the command-line options indicate that we're to generate a query string for a CGI script, we append the random data to the base URL after a ? character. If the user wishes to generate a random URL instead, we append the data after a / character.

On line 88, we perform the actual network fetch by calling the UserAgent object's request method. The response is returned as an HTTP::Response object, and stored in a like-named variable. We use this object on line 91 to print the result code (e.g. 500) and result message (e.g., Internal Server Error).

Lines 95–99 define the random_string function, which generates an array of random numbers between 0 and 255, then transforms the array into a random ASCII character string using Perl's map and chr functions. Notice that this function isn't particularly memory efficient, since it generates a temporary integer array as long as the requested random string. Replace it with a loop if this bothers you.

Wrapping Up

That's all there is to it. Point the script at your favorite server and let it rip! For best results I recommend that you run the torture script overnight, using at least a thousand test repetitions (the more the better). Redirect its output to a file so that you can analyze the results at your leisure. Be careful not to run the tests on a server that's being used for a live web site. Even if there aren't any bugs to trigger, the script will load down the server and might hurt its performance.

In the next article, I'll show you how to secure your CGI scripts, ensuring that evildoers can't exploit them to wreak havoc on your system.

## CHAPTER 18

Securing Your CGI Scripts

Lincoln D. Stein

 Since this article was written, a new module has become available: Roland Giersig's `Expect.pm`, available on CPAN. I recommend it over both `chat2.pl` and `Comm.pl`; not only is it a full-fledged module, but it uses IO::, which renders Lincoln's workaround in the section "Oops" unnecessary.

I like to keep my CGI scripts puny and weak, and you should too. CGI scripts are a gateway into your system from the Internet, and are, unfortunately, all too often exploited by unscrupulous people for nefarious ends. The more access a CGI script has to your system, the more dangerous it becomes when used for unintended purposes.

To keep CGI scripts under control, most webmasters, myself included, run the web server under an unprivileged user account. On Unix systems, this is often an account called *nobody*. On Windows, it's an anonymous account with guest logon access. On correctly configured systems, the web server user account has even fewer privileges than an ordinary user. It doesn't own a home directory, have a shell, or even have the ability to log in as a normal user.

Under most circumstances you'll never notice the fact that CGI scripts run as an unprivileged user. However, sometimes this fact becomes inconvenient. For example, what if you want to give remote users read/write access to their home directories from across the web, allow web access to a database that uses account privileges for access control, or perform administrative tasks that require superuser privileges? When you face challenges like these, your only choice is to give the script a little more power than usual. In this article I'll show you how to accomplish this without creating a monster.

The Example Script

The example I use here lets Unix users change their login passwords remotely via a web page. When the user first accesses the script, the screen shown in Figure 18-1 prompts him for the account name, old password, and new password (twice). After pressing the Change Password button, the script verifies the input and then attempts to make the requested change. If the change is successful, the user is presented with a confirmation screen. Otherwise, an error message (in large red letters) is displayed, and the user is prompted to try again, as shown in Figure 18-2.

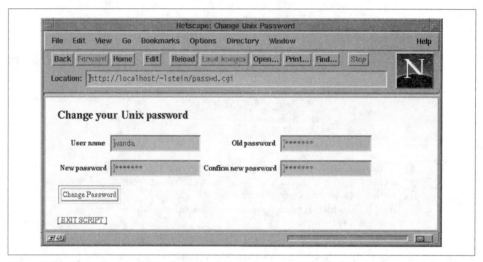

Figure 18-1. Changing your system password

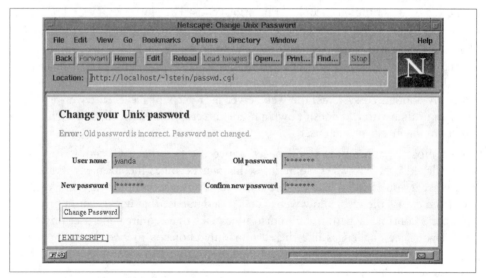

Figure 18-2. An unsuccessful attempt

Note that this password-changing script is designed to change not the user's web access password, but his system login password. An Internet service provider might use something like this to allow users to change their POP (Post Office Protocol), NNTP (Net News Transfer Protocol), or dialup passwords without bothering the system administrator or accessing a shell.

Designing the Script

An ordinary CGI script has a snowball's chance in hell of accomplishing this password-changing task. It can't modify the system password file directly, because write access to the file is off-limits to anyone but the superuser. It can't even run the system passwd utility on the remote user's behalf, because passwd prevents one user from changing another's password, and will detect the attempt by the web server account to do so as a security violation.

To get around these problems, we have several choices:

1. Launch the CGI script as the superuser (with *suid*), and modify the system password files directly.

2. Launch the CGI script as the superuser (with *suid*), and run the system passwd utility to change the user's password.

3. Launch the CGI script as the superuser (with *suid*), immediately change to the remote user's access privileges, and run the system passwd utility to change the password.

4. Launch the CGI script normally, and call the su program to run the passwd utility under the privileges of the remote user.

The first solution is by far the worst. Running a CGI script as the superuser and then using its far-reaching powers to modify essential system files is an invitation to disaster. The solution is also extremely nonportable, since many Unix systems use shadow password systems or Network Information System (NIS) databases to hold user account information.

The second solution is somewhat more appealing. Instead of modifying system files directly, we call the system passwd utility to change the user's password on our behalf. This avoids many of the portability problems because the passwd program presumably knows all about the fiddly details of the system password database. However, it still requires that the script be run as root, and this makes me nervous.

The next solution isn't much different. The CGI script is again launched with root privileges, but it quickly changes its identity to run as the remote user. With the remote user's account privileges, it then invokes passwd. This is an improvement because the script gives away its superuser privileges as soon as possible. However, the script is still launched as root, and this is a Bad Thing.

I like the last solution the best. The script isn't run as root at all. Instead, after parsing the CGI parameters and deciding what to do, it calls the su program to change its identity to that of the remote user. In order to run su, the script needs the remote user's password, which, conveniently enough, he has already provided. If su grants the request, the script calls the passwd program to change the user's password. Not only does this solution avoid the problem of becoming root, but it works with systems that have disabled *suid* scripts and even with servers that don't run CGI scripts as separate processes, such as Apache equipped with mod_perl (see the article *mod_perl* earlier in this book).

This is the design I use here.

The chat2.pl Library

Unfortunately, there's one little problem. Both su and passwd are interactive programs. They read their input directly from the terminal rather than from standard input, so you can't just send them input via a pipe. Instead, you have to trick them into thinking they're talking to a human typing at a terminal rather than to a Perl script.

Happily, there's a ready-made solution. The chat2.pl library, part of the standard Perl 5.004 distribution, allows you to open up a pseudo tty to any program on the system and hold an interactive conversation with it. All we have to do is to figure out what prompts the program produces and what inputs to provide.

In preparation for writing a script that uses chat2.pl, it's good to run the desired program from the command line a few times and provide it with a range of inputs so that you can see all the possible outcomes. Here's a transcript of the session that I used to design the password-changing script:

```
1> su -c /usr/bin/passwd impostor
su: user impostor does not exist

2> su -c /usr/bin/passwd wanda
Password: wrong_password
su: incorrect password

3> su -c /usr/bin/passwd wanda
Password: llamas2
Changing password for wanda
Enter old password: wrong_password
Illegal password, impostor.

4> su -c /usr/bin/passwd wanda
Password: llamas2
Changing password for wanda
Enter old password: llamas2
Enter new password: zebras
The password must have both upper- and lowercase letters, or non-letters; try again.
Enter new password: zeBrAs
Re-type new password: zeBras
You misspelled it. Password not changed.

5> su -c /usr/bin/passwd wanda
Password: llamas2
Changing password for wanda
Enter old password: llamas2
Enter new password: ZeBrAs
Re-type new password: ZeBrAs
Password changed.
```

In each attempt, I called su with the -c flag to make it run the passwd program with the privileges of the indicated user. In the first attempt, I deliberately gave su the name of a bogus user, and it replied with an error message. In the second attempt, I gave su the name of a legitimate user of the system, but deliberately mistyped her password.

In the third try, I gave su the correct password; it accepted the password and passed me on to the passwd program, which printed Changing password for wanda. I then deliberately entered the incorrect password at this point, to see the message Illegal password.

Continuing to work my way through the possibilities, I invoked the program again, this time giving the correct password both times. This got me to the Enter new password: prompt. When I typed in zebras, however, the passwd program rejected it because it was too easy (my system rejects passwords that are too short or consist only of lowercase letters; other systems may have even more stringent rules). The system accepted ZeBrAs as a password, but when I confirmed it, I made a spelling error and was booted out.

Finally, on trial 5, I was able to work my way through the password changing process, getting to the final confirmation Password changed.

Armed with this information, we can design a series of calls to chat2.pl that automate the password changing operation.

Oops

But not quite yet. Soon after I began writing this script I discovered that the chat2.pl library, which was originally written for Perl 4, hasn't been brought up to date for a long time. As a result, it's not as portable as other parts of Perl 5. chat2.pl uses a number of system-specific constants for creating sockets and pseudo ttys. Some of the constants are obtained from .ph files (system include files that have been run through the h2ph converter), while others are, unfortunately, hard coded. h2ph is notoriously difficult to run correctly, and the .ph files it produces often have to be tuned by hand. Worse, the hardcoded value for one essential constant, TIOCNOTTY, was just plain wrong for my Linux system, causing chat2.pl to fail miserably.

To get things working, I patched my copy of chat2.pl slightly to bring it up to date. The patch replaces hardwired and .ph constants with ones imported from the Socket.pm and Ioctl.pm modules. You can find a copy of this patch file on the web site for this book.

Although Socket.pm is a standard part of Perl, Ioctl.pm isn't in all distributions, so you may have to download it from CPAN. Be warned that installing Ioctl.pm is not as straightforward as most other modules. After the standard perl Makefile.PL and make steps, you must open a file named *Ioctl.def* and define a comma-delimited list of those constants you wish to make available. A good list can be found in the autogenerated file *genconst.pl*, where it is, inexplicably, commented out. I created an *Ioctl.def* for my system by cutting and pasting between the two files. After this, you must make again and then make install.

Recently, Eric Arnold wrote an alternative to chat2.pl called Comm.pl. Its advantages over chat2.pl include a more intuitive interface that resembles Tcl's expect program, and includes some extra goodies like an interact function for interactively getting input from the user. However, Comm.pl is still a Perl 4 library with lots of hardcoded system-specific constants. Until Comm.pl is updated to use Perl 5's Socket and Ioctl modules, I'll continue to use my patched copy of chat2.pl. For those who want to investigate Comm.pl further, it can be found on CPAN.

The CGI Script

The complete password-changing script is shown in below. We'll focus first on lines 58 through 110, where the subroutine named set_passwd is defined. This is the core of the script, where the password is actually changed.

```
0    #!/usr/bin/perl -T
1
2    # Preliminaries to satisfy taint checks
3    $ENV{PATH} = '/bin:/usr/bin';
4    $ENV{IFS} = '';
5
6    # Prevent buffering problems
7    $| = 1;
8
9    use CGI qw/:standard :html3/;
10
11   print header,
12   start_html(-title => 'Change Unix Password', -bgcolor => 'white'),
13
14   h1('Change your Unix password');
15
16   import_names('Q');
17
18   TRY: {
19     last TRY unless $Q::user;
20     my ($rv, $msg) = check_consistency();
21     do_error($msg), last TRY unless $rv;
22
23     # Change the password, after temporarily turning off
24     # an annoying (and irrelevant) error message from su
25     open(SAVERR, ">&STDERR");
26     open(STDERR, ">/dev/null");
27     ($rv, $msg) = set_passwd($Q::user,$Q::old,$Q::new1);
28     open(STDERR, ">&SAVERR");
29     do_error($msg),last TRY unless $rv;
30
31     print $msg;
32     $OK++;
33   }
34
35   create_form() unless $OK;
36
37   print
38         p,
```

```
39       a({href=>"$Q::referer" || referer() },"[ EXIT SCRIPT ]");
40       hr,
41       a({href=>'/'},'Home page'),
42       end_html;
43
44   sub check_consistency {
45     return (undef,'Please fill in the user name field.') unless $Q::user;
46     return (undef,'Please fill in the old password field.') unless $Q::old;
47     return (undef,'Please fill in the new password fields.') unless $Q::new1 && $Q::new2;
48     return (undef,"New password fields don't match.") unless $Q::new1 eq $Q::new2;
49     return (undef,"Suspicious user name $Q::user.") unless $Q::user=~/^\w{3,8}$/;
50     return (undef,'Suspiciously long old password.') unless length($Q::old) <= 30;
51     return (undef,'Suspiciously long new password.') unless length($Q::new1) <= 30;
52     my $uid = (getpwnam($Q::user))[2];
53     return (undef,"Unknown user name $Q::user.") if $uid eq '';
54     return (undef,"Can't use this script to set root password.") if $uid == 0;
55     return 1;
56   }
57
58   sub set_passwd ($$$) {
59     require "chat2.pl";
60     my $TIMEOUT = 2;
61     my $PASSWD = "/usr/bin/passwd";
62     my $SU = '/bin/su';
63
64     my ($user, $old, $new) = @_;
65
66     my $h = chat::open_proc($SU,'-c',$PASSWD,$user)
67       || return (undef,"Couldn't open $SU -c $PASSWD: $!");
68
69     # Wait for su to prompt for password
70     my $rv = chat::expect($h, $TIMEOUT,
71                           'Password:' => "'ok'",
72                           'user \w+ does not exist' => "'unknown user'"
73                           );
74     $rv || return (undef,"Didn't get su password prompt.");
75     $rv eq 'unknown user' && return (undef,"User $user unknown.");
76     chat::print($h, "$old\n");
77
78     # Wait for passwd to prompt for old password
79     $rv = chat::expect($h, $TIMEOUT,
80                        'Enter old password:' => "'ok'",
81                        'incorrect password' => "'not ok'");
82     $rv || return (undef, "Didn't get prompt for old password.");
83     $rv eq 'not ok' && return (undef,"Old password is incorrect.");
84
85     # Print old password
86     chat::print($h, "$old\n");
87     $rv = chat::expect($h, $TIMEOUT,
88                        'Enter new password: ' => "'ok'",
89                        'Illegal' => "'not ok'");
90     $rv || return (undef,"Timed out without seeing prompt for new password.");
91     $rv eq 'not ok' && return (undef,"Old password is incorrect.");
92
```

```
 93     # Print new password
 94     chat::print($h,"$new\n");
 95     ($rv, $msg) = chat::expect($h, $TIMEOUT,
 96                                  'Re-type new password: ' => "'ok'",
 97                                  '([\s\S]+)Enter new password:' => "('rejected',\$1)"
 98                                );
 99     $rv || return (undef,"Timed out without seeing 2d prompt for new password.");
100     $rv eq 'rejected' && return (undef,$msg);
101
102     # Reconfirm password
103     chat::print($h, "$new\n");
104     $rv = chat::expect($h, $TIMEOUT,
105                          'Password changed' => "'ok'");
106     $rv || return (undef,"Password program failed at very end.");
107     chat::close($h);
108
109     return (1,"Password changed successfully for $user.");
110 }
111
112 sub create_form {
113    print
114          start_form,
115          table(
116              TR({ align => RIGHT },
117                  th('User name'),
118                  td(textfield(-name => 'user')),
119                  th('Old password'),
120                  td(password_field(-name => 'old'))),
121              TR({ align => RIGHT },
122                  th('New password'),
123                  td(password_field(-name => 'new1')),
124                  th('Confirm new password'),
125                  td(password_field(-name => 'new2'))),
126              ),
127          hidden(-name => 'referer',-value => referer()),
128          submit('Change Password'),
129          end_form;
130 }
131
132 sub do_error ($) {
133    print font({ -color => 'red',-size => '+1' },
134    b('Error:'), shift, " Password not changed.");
135 }
```

Our first step is to bring in chat2.pl, which we do using an old-fashioned require, because chat2.pl is still a Perl 4 library file. It's not a real module, so we can't use use. We also define some constants: $PASSWD and $SU give the absolute path to the passwd and su programs, respectively, and $TIMEOUT specifies a timeout of two seconds for our conversation with the su and passwd programs. If an expected output is not seen within this time, the subroutine aborts.

On line 64, we recover the name of the account to change as well the old and new passwords. We call the chat::open_proc function to open up a pseudo tty to the command

---

`su -c /usr/bin/passwd` *username*. If successful, the chat package returns a filehandle we use for the subsequent conversation. Otherwise, we abort with an error message.

We wait for su to prompt for the original password (lines 69 through 73) by calling the function chat::expect. This function takes the pseudo tty filehandle, a timeout value, and a series of pattern/expression pairs, and scans through the opened program's output looking for a match with each of the provided patterns. When a match is found, its corresponding expression is eval'd and the result is returned. If no pattern is matched during the specified timeout period, an undef value is returned.

In the first call to expect, we're looking for two possible patterns. The first pattern is the string Password:, indicating that su is prompting for the user's current password. The second possible pattern is user \w+ does not exist, which means that the account name we are attempting to su to is invalid. In the first case, we return the string ok. In the second case, we return the string unknown user. Notice that because these expressions will be passed to eval, we must enclose them in quotes in order to prevent Perl from trying to execute them as functions or method calls.

Next, in lines 74 to 76, we examine the return value from chat::expect and act on it. If there's no return value at all, we return an error indicating that we timed out before seeing one of the expected patterns. If the return value is the unknown user string, we abort with an appropriate error message. Otherwise, we know that su is waiting for the password. We oblige it by calling chat:print to send the old password to su.

We now repeat this chat::expect and chat::print sequence several times. First we await confirmation from su that the password was correct (lines 78–83). Next we provide passwd with the old and new passwords (lines 85–106) and wait for confirmation that they were acceptable. When done, we close the pseudo tty by calling chat::close (line 107).

The only trick worth noting here is the call to chat::expect on lines 95 to 98, where we provide passwd with the user's new password. With my version of passwd, there's a chance of the new password being rejected as too simple. Sometimes the password is rejected as too short, sometimes for being composed of lower-case letters only, and sometimes for other reasons. In addition to detecting the fact that the password has been rejected, we'd like to capture the reason given by passwd. We do this using parentheses in the regular expression match to create a backreference. The matched string is then returned from expect when the expression $1 is evaluated.

The return value from set_passwd is a two-element array. The first element is a numeric result code, where a true value indicates a successful outcome. The second element is a string that gives the reason for failure, if any.

The Rest of the Script

Changing the password was the hard part. Let's step back now and walk through the rest of the script. At the top of the script we invoke Perl with the -T switch to turn taint checks on. Taint checks cause Perl to abort if we attempt to pass unchecked user input to external programs or shells. Since we invoke the su and passwd programs, it is a good idea to include these checks. We'd use the -w warning switch too, but chat2.pl generates many noise warnings about unused variables.

Lines 2 through 4 are there to make the taint checks happy. Explicitly setting the PATH and IFS environment variables prevents programming practices that rely on unsafe assumptions about the environment. We turn off I/O buffering on line 7, to avoid conflicts between the standard I/O buffering used by Perl and the external programs we launch.

On line 9 we load the standard CGI library and import the standard and HTML3 sets of functions. The HTML3 set gives us access to HTML table definition tags. We now print the standard HTTP header, and begin the HTML page (lines 11 through 14).

Line 16 calls CGI::import_names to import all the current CGI parameters into like-named Perl variables in the Q:: namespace. This script expects five different CGI parameters:

user
  The name of the user

old
  The user's old password

new1
  The user's new password

new2
  Confirmation of the user's new password

referer
  The URL of the page that originally linked to the script

After import_names is called, there will be variables named $Q::user, $Q::old, and so forth.

Lines 18 through 33 define a block labeled TRY. In TRY we attempt to recover the user's information and set the password. If we encounter an error during this process, we call last TRY to fall through to the bottom of the block immediately (this is essentially a goto written in a structured manner). First, we test whether the $Q::user parameter is defined at all. If it isn't, we just jump to the end of the block. Otherwise, we call a routine named check_consistency to check whether all the other parameters are present and are in the expected format. If check_consistency fails, we print out an error message and exit the block.

If we pass the consistency check, we call the set_passwd routine that we looked at in detail above. If set_passwd is successful, we print an acknowledgment message and set the variable $OK to true.

The actual call to set_passwd is on line 27. The mess above and below it are a workaround for an error message that I found appearing in my server's error log: stty: standard input: Invalid argument. This error message is issued when su tries to suppress the terminal's echo of the user's typed password. Since this error is irrelevant, we suppress it by temporarily redirecting standard error to /dev/null.

Outside the TRY block, line 35 calls create_form to generate the fill-out form. We do this when $OK is false, causing the form to be displayed the first time the script is called, and regenerated if any errors occur during the TRY block. Because CGI.pm generates "sticky" fill-out forms automatically, the values the user previously typed into the form fields are retained.

Lines 37–42 generate the end of the page, a hypertext link labeled EXIT SCRIPT that takes the user back to the page that originally linked to the script, and a link to the site's home page. The URL for the EXIT SCRIPT link is generated from a CGI parameter named "referer." If that isn't defined, it uses the value returned by the referer function. The rationale for this is discussed below.

Finally, let's look at the definitions of check_consistency and create_form. The check_consistency subroutine, defined in lines 44 to 56, performs various sanity checks on the username and other CGI parameters. First, it checks that the $Q::user, $Q::old, $Q::new1, and $Q::new2 fields are all present, and returns a warning message if any are missing. Next, it checks that the $Q::new1 and $Q::new2 passwords are identical. If not, it warns the user that the new password and its confirmation don't match. The routine now verifies that the username has printable nonwhitespace characters only, and is no longer than 8 characters (this is the limit on my Linux system; it may be different on yours). Passwords must be no more than 30 characters in length. Finally, the routine uses getpwnam to check that the username provided is a valid account name on this system. If getpwnam returns an empty list, the name is unknown and we return an error message to that effect. If the user name corresponds to the root user (user ID equals 0), we also return an error. It's not a good idea to let anyone change the superuser password via the web!

Lines 112 to 130 define create_form, the routine responsible for creating the fill-out form. Using CGI's HTML shortcuts, it generates a straightforward two-row by four-column table that prompts the user for her account name, and old and new passwords. We use call textfield to generate the field that prompts the user for her account name, and call password_field to create input fields for the passwords. (Password fields differ from ordinary text fields in that the letters the user types in are displayed as stars.)

The only trick in this form appears on line 127, where we create a hidden field named referer. This field stores the value returned by CGI::referer, the URL of the page that linked to the script. We use the hidden field to turn this value into an invisible CGI parameter the very first time the script is called, which we later retrieve and use to generate the link labeled EXIT SCRIPT. We have to store this value when the form is first generated because later, after the form has been submitted and the script reinvoked, referer will return the URL of the script itself rather than the original page. The stickiness of CGI form fields guarantees that the original value of referer will be maintained through all subsequent invocations.

Lines 132 to 135 define do_error, which creates a standard error message. The call to CGI::font creates an HTML tag that causes the text to be enlarged and colored red.

Caveats

Before you install this script on your own system, you may need to make a few changes. Your versions of su and passwd may not behave exactly like mine. You may need to experiment a bit and change the prompt strings that chat::expect scans for. This is particularly likely to be true if you use NIS or a shadow password system.

You should also be aware that web communications are not, by default, encrypted. When the remote user fills out the form and sends in her account name and passwords, this information could, theoretically, be intercepted by someone armed with a packet sniffer who had somehow gained access to one of the computer systems on the link between the remote user and the web server. If this bothers you, you can avoid the risk by installing the script on a server that uses the SSL (Secure Sockets Layer) encryption protocol, and configuring the server so that users can only access the page when SSL is active.

If you run a Windows system, this script won't work at all because, thankfully, the Windows interfaces to user account databases are quite different from their Unix counterparts. Thanks to David Roth's excellent Win32::AdminMisc module, you can change Windows passwords simply by replacing the set_passwd routine with this much simpler piece of code:

```perl
sub set_passwd ($$$) {
    use Win32::AdminMisc;
    use Win32::NetAdmin;
    my $DOMAIN = "NT Domain";
    my $CONTROLLER = '';
    my ($user, $old, $new) = @_;

    return (undef, "Couldn't get primary domain controller name.")
      unless Win32::NetAdmin::GetController('', '', $CONTROLLER);

    return (undef, "Couldn't log in as $user.")
      unless Win32::AdminMisc::LogonAsUser($DOMAIN, $user, $old);

    return (undef, "Couldn't change password for $user.")
      unless Win32::AdminMisc::SetPassword($CONTROLLER, $user, $new);

    return (1, "Password changed successfully for $Q::user.");

}
```

You'll need to change $DOMAIN to whatever the correct domain is for your system.

## CHAPTER 19

Building Web Sites with Mason

Joe Johnston

 When this introduction to HTML::Mason was first published, Version 0.80 was the state of the art. The examples in this article still work under the current version, 1.04. I have corrected the anachronisms where possible and note them when not.

The scene: a dusty afternoon in a rickety one horse town. The sign over the "Last Chance" saloon leans drunkenly forward and tumbleweed skips lazily across your path. You've fought your way through seven ambushing web projects and just barely escaped to tell about them. To your left, a shifty-eyed city slicker named ASP hawks his miracle invention to eliminate work-a-day web drudgery. To your right, a young, ruddy-faced preacher thumps his ham fist righteously on his leather bound Cold Fusion manual. All around you, the young and blind pound the dry earth, desperately trying to hold together their company's legacy home page with NotePad and Frontpage. And staring down at you from the end of the street, is the meanest, neediest, most market-driven web site east of the Mississippi that threatens to eat your lunch.

Yep, there's no doubt about it. You're in web country.

What Is Mason?

When the person responsible for designing an appealing web site is different from the person who writes the code to make it happen, traditional hard-wired CGI scripts just get in the way. As a web programmer, you probably don't have much trouble adding print statements to spew HTML. But every time the designer wants to alter the site, a traditional CGI script requires the programmer to implement those changes, no matter how small. Wouldn't you rather give control of the HTML to the designer so that you're not in the critical path? Mason solves this problem.

Mason (*http://www.masonhq.com*) is an open source project authored by Jonathan Swartz which, together with mod_perl and Apache, offers web developers a tool to slay the maintenance dragon. In the words of the FAQ, Mason is "a Perl-based web site development and delivery engine." HTML::Mason is a freely available Perl module that makes Mason available to your Perl programs.

SSI Redux

Mason accomplishes its magic with a venerable trick. It allows Perl code to be embedded in an otherwise ordinary HTML file. In fact, these bits of embedded Perl can be collected into files called *components* which in turn can be called from other Mason-rendered HTML files. Components are to Mason what subroutines are to Perl.

Yes, Server Side Include (SSI) technology is alive and well. In fact, Mason has some very successful closed-source brethren. Microsoft's Active Server Pages and Allaire's Cold Fusion also use a special SSI language. Let's not forget about open source competitors like Python's Zope, Java Server Pages, or PHP! SSI is here to stay.

Form Versus Function

To tame the wild beast of creating and maintaining a living web site, traditional HTML-spewing CGI programs are not enough. Even with a flexible language like Perl, changing the look and feel of a traditional CGI script often requires an experienced coder. "Vital" changes thought up by marketing folks and their graphic designers can often amount to several hours of patching and testing new CGI code. Even simple changes like moving a button or adding text can take time when a web site's presentation is tied to its functionality. This is the issue that transcends the choice of implementation language and speaks to the core of dynamic web site design.

Any SSI technology will greatly reduce the friction between coders and graphics people because site functionality (a navigation widget, for example) can be encapsulated into a component which is then called from an otherwise static web page. The graphic designer can simply treat this code, which looks like a funny HTML tag, as a black box and move this widget to wherever his fickle heart desires. The good news is that, after implementing the navigation widget, the coder is no longer required.

For those that want the benefits of code reusability and data hiding, HTML::Mason components can be used in an object-oriented fashion.

Installation

 My, how time flies. I successfully tested this code on the same machine that is now running Red Hat 7.1, Apache 1.3.20, mod_perl 1.26 and HTML::Mason 1.04.

Mason works best with Apache and mod_perl. For the record, the system I used was a Celeron 400 running Red Hat 6.0 with 128M of RAM, Apache 1.3.9 compiled from source, mod_perl 1.21, and HTML::Mason 0.8. If you don't already have mod_perl, install mod_perl first. Normally, I don't use the CPAN module to install mod_perl, since I often play with various configuration options for both mod_perl and Apache. You can get a copy of mod_perl from CPAN or the web (*http://www.cpan.org/ modules/by-module/Apache/*). When you are ready to build mod_perl, make sure to build all the mod_perl options like so:

```
$ perl Makefile.PL EVERYTHING=1 && make
```

HTML::Mason likes to use Apache::Table, which isn't normally built with the default mod_perl install.

Building Mason is usually very easy. To get the source, try your local CPAN mirror at *http://www.cpan.org/modules/by-module/HTML*. Better yet, use the CPAN module. From your shell, and with administrator privileges if necessary, type:

```
perl -MCPAN -e "install HTML::Mason"
```

Have I mentioned how much I love the CPAN.pm module? A lot.

Mason comes with a complete installation guide in the file *Mason.html*. For those familiar with Apache, the *httpd.conf* changes are trivial, although I'm not sure I'd commit my entire web directory to Mason, as this installation guide suggests. I made a directory off the root of my *htdocs* called *mason*.

The changes I made to *httpd.conf* amounted to this:

```
PerlSetVar MasonCompRoot /home/jjohn/src/apache_1.3.20/htdocs/mason
PerlSetVar MasonDataDir /home/jjohn/tmp/mason_data
PerlModule HTML::Mason::ApacheHandler

<Directory /home/jjohn/src/apache_1.3.20/htdocs/mason>
  <FilesMatch "*.html">
     SetHandler perl-script
     PerlHandler HTML::Mason::ApacheHandler
  </FilesMatch>
  <FilesMatch "*.pl">
     SetHandler perl-script
     Options +ExecCGI
     PerlHandler Apache::Registry
  </FilesMatch>
</Directory>
```

The first two lines are simply configuration variables Mason needs to oriented itself to your system. *MasonCompRoot* is the real filesystem path to the directory from which Mason components will be served. This directory typically needs to be under Apache's DocumentRoot (I have an Apache installation in my home directory which isn't standard). *MasonDataDir* is a directory writable by Apache where Mason stores compiled components. It shouldn't be under your DocumentRoot. The Mason Apache handler module is then pulled in.

I only want files with the extension "html" under my Mason directory to be parsed by Mason, and any "pl" files to be handled by the standard Apache::Registry module. The final lines of the *httpd.conf* section handle these requirements.

Next, you'll want to create a *handler.pl* file in your new *mason* root directory. This is where you'll use modules common to all your components, avoiding the overhead of including the same module in multiple components. You'll find a very serviceable *handler.pl* file in the *eg* subdirectory in the unpacked Mason directory. I recommend uncommenting this line in the `handler` subroutine:

```
#return -1 if $r->content_type && $r->content_type !~ m|^text/|io;
```

This prevents Mason from trying to parse nontext files served from your *mason* directory. I suppose an entry for next year's Obfuscated Perl Contest might include a carefully engineered GIF meant to be parsed by Mason to produce *The Perl Journal*, but it won't be submitted by me.

Another source of confusion about configuring *handler.pl* has to do with the initialization of Mason's Interp (Interpreter) object, which requires a few user-dependent paths. Because this file will execute under mod_perl, we can use the Apache::Request object to get the configuration variables from *httpd.conf*. In the default *handler.pl* file, find the section where the parser and interpreter objects are created and substitute these lines:

```
my $r = Apache->request;
my $parser = new HTML::Mason::Parser;
my $interp = new HTML::Mason::Interp (parser=>$parser,
                              comp_root =>
                                  $r->dir_config('MasonCompRoot'),
                              data_dir =>
                                  $r->dir_config('MasonDataDir'));
```

By calling Apache::Request's *dir_config* method, you can find the values for any variable defined in *httpd.conf* with a PerlSetVar directive.

Although most new users won't need to directly manipulate it, the Interpreter object is responsible for executing the components and directing the resulting output.

 Unless you're using HTML::Mason Version 0.80, you may skip this last section.

Mason 0.8 has some new syntax than earlier versions. While I believe the development is heading in the right direction, there are some issues worth noting. For instance, Mason 0.8 won't send HTTP headers for a page with no text. This makes redirection and issuing cookies less than ideal, since you would need to write a dummy page just to serve the HTTP headers. There is a workaround on the Mason mailing list, but I'd recommend staying with the last 0.7x version or downloading 0.81.

Building a Dynamic Site

The site I designed demonstrates some common tasks that most web designers face. Please note: I'm no layout expert; one of the compelling reasons to use Mason is to bridge the gap between coders and designers, and I'm a coder. The task I most commonly tackled was to have a web page display information stored in a database. The designer wants the coder to provide a method for accessing this data, and this is where a Mason component comes in handy. I will be querying my web site Aliens, Aliens, Aliens (A3). It's about aliens. It is a MySQL-driven web site with a mod_perl frontend.

Headers and Footers

The best place to begin a discussion of components is with the Mason equivalent of "Hello, World". Many sites have standard headers and footers that provide a common look and feel to pages on the site. Here's my header (stored in a file called *header.html*):

```
<html>
<title><%$title%></title>
<body bgcolor="<%$color%>">
<h1><%$title%></h1>

<%args>
$title => 'Nonsuch'
$color => 'FFFFFF'    # White
</%args>
```

From Mason's perspective, this is a component, because it's a mixture of HTML and specially delimited Perl code. For the most part, it looks like boring HTML.

There are two different Mason tags to notice here. The first is the ubiquitous <% %> tag. Any arbitrary Perl code found inside will be evaluated and the resulting value displayed in the render page. <% 2 + 2 %> will display in a browser as 4.

Mason also has a small set of special tags used for more complex or special purpose blocks of code. Here, the <%args>...</%args> section is used to prototype the two expected arguments for this component: $title and $color. In this case, two scalars may be passed to the header component; if they aren't, "Nonsuch" and white will be used as defaults. You may declare arguments without defaults, which forces the caller to pass parameters. These parameters are lexically scoped, which means these variables cease to exist outside of the component. If you've wanted stronger subroutine prototyping in Perl, this may appeal to you.

The footer component, stored in the file *footer.html*, is even simpler, since it takes no arguments at all:

```
<hr>
<div align=center>
<address>
&copy; <% 1900+(localtime)[5] %> Joe Johnston<BR>
Use this code to your maximium advantage, but
due credit is always appreciated.
<address>
</div>
</body>
</html>
```

Passing Parameters

Mason provides many flexible ways to pass arguments to components. One way is to simply attach URL-encoded arguments (spaces become %20, for example) to the URL of the component, just like in a GET query. Another is to call the component directly from another component, as seen in the first line of my index page:

```
<& header.html, title=>'Welcome to the World of Mason', color=>'tan' &>

<P>Gawk in amazement as I build an interactive, database driven site before your eyes!

<P>Here's a link to a nonexistent <a href="microsoft">subdirectory</a>.
<P>Pssst! Want to look at some headlines from other sites?
<UL>
  <LI><a href="news/slashdot">Slashdot</a>
  <LI><a href="news/perl_news">Perl News</a>
  <LI><a href="news/a3">Aliens, Aliens, Aliens</a>
  <LI><a href="news/missing_uri">Microsoft News</a>
  <LI><FORM Method=post Action="news/dhandler">
       URL to your favorite RDF: <input type=text name=RDF>
<input type=submit>
</FORM>
</UL>
<& departments.html &>
<& footer.html &>
```

Mason's <& &> is similar to Perl's ampersand operator in that it calls a component much like a subroutine. The return value is discarded; the side effects are what's important. Let's look at the first line of this component more closely:

```
<& header.html, title => 'Welcome to the World of Mason', color => 'tan' &>
```

This inserts the rendered version of the header, modified with the appropriate parameters, onto the web page. The rendered version of this page appears in Figure 19-1. Yet another way to pass arguments is to use default handlers and extra path information.

Default Handlers and XML

When a component is called that Mason can't find, it looks in that directory for a file called *dhandler* (notice there's no *.html*). For example, I have the *dhandler* shown below in the *mason* directory:

```
<& header.html &>

<b>Oops! I'm not certain where you were going!</b>

<p><a href="index.html">Back</a>
<& footer.html &>
```

This is just a custom "404 Not Found" document. The generated page is shown in Figure 19-2.

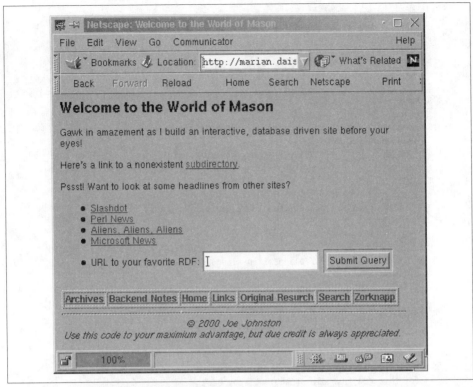

Figure 19-1. A web page generated by Mason

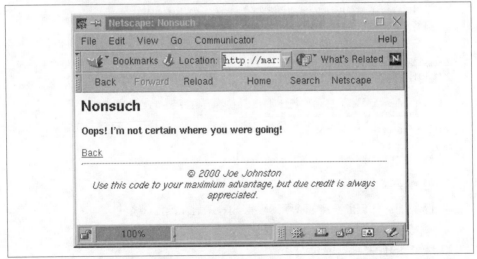

Figure 19-2. A customized "File Not Found" page

In the *news* subdirectory, I have another *dhandler*, which is meant to be called with extra path information.

```
<%init>
use XML::RSS;
use LWP::Simple qw(get);

my $news_site = $m->dhandler_arg;

my $rss = new XML::RSS;
my $rdf;

for ( $news_site ) { # This is like a 'switch' statement
    /slashdot/ && do {
        $rdf = get('http://slashdot.org/slashdot.rdf');
        last;
    };
    /perl_news/ && do {
        $rdf = get('http://www.news.perl.org/perl-news.rdf');
        last;
    };
    /a3/ && do {
        $rdf = get('http://aliensaliensaliens.com/a3.rdf');
        last;
    };
}

$rdf ||= get($ARGS{RDF}); # Was I passed in something?

unless ( $rdf ) {
    # a little tricky, use the existing mechanism
    # for this 404, use old standby CGI env hack

    use CGI qw/:all/;
    print redirect("http://$ENV{SERVER_NAME}/mason/tpj/404");
    return;
}

$rss->parse($rdf);
</%init>

<& ../header, title=> ($news_site||$rss->{'channel'}->{'title'}) &>

<p>See the rest of <a href="<% $rss->{'channel'}->{'link'} %>">

<UL>

% for my $bit ( @{ $rss->{'items'}} ){   # Not very OO ;-)

  <LI><a href="<% $bit->{'link'} %>"><% $bit->{'title'} %></a>

%  if( $bit->{'description'} ) {
    : <% $bit->{'description'} %>
%  }

% }
```

```
</UL>
<a href="/mason/">Back</a>
<& ../footer.html &>
```

In this case the *dhandler* will try to retrieve an RSS (Rich Site Summary) file, an XML description that many news sites (including Perl News) use to broadcast their headlines. Looking back at the *index.html* component shown earlier, you can see that the *dhandler* parameter resembles a file in the news subdirectory. Selecting the A3 link produces the page seen in Figure 19-3. This is the kind of magic that makes some coders soil themselves. Unfortunately there's equal and opposite kind of magic that can burn you here: those leading percent signs that indicate Perl code needs to be in the first column of the line in your component to be correctly interpreted.

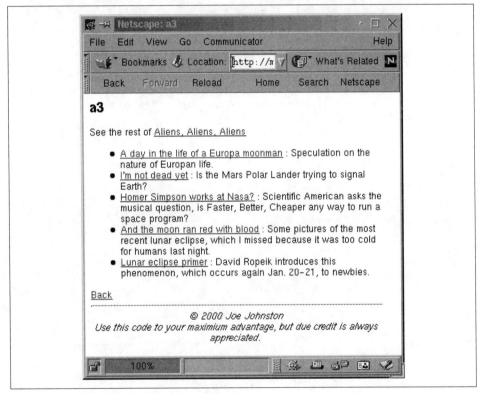

Figure 19-3. Aliens, aliens, aliens

Something else is going on in this *news/dhandler* component. Because we want users to be able to enter an arbitrary URL to an RDF (Resource Description Framework) file, this component also accepts the more traditional parameter-passing method in a variable called %ARGS.

Accessing MySQL

If you're familiar with DBI, database access is performed no differently in Mason. In fact, you can use Apache::DBI to transparently give you persistent database handles. Aliens, Aliens, Aliens is divided up into several departments, which themselves contain other departments. The departments component generates a nice table with links to all the top level departments:

```
<%init>
    my $dbh = DBI->connect("DBI:mysql:aliens:nfs.daisypark.org",
                            "username", "password")
        or die "ERROR: Couldn't connect to DB $DBI::errstr";

# Find all the top level departments
# All top level departments have 'home' as a parent
my $sql = "select homepage_id,segment from departments
            where parent_id=1 order by segment";

my $sth = $dbh->prepare($sql)
        or die "ERROR: prepare failed " . $dbh->errstr;

$sth->execute or die "ERROR: couldn't get departments! " . $dbh->errstr;
</%init>

<TABLE Border=1>
<TR>
% while ( my $hr = $sth->fetchrow_hashref ) {

<TH><A HREF="http://nfs.daisypark.org/cgi-bin/render_article.pl?
                        article_id=<%$hr->{homepage_id}%>">
<% $hr->{segment} %></A></TH>

% }

</TR>
</TABLE>

<%cleanup>
# $dbh->disconnect;
</%cleanup>
```

I'll skip the discussion of DBI and SQL and draw your attention to the embedded fetchrow loop which retrieves all the pertinent links and labels. Notice how even though the while statement is preceded by the % symbol (meaning that the rest of the line is Perl code), the plain HTML is repeated as needed. Compare this to a more traditional Perl CGI program in which the loop has a print statement outputting HTML. Although this may seem like two sides of the same coin, the difference with Mason is that your layout expert can now tweak the non-code bits without bothering you. This generally leads to more beer time, which is the second thing any good job should give you.

Finally, you'll notice the <%cleanup> section. This is Perl code to be executed when the component has finished. Here, I would normally kill my database handle, close filehandles, or free objects. However, since Apache::DBI (which should be included in the *httpd.conf* file) lets me keep database handles open from visit to visit, I have commented this out.

What Now?

I have provided only a brief introduction to this great tool. Other topics that await you in Mason-land are the fabulous Component Manager (written by Mark Schmick), lots of documentation, component debugging files, and component staging. Do yourself a favor and check Mason out.

Not surprisingly, Mason has been under constant development since this article first appeared. Included in HTML::Mason archive file is a sample shopping cart system and examples of the very excellent Apache::Session module. Check out *masonhq.com* for the most recent news.

CHAPTER 20
Surreal HTML

Lincoln D. Stein

If you've poked around the *eg* directory in old Perl distributions, you might have noticed a small program called travesty. This program takes any regular text file, processes it, and spews out a curious parody of the original. For example, here's a small part of what you get when you feed it this article:

```
Travesty achieves this by calling the Perl distribution's eg
directory, you may have noticed a small program called travesty. This
program takes any regular text file, processes it, and spews out a
curious parody of the number of words to generate (lines 81 to
82). Travesty::regurgitate returns a parse tree in turn, calling
ref to determine whether the node is any of the tree by returning a
value of 0 from the LWP modules, as well as back to Mangler's fill-out
form.
```

Travesty's output is almost, but not quite, English. Reasonable phrases and some-times whole sentences pop out, but the whole makes no sense at all. However, if you were to analyze the word frequency of the output, you'd find it identical to the original. Furthermore, if you were to count the frequency of word pairs, you'd find them the same as well. Travesty achieves this by using the original text to create a lookup table of word triples (A,B,C), in which C is indexed on the (A,B) pair. After creating this table, it spews out a parody of the text using a *Markov chain*: the program chooses a random (A,B) pair and uses the lookup table to pick a C. The new (B,C) pair is now used to look up the fourth word, and this process continues *ad infinitum*.

This article presents the Mangler, a CGI script that runs any web page on the Internet through the travesty program and returns the result.

How It Works

You can see Mangler's entry page in Figure 20-1. When the user connects, she's shown a page that prompts her to type in the URL for a web page with text. When she presses the "Mangle" button, the script extracts the text from that page, slices and dices it with the travesty algorithm, and displays the result, shown in Figure 20-2.

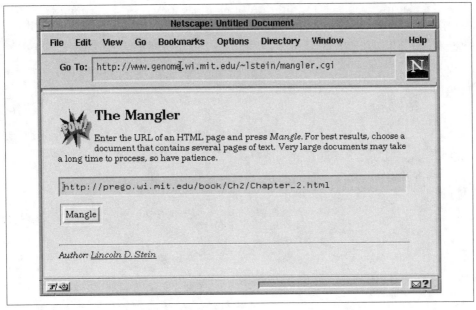

Figure 20-1. The Mangler's introductory page

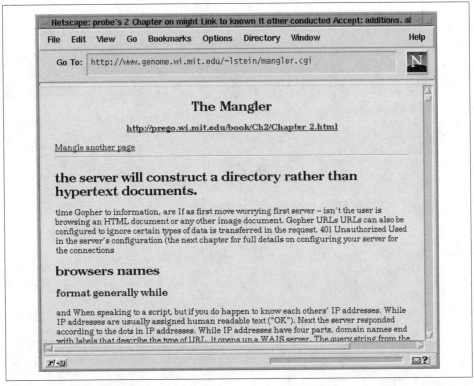

Figure 20-2. A Mangled page

The Mangler uses routines from the LWP modules (described in *Scripting the Web with LWP*), as well as from the CGI.pm module discussed in *CGI Programming*. Both of these libraries are available from CPAN, and the full source code is shown in Example 20-1.

Example 20-1. The Mangler

```
0    #!/usr/bin/perl
1    # File: mangler.cgi
2
3    use LWP::UserAgent;
4    use HTML::Parse;
5    use HTTP::Status;
6    use CGI qw(:standard :html3);
7    $ICON = "pow.gif";
8
9    srand();
10
11   $url_to_mangle = param('mangle') if request_method() eq 'POST';
12
13
14   print header();
15
16   if ($url_to_mangle && mangle($url_to_mangle)) {
17       ; # nothing to do
18   } else {
19       prompt_for_url();
20   }
21
22   # ---------------------------------------------------
23   # THIS SECTION IS WHERE URLs ARE FETCHED AND MANGLED
24   # ---------------------------------------------------
25   sub mangle {
26       my $url = shift;
27       my $agent = new LWP::UserAgent;
28       my $request = new HTTP::Request('GET', $url);
29       my $response = $agent->request($request);
30
31       unless ($response->isSuccess) {
32           print h1('Error Fetching URL'),
33               "An error occurred while fetching the document located at ",
34               a({href=>$url},"$url."),
35               p(),
36               "The error was ",strong(statusMessage($response->code)),".",
37               hr();
38           return undef;
39       }
40
41       # Make sure that it's an HTML document!
42       my $type = $response->header('Content-type');
43       unless ($type eq 'text/html') {
44           print h1("Document isn't an HTML File!"),
45               "The URL ",a({href=>$url},"$url"),
46               " is a document of type ",em($type),". ",
```

Example 20-1. The Mangler (continued)

```
47                "Please choose an HTML file to mangle.",
48                hr( );
49                return undef;
50      }
51
52      print start_html(-title => 'Mangled Document',
53                       -xbase => $url),
54          div({ -align => CENTER },
55              h1("The Mangler"),
56              strong( a({-href => $url},$url) )
57          ),
58          p( ),
59          a( {-href => self_url() },"Mangle another page"), hr( );
60
61      my $parse_tree = parse_html($response->content);
62      $parse_tree->traverse(\&swallow);
63      $parse_tree->traverse(\&regurgitate);
64      $parse_tree->delete( );
65      1;
66  }
67
68  sub swallow {
69      my ($node, $start, $depth) = @_;
70      return 1 if ref($node);
71      return &Travesty::swallow($node);
72  }
73
74  sub regurgitate {
75      my ($node, $start, $depth) = @_;
76      if (ref($node)) {
77          return 1 if $node->tag =~ /^(html|head|body)/i;
78          return 0 if $node->isInside('head');
79          &Travesty::reset() if $start;
80          print $node->starttag if $start;
81          print $node->endtag unless $start;
82      } else {
83          my @words = split(/\s+/,$node);
84          print &Travesty::regurgitate(scalar(@words));
85      }
86      1;
87  }
88
89  # ---------------------------------------------------
90  # THIS SECTION IS WHERE THE PROMPT IS CREATED
91  # ---------------------------------------------------
92  sub prompt_for_url {
93      print start_html('The Mangler'),
94          -e $ICON ? img({-src=>$ICON,-align=>LEFT}) : '',
95          h1('The Mangler'), "Enter the URL of an HTML page and press ",
96          em("Mangle. "), "For best results, choose a document containing ",
97          "several pages of text.  Very large documents may take a long ",
98          "time to process, so have patience.",
99
```

Example 20-1. The Mangler (continued)

```
100        start_form( ),
101        textfield(-name => 'mangle', -size => 60),
102        submit(-value => 'Mangle'),
103        end_form( ),
104        hr( ),
105        address("Author: ",
106               a( { -href => 'http://www.genome.wi.mit.edu/~lstein/' },
107                  'Lincoln D. Stein'),
108               ),
109        end_html( );
110 }
111
112 # derived from the code in Perl's eg/ directory
113 package Travesty;
114
115 sub swallow {
116     my $string = shift;
117     $string =~ tr/\n/ /s;
118
119     push(@ary, split(/\s+/, $string));
120     while ($#ary > 1) {
121         $a = $p;
122         $p = $n;
123         $w = shift(@ary);
124         $n = $num{$w};
125         if ($n eq '') {
126             push(@word, $w);
127             $n = pack('S', $#word);
128             $num{$w} = $n;
129         }
130         $lookup{$a . $p} .= $n;
131     }
132     1;
133 }
134
135 sub reset {
136     my ($key) = each(%lookup);
137     ($a,$p) = (substr($key,0,2), substr($key,2,2));
138 }
139
140 sub regurgitate {
141     my $words = shift;
142     my $result = '';
143     while (--$words >= 0) {
144
145         $n = $lookup{$a . $p};
146         ($foo, $n) = each(%lookup) if $n eq '';
147         $n = substr($n,int(rand(length($n))) & 0177776, 2);
148         $a = $p;
149         $p = $n;
150         ($w) = unpack('S', $n);
151         $w = $word[$w];
152
```

Example 20-1. The Mangler (continued)

```
153          # Most of this formatting is only for <PRE> text.
154          # We'll leave it in for that purpose.
155          $col += length($w) + 1;
156          if ($col >= 65) {
157              $col = 0;
158              $result .= "\n";
159          } else {
160              $result .= ' ';
161          }
162          $result .= $w;
163          if ($w =~ /\.$/) {
164              if (rand() < .1) {
165                  $result .= "\n";
166                  $col = 80;
167              }
168          }
169
170      }
171      return $result;
172 }
```

Prompting the User

The Mangler uses CGI.pm to parse the CGI parameters and create the fill-out form. We pull in CGI.pm on line 6 and import both the standard and HTML3-specific subroutines. On line 11 we look for a parameter named "mangle." If defined, we call the mangle subroutine (line 16). Otherwise, we call prompt_for_url. As an aside, line 11 shows a technique for initializing field values in a fill-out form. Only if the request method is a POST resulting from the user pressing the "Mangle" button do we actually do the work. Otherwise, if the request method is a GET, we ignore it and let CGI.pm's "sticky" behavior initialize the text field automatically. This allows you to create a default URL for Mangler by creating a link to it like this one:

```
<A HREF="/cgi-bin/mangler?mangle=http://www.microsoft.com/">
 Mangle Uncle Bill
</A>
```

The prompt_for_url routine is defined in lines 92 through 110. It follows the form that should be familiar to readers of my previous columns. Using CGI.pm's fill-out form and HTML shortcuts, we create a form containing a single text field labeled "mangle" and a submit button.

Fetching the Document

The first half of the mangle subroutine (lines 25–50) does the work of fetching the remote document. We use the LWP::UserAgent library to create an HTTP request and to retrieve the document across the net. Several things may go wrong at this point. For example, the user may have typed in an invalid URL, or the remote server may be down. On line 31, we check the success status of the transfer. If the transfer fails, the subroutine prints out the nature of the error using LWP's statusMessage subroutine and returns. When the script sees that the subroutine has returned a false value, it regenerates the fill-out form by invoking prompt_for_url again.

Next, we extract the retrieved document's MIME type from its Content-type header field. We get the field on line 42 by making a call to the LWP::Response header method. We can only process HTML files, so if the type turns out not to be "text/html" we print an error message and again return false.

If all has gone well so far, we print out a small preamble before the mangled document itself (lines 52–59). The preamble creates a title for the page, a descriptive header, and links to the original document location and to Mangler's fill-out form. One interesting question: How do we ensure that the document's relative URLs and in-line images work properly? We set the document's BASE attribute to the URL of the unmodified document by passing -xbase to the start_html method in CGI.pm.

Running the Travesty Algorithm

This is the most interesting part of the program. If we were to pipe the retrieved HTML through the travesty generator, it would scramble the tags with the text, creating an illegible mess. We want to mangle the text of the file but leave its HTML structure, including tags and in-line images, intact.

We do this using the HTML manipulation routines defined in LWP. On line 61, we call parse_html, a routine defined in HTML::Parse. This parses the HTML document and returns a parse tree object, which we store in the scalar $parse_tree.

On line 62, we make the first of two calls to the parse tree's traverse method. This method performs a depth-first traversal of the parse tree, calling the subroutine of our choosing for each element of the tree. In this case, we pass it a reference to our swallow subroutine (lines 68–72). swallow examines each node in turn and extracts the ones that contain straight text, passing them to the travesty algorithm. There are two types of node to worry about: those that are branches in the tree (tag pairs surrounding content), and those that are leaves (plain text). We can distinguish between branches and leaves by calling Perl's ref function on the node. If the node is a reference, it's a branch and we return immediately. Otherwise we know that the node is a leaf. We pass its text to the subroutine Travesty::swallow which breaks up the string into an array of words using split and adds them to the travesty algorithm's lookup table.

The travesty algorithm itself is defined in the last sixty lines of the Mangler. The code here is a slight modification of the original code in Perl's *eg* directory, and I won't go into the details here. It's worth studying, particularly if you're interested in entering the Obfuscated Perl contest.

Printing the Mangled Document

The last task is to print out the mangled document. In line 61, we make the second call to traverse, this time passing it a reference to the regurgitate subroutine (lines 74–87). As before, the subroutine examines each node of the parse tree in turn, calling ref to determine whether the node is a leaf or a branch. If the node is a branch corresponding to any of the tags <HTML>, <HEAD>, or <BODY> we skip it completely—we've already begun to create the HTML document and we don't need to repeat these sections. Similarly, we skip the entire contents of the HTML head section by asking the parse tree's isInside method (line 78) whether the node lies within a <HEAD> tag. If it does, we abort the traversal of this part of the tree by having regurgitate return 0. Otherwise, we print out the tag, using the node's starttag and endtag methods to produce the appropriate opening and closing tags.

Whenever we encounter a leaf node containing text, we pass the number of desired words we'd like ($words) to Travesty::regurgitate (lines 83 to 84). It returns a series of scrambled words, which we simply print out. That's it!

CHAPTER 21
Web Page Tastefulness

Lincoln D. Stein

The Web is slowly but surely turning into a cyber-stripmall, complete with flashing neon signs, tasteless ads, and outlet stores. Snazzy graphics crowd out textual information, giving both myself and my low-bandwidth modem a headache. A page purporting to be the definitive guide to some subject turns out to consist of lists of links, most of which are dead. Frames proliferate like weeds, crowding out the page content with scrollbars within scrollbars within scrollbars. Meanwhile, hopping, jittering, flashing, bleeping, and morphing applets dance in and out of my visual field, jerking my attention away from whatever mindless promotional copy I was trying to wade through.

What to do about the proliferation of web junk? Will the Internet actually collapse under its own weight as technology pundit Bob Metcalfe predicted way back in 1995?

Perl to the rescue. You don't have to wade through 19 pages of trash to find the gem buried in the twentieth. You can have a Perl agent do the wading for you. In a column that I wrote for WebTechniques in May 1997, I suggested a series of indexes to measure the tastefulness of a web page. Some of the indexes were serious, such as the ratio of words in hyperlinks to total words on the page (pages with sparsely scattered links are more likely to contain real information than pages consisting almost entirely of links), or the number of potential advertisements on the page. Others were tongue-in-cheek, such as the TutieFrutie Index to measure the number of clashing color changes on the page, or the "Cool!" Index to count the times the words "cool," "neat," or "awesome" appeared. Nevertheless, the intent was sincere: to have a script capable of screening out frivolous or tasteless pages according to whatever your personal criteria happen to be. See "Tastefulness Indexes" for a listing of the indexes that I proposed.

The agent might be something that you invoke on the spur of the moment. ("Hmmm. That URL looks like it might be interesting. Let's have Perl give it the once-over.") A more likely prospect would be to incorporate the agent into a search engine. At the same time the search engine is indexing the keywords on a remote site's pages, it can be calculating and recording the site's tastefulness.

Tastefulness Indexes

Information Index (II)

Basic measure of the word to link ratio, defined as:

```
II = 100 x (1 - (words inside links / total words in document))
```

Graphics Index (GI)

Measure of the graphics usage of a page, defined as:

```
GI = number of IMG tags / number pages
```

Doodads Index (DI)

Measure of the number of applets, controls, and scripts, defined as:

```
DI = number of doodads / number pages
```

TutieFrutie Index (TFI)

Measure of how "colorful" a document is, defined as:

```
TFI = number of color changes / number of pages
```

Frames Index (FI)

Measure of the use of frames, defined as:

```
FI = number of frame tags
```

Cool! Index (C!I)

Measure of how excited a page is about itself, defined as:

```
C!I = 100 x ( exclamation marks + superlatives ) / total sentences
```

Crass Commercialism Index (CCI)

Indication of banner advertising on the page, defined as:

```
CCI = number of ads / number of pages
```

This program uses heuristics to count banner advertisements and may not always guess correctly.

Reactions to the proposal have ranged from the mildly amused to the wildly enthusiastic. It will probably never become part of a commercial product, but at the very least the agent is a good example of how to write a robot with the LWP library.

For fun, I implemented the agent as a CGI script. When you first invoke it, it displays a screen prompting the user to type in a URL, as shown in Figure 21-1. When the user presses the submit button, the script fetches the page, rates it, and displays the results in a table. If the URL contains links to other local pages at the same or lower level in the document tree, the script recurses into them and adds them to the aggregate listing. Since processing lots of pages can take significant time, the script updates the web page as it goes along, displaying each URL as it is processed. To allow people to see what others have been rating, the page also displays the results from the last thirty URLs fetched; you can see a screenshot in Figure 21-2.

I'll spend the rest of this article walking through the script. Although more complex than other example scripts in this series, it's a good example of how to write a web-walking robot with LWP. It also illustrates a few CGI tricks that haven't popped up in these pages before.

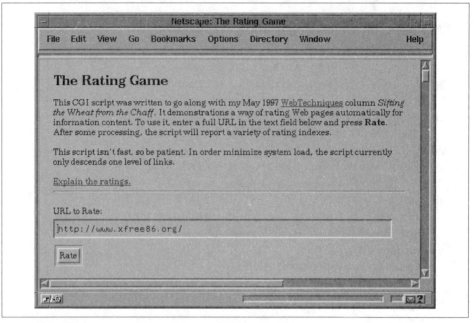

Figure 21-1. The Rating Game

The script has four objectives:

1. Display the welcome page and prompt for input.
2. Fetch the provided URL and all pages linked from it.
3. Collect statistics on the pages and crunch them into rating indexes.
4. Record recent results into a file that can be displayed at the bottom of the page.

How It Works

Because this script is 400 lines long, I'll intersperse the code with explanations of what's going on. In some places, I depart from the strict linear order of the code in order to make the explanations clearer. If you find this hopelessly confusing, don't despair: you can fetch the entire listing online from this book's web page at *http://www.oreilly.com/catalog/tpj2*.

```
0    #!/usr/bin/perl
1
2    # File: nph-rater.cgi
3    # Copyright 1997, Lincoln D. Stein. All rights reserved.
4    # Permission is granted to use, modify and redistribute
5    # in whole or in part, provided that the above
6    # copyright statement remains prominently displayed.
7    use LWP::UserAgent;
8    use HTML::Parse;
9    use HTTP::Status;
10   use CGI qw/:standard :html3 :nph/;
11   use CGI::Carp;
12
```

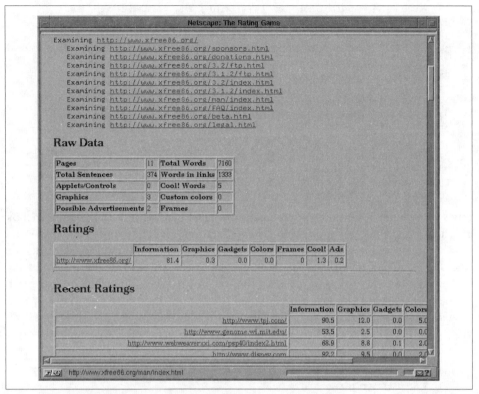

Figure 21-2. Tastefulness ratings of selected web pages

The beginning of the script (lines 7 through 11) loads all the modules we need for the agent. We use the LWP::UserAgent module for fetching URLs, the HTML::Parse module for creating a parse tree of the document's HTML, and the HTTP::Status module for access to various HTTP status code constants. In addition, we load the CGI and CGI::Carp modules. The first provides us with shortcuts for processing CGI variables and writing HTML, while the second makes any error messages generated by the script more informative. A new feature of the CGI library that's not been previously demonstrated in these articles is support for no-parsed header (NPH) scripts, a dialect of CGI in which the script's output is forwarded directly to the browser without extra processing by the web server. When the symbol :nph is imported from the CGI module, it will automagically generate the HTTP header information necessary to run as an NPH script. In this case, the only reason we want an NPH script is to turn off buffering at the web server's side of the connection so that we can update the page incrementally. In most cases the server also has to be told that the script is of the NPH variety, usually by tacking the prefix nph- to its name.

```
13  $MAX_DEPTH = 2;            # How deeply to recurse
14
15  # Words counted towards the cool! index
```

```
16  @COOL_WORDS = qw/cool hot groovy neat wild snazzy great awesome wicked/;
17
18  # Words that might indicate an advertisement
19  @AD_WORDS = qw/promotion ad advertisement sponsor banner
20               banner commercial promotions ads advertisements
21               banners sponsors commercials doubleclick/;
22
23  # The attributes to count towards tutie-frutie
24  @COLOR_ATTR = qw/color bgcolor text link alink vlink background/;
25
26  # The number of previous rankings to list
27  $PREVIOUS_RANKS = 30;
28
29  # The file containing the previous rankings
30  $RANK_FILE = '/usr/local/etc/www/INDEXER.RANKS';
```

Lines 13 through 30 contain various user-adjustable globals, including strings to look at when trying to decide if a graphic is an advertisement, and words like "cool" and "snazzy" that might indicate a hyped-up web page. An important constant here is $MAX_DEPTH, which tells the script how deeply to recurse into linked pages. In the code listing here it's set to 2, meaning that only one level of links will be traversed. Higher values make the script investigate a site more thoroughly, at the cost of a longer wait. Also defined here is the name of the file containing the results from previous ratings. You'll need to create this file and make it writable by your web server before you run this script for the first time.

```
32  #-------------------------------------------------------
33  # No user serviceable parts below
34
35  # Global for collecting statistics
36  %COUNTS = (
37                    'pages' => 0,
38                   'images' => 0,
39                  'doodads' => 0,
40                   'colors' => 0,
41                   'frames' => 0,
42                      'ads' => 0,
43               'link_words' => 0,
44               'cool_words' => 0,
45              'total_words' => 0,
46          );
47
48  grep ($COLOR_ATTR{$_}++, @COLOR_ATTR);
49  $LEVEL = 0;                              # Recursion level
50  $HTML::Parse::IGNORE_UNKNOWN = 0;        # Don't ignore unknown tags
51
52  $COOL_PATTERN = join("|", @COOL_WORDS);
53  $AD_PATTERN   = join("|", @AD_WORDS);
54  $SIG{ALRM}    = \&do_alarm;
55  $FH           = 'FH0000';                # Just a filehandle
56  $|            = 1;                       # Turn off buffering
```

Lines 35 through 56 set up various internal globals. We initialize the %COUNTS hash to keep track of web page statistics. Among the things we record are the number of pages counted, the number of images, the number of applet tags, the number of words in links, and so on. We also create some patterns to find advertisements and hyped-up pages. Several obscure globals are also set here. We zero the variable $LEVEL, which monitors the recursion level, and we set the internal HTML::Parse global $IGNORE_UNKNOWN to false, because by default the parser skips over any HTML tags that it's unfamiliar with, including some of the newer tags that matter to us, such as <FRAME>. We also set up a signal handler for alarm—this becomes important later. Finally, we unbuffer output by setting $| to true, allowing partial pages to be sent to the browser.

```
58  print header,
59  start_html('The Rating Game'),
60  h1('The Rating Game');
61
62  if (param('action') eq 'explain') {
63    print 'The idea is to automatically collect information about a linked set of ',
64      'pages that gives the reader some idea of the flavor of the document. The ',
65      'ratings measure pages\' information content, the amount of graphics they ',
66      'use, the presence of applets, and the presence of commercial content.',
67    p(),
68    h2('Key'),
69    dl(
70      dt(strong('Information Index (II)')),
71      dd('Basic measure of the word to link ratio, defined as:', p(),
72        pre('II = 100 x (1 - (words inside links / total words in document))'),
73        p()),
74      dt(strong('Graphics Index (GI)')),
75      dd('Measure of the graphics usage of a page, defined as:',p(),
76        pre('GI = number IMG tags / number pages'),
77        p()),
78      dt(strong('Doodads Index (DI)')),
79      dd('Measure of the number of applets, controls and scripts, defined as:',p(),
80        pre('DI = number of doodads / number of pages'),
81        p()),
82      dt(strong('TutieFrutie Index (TFI)')),
83      dd('Measure of how "colorful" a document is, defined as:',p(),
84        pre('TFI = number of color changes / number of pages'),
85        p()),
86      dt(strong('Frames Index (FI)')),
87      dd('Measure of the use of frames, defined as:',p(),
88        pre('FI = number of frame tags'),
89        p()),
90      dt(strong('Cool! Index (C!I)')),
91      dd('Measure of how excited a page is about itself, defined as:',p(),
92        pre('C!I = 100 x (exclamation marks + superlatives) / total sentences'),
93        p()),
94      dt(strong('Crass Commercialism Index (CCI)')),
95      dd('Indication of banner advertising on the page, defined as:',p(),
96        pre('CCI = number of ads / number of pages'),
```

```
97          p( ),
98          'This program uses heuristics to count banner advertisements and may ',
99          'not always guess correctly.'
100         )
101    );
102  } else {
103    print
104      'This CGI script was written to go along with my May 1997',
105      a({-href=>'http://www.webtechniques.com/'}, 'WebTechniques'),' column',
106      cite('Sifting the Wheat from the Chaff'),'. It demonstrates a way of ',
107      'rating Web pages automatically for information content. To use it, ',
108      'enter a full URL in the text field below and press', strong('Rate'),
109      '. After some processing, the ',
110      'script will report a variety of rating indexes.',
111      p( ),
112      'This script isn\'t fast, so be patient. In order to minimize system load, ',
113      'the script currently only descends one level of links.',
114      p( ),
115      a({-href=>script_name( ) . '?action=explain', -target=>'explanation'},
             'Explain the ratings.');
```

Lines 58 through 115 print out the welcome page and instructions for the user. This part of the script makes extensive use of the HTML shortcuts provided by the CGI module; see the article *CGI Programming* for details. If you don't know what's going on, suffice it to say that h1 produces a level 1 header, a produces a link, and so on. The script actually includes its own documentation; if called with the CGI parameter named action set to explain (i.e., *cgi-bin/nph-rater.cgi?action=explain*), it displays text explaining the rating system. Otherwise, it prints the normal welcome page. The check for this parameter is in line 62. An interesting trick related to this can be found on line 115, where you'll find this bit of code used to generate the self-referencing URL that summons up the explanatory text:

```
a({-href => script_name( ). '?action=explain', -target => 'explanation'},
   'Explain the ratings.');
```

This generates a link with the TARGET attribute set. On frames-aware browsers (primarily Netscape and Internet Explorer), this causes the explanatory text to be displayed in a newly-created browser window.

```
117    print_prompt( );
118    %stats = process_url($URL) if $URL = param('url_to_process');
119    print_previous(%stats);
120  }
121
122  print_tail( );
123
124  exit 0;
125
126  sub print_prompt {
127    print hr,
128      start_form,
129      'URL to Rate:', br,
```

```
130    textfield(-name=>'url_to_process',-size=>60),br,
131    submit('Rate'),
132    end_form;
133 }
...
146 sub print_tail {
147    print hr(),
148    address(a({-href=>'/~lstein'},"Lincoln D. Stein"), br,
149    a({-href=>'http://www.genome.wi.mit.edu/'},'Whitehead Institute/MIT
                                        Center for Genome Research'));
150 }
```

Line 117 invokes the print_prompt subroutine (lines 126–133), which uses standard CGI module calls to create a small fill-out form. Aside from the submit button, only one form element is defined: a text field named url_to_process. After the form is submitted, a like-named CGI parameter will contain the URL to process. Line 118 checks this parameter, and, if present, passes its value to the aptly-named process_ url function for processing and display. The previous thirty statistics are next fetched from a disk file and printed at the bottom of the page. Finally, the script prints out the bottom of the HTML page (subroutine print_tail, lines 146–150) and exits.

```
135 sub process_url {
136    my $url = shift;
137    print hr(),
138       h2('Progress');
139    print "<PRE>\n";
140    collect_stats(new URI::URL $url);
141    print "</PRE>\n";
142
143    return summary_statistics($url) if $COUNTS{'pages'};
144 }
```

The clever LWP agent begins with the call to process_url (lines 135–144). Because the script may take some time to traverse the linked pages, we're careful to keep the user on top of what's going on. We print out a level 2 header labeled "Progress" and then start a preformatted section with the <PRE> HTML tag. In line 140, we call the LWP library to create a new URI::URL object, and pass this object to the subroutine collect_stats. As collect_stats traverses the document tree, it prints out an indented set of URLs, which are immediately displayed. As collect_stats works, it adds the collected statistics to the global variable %COUNTS. When it's finished, we call the routine summary_statistics to crunch the numbers and format them.

```
245 sub collect_stats {
246    local $CURRENT_DOC = shift;
247    return undef unless $LEVEL < $MAX_DEPTH;
248
249    my $path = $CURRENT_DOC->abs->path;
250    return undef if $BEEN_THERE{$path}++;
251
252    my $href = $CURRENT_DOC->abs->as_string;
253
```

```
254   print ' ' x ($LEVEL*3), "Examining ", a({-href => $href}, $href)," ";
255
256   $LEVEL++;
257   my $agent    = new LWP::UserAgent;
258   my $request  = new HTTP::Request('GET', $CURRENT_DOC);
259   my $response = $agent->request($request);
260
261   local ($BASE,$INSIDE_A_LINK,$TEXT);
262
263 TRY:
264   {
265     # Replace with a more informative error message later
266     do { print em("unable to fetch document\n"); last TRY }
267       unless $response->is_success;
268     # This guarantees that we get the correct base document
269     # even if there was a redirect thrown in there.
270     if ($response->request->url->abs->path ne $path) {
271       $CURRENT_DOC = $response->request->url;
272       last TRY if $BEEN_THERE{$CURRENT_DOC->abs->path}++;
273     }
274
275
276     # Make sure that it's an HTML document!
277     my $type = $response->header('Content-type');
278     do { print em("not an HTML file\n"); last TRY; }
279       unless $type eq 'text/html';
280     my $parse_tree = parse($response->content);
281     do { print em("unable to parse HTML\n"); last TRY; }
282       unless $parse_tree;
283     print "\n";
284
285     $COUNTS{'pages'}++;
286     $parse_tree->traverse(\&process_page);
287
288     # For non-obvious reasons, we have to collect all
289     # the text before we can count the sentences.
290     $COUNTS{'sentences'} += sentences($TEXT);
291
292     $parse_tree->delete;
293   }
294   $LEVEL--;
295   return 1;
296 }
```

Lines 245 through 296 contain the code for collect_stats, the subroutine responsible for fetching the document at the indicated URL and its linked pages. We begin by loading the URI::URL object previously created in the call to process_url into a dynamically-scoped variable named $CURRENT_DOC. Although lexically-scoped variables created with my are usually preferable, dynamic scoping with local comes in handy when you want to create a set of variables that can be shared among a series of recursive subroutines. We use the same trick on line 261, where the values of pseudo-globals $BASE, $INSIDE_A_LINK, and $TEXT are defined.

Next, we perform a check for the depth of recursion. We return immediately if the global variable $LEVEL reaches $MAX_DEPTH (line 247). Following this is another important check: If we've seen this URL before, we must also return without processing the page. Because tasteless web pages often contain a series of tangled self-referential links, we have to be careful not to count the same page twice. This is done by calling the URL object's abs and path methods. Together, these methods resolve relative URLs into absolute ones (taking the BASE tag, if any, into account), strip off the protocol, host name, query string and "#" parts of the URL, and return the naked URL path. We compare this path to %BEEN_THERE, a hash of visited URLs, and exit if we've seen it already.

On lines 252 through 254, we convert the URL object into a string by calling the URL's as_string method, and print it out, tabbing over an appropriate number of spaces according to the recursion level. When this is done, we bump up the $LEVEL global.

The section between lines 257–259 creates a new LWP UserAgent and attempts to fetch the document at the current URL. The HTTP response from the attempt (whether successful or unsuccessful) is stored in the variable $response. We now attempt to process the response (lines 263–296). First, we check the HTTP result code by calling the response's is_success method. If unsuccessful, we print an error message and bail out. Next, we fetch the actual URL associated with the response and update the $CURRENT_DOC variable if it is different from what we attempted to fetch. Usually, an HTTP request returns the same URL that we attempted to fetch, but redirections muddy the waters. Again, we need to check that we aren't counting the same document twice. The final sanity check is for the returned document's MIME type (lines 277 and 278). If it's an HTML file we proceed; otherwise, we exit the subroutine.

Now that we have an HTML document in hand, we parse it (line 280) by passing it to parse. If successful, this returns an HTML::Parse object containing a tree of the document's HTML. We bump up the page count (line 285) and scrutinize the document by calling the traverse method.

```
378 sub parse {
379    my $content = shift;
380    return eval <<'END';
381 alarm(10);
382 my $f = parse_html($content);
383 alarm(0);
384 $f;
385 END
386 }
```

The parse subroutine (lines 378 through 386) is worth a quick look. A problem with the LWP HTML parsing routines is that bad HTML (which, sadly, is far from uncommon!) causes them to hang indefinitely. For this reason, we wrap LWP's parse_html function in an eval statement containing an alarm. If LWP hasn't finished parsing the document after ten seconds has elapsed, we print a warning message and return an undefined value.

The HTML::Parser module (as opposed to HTML::Parse) is now available and is more robust.

```perl
298 sub process_page {
299   my ($node, $start, $depth) = @_;
300   if (ref($node)) {                      # We have subparts
301
302     $BASE = $node->attr('href') if $node->tag eq 'base';
303
304
305     $COUNTS{'images'}++ if $start && $node->tag eq 'img';
306     $COUNTS{'doodads'}++ if $start && $node->tag =~ /^(applet|object|script)/;
307     #
308     # count the number of color changes
309     grep($COLOR_ATTR{$_} && $COUNTS{'colors'}++, keys %{$node}) if $start;
310
311     $COUNTS{'frames'}++ if $start && $node->tag eq 'frame';
312     $COUNTS{'ads'}++ if $start && $node->tag eq 'img' && is_ad($node->
                                                                attr('src'));
313
314     # Here's where we handle links and recursion
315     if ($node->tag eq 'a') {
316       my $href = $node->attr('href');
317       if ($href) {
318         if (is_child_url($href)) {
319           my $newdoc = new URI::URL($href,$BASE || $CURRENT_DOC->abs);
320           collect_stats($newdoc) unless $start;
321         }
322         $INSIDE_A_LINK = $start;
323       }
324     }
325
326     # Step into frames correctly
327     if ( $start && ($node->tag eq 'frame') ) {
328       my $href = $node->attr('src');
329       if ($href && is_child_url($href)) {
330         my $newdoc = new URI::URL($href,$BASE || $CURRENT_DOC->abs);
331         collect_stats($newdoc);
332       }
333     }
334
335   } else {                              # If we get here, we've got plain text
336     my @words = $node =~ /(\S+)/g;
337     $COUNTS{'link_words'}  += @words if $INSIDE_A_LINK;
338     $COUNTS{'total_words'} += @words;
339     $COUNTS{'cool_words'}  += is_cool($node);
340     $TEXT .= $node . " ";
341   }
342
343   return 1;
344 }
345
```

```
346 sub is_cool {
347    my $text = shift;
348    my ($exclamation_marks) = $text=~tr/!/!/;
349    my (@cool_words) = $text =~ /\b($COOL_PATTERN)\b/oig;
350    return $exclamation_marks + @cool_words;
351 }
352
353 sub sentences {
354    my $text = shift;
355    # Count capital letters followed by some non-punctuation,
356    # followed by punctuation and a space.
357    my (@sentences) = $text =~ /([A-Z].+?[.!?]\s)/gm;
358    return scalar(@sentences);
359 }
360
361 sub is_ad {
362    my $url = shift;
363    return undef unless $url;
364    return $url =~ /\b($AD_PATTERN)\b/oi;
365 }
366
367 sub is_child_url {
368    my $url = shift;
369    return undef if $url =~ /^\w+:/;
370    return undef if $url =~ m!^/!;
371    return undef if $url =~ /^\.\./;
372    1;
373 }
```

The statistics-gathering takes place in the subroutine named process_page (lines 298–344). process is called recursively by the HTML object's traverse method. Each time it's invoked, process is passed three parameters: a node corresponding to the current HTML element, a flag indicating whether the element is an opening tag or a closing tag, and the depth of the element in the parse tree. The subroutine's main task is to collect statistics about the page.

First, we check whether the node is a reference to an HTML object, which occurs when we're inside a tag of some sort. If we are, we can extract the tag's name by calling the object's tag method and the values of any attributes with its attr method. In most cases the statistics we gather are pretty simple. For example, if we see an <IMG> tag (line 305), we bump up the images field in the %COUNTS global. Similarly, we bump the doodads field if we find an <APPLET>, <OBJECT>, or <SCRIPT> tag.

Detecting potential advertisements is a little more difficult. We look for an <IMG> tag whose SRC URL contains one or more of the words "promotion," "ad," "advertisement," "sponsor," "banner," or "commercial." The majority of banner ads contain one of these telltale strings. We also specifically check for URLs from the ubiquitous DoubleClick advertising agency.

The \<BASE\> Tag

A few tags are special. If we encounter a \<BASE\> tag, we extract its HREF attribute and store it in the packagewide variable $BASE. This allows us to properly resolve relative URLs detected anywhere in the document. If we find a hyperlink anchor (lines 315 to 324), we extract its HREF attribute and check whether it is a relative reference to a document on the same or lower level as the current one. If it satisfies this test, we create a new URL object (line 319), being careful to resolve the relative reference with $BASE if defined, or the URL of the current document if not. We then recursively pass the resolved URL object to collect_stats, processing the linked document in a depth-first manner.

On line 322, we set the $INSIDE_A_LINK dynamically-scoped global to true when we encounter the opening tag of a link, and false when the corresponding closing tag is encountered. This flag allows us to identify words that are inside links for the purposes of creating the Information Index.

Lines 326 to 333 contain code for handling frames correctly. The code here is almost identical to that used for handling links.

Lines 335 to 341 are executed when the parse tree traverses the plain text part of the HTML page. This section tallies various word counts, keeping track of total words, words inside links, and words of the "cool" persuasion. We also need to tally the number of sentences on the page. Since the HTML parser, by its nature, breaks sentences into chunks and presents them to process in discontinuous pieces, we simply concatenate the sentence fragments into the dynamically-scoped variable $TEXT, and defer tallying sentences until the entire HTML tree traversal is finished (line 290).

```
152 sub summary_statistics {
153   my $href = shift;
154   print h2('Raw Data'),
155     table({-border=>''},
156         TR({-align=>LEFT},
157           th('Pages'), td($COUNTS{'pages'}),
158           th('Total Words'), td($COUNTS{'total_words'})),
159         TR({-align=>LEFT},
160           th('Total Sentences'),td($COUNTS{'sentences'}),
161           th('Words in links'),td($COUNTS{'link_words'})),
162         TR({-align=>LEFT},
163           th('Applets/Controls'), td($COUNTS{'doodads'}),
164           th('Cool! Words'), td($COUNTS{'cool_words'})),
165         TR({-align=>LEFT},
166           th('Graphics'), td($COUNTS{'images'}),
167           th('Custom colors'), td($COUNTS{'colors'})),
168         TR({-align=>LEFT},
169           th('Possible Advertisements'), td($COUNTS{ads}),
170           th('Frames'), td($COUNTS{'frames'}))
171         );
172   my %i = (compute_indices(%COUNTS), 'href' => $href);
173   print h2('Ratings'),summary_table(\%i);
```

```
174    return %i;
175 }
176
177 sub summary_table {
178    my (@row) = @_;
179    my (@rows, $i);
180    foreach $i (@row) {
181      push(@rows,
182          td([ a({-href => $i->{href}}, $i->{href}),
183                sprintf("%2.1f",$i->{II}),
184                sprintf("%2.1f",$i->{GI}),
185                sprintf("%2.1f",$i->{DI}),
186                sprintf("%2.1f",$i->{TFI}),
187                $i->{FI},
188                sprintf("%2.1f",$i->{'C!I'}),
189                sprintf("%2.1f",$i->{CCI}) ]
190          )
191        );
192    }
193    return join("\n",
194                    table( {-border => ''},
195                        TR(th(),
196                            th('Information'),
197                            th('Graphics'),
198                            th('Doodads'),
199                            th('Colors'),
200                            th('Frames'),
201                            th('Cool!'),
202                            th('Ads')),
203                        TR({-align=>RIGHT},\@rows)
204                    )
205            );
206 }
...
231 sub compute_indices {
232    my (%COUNTS) = @_;
233    my %indices = (
234      II => 100 * (1-$COUNTS{'link_words'}/($COUNTS{'total_words'} || 1)),
235      GI => $COUNTS{'images'}/$COUNTS{'pages'},
236      DI => $COUNTS{'doodads'}/$COUNTS{'pages'},
237     TFI => $COUNTS{'colors'}/$COUNTS{'pages'},
238      FI => $COUNTS{'frames'},
239    'C!I'=> 100 * ($COUNTS{'cool_words'}/($COUNTS{'sentences'} || 1)),
240     CCI => $COUNTS{'ads'}/$COUNTS{'pages'},
241    );
242    return %indices;
243 }
```

When collect_stats has finished processing all the linked documents, %COUNTS contains the final tallies. The subroutine summary_statistics (lines 152 through 175) creates an HTML table showing the raw statistics, and invokes compute_indices (lines 231–243) to crunch these numbers according to the rating scheme. The crunched results are passed on to summary_table (lines 177–206) to format the results into a nice HTML table.

```
208 sub print_previous {
209   my (%current) = @_;
210   my $fh = open_and_lock($RANK_FILE);
211   my (@previous_ranks);
212   chomp(@previous_ranks = <$fh>);
213   if (@previous_ranks) {
214     my (@processed) = map { {split("\t")} } @previous_ranks;
215     print hr( ), h2('Recent Ratings'), summary_table(@processed);
216   }
217
218   unless ($COUNTS{'pages'}) {
219     unlock($fh);
220     return;
221   }
222
223   unshift(@previous_ranks, join("\t", %current));
224   pop(@previous_ranks) if @previous_ranks > $PREVIOUS_RANKS;
225   seek($fh, 0, 0);
226   print $fh join("\n", @previous_ranks), "\n";
227   truncate($fh,tell($fh));
228   unlock($fh);
229 }
```

The script's last task is to add the current site's rating results to a list of the last thirty ratings. We do this in a fairly crude manner in the subroutine print_previous, which you'll find in lines 208 through 229. We keep the results as a simple text file, one line per rating. Using Perl's flock call, we gain exclusive read/write access to the text file. This is necessary to avoid multiple instances of the CGI script from trying to update the file simultaneously.

```
392 # ------------------- File locking code ------------
393 # This bit of code creates an advisory lock on the
394 # indicated file and returns a file handle to it.
395 sub LOCK_SH { 1 }
396 sub LOCK_EX { 2 }
397 sub LOCK_NB { 4 }
398 sub LOCK_UN { 8 }
399
400 sub open_and_lock {
401   my $path = shift;
402   my $fh;
403
404   local ($msg)    = '';
405   local ($oldsig) = $SIG{'ALRM'};
406   $SIG{'ALRM'} = sub { $msg='timed out'; $SIG{ALRM}=$oldsig; };
407   alarm(5);
408
409   $fh = ++$FH;
410   open ($fh,"+<$path") or die("Couldn't open $path: $!");
411
```

```
412    # Now try to lock it
413    die("Couldn't get write lock (" . ($msg || "$!") . ")")
414        unless flock ($fh,LOCK_EX);
415
416    $fh;
417 }
418
419 sub unlock {
420    my $fh = shift;
421    flock($fh, LOCK_UN);
422    close $fh;
423 }
```

Lines 392–423 contain the boilerplate code that I use for this type of file locking. If we successfully obtain a lock, we read the entire contents of the file into list, and format it into an HTML table by calling summary_table once more to do the dirty work. When this is done, we throw out the first entry in the list and add the current document's ratings to the end of the list. We then format the numbers into a table and write the results back to the file. Finally, we unlock the file and return.

For Extra Credit

The demonstration script on my web site is slightly more sophisticated than what I've shown here. It turns out that many high-end web sites customize their content for their user's browser. Browsers that identify themselves as Netscape or Internet Explorer get snazzy graphics, frames, and applets. Other browsers get a toned-down page. With a little extra programming effort, the rater script can pretend to be various popular brands of browser. Try rating the same pages while impersonating different browsers and see what happens!

## CHAPTER 22

Summarizing Web Pages with HTML::Summary

Tony Rose and Ave Wrigley

Canon, like many other large companies, is a multinational organization with multiple web sites, each managed by a different part of the company. This is a problem for the typical Canon customer, who knows nothing about Canon's internal organization and simply wants to find information about their cameras or download a new printer driver. They need a single clear way to find what they want.

CS-Web: A Search Engine for Canon's Web Space

Back in 1997, we wrote CS-Web, a set of Perl programs to collect information from all of Canon's web sites, index it, and make it searchable from the web. We wrote our own solution because at the time the available products were either services designed for searching the entire web (such as AltaVista), or tools for indexing and searching a single web site.

CS-Web consists of a robot, a database, and a web interface (written in mod_perl). The robot traverses all of Canon web sites and stores a description of each page in the database. The search engine queries the database and gives you a list of candidate documents, and their descriptions. You can try CS-Web for yourself: it is linked from the main "gateway" page for Canon (*http://www.canon.com/*). You can also access it directly at *http://csweb.cre.canon.co.uk/*.

CS-Web presented a variety of challenges, many of which make suitable war stories for TPJ. However, for this article, we will focus on one crucial problem: generating the summary of an HTML document.

META Tags

Unlike some other search engines, CS-Web doesn't index the full text of the document. Instead, it indexes document descriptions. When web page authors use the META tag's NAME and CONTENT attributes to encode information about the document, CS-Web will use it. However, when no such information is conveniently provided by the author, CS-Web tries to boil down the text of the document into a description it can use.

One important limitation on a document's description is length; each web page corresponds to a row in a relational database table, and for performance reasons the size of each field in each row is fixed in advance. This is because with the database engine we were using at the time, MySQL, fixed-width fields were much quicker to search than variable-width fields. You'll see later how this length constraint introduced its own problems.

If we were deploying CS-Web across a lot of public web sites, we'd have quickly found that very few web page authors consistently provide accurate metadata. In fact, deliberately misleading metadata is often included by unscrupulous authors to enhance the page's prominence in search engine results.

However, the outlook for CS-Web was a little more promising. Since Canon's webmasters are generally working together, we could expect a certain level of integrity, and assume that they were not trying to deceive the CS-Web robot. In turn, the CS-Web robot could acknowledge this trust: if it found a page description within a META tag, it would accept it as legitimate. However, the task of adding these META tags to existing pages can be a time-consuming process, and we couldn't rely on their presence on all of the pages.

So how could we generate a text description from the raw HTML when no metadata are present? By using a combination of some natural language processing techniques and Perl. The result was the HTML::Summary module. We'll explore it shortly, but before we do we'll look at some basic summarization methods for text.

Basic Summarization Methods

The basic approach of most summarization systems is to examine each sentence in the original document, assess its importance (using one or more known heuristics) and then output a summary of the desired length by omitting the less important sentences. Obviously, our success relies on how well we can measure importance. Usually, a combination of the following six simple methods is used:

Location method

    Sentences are scored according to their position or location within the document. For example, sentences occurring at the beginning or end of the first paragraph, or within a heading, are given a higher score than sentences in the middle of a paragraph.

Cue method

    Certain words in the document indicate the presence of more (or less) important material. For example, strongly positive words like "best," "significant," and "greatest" increase the sentence score. By contrast, negative words like "impossible" or "hardly" decrease the sentence score.

Title-keyword method

    The title of the document is assumed to be a reliable indication of the focus of its contents; sentences referring to those concepts are given a higher score. To help out, some pre-processing can be used; for example, a stemmer can conflate inflected terms to a single root ("runs" and "running" become "run"). Similarly, a stop list may be used to filter out stop words ("the," "of," "and," and so on).

Frequency-keyword approach

The important concepts in a document will yield particular keywords that occur with a greater-than-expected frequency, so sentences containing these words are given a higher score. The keywords are usually identified by sorting word frequencies and removing the stop words. A slightly more sophisticated variant involves the use of "distinctiveness" rather than raw frequency—normalizing the frequency counts by *a priori* frequencies taken from an independent large text corpus.

Indicator phrase method

This method is similar to the cue method, except that in this case one looks for certain phrases rather than words. For example, "The aim of this paper is…" and "This document attempts to review…" both indicate that the important concept is about to be introduced, so documents containing such constructions should receive higher scores. There are obviously many different indicator phrases, but research suggests that these are usually derived from a small number of underlying templates.[*]

The syntactic method

Experiments from up to thirty years ago have attempted to correlate sentence importance with syntactic structure, so far without conclusive results.[†]

Edmundson performed a comparative evaluation of the above six methods, and found the first four to be superior, in the order shown above. In addition, he evaluated their performance in combination, and found a linear combination of the first three (with an appropriate weighting given to the scores obtained from each method) to be even better.[‡]

HTML::Summary

HTML::Summary is available from CPAN; Version 0.016 is described in this article. This is how it is used.

First, you create an HTML::Summary object, using the new method. You can provide configuration parameters as arguments to new:

```
my $html_summarizer = new HTML::Summary LENGTH => 200;
```

---

[*] Paice, C. "Constructing literature abstracts by computer." *Information Processing and Management*, Volume 26(1), 1990. Emundson 1969.

[†] Earl, L.L. "Experiments in automatic extracting and indexing." *Information Storage and Retrieval*, Volume 6, 313–334, 1970.

[‡] Edmundson, H. P. "New methods in automatic extracting." *Journal of the ACM*, 16(2):264-285, 1969.

The LENGTH parameter is the maximum length in bytes for the generated summary. Next, you need an HTML::Element object corresponding to the HTML page that you want to summarize. You can generate one with HTML::TreeBuilder:

```
my $html_tree = new HTML::TreeBuilder;
$html_tree->parse( $html_document );
```

$html_document is a string containing the HTML of the web page; this could have been read in from a file, or returned as the contents of an HTTP request, such as through LWP::Simple's get method.

Finally, you call the generate method of the HTML::Summary object, with the HTML::Element object as an argument, which returns the summary of the page as a string:

```
$html_summary = $html_summarizer->generate( $html_tree );
```

That's how you use it. But how does it work?

The Summarization Algorithm

One of the main tasks before us was generating a good fixed-length abstract from arbitrary text. As described above, this is known to be a important and difficult problem, and a quality solution requires sophisticated natural language techniques that can analyze the structure of the original, identify key phrases and concepts, and regenerate them in a more succinct format.

Luckily for us, there are some quick and dirty ways to generate summaries. We only needed to provide a gist of the original for someone browsing the CS-Web search results. In addition, for retrieval purposes, we want the summary to contain representative keywords.

One advantage that we had over people trying to generate summaries from plain text is that HTML pages contain *markup information*—the HTML tags. Markup tells us about the structure of the content, and often about its relative importance as well. For example, it is usually clear in HTML pages where paragraphs begin and end, and when important text is *italicized*, **emboldened**, or made into a heading.

The HTML::Summary module uses the *location method* of text summarization described above. This identifies important sentences (based primarily on their location in the text), and concatenating them together to produce an abstract. A simple example of this would be to take the first sentence of every paragraph in an article and string them together. This can sometimes be surprisingly effective:

```
Canon, like many other large companies, is a multi-national
organization with multiple (26) web sites, each managed by a different
part of the company.  In 1997 we wrote CS-Web, a set of Perl programs
to collect information from all of Canon's web sites, index it, and
make it searchable from the web.  CS-Web consists of a robot, a
database, and a web interface (written in mod_perl).  CS-Web presented
a variety of challenges, many of which would make suitable war stories
for TPJ.
```

The text summarization method used in HTML::Summary is an adaptation of the location method. It works as follows:

Split into sentences

First, the text is split into sentences. (More about this later.)

Score the sentences

The sentences are scored according to what HTML element they appear in, and whether or not they are the first sentence in that element. The algorithm here is pretty simple: each element has a score. The first sentence in that element gets this score; the rest of the sentences get nothing.

Sort the sentences by score

The sentences are stored in an array of hashes. Each hash corresponds to a sentence, and contains information about the text in the sentence, its length, the HTML element it appeared in, its score, and its original order in the text.

```
$summary[ scalar( @summary ) ] = {
    'text'        => $text,
    'length'      => length( $text ),
    'tag'         => $tag,
    'score'       => $score,
    'order'       => scalar( @summary ),
};
```

The scores, as described above, are based on the HTML element that the sentences appear in. These scores are stored in a global hash:

```
my %ELEMENT_SCORES = (
    'p'         => 100,
    'h1'        => 90,
    'h2'        => 80,
    'h3'        => 70,
);
```

These scores were arrived at by empirical investigation; we have no theoretical justification for them.

Truncate the list of sentences

Calculate how many sentences are needed before the requested summary length is met (or exceeded).

Sort the sentences by original order again

Having remembered the original sentence order in the text in the hash for that sentence, we can now re-sort the sentences in that order.

Concatenate the sentences to create the summary

Spaces are added between the sentences, since whitespace was stripped when the sentences were split.

Truncate the summary at the requested length

This last step assumes that if you want a summary of 200 characters, 201 characters are not acceptable—even if it means chopping the summary off midsentence. This is what we wanted in CS-Web. Maybe in other applications a less severe approach would be appropriate—it's easy to add more options to HTML::Summary, so let us know what you think.

Sentence Splitting

Now for the nitty gritty. The remainder of this article focuses on just one aspect of the HTML::Summary: splitting the element contents into sentences. Japanese character encodings were a particular problem for CS-Web; our approach is described in the section "Afterword: Truncating Japanese Text."

The task of splitting text into sentences seemed like a more general problem than its application to text summarization, so this is contained in a separate module, Text::Sentence (also available from CPAN).

Text::Sentence is basically just a regex. It is has a non-object–oriented interface that exports one function, split_sentences, that takes the text to be split into sentences as an argument, and returns a list of the sentences.

```
sub split_sentences {
    my $text = shift;
    return () unless $text;
```

The function first checks if there really is any text to split into sentences; if not, it just returns an empty list.

```
# $capital_letter is a character set; to account for locale, this
# includes all letters for which lc is different from that letter.

my $capital_letter =
    '[' .
        join( '',
            grep { lc( $_ ) ne ( $_ ) }
            map { chr( $_ ) } ord( "A" ) .. ord( "\xff" )
        ) .
    ']'
;
```

Although it would be more efficient to compute this regex component once at the package level, doing it in split_sentences allows the user to change locales between calls.

The next few lines build up the components of the regex that split the text into sentences. The first of these components is the capital letter found at the start of a sentence. Instead of using the character class [A-Z] as you would normally, Text::Sentence accounts for locale-specific capital letters. For example, in French, a capital A acute (Á) won't be matched by [A-Z]. The method used in Text::Sentence makes use of the fact that lc is sensitive to locale settings, and returns a lowercase version of all capitalized characters. A set of locale-specific capital letters can be built up for the extended ASCII range by filtering any characters changed by lc. For more information on how Perl handles locales, see the perllocale documentation bundled with Perl.

```
@PUNCTUATION = ( '\.', '\!', '\?' );
```

The @PUNCTUATION array is a global variable in Text::Sentence containing any punctuation used to indicate the end of a sentence. The fact that it's a global means that you're able to change it (although the interface could be improved—an options hash

passed to split_sentences, perhaps. For example, you might want to add locale specific punctuation for the Spanish ¡.

```
push( @Text::Sentence::PUNCTUATION, chr( 161 ) );
```

Back to split_sentences:

```
# This needs to be alternation, not a character class,
# because of multibyte characters
my $punctuation = '(?:' . join( '|', @PUNCTUATION ) . ')';
```

As mentioned above, one of our concerns was dealing with multibyte character
encodings (see "Afterword: Truncating Japanese Text"). Japanese punctuation characters may be more than one character long, so we can't use a character class for
punctuation in the sentence splitting regex. For example, an exclamation point in the
EUC Japanese encoding is "\xA1\xAA".

```
# Return $text if there is no punctuation ...
return $text unless $text =~ /$punctuation/;
```

If these isn't any end-of-sentence punctuation in the text, then we might as well
return the text now.

```
my $opt_start_quote = q/['"]?/;
my $opt_close_quote = q/['"]?/;

# These are distinguished because (eventually!) I would like to do
# locale stuff on quote characters

my $opt_start_bracket = q/[[({]?/; # }{
my $opt_close_bracket = q/[\])}]?/;
```

Sentences sometimes have quotation marks or parentheses that come before the capital letter at the beginning, or after the full stop (period, question mark, or exclamation point) at the end. For example, the following sentence:

```
Larry said "let there be light!" (And there was.)
```

is two sentences; the first ends after the second double quote. However, this is one
sentence:

```
Larry said "let there be light!" (and there was).
```

Here is the regex in all its glory:

```
my @sentences = $text =~ /
(
                        # Sentences start with ...
    $opt_start_quote    # an optional start quote
    $opt_start_bracket  # an optional start bracket
    $capital_letter     # a capital letter ...
    .+?                 # at least some (non-greedy) anything ...
    $punctuation        # ... followed by any one of !?.
    $opt_close_quote    # an optional close quote
    $opt_close_bracket  # and an optional close bracket
)
```

```
    (?=                          # with lookahead that it is followed by ...
        (?:                      # either ...
            \s+                  # some whitespace ...
            $opt_start_quote     # an optional start quote
            $opt_start_bracket   # an optional start bracket
            $capital_letter      # an uppercase word character (for locale
                                 # sensitive matching)
        |                        # or ...
            \n\n                 # a couple (or more) of CRs (i.e. a new para)
        |                        # or ...
            \s*$                 # optional whitespace, followed by end of string
        )
    )
    /gxs
    ;
    return @sentences if @sentences;
    return ( $text );
        }
```

This regex makes use of the lookahead feature of regular expressions. In this case, it allows us to specify that a sentence must not only start with a capital letter, and end in a full stop, but that there must be another capital letter that follows the full stop. The only exception to this is when the sentence is either at the end of a paragraph, or at the end of the string.

The lookahead accounts for the whitespace between sentences, so it's not part of the matched patterns that end up in the @sentences array. That's why concatenating the sentences won't give you back the exact original text.

The main problem with trying to split text into sentences is that there are several uses for periods, such as abbreviations.

```
    Dr. Livingstone, I presume.
```

This phrase counts as two sentences according to Text::Sentence—the first sentence is three characters long. The performance of Text::Sentence could be improved by taking into account special cases like honorifics (Mr., Mrs., Dr.), common abbreviations (e.g., etc., i.e.), and so on. However, as with many natural language problems, this obeys the law of diminishing returns; a little bit of effort will do a decent 90% job, but that last 10% is pretty difficult. For our purposes, the 90% is good enough.

Conclusion

We chose to use Perl for CS-Web because of the obvious benefits: the LWP modules for web programming, DBD/DBI, mod_perl, and so on. We found that Perl is also a useful tool for doing natural language work. Its text processing features, rapid development cycle, and ability to generate complex data structures on the fly make it particularly appropriate.

A lot of interesting work in natural language research involves analyzing corpus data; collecting statistics about language use over large databases of typical usage. The web is an obvious rich source of this type of data, and in view of this, it is a little surprising how few tools and modules appeared to be available in Perl for this field. Certainly, when we posted about Text::Sentence to a language processing mailing list, there seemed to be quite a lot of interest in what we were doing, as well as extensive Perl expertise in that community. Hopefully, natural language processing will become yet another nut for Perl to crack!

Afterword: Truncating Japanese Text

Canon is a Japanese company, with Japanese text on many of its web pages. Japanese text is usually encoded in one of several possible multibyte encoding schemes (not including Unicode!), and some of these schemes use variable numbers of bytes to represent single Japanese characters, or intermingle Japanese and regular ASCII characters. This was a problem.

The summaries generated by Text::Summary are truncated at a fixed length, and this length is specified in bytes, not characters. If Japanese text is truncated at an arbitrary byte length, this might mean truncation *in the middle of a character*.

Worse, our page abstracts can appear in result listings for keyword searches. If a page summary broken midcharacter is inserted into running text, the byte *immediately following the summary* could be interpreted as the next byte of the previously uncompleted Japanese character, upsetting the character boundaries for the rest of the text.

The Text::Sentence used another module, Lingua::JA::Jtruncate (also available on CPAN), which addresses this problem. Lingua::JA::Jtruncate contains just one subroutine, jtruncate, used as follows:

```
use Lingua::JA::Jtruncate qw( jtruncate );
$truncated_jtext = jtruncate( $jtext, $length );
```

where $jtext is some Japanese text that you want to truncate, $length is the maximum truncation length, and $truncated_text is the result. Here's how it works.

First, some regexes are defined that match characters in each of the three main Japanese coding schemes: EUC, Shift-JIS, and JIS.

```
%euc_code_set = (
    ASCII_JIS_ROMAN     => '[\x00-\x7f]',
    JIS_X_0208_1997     => '[\xa1-\xfe][\xa1-\xfe]',
    HALF_WIDTH_KATAKANA => '\x8e[\xa0-\xdf]',
    JIS_X_0212_1990     => '\x8f[\xa1-\xfe][\xa1-\xfe]',
);

%sjis_code_set = (
    ASCII_JIS_ROMAN     => '[\x21-\x7e]',
    HALF_WIDTH_KATAKANA => '[\xa1-\xdf]',
    TWO_BYTE_CHAR       => '[\x81-\x9f\xe0-\xef][\x40-\x7e\x80-\xfc]',
);

%jis_code_set = (
    TWO_BYTE_ESC        =>
```

```
                '(?:' .
                join( '|',
                    '\x1b\x24\x40',
                    '\x1b\x24\x42',
                    '\x1b\x26\x40\x1b\x24\x42',
                    '\x1b\x24\x28\x44',
                ) .
                ')'
            ,
            TWO_BYTE_CHAR       => '(?:[\x21-\x7e][\x21-\x7e])',
            ONE_BYTE_ESC        => '(?:\x1b\x28[\x4a\x48\x42\x49])',
            ONE_BYTE_CHAR       =>
                '(?:' .
                join( '|',
                    '[\x21-\x5f]',              # JIS7 Half width katakana
                    '\x0f[\xa1-\xdf]*\x0e',     # JIS8 Half width katakana
                    '[\x21-\x7e]',              # ASCII / JIS-Roman
                ) .
                ')'
        );

    %char_re = (
        'euc'   => '(?:' . join( '|', values %euc_code_set ) . ')',
        'sjis'  => '(?:' . join( '|', values %sjis_code_set ) . ')',
        'jis'   => '(?:' . join( '|', values %jis_code_set ) . ')',
    );
```

Each of the regexes in %char_re matches one character encoded in the scheme corresponding to the keys of the hash.

Now for the definition of the jtruncate subroutine; first, some fairly obvious sanity checks:

```
    sub jtruncate
    {
        my $text            = shift;
        my $length          = shift;

        # sanity checks

        return '' if $length == 0;
        return undef if not defined $length;
        return undef if $length < 0;
        return $text if length( $text ) <= $length;
```

Now we save the original text; this is used later if the truncation process fails for some reason.

```
    my $orig_text = $text;
```

Now we use Lingua::JA::Jcode::getcode to detect which encoding the text uses. Lingua::JA::Jcode::getcode is a simple wrapper around the jcode.pl Perl library for Japanese character code conversion. Kazumasa Utashiro kindly agreed to let us distribute the code with HTML::Summary.

```
    my $encoding = Lingua::JA::Jcode::getcode( \$text );
```

If getcode returns undef, or a value other than euc, sjis, or jis, then it has either failed to detect the encoding, or detected that it is not one of those that we are interested in. We then take the brute force approach, using substr.

```perl
if ( not defined $encoding or $encoding !~ /^(?:euc|s?jis)$/ )
{
    return substr( $text, 0, $length );
}
```

The actual truncation of the string is done in chop_jchars—more on this subroutine in a bit.

```perl
$text = chop_jchars( $text, $length, $encoding );
```

chop_jchars returns undef on failure. If we have failed to truncate the Japanese text properly, we resort to substr again. We had to decide whether it was more important to meet the $length constraint or risk returning a Japanese string with broken character encoding. We chose the former:

```perl
return substr( $orig_text, 0, $length ) unless defined $text;
```

Next, a special case: JIS encoding uses escape sequences to shift in and out of single-byte and multibyte modes. If the truncation process leaves the text ending in multibyte mode, we need to add the single-byte escape sequence. Therefore, we truncate (at least) three more bytes from JIS encoded string, so we have room to add the single-byte escape sequence without going over the $length limit.

```perl
if ( $encoding eq 'jis' and
    $text =~ /$jis_code_set{ TWO_BYTE_CHAR }$/ ) {
    $text = chop_jchars( $text, $length - 3, $encoding );
    return substr( $orig_text, 0, $length ) unless defined $text;
    $text .= "\x1b\x28\x42";
}
```

And we're done!

```perl
    return $text;
}
```

Now for chop_jchars, which simply lops off Japanese characters from the end of the string until it is shorter than the requested length. It's pretty ugly, and slow for large strings truncated to small values, but it does the job!

```perl
sub chop_jchars
{
    my $text = shift;
    my $length = shift;
    my $encoding = shift;

    while( length( $text ) > $length )
    {
        return undef unless $text =~ s!$char_re{ $encoding }$!!o;
    }

    return $text;
}
```

## CHAPTER 23

Wireless Surfing with WAP and WML

Dan Brian

Mobility! In my day we had to pick up the phone and put it on the acoustic modem. Now you can get stuff any time, anywhere. These kids...

I bought a new mobile phone with wireless Internet not long ago. The prospect of tracking news headlines, stock prices, and checking email over the phone seemed appealing. But after only a few minutes of browsing, I felt disappointed. Navigation was cumbersome, the viewscreen very small, and most frustrating of all, it took a really long time to get all the information I wanted. I read a bit more about the various portals that consolidate data from various sources, but after using one of them, I realized that no existing service would give me the variety of content I wanted. Besides, I've never much liked the idea of my username, passwords, and messages passing through someone else's servers. And this was about the same time I read the fine print on my service contract, explaining that I was paying for talk-time whenever I used my wireless Internet access.

In this article, I'll explore application development for wireless devices, first providing an overview of the WAP (Wireless Application Protocol) architecture, and then introducing some Perl modules to help create WAP applications.

A Quick Look at WAP

Wireless web browsers are the embodiment of a dominant trend in modern information technology. This trend is to equate "client" with "accessor," and "server" with "provider". While that definition might apply to most network applications, it has one of its simplest models in WAP, where dynamic functionality is best executed at the server, and no data is typically stored at the client. (Granted, you *can*, if you try hard enough, use cookies with wireless devices, but such processing is interface-centric, like client-side JavaScript. Furthermore, support for such features is inconsistent.) This paradigm shift from client-distributed computing is evidenced by the popularity of personalized "my-" portals, web-based messaging, centralized file storage services, and the porting of major applications to the web.

WAP (Wireless Application Protocol) is a communications standard that includes specifications for markup, session, transaction, security, and transport application layers. These standards are maintained by the WAP Forum, founded by Ericsson, Nokia, Motorola, and Phone.com. (Phone.com was originally Unwired Planet, the company that pioneered wireless Internet services in the mid-1990s. Consequently, most of the browsers within modern phones run the Phone.com software.) Although the WAP Forum is currently working on Version 1.3 of the specifications, most phones currently support only Version 1.1.

The basics of WAP architecture are shown in Figure 23-1. An application server on the Internet receives WAP requests and responds with data (typically WML documents), sent over the Internet between the application server and a WAP gateway. The gateway routes and translates WAP requests to HTTP requests, determining what WAP data gets sent over a wireless network to a communications tower and eventually to your phone.

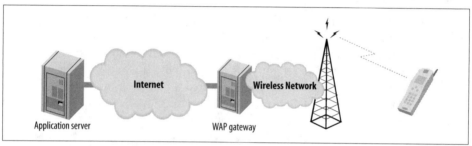

Figure 23-1. WAP architecture

Enabling WAP on Apache

Thanks to the WAP gateway, any web server can deliver WML-formatted documents over HTTP by simply adding them to the MIME types for the server. In the case of Apache, you can add the following to an *.htaccess* file to WAP-enable the server (most newer Apache servers already have these types in their *mime.types* file):

```
addtype text/vnd.wap.wml            wml
addtype text/vnd.wap.wmlscript      wmls
addtype application/vnd.wap.wmlc    wmlc
addtype application/vnd.wap.wmlscriptc  wmlsc
addtype image/vnd.wap.wbmp          wbmp
```

When a wireless user wants to visit your site, they enter the URL. Unless you want to require your visitors to type .wml after a request, Apache will usually serve up an HTML document by default. To remedy this situation, we could use Apache's mod_ rewrite engine to rewrite every request for an *.html* file to look for a *.wml* file in the same directory.* Again, since the WAP gateway supports HTTP headers, we can do

---

* If mod_rewrite isn't part of your Apache installation, and you've compiled the Apache apxs utility, you can add mod_rewrite from the Apache 1.3.12 source directory with: apxs -i src/modules/standard/mod_rewrite.c.

this easily by adding the following to *httpd.conf*. Additional `HTTP_USER_AGENT` entries would need to be added, since this one will only rewrite Phone.com's UP.Browser client (*http://www.phone.com/developers/index.html*):

```
RewriteEngine on
RewriteLog logs/rewrite
RewriteLogLevel 9
RewriteCond %{HTTP_USER_AGENT} UP\.Browser
RewriteRule ^(.+)\.html$ $1.wml
```

There is another option, which makes use of Apache's `HTTP_ACCEPT` variable to list the MIME types that the connecting browser supports. However, most WAP clients report the ability to accept responses of type `text/html`, even though they lack the ability to translate the data. A better option is to determine if the connecting browser supports WML, since most HTTP browsers cannot read WML.

```
RewriteCond %{HTTP_ACCEPT} text\/vnd\.wap\.wml
```

Of course, to serve any dynamic content will require a bit more work. Before delving into that, let's look a bit at WML.

WML Basics

WML (Wireless Markup Language) is a standard set of XML tags for the display of documents on mobile devices. Similar in function to HTML, these tags allow content to be formatted and linked. But given the limitations of wireless displays, the feature set is much more limited than HTML. And this is a good thing.

Since it is XML, WML requires strict formatting. Any errors in the markup, such as unterminated paragraph tags (`<p></p>`), should cause a client to return an error. (So long as we're talking about them, note that *all* text content must be within paragraph tags.) XML is usually explained to novices as the opposite of display data: rather than containing information about the formatting of data, as in HTML, XML contains information about the data itself: its structure, interrelation, and organization. WML would seem to be an exception—but when it comes to wireless applications, the appearance of the data and its structure become intertwined.

A simple WML document is shown below. If you aren't familiar with XML, all you need to know about the document header is that it occurs within every WML document, and provides a data type definition for the client parsing the code. This header will only change if documents use different versions of WAP. Most do not.

```
<?xml version="1.0"?>
<!DOCTYPE wml PUBLIC "-//WAPFORUM//DTD WML 1.1//EN"
    "http://www.wapforum.org/DTD/wml_1.1.xml">

<wml>
<card id="main" title="First Example">
  <p>
    Hello WAP World!
  </p>
</card>
</wml>
```

When saved as *hello.wml* in a web server directory and requested from a wireless client, it will display what's shown in Figure 23-2.

Figure 23-2. hello.wml

If our web server enabled rewrites using the *httpd.conf* directives shown earlier, this document could be requested as *hello.html*, and still produce the desired result.

There are many tools available to developers to aid in wireless development. The screenshots in this article are taken from Phone.com's Up.Simulator program, which allows you to browse the wireless web without using your phone (or the precious minutes you pay for if you share my service plan). Keep in mind that no two wireless browsers are identical. Although there are far fewer hornet's nests in the nested tags of WML than there are for HTML, there is no real consolation here for those craving a "write-once, read-the-same-everywhere" environment. But it is a standard that is adhered to between enterprises, if not functionally, at least syntactically. (Are you out there, XHTML?)

WAP Cards

Latency is a bigger issue for WAP than for HTTP, since the system architecture itself is a many-hop, many-protocol network. In part to address the problem of delivery time, but also to fit markup to the WAP model, WAP applications don't use pages as they exist on the web. Instead, WAP has *cards*. A card is simply what is displayed on a device at any given time. A single WML document might contain many cards. A collection of cards within a document is referred to as a *deck*, and can be explained as many analogous web pages folded into a single document with hyperlinks between the cards. The following example shows a WML document containing three cards and a menu to navigate between them, defined in the <template></template> element.

```
<?xml version="1.0" encoding="iso-8859-1"?> <!DOCTYPE wml PUBLIC "-//WAPFORUM//DTD
WML 1.1//EN"
"http://www.wapforum.org/DTD/wml_1.1.xml">
<wml>
<template>
  <do type="accept" label="Back">
    <prev/>
  </do>
  <do type="accept" label="Football">
```

```
      <go href="#football"/>
    </do>
    <do type="accept" label="Basketball">
      <go href="#basketball"/>
    </do>
</template>

<card id="main" title="Main">
  <p>
    Use the option menu to find sports scores.
  </p>
</card>

<card id="football" title="football">
  <p>
    Saints <b>31</b>, Rams <b>24</b><br/>
    Chargers <b>17</b>, Chiefs <b>16</b><br/>
    Eagles <b>23</b>, Redskins <b>20</b><br/>
  </p>
</card>

<card id="basketball" title="Basketball">
  <p>
    Lakers <b>102</b>, Clippers <b>98</b><br/>
    Timberwolves <b>88</b>, Magic <b>87</b><br/>
  </p>
</card>
</wml>
```

I won't touch on the markup here much, other than to explain that the do/ tags specify an options menu to be displayed when the "Options" button on a phone is selected. Note that the href links specify a link within the local document, prefixed with the #. (These links could also be fully-qualified URLs to non-local cards.) Also, the <template> tags enclose data that will be applied to every card in the deck, saving space.

Initially, this document will display what's shown in Figure 23-3.

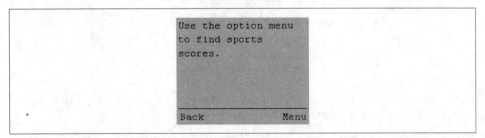

Figure 23-3. The initial sports scores menu

Pushing the button beneath "Menu" will bring up the <do/> option menu, enclosed in the <template/> element (see Figure 23-4). Selecting the "Football" option from the list will take us to the card labeled football (see Figure 23-5).

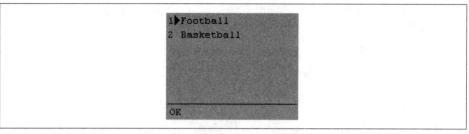

Figure 23-4. The do/ option menu

Figure 23-5. The "football" menu

A set of cards organized into a tree can collect many pages of data before sending a network request back to the web server, resulting in quicker WAP applications.

WML has other features intended to eliminate costly round-trips between mobile devices and WAP application servers. For example, WML has a `<select/>` element that is much more functional than its HTML cousin, with `<option/>` elements that may contain events to handle a given selection. For example:

```
<card id="products" title="Products">
  <p>
    <select title="Flavors">
      <option onpick="#vanilla">Vanilla</option>
      <option onpick="#chocolate">Chocolate</option>
    </select>
    <do type="accept" label="Go">
      <noop/>
    </do>
  </p>
</card>
```

In this example, selecting an option from the `<select>` menu loads a different card from the deck, without another trip to the server and back.

Variables are another part of the core WML specification, and use a familiar syntax:

```
<setvar name="phone" value="432-0911">
<p>
  Call me at $phone.
</p>
```

Variables can even be used within select lists to carry variables between cards, much the same way as the HTML `<input type="hidden">` tag is often used to make data persistent across requests.

```
<select title="products" name="product">
  <option value="Model B">Model </option>
  <option value="Model D">Model </option>
</select>
```

A subsequent card can then use the selected value, stored in $product:

```
Are you <b>sure</b> you want to buy a $(product) Steinway?<br/>
```

And finally, variables can be posted to a server using the WML `<go/>` elements with `<postfield/>` tags, placed inside an `<anchor/>` element in order to link responses of "Yes" or "No" to their appropriate locations:[*]

```
<anchor>
  Yes
  <go method="post" href="http://www.mypianostore.com/buy.cgi">
    <postfield name="product" value="$(product)"/>
  </go>
</anchor>
<anchor>
  <go href="#products"/>
  No
</anchor>
```

For a comprehensive look at WML, I recommend the new O'Reilly text *Learning WML & WMLScript* by Martin Frost. Wrox's *Professional WAP* contains more information on general mobile phone development (beyond WML), but is not as concise a read as the Frost book, probably due to the many-author model that Wrox seems to favor.

Developing WAP Applications

Typically, the purpose of a display markup language is to enhance the appearance of data, sometimes to a fault. This is true of WML. However, the simplicity of wireless displays demands that the formatting of display elements be basic and straightforward. For this reason, it is generally not too much work to develop an entire WAP site using a simple text editor. Introducing dynamic content into a document, however, presents many breeds of challenges. With HTML, creating dynamic content usually means adding one type of markup to another; for instance, adding Perl or PHP "programmatic markup" to the conventional display markup. An alternative solution is to print the HTML directly from a program either by embedding HTML within the program code, or by calling functions that create the interface themselves, much as CGI.pm's printing functions automate the creation of HTML. A third approach is a total separation of content (such as XML) from interface (such as HTML/CSS or XSL), with application data stored elsewhere.

---

[*] WML also supports some traditional HTML tags for ease of use. For example, `<a/>` tags may be used in place of `<anchor/>`.

I won't argue here for a particular model. As is the case with HTML, each has its own strengths for WML development. Because of the simplicity of WML, display code generally represents a smaller portion of the total application than with HTML development. On the other hand, WML's notion of cards moves much of the application logic to the interface, simplifying the server. In the case of using XML with XSL to generate WML, there are serious issues of complexity and overhead, especially considering the limited information being generated.* There are many such considerations to be made when choosing a design model for WAP applications. For the remainder of this article, I'll explore three styles of WML generation: using the CGI::WML module to automate the creation of WML, marking up WML with Perl using a web development kit like Mason, and embedding WML directly within Perl programs. I'll show examples of each.

CGI::WML

If you ever shied away from using CGI.pm's printing functions, you probably justified it because of the complexity of your HTML. No such excuse can be made when delivering WML. The CGI::WML module, by Angus Wood, subclasses Stein's CGI.pm to give users a familiar interface to WML programming. All of the input parameter processing functions remain, as well as new functions to help you create WML documents:

```
use CGI::WML;
$cgi = new CGI::WML;

print
$cgi->header( ),
$cgi->start_wml( ),
$cgi->template(-content=>$cgi->prev( )),
$cgi->card(-id=>"first_card",
        -title=>"First card",
        -content=>"<p><b>No one</b> when he has got <i>sufficient</i> ".
            "furniture for his house <b>dreams</b> of making further ".
            "purchases on this head, but of silver no one <i>ever</i> ".
            "yet possessed so much that he was forced to cry ".
            "\"enough.\"</p>"),
$cgi->end_wml( );
```

This example displays:

```
Content-Type: text/vnd.wap.wml; charset=ISO-8859-1
<?xml version="1.0" encoding="iso-8859-1"?> <!DOCTYPE wml PUBLIC "-//WAPFORUM//DTD
WML 1.1//EN"
"http://www.wapforum.org/DTD/wml_1.1.xml">
<wml>
```

---

* While I'm a big fan of XSLT, being able to transform a single data set to many types of interfaces does not necessarily address the core issue here. A WAP application will hopefully not differ from an HTTP application only in its presentation, but also in its design, flow, and function. WAP usability concerns require that applications go far beyond simply translating data for presentation.

```
<template>
  <do type="accept" label="Back">
    <prev/>
  </do>
</template>
<card id="first_card" title="First card" >
  <p><b>No one</b> when he has got <i>sufficient</i> furniture for
  his house <b>dreams</b> of making further purchases on this head,
  but of silver no one <i>ever</i> yet possessed so much that he was
  forced to cry "enough."</p>
</card>
</wml>
```

See Figure 23-6 to see how this is viewed within a browser window.

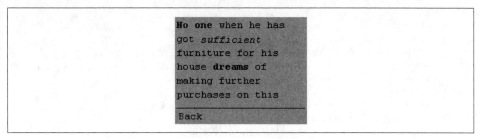

Figure 23-6. WML document

(For those interested, the text is from "On Revenues" by Xenophon. Good stuff. Emphasis mine.)

The CGI::WML module also has functions for automated HTML-to-WML conversion and WML-to-WMLC conversion. WMLC documents compress deck content for quicker delivery, a task usually performed by a WAP gateway. WMLC conversion is also useful for testing the size of a compiled WML deck, since most WAP browsers have a maximum compiled deck size around 2000 bytes. Using the `wml_to_wmlc()` function, you can continually check what size your deck will be after it has passed through the WAP gateway:

```
if (length($cgi->wml_to_wmlc($wml)) > 2000) {
    # do something
}
```

For the moment, CGI::WML lacks functions to automate the creation of many WML 1.1 elements, including option menus and variables. These will be added in a future version, according to Wood.

A Small File Browser with CGI::WML and mod_perl

To use CGI::WML within an application, we'll write a short file browser. Often, when an HTTP browser accesses a web server directory without an index file, Apache's mod_autoindex module generates a file list. WAP browsers can't display a listing unless the WAP gateway being used is translating HTML responses, which is unlikely. We'll write a very basic module to provide this capability.

To start, we need a way for our module to know whether to handle this request. In a production environment, we'd want to determine if the requesting browser was a WAP client, as well as look for any index files within that directory prior to handling the request. Look at the Apache::AutoIndex module for code to perform such tasks. For now, we're going to treat any incoming request that ends in *filelist.wml* as a directory request. Here's the module:

```
package Apache::WAP::AutoIndex;
use strict;
use CGI::WML;
use Apache::Constants qw(:common);

sub handler {
    my $r = shift;
    my $cgi = new CGI::WML;

    my $filename     = $r->filename;
    my $url_filename = $r->uri;
    $filename     =~ s/filelist\.wml$//;
    $url_filename =~ s/filelist\.wml$//;
    unless (opendir DH, $filename) { return FORBIDDEN; }

    my $content = "<p>Directory $url_filename:<br/>";
    my $filelink;
    foreach my $file ( readdir DH ){
        if (-d "$filename/$file")
            { $file .= "/"; $filelink = $file . "filelist.wml"; }
        else { $filelink = $file; }
        $content .= CGI::a({href => "$filelink"}, "$file");
    }
    $content .= "</p>";
    close DH;

    $r->print( $cgi->header(),
        $cgi->start_wml(),
        $cgi->template(-content=>$cgi->prev()),
        $cgi->card(-id=>"dirlist",
            -title=>"Directory $filename",
            -content=> $content),
        $cgi->end_wml() );
}
1;
```

To enable it, we need to add the following to *httpd.conf*:

```
PerlModule Apache::WAP::AutoIndex
<Location ~ "filelist\.wml$">
  SetHandler perl-script
  PerlHandler Apache::WAP::AutoIndex
</Location>
```

Figure 23-7 is the result when pointed at */wap/filelist.wml* on the site.

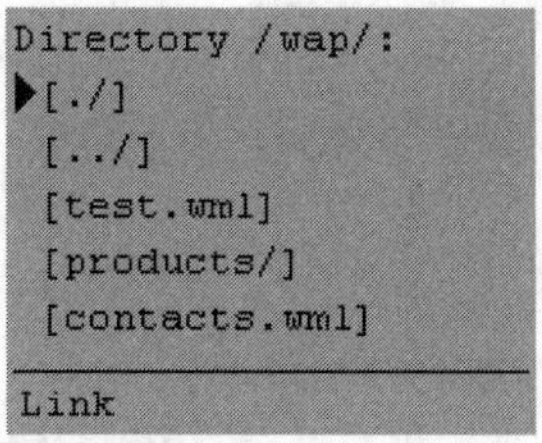

Figure 23-7. /wap/filelist.wml

Generating WML with HTML::Mason

Sometimes it is easier to work directly with the WML markup and surround with it program code. If you'd prefer to mark up WML code with Perl, Mason is a good choice.

Mason is a comprehensive site development and delivery engine in pure Perl. Running with mod_perl under Apache, it allows you to create dynamic and modular web sites easily. Incorporating programmatic features into web pages is as simple as importing a module and directly calling its functions from within that page, and component-based development means that you can reuse and consolidate information that appears within many pages (or decks, in our case).

For those who haven't used Mason, you can download and install it from CPAN using the standard perl Makefile.PL, make, make test, and make install commands. There are a few prerequisites, and you need to configure mod_perl to load the HTML::Mason modules. Consult the Mason documentation for help on this; it's quick and painless. Once installed and loaded, you simply tell Mason which directories or files to handle, and then write your pages. You embed Perl directly into your HTML, by placing it within some predefined Mason tags, such as a %perl block:

```
<%perl>
  use DBI;
  my $DSN = 'dbi:mysql:books';
  my $dbh = DBI->connect($DSN, "user", "pass", { RaiseError => 1 } )
        or die "Couldn't connect to database: $!\n";
</%perl>
```

Single lines of Perl can be placed into pages by prefixing them with a %:

```
% my $query = $dbh->prepare("select name,author from books");
% $query->execute;
```

Mason treats anything not beginning with % as HTML to be displayed. Mason's ability to understand blocks of Perl code, interspersed with HTML, makes this a powerful feature for program flow:

```
% # Print out all the books and authors
% while (my $dat = $query->fetchrow_hashref) {
    <% $dat->{name} %> by <% $dat->{author} %><br>
% }
```

If you let Mason handle your HTTP headers, it trusts Apache to print a header appropriate for the type of file (determined by the extension). More to the point, if Mason is handling all requests for a given directory by having this in your *httpd.conf* file:

```
<Location /mason>
    SetHandler perl-script
    PerlHandler HTML::Mason
</Location>
```

then you can simply save Mason files in this directory with a *.wml* extension, and they will be delivered with the proper MIME type. You can also test the user agent within a Mason file, and thereby deliver the MIME type and content appropriate for the browser. This is done using the Mason %init section, which makes an Apache request object available as the familiar $r:[*]

```
<%init>
  my $content_type;
  if ($r->header_in('Accept') =~ /text\/vnd\.wap\.wml/) {
      $content_type = "wml";
      $r->content_type('text/vnd.wap.wml');
  } else {
      $content_type = "html";
      $r->content_type('text/html');
  }
</%init>
```

Note what happens here: to determine the browser type, we're using the HTTP header HTTP_ACCEPT (seen by mod_perl as Accept), rather than the User Agent. (The only potential problem here: if future HTTP browsers support WML, they'll display the WML instead of the HTML.)

In the rest of the document, different content could be served for the two content types:

```
% if ($content_type eq "wml") {
    <card id="first_card" title="First card" >
        <p>The weather for today is cold and hard.</p>
    </card>
% } else {
    <p><font size=3>The weather for today is cold and hard.</font></p>
% }
```

A WML Phone Directory with Mason

The real benefits of placing program code markup within interface documents arises when the bulk of the content is dynamic. Assume we had an address book, and we wanted users to be able to browse it on WAP devices and directly call numbers in the address book. In the following example, the list of addresses is being generated from a MySQL database. We've stored the WML header information in a file, *header.wml*, which is loaded as a component using the <& &> syntax.

---

[*] If you aren't familiar with the Apache API as in mod_perl, consult O'Reilly's *Writing Apache Modules with Perl and C* by Stein and MacEachern for information that will change your development life and world view.

```
<%perl>
  use DBI;
  my $DSN = 'dbi:mysql:directory';
  my $dbh = DBI->connect($DSN,"user","pass", { RaiseError => 1 } )
        or die "Couldn't connect to database: $!\n";
  my $query = $dbh->prepare("select name,phone from addresses");
  $query->execute;
</%perl>

<& header.wml &>
<wml>
  <card id="phonelist">
    <p>Place a call to:
    <do type="accept">
      <go href="wtai://vc/sc;$number;1" />
    </do>
    <select name="number">

% while (my $dat = $query->fetchrow_hashref) {
        <option value="<% $dat->{phone} %>"><% $date->{name} %></option>
% }

    </select>
    </p>
  </card>
</wml>
```

The href tag here makes use of the WTAI standard WAP libraries, which contain functions for interacting with the phone itself. This example accesses the vc (Voice Call Control) library to dial the number stored in variable $number. The resulting display appears as shown in Figure 23-8, and selecting a name from the list causes the phone to dial that number.

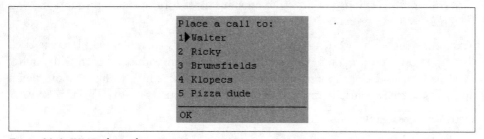

Figure 23-8. WMP phone directory

Of course, this could easily be extended to include more information from the address book, placing different types of information in different cards.

WML with Straight Perl

When working with a markup language as simple as WML, there's something to be said for developing an application entirely in plain Perl, and embedding the WML tags directly into your program. While that may sound like a regression to the hardcoded

CGIs of our youth, the simplicity of WML actually makes such interfaces easy to update and manage. Speaking of hardcoded CGIs, remember how useful that `printenv` or `env.cgi` script was? It's just as useful for debugging environments for WAP applications. Here it is in straight Perl with WML output:

```perl
#!/usr/bin/perl
$output = <<EOF; Content-type: text/vnd.wap.wml
<?xml version="1.0" encoding="iso-8859-1"?>
<!DOCTYPE wml PUBLIC "-//WAPFORUM//DTD WML 1.1//EN"
                "http://www.wapforum.org/DTD/wml_1.1.xml">
<wml><card id="env"><p>
EOF
foreach $var (sort(keys(%ENV))) {
$val = $ENV{$var};
$val =~ s|\n|\\n|g;
$val =~ s|"|\\"|g;
$val =~ s|<|\<|g;
$val =~ s|>|\>|g;
$output .= "${var}=\"${val}\"<br/>\n";
}
$output .= "</p></card></wml>";
print $output;
```

A Remote Control for Home Automation

Accessing information is only one use for wireless browsers. Wouldn't it be great if you could also use your phone to perform tasks? An interface to the Perl home automation package Control::X10 makes that possible.

Our application will have the user choose a house location and an appliance, and then be prompted to turn it on or off. The deck will consist of eight cards; the last card (turn on/off) will use values from previous cards for the action prompt, and will then post to the web server.

Translating this to a WML expression is trivial. In this example, we place the deck directly in our Perl program. This excerpt could be run within a Perl module under mod_perl, or as a CGI script (gasp!). In our example, it's running within a module, with an Apache directive causing this module to handle all requests to /mister on the server.

First, we'll create our main card (see Figure 23-9).

```perl
my $main_card = <<EOF;
    <card id="main" title="Main">
      <p>
        Select an area:
        <select title="Areas">
            <option onpick="#outside">Outside</option>
            <option onpick="#living">Living Room</option>
            <option onpick="#kitchen">Kitchen</option>
        </select>
      </p>
      <do type="accept" label="Back">
```

```
            <prev/>
        </do>
        <do type="accept" label="Go">
            <noop/>
        </do>
    </card>
EOF
```

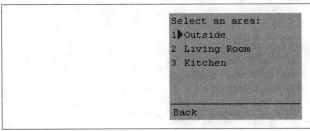

Figure 23-9. Home automation card

Next, the "outside" card (see Figure 23-10):

```
my $outside_card = <<EOF;
    <card id="outside" title="Outside">
      <p>
        Select an appliance:
        <select name="appliance" title="Outside">
            <option value="flood light">Flood light</option>
            <option value="christmas lights">Christmas lights</option>
        </select>
      </p>
      <do type="accept" label="Back">
          <prev/>
      </do>
      <do type="accept" label="Go">
          <go href="#toggle"/>
      </do>
    </card>
EOF
```

Figure 23-10. Outdoor lighting card

We'll skip the cards for "Living Room" and "Kitchen," and go directly to the last card of the deck (Figure 23-11).

```
my $toggle_card = <<EOF;
    <card id="toggle" title="Toggle appliance">
        <p>
            Turn on/off the \$(appliance)?<br/>
            <a href="/mister?toggle=\$(appliance:e)">Yes</a>
        </p>
        <do type="accept" label="Back">
            <prev/>
        </do>
    </card>
EOF
```

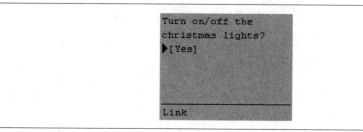

Figure 23-11. Christmas light control

The $(appliance:e) syntax above causes the value of $appliance to be escaped for inclusion on the URL line. Keep in mind that this entire deck will be sent to the client at once. The server will not hear back from the client until the user gets to the last card and selects the "Yes" href link, which will repost to the same program. Assuming that we are running this code as a mod_perl module, here's the rest of the program.

```
package MisterHouseWAP;
use Apache::Constants qw(:common);
use CGI::WML;
require 'start_port.pl';
use ControlX10::CM17;

our %appliances = ('christmas lights' => 'A1J',
                   'flood light'      => 'A4J');
sub handler {
  my $r      = shift;
  my @msgnos = ();
  my %params = $r->method eq 'POST' ? $r->content : $r->args;

  if ($params{'toggle'}) {
      toggle($params{'toggle'});
  }

  my $deck = CGI::WML::header() . "<wml>\n" . $main_card .
          $outside_card . $toggle_card . "</wml>";

  $r->send_http_header('text/vnd.wap.wml');
  $r->print($deck);
}
```

```
sub toggle {
  # pseudo-sending code; see the X10 modules for real examples
  my $serial = open_port('COM1');
  send_cm17($serial, $appliances{$_[0]});
  $serial->close;
}
1;
```

Creating a Personal Portal

Finally, we come to my personal motivation for this article. The difficulty of navigating information on commercial portals prompted me to create my own. It's really quite simple, consisting of eight cards, and using CPAN modules to interface with stock quotes (Finance::Quote), news, new mail summaries (Mail::Cclient), and DBM files for everything else. Everything is delivered in a single deck, so I can connect with my phone, download the deck, disconnect, and be able to browse the updates offline.

The following example allows a user to browse unread mail messages by first prompting for a username and password, and then using the Mail::Cclient module by Malcolm Beattie to fetch the unread messages from an IMAP server.

First, the login screen, which we'll call *login.wml*:

```
<?xml version="1.0"?> <!DOCTYPE wml PUBLIC
"-//WAPFORUM//DTD WML 1.1//EN"
"http://www.wapforum.org/DTD/wml_1.1.xml">
<wml>
<card title="Login">
    <!-- Reset fields when entered backwards. -->
    <onevent type="onenterbackward">
        <refresh>
            <setvar name="username" value=""/>
            <setvar name="password" value=""/>
        </refresh>
    </onevent>

    <!-- Read login and password from user. -->
    <p>Username: <input name="username"/></p>
    <p>Password: <input type="password" name="password"/></p>

    <!-- Submit button sends data to server. -->
    <do type="accept" label="Submit">
        <go href="/wmlmail/" method="post">
            <postfield name="username" value="$(username)"/>
            <postfield name="password" value="$(password)"/>
        </go>
    </do>
</card>
</wml>
```

This will prompt for a username and password as shown in Figure 23-12 and Figure 23-13.

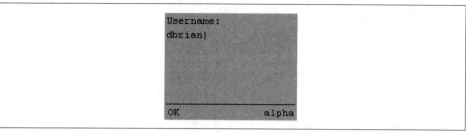

Figure 23-12. Username prompt

Figure 23-13. Password prompt

The module that handles the post from the above deck is also handling all requests to /wmlmail/ using a Location directive in *httpd.conf*. If the login is successful, the user gets a list of unread mail messages with the sender and the subject. (See Figure 23-14.)

```
package Apache::WAP::MailPeek;
use strict;
use Apache::Constants qw(:common);
use Mail::Cclient;

our $mail_server = 'brians.org';
Mail::Cclient::parameters(
'NIL',
RSHTIMEOUT     => 0,
OPENTIMEOUT    => 1,
READTIMEOUT    => 1,
CLOSETIMEOUT   => 1,
MAXLOGINTRIALS => 1,
);
sub handler {
my $r     = shift;
my @msgnos = ( );
my %params = $r->method eq 'POST' ? $r->content : $r->args;

Mail::Cclient::set_callback
      login     => sub {
          return $params{'username'}, $params{'password'}
      },
      searched => sub {
```

```
            push (@msgnos, $_[1]);
    },
    log        => sub { print @_ }, dlog => sub { print @_};

my $mail = Mail::Cclient->new("{$mail_server/imap}") or die $!;

$r->content_type('text/vnd.wap.wml');
$r->send_http_header;

$r->print(<<END);
  <?xml version="1.0" encoding="iso-8859-1"?>
    <!DOCTYPE wml PUBLIC "-//WAPFORUM//DTD WML 1.1//EN"
                  "http://www.wapforum.org/DTD/wml_1.1.xml">
  <wml><card id="mail">
END
  $mail->search("UNSEEN");
  foreach my $msgno (@msgnos) {
      my ($envelope,$body) = $mail->fetchstructure($msgno);
      my $subject = $envelope->subject;
      my $from    = ${$envelope->{from}}[0]->{personal} ||
              ${$envelope->{from}}[0]->{mailbox} . "@" .
              ${$envelope->{from}}[0]->{host};
      $from =~ s/\&/\&amp\;/g; $subject =~ s/\&/\&amp\;/g;
      $from =~ s/\$/\$\$/g; $subject =~ s/\$/\$\$/g;
      $r->print ("<p><b>", $from, "</b>: ", $subject, "</p>\n");
  }
  $mail->close;
  $r->print("</card></wml>");
} 1;
```

Figure 23-14. Unread email messages

In time, I'll abstract the entire portal enough to get it on CPAN. But as you can see, creation of such a system is quite straightforward, thanks to the compact nature of WML and the ease of developing applications in Perl.

PART II

Graphics

In this section, nine articles will demonstrate some of the ways that Perl can be used for graphics programming. By "graphics programming," I don't mean graphical *applications* like those you'd create with Perl/Tk, but rather the creation and manipulation of raw pictures: graphs, logos, art, scenes, and video.

We begin with two articles about graphs: Lincoln Stein's article demonstrating how to glue the Gnuplot graphing program into a CGI program (*Web Plots with Gnuplot*), and Jeremy Wadsack's article (*GD-Graph3d*) showing how to create three-dimensional graphs from your Perl programs using the gd library. Jason Reed follows with an article about how you can use that library to evolve your own images of plants in *GD and L-Systems*.

Two articles about three-dimensional graphics follow: Alligator Descartes's *OpenGL* introduces the OpenGL library and its use from Perl, and Mark Jason Dominus explains a popular rendering technique in *Ray Tracing*.

The Gimp is a popular image manipulation program similar to Adobe Photoshop, but free. You can create plug-ins for it that enable you to control Gimp from Perl. Aaron Sherman's article, *Perl and the Gimp*, shows you how.

Next, Ace Thompson writes about the Perl interface to Glade in *Glade*. Glade is a graphical interface designer for GTK, a GUI library used by Gnome, one of the two popular graphical user environments on Linux (the other is KDE). Joe Nasal follows with *Gnome Panel Applets*, which shows you how to create applications that reside on the Gnome panel visible on your desktop.

Finally, Marc Lehmann concludes the section with one of the more bizarre articles ever to appear in TPJ. Marc uses Perl, PDL, the venerable Kermit protocol, an HP-48 calculator, and information extracted from the vertical blanking interval (the horizontal stripe you see when your television is out of sync) to create a Frankenstein system that records television programs appearing at hard-to-predict intervals—kind of a Perl TiVo. His article demonstrates how to frame-grab television in *Capturing Video in Real Time*.

## CHAPTER 24

Web Plots with Gnuplot

Lincoln D. Stein

With all the excitement over the things that we can make Perl do, we sometimes lose sight of the fact that Perl's greatest strength is the ease with which you can use it to glue independent programs together into a single powerful application. This toolkit philosophy, in which large applications are built from many small command-line tools, is the great simplifying principle of the Unix operating system, and one that Perl readily takes advantage of.

This column addresses a case in point. Say you're interested in seeing the hourly breakdown of accesses to your web site in order to do capacity planning. When does traffic peak and when is it at a minimum? Say that you want to be able to view this data graphically as a bar chart and that you'd like the chart to be generated on the fly from a CGI script. How would you go about doing this?

One approach would be to do all the work in Perl. Running as a CGI script, Perl can parse the server's access log file, tally up the hourly hits, generate the bar chart using the graphics primitives in the GD or Image::Magick modules, and output the plot as a GIF image. The script would be responsible for drawing the plot axes, calculating the width and position of the bars, creating the X and Y tics, and drawing the labels. Although the job is relatively straightforward, the program would likely take at least half a day to write and debug and would certainly be several pages of code by the time you were finished.

But why reinvent the wheel? There are many plotting packages available for Unix and Windows systems, and most of these can be called as subprocesses from within Perl. One of the more ubiquitous plotting packages is Gnuplot, an open source package that comes preinstalled on many Linux systems, and is available as source and precompiled binaries for a variety of Unix and Microsoft Windows architectures. By taking advantage of this existing tool, we can write this CGI script in just a few minutes. The complete application comes to just 46 lines of code.

Using Gnuplot

Before we dive into the log-processing application itself, let's look at a simple use of Gnuplot from within Perl. Gnuplot was designed to draw complex mathematical functions and plot scientific data. It can be run interactively under the X Windows and Microsoft Windows systems, in which case plots are displayed in a graphics window, or run in batch mode from the command line, in which case the output graphics are written to standard output or a file. Gnuplot is able to generate a large variety of graphics file formats, including GIF and Postscript.

Gnuplot has a command language that can be used to control the graphs it generates. In interactive mode, you can type in commands and watch them take effect immediately. In batch mode, you feed Gnuplot commands from a file or standard input.

Let's look at an example. From the Gnuplot command line, here's how to graph the equation $y = \sin(x)/\cos(x)$:

```
gnuplot> plot sin(x)/cos(x)
```

In a fraction of a second, Gnuplot displays the graph shown in Figure 24-1.

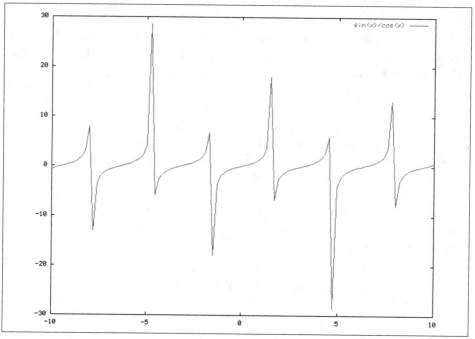

Figure 24-1. Gnuplot output

It's almost as easy to call Gnuplot as a subprocess from within Perl. Just open up a pipe to Gnuplot, and send it the commands. For example, here's a 6-line program to plot $\sin(x)/\cos(x)$ from within Perl and output the result in GIF format:

```
0 #!/usr/bin/perl

1 use strict;
2 use constant GNUPLOT => '/usr/local/bin/gnuplot';
3 open (GP,'|'.GNUPLOT) || die "Gnuplot: $!";
4 print GP "set terminal gif\n";
5 print GP "plot sin(x)/cos(x)\n";
6 close GP;
```

The script begins by defining a GNUPLOT constant indicating the path to the Gnuplot executable. It then opens up a pipe to Gnuplot by calling Perl's open function with a pipe symbol as the first character in the command's name. The program next sends two commands to Gnuplot. The first (line 4) changes the default terminal type to gif, telling Gnuplot to output the graph as a GIF format image. Next, the script sends the plot command as before. The pipe is now closed and the program exits.

Note that you'll need Gnuplot Version 3.7 or higher to get GIF support, plus Tom Boutell's libgd graphics library.

Gnuplot can graph experimental data as well as equations. The simplest format it accepts consists of a two-column table indicating the X and Y values of a data series. Comment lines beginning with the # symbol are ignored. As an example, here's a data table containing one day's worth of hourly tallies on my laboratory web site. The first column is the hour (using the 24-hour clock), and the second column is the total number of hits:

#hour	hits
00	309
01	408
02	427
03	353
04	342
05	450
06	326
07	332
08	385
09	527
10	751
11	849
12	657
13	566 ...

Plotting this data as a bar chart is a matter of setting the chart type by providing the set data style command with boxes, and then issuing the plot command with the data file name as its argument:

```
gnuplot> set data style boxes
gnuplot> plot 'hours.dat'
```

By fussing with various set commands, you can adjust many aspects of Gnuplot's display, including the graph and axis labels, the position of the key, the positioning and frequency of tics, and so forth. However, Gnuplot is oriented towards scientific rather than business applications, so the number of plot types is limited. For example, pie charts aren't supported.

What if you want the data table to be computed dynamically by an external program? Gnuplot provides the equivalent of Perl's open pipe syntax. By prepending the < symbol to the filename passed to the plot command, Gnuplot treats the filename as a command to execute. For example, if we had a Perl script named tally_log.pl whose job was to parse a web access log and produce a tabular list similar to the columns above, we could plot its output dynamically with this command:

```
gnuplot> plot '< tally_log.pl ~www/logs/access_log'
```

Parsing Log Files

Running Gnuplot is half of our CGI script. The other half is the part that parses the web server's log file. Table 24-1 shows the fields in the "common" web access log file format.

Table 24-1. Fields in the "common" web access log file format.

Field name	Description
Remote host	DNS name or IP address of the remote host.
RFC931	Login name of the remote user, determined using the RFC1413 protocol. This protocol relies on a correctly configured and running identd daemon on the remote user's side. Since most systems don't run this daemon, this field is usually blank (a hyphen).
Username	If the requested document was password protected, this field contains the username the remote user provided for authentication. Otherwise the field contains a hyphen.
Date	The date of the request, in local time.
Request	The text of the HTTP request, usually GET, POST, or HEAD followed by the requested URL.
Status	The status code that the server responded to the request with, usually 200 for OK.
Response size	The total number of bytes transferred from server to browser.

The standard or common log file format used by most web servers was established years ago by the NCSA *httpd* and CERN servers. Each line of the access log records a single hit on your site and is subdivided into the seven fields described in Table 24-1. A typical entry looks like this one:

```
phage.cshl.org - - [07/May/1999:01:17:19 -0400] "GET / HTTP/1.0" 200 6118
```

To parse the various fields from within Perl, just match each line against the following regular expression:

```
$REGEX = /^(\S+) (\S+) (\S+) \[([^]]+)\] "(\w+) (\S+).*" (\d+) (\S+)/;
while (<>) {
    ($host,$rfc931,$user,$date,$request,$URL,$status,$size) = m/$REGEX/o;
}
```

You can then tally or otherwise manipulate the fields in any way you choose.

Putting It All Together

The tally_hourly.pl script parses the web server's access log, tallies the hourly hits, and passes the result to Gnuplot. It's intended to be called from an inline <img> tag:

```
<img src="/cgi-bin/tally_hourly.pl?file=access_log.1">
```

The script expects a single CGI parameter named file, which tells the script what access log file to open and parse. On my web site, log files are rotated once a day, *access_log* becoming *access_log.1*, *access_log.1* becoming *access_log.2*, and so forth. So *access_log.1* always holds the complete record of yesterday's activities. You can put multiple days' graphs on the same page just by repeating the <img> tag with different file parameters.

A page created by tally_hourly.pl is shown in Figure 24-2. For the day plotted, accesses peaked at 11:00 in the morning, and then peaked again at about 5:00 in the afternoon. This pattern is typical of scientific sites that are most heavily accessed during the work day. Recreational sites are more heavily used in the evenings.

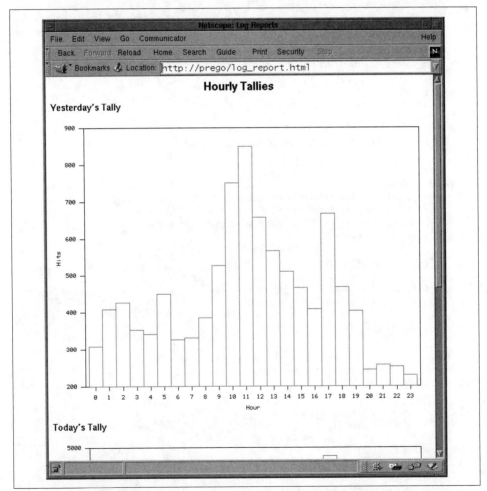

Figure 24-2. tally_hourly.pl is actually two programs: a CGI script that calls Gnuplot, and a log file parser that is called by Gnuplot

Example 24-1 shows the code for tally_hourly.pl. The main trick used here is that the script is actually two programs which execute independently of one another (see Figure 24-3). The first program is a CGI script that processes the CGI file parameter and invokes Gnuplot. The second program is the log file parser. It is invoked *by* Gnuplot when Gnuplot runs its plot command. The script determines which context it's running in by looking at the @ARGV array. If @ARGV is not set, then the script is running in the CGI context. Otherwise, it's been invoked by Gnuplot in order to process the log file given by the first @ARGV argument.

Example 24-1. tally_hourly.pl collates log file entries and displays them as a bar chart

```
0    #!/usr/bin/perl -T

1    use strict;
2    use CGI qw(param header -no_debug);
3    use CGI::Carp qw(fatalsToBrowser);
4    $ENV{'PATH'} = '/bin:/usr/bin';

5    use constant GNUPLOT  => '/usr/local/bin/gnuplot';
6    use constant LOGFILES => '/home/www/logs';
7    $| = 1;

8    # If REQUEST_METHOD is set, then we're a CGI script,
9    # so we get the logfile name with param() and generate
10   # the GIF image.
11   unless (@ARGV) {
12       my $logfile = param('file');
13       die "Bad log file name: $logfile\n"
14         unless $logfile =~ /^([a-zA-Z][\w.-]*)$/;
15       $logfile = LOGFILES . "/$1";
16       die "Can't open log file $logfile\n" unless -r $logfile;
17       generate_gif($logfile);
18   }
19   # Otherwise we're running as a regular program, and we
20   # parse the log file for use by GNUPLOT
21   else {
22       generate_data();
23   }

24   # Make the GIF image (as a CGI script)
25   sub generate_gif {
26       my $logfile = shift;
27       print header('image/gif');
28       open (GP, "|".GNUPLOT) || die "Couldn't open GNUPLOT: $!";

29       while (<DATA>) {
30           print GP $_;
31       }
32       print GP "plot '< $0 $logfile'";
33       close GP;
34   }
```

Example 24-1. tally_hourly.pl collates log file entries and displays them as a bar chart (continued)

```
35   # Generate the data for use by GNUPLOT
36   sub generate_data {
37       my %HITS;
38       while (<>) {
39           next unless m!\[\d+/\w+/\d{4}:(\d+):\d+:\d+ [\d+-]+\]!;
40           my $hour = $1;
41           $HITS{$hour}++;
42       }
43       foreach (sort {$a<=>$b} keys %HITS) {
44           print join("\t", $_, $HITS{$_}), "\n";
45       }
46   }


__DATA__
set terminal gif small size 640,480 interlace
set border
set boxwidth
set nogrid
set nokey
set nolabel
set data style boxes
set noxzeroaxis
set noyzeroaxis
set tics out
set xtics nomirror 0,1,23
set ytics nomirror
set xlabel "Hour" 0,0
set xrange [ -0.75 : 23.75]
set ylabel "Hits" 0,0
```

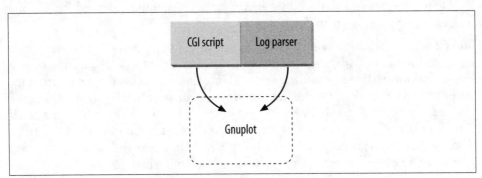

Figure 24-3. A bar chart produced by tally_hourly.pl

Turning to the listing, the script begins by activating Perl's taint check features with the -T switch. This is particularly important to do in this script, because it will be shelling out to a subprocess using untrusted user-provided data (the value of the file parameter). The script then turns on strict syntax checking and imports various functions from the CGI and CGI::Carp libraries. Among the functions imported from CGI is the -no_debug pragma, which disables CGI.pm's command-line debugging features. This is important to do; otherwise, CGI.pm might enter command-line debugging mode when it was invoked by Gnuplot. We bring in the `fatalsToBrowser` function from CGI::Carp, which automatically redirects fatal errors to the browser, helping track down any script failures.

Line 4 hard-codes the `PATH` environment variable. This is necessary in order for the script to pass Perl's taint checks.

Lines 5–6 define file paths for Gnuplot and the directory that contains the server's log files. These constants will need to be adjusted for your system. Line 7 puts standard output into unbuffered (autoflush) mode. This is necessary when calling out to subprocesses to ensure that the output produced by the script and the subprocess appear in the order you intend rather than the order determined by incompatible I/O buffering schemes.

Line 11 examines the `@ARGV` array. If it is not set, then the script is running in the CGI environment. Otherwise, the script is running under Gnuplot. In the former case, the script recovers the log file name from the `file` parameter, untaints it using a pattern match, and prepends the log directory path to the untainted file name. The pattern match is set up to match any file name beginning with an alphabetic character and followed by zero or more alphanumeric characters, the hyphen, or the dot. This specifically excludes filenames containing shell metacharacters such as `>` and relative path names such as `..` to indicate the parent directory. The script tests that the file exists and is readable. If so, it calls a function named `generate_gif` to create the bar chart (line 17).

If there is a command-line argument in the `@ARGV` array, then the script knows it has been invoked by Gnuplot. The command-line argument contains the full path to the log file to process. The script calls `generate_data` to tally the indicated log file and produce the tabular summary for Gnuplot's use (line 22).

Lines 24–34 contain the definition of `generate_gif`. It emits an HTTP header with a content type field of `image/gif`. It then opens up a pipe to Gnuplot and sends it graphing commands. Most of the commands are constant boilerplate read from the script's `__DATA__` section. I arrived at this set of commands by playing with Gnuplot interactively until the graph looked the way I wanted it. Then the subroutine sends Gnuplot the `plot` command, telling it to run a pipe constructed from the `$0` variable, which holds the name of the currently running script and the value of the `file` parameter. The plot command ends up looking something like this:

```
plot '< /www/cgi-bin/tally_hourly.pl/www/logs/access_log.1'
```

The subroutine closes the Gnuplot pipe and exits. Gnuplot sends its output to standard output, which then forwarded to the waiting browser.

Lines 35–46 define `generate_data`, which is called on to process the log file and produce a summary in Gnuplot data format. It reads through the log file line by line using the `<>` operator and parses out the hour component of the request time. In this case, we don't need any of the other fields, so the more general regular expression that we looked at previously isn't needed. The parsed hour is added to a hash named %HITS, which keeps track of how many hits we've seen in each interval. When the subroutine reaches the end of the log file, it sorts the keys of %HITS numerically and prints out a two column table in Gnuplot format.

Simple Things Made Easy

The tally_hourly.pl script is another example of how Perl makes simple things easy and hard things possible. By using a preexisting tool rather than rolling our own, a script that might have been a bear to write became almost trivial.

With a little more work, you could adapt this script for other sorts of log processing tasks, such as plotting hits by day of the week, summing over domain names, or tallying up the bandwidth used by the web server. By replacing Gnuplot with a charting package oriented towards business graphics, you can produce pie charts, stacked column charts, and other displays with little additional effort.

## CHAPTER 25

GD-Graph3d

Jeremy Wadsack

When it comes to understanding large amounts of data, we humans have two stages of interpretation. First, we analyze the data, organizing it in myriad ways to find the hidden relationships, quantities, and trends that deliver meaning to our world. Second, we present it somehow, often by displaying it visually. With graphs and charts we can visualize trends, understand relationships, and compare quantities at a glance.

I developed the Perl package GD-Graph3d to accompany some statistics presentation tools I work on for analyzing the huge amounts of data available to and generated by web servers. Our freely available Report Magic presentation package uses GD-Graph3d to present analyses in a friendly manner with graphs like Figure 25-1.

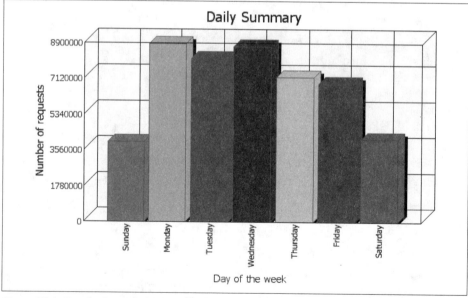

Figure 25-1. Sample GD-Graph3d output.

GD-Graph3d is an extension to Martien Verbruggen's GDGraph package. GDGraph draws only two-dimensional images (except for the 3d option on pie charts) but provides the basis for data management, labeling, legends, and other routine graph operations that are common to both packages.

Using GD-Graph3d

In order to use GD-Graph3d, you will need to install several packages: at a minimum, the GDGraph, GD-TextUtil, and GD Perl modules, and the libgd library. Fortunately for Windows and Mac users, GD and the libgd library are included in ActivePerl and MacPerl. If you have ActivePerl, you can use the PPM or VPM tool to acquire the latest version of GD. With PPM you can simply use this command:

```
> ppm install GD
```

On Unix (and Unix-like) systems, the installation is a lot more complex. libgd itself is a C library that depends on the libpng and zlib libraries. If you want TrueType font support (recommended if you're using a character set other than Latin-1), you'll need FreeType's libfreetype. In order to build GD on top of libgd, you will also need to install the jpeg-6b library. Complete details for installing this are listed on the libgd web site (*http://www.boutell.com/gd/*); a summary is available at the end of this article.

Installing GDGraph and GD-Graph3d is simple. They're on CPAN and can be found with the CPAN search engine at *http://search.cpan.org*. Install the GDTextUtil package, which you can find there as well. Once you have the proper modules and libraries installed, write some code and make some pictures. Example 25-1 contains a simple script to generate the graph in Figure 25-2. We'll go through the script line by line.

Example 25-1. A sample GDGraph3D program

```
#!/usr/bin/perl -w
##########################################################
#
# Description:
# Draws a basic multi-set line chart with GD-Graph3d
#
# Created: 31.May.2000 by Jeremy Wadsack for Wadsack-Allen Digital Group
# Copyright (C) 2000 Wadsack-Allen. All rights reserved.
#
# This script is free software; you can redistribute it and/or
# modify it under the same terms as Perl itself.
##########################################################
use strict;

# **** Line numbering in the article starts here ****
use GD::Graph::lines3d;

# Create an array of data
my @data = (
  [ "Jan", "Feb", "Mar", "Apr", "May", "Jun", "Jul", "Aug", "Sep", "Oct", "Nov", "Dec"],
  [  860,   813,   1694,  957,   1805,  1835,  2335,  1272,  1562,  2296,  2123,  1882,],
```

Example 25-1. A sample GDGraph3D program (continued)

```
[  1249,  483,   1731,  1617,  1166,  1761,  1111,  1635,  2158,  2007,  2250,  2858,],
[  747,   1216,  525,   1028,  1053,  1860,  2282,  1871,  2143,  1845,  2924, 2858,],
[  1220,  864,   1325,  967,   1200,  1371,  1759,  1512,  1484,  1683,  1965,  2458,],
[  1276,  639,   931,   1288,  2049,  909,   1617,  1432,  1615,  2605,  2712,  2429,],
);

# Make a new graph object that is 600 pixels wide by 400 pixels high
my $graph = new GD::Graph::lines3d( 600, 400 );

# Set some labels
$graph->set(
            x_label => 'Month, 1999',
            y_label => 'Revenue ($US)',
             title => 'Monthly revenue for 1999',
);

# Plot the graph to a GD object
my $gd = $graph->plot( \@data );

# Figure out what the default output format is
my $format = $graph->export_format;

# Now open a file locally and write it
open(IMG, ">sample.$format") or die $!;
binmode IMG;
print IMG $gd->$format();
close IMG;
```

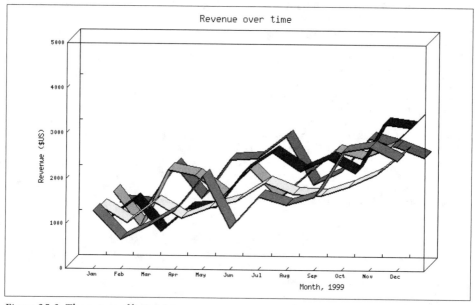

Figure 25-2. The output of listing 1

The first line tells Perl which graph module you want to use. With both GDGraph and GD-Graph3d, you use the type of graph you wish to make. So in this instance, because we are making a line graph, we use GD::Graph::lines3d.

The next set of lines creates a data structure containing the data to be graphed. GD-Graph3d uses an array of an array of values. The first row holds the labels for the x-axis, and the subsequent rows are the data for each line of the graph. In this example, we've coded the values by hand, but in a real application, you'd get these from a database, an external file, or some other source. Check out the GD::Graph::Data class for methods that make it easy to read data from delimited text files and DBI sources.

On line 14, we create a new graph lines3d object. GD-Graph3d objects cannot be reused—you create a new one for each set of data you wish to plot. Lines 17 to 21 set several self-explanatory options for the graph. GD-Graph3d supports all the options that GDGraph does (and there are many), as well as a few options specifically for three-dimensional output (such as the z-directional depth of the lines). We go into more detail later about using options to improve the look of the graph. Line 24 tells GD-Graph3d to plot the data to an image. The plot method returns a reference to a GD image object. If you wish, you can further process this image with additional GD methods.

Because the GD library can output in different formats (GIF, PNG, JPEG, and so on) GD-Graph3d offers the export_format method to return the default format. For new installations, this call will return png. If you happen to have an old version of GD and libgd on your system, this returns the patent-infringing gif.

Now, using the format that GD-Graph3d found for us, we can write the contents of the image to a file on the system: in our example, either sample.png or sample.gif. The binmode call is included for systems that make a distinction between binary and text files (like Windows). On other systems, this has no effect.

GDGraph and GD-Graph3d allow you to adjust the graph in many ways. We start by setting some colors. GD-Graph3d has 29 predefined colors (white, lgray, gray, dgray, black, lblue, blue, dblue, gold, lyellow, yellow, dyellow, lgreen, green, dgreen, lred, red, dred, lpurple, purple, dpurple, lorange, orange, pink, dpink, marine, cyan, lbrown, and dbrown) or can accept any RGB color defined with HTML syntax. To set the colors, add some key/value pairs to the $graph->set statement so it looks like this:

```
# Set some labels
$graph->set(
      x_label  => 'Month, 1999',
      y_label  => 'Revenue ($US)',
        title  => 'Monthly revenue for 1999',
         dclrs => ['#9999CC', '#CCCC66', '#339900', '#990000', '#FFCC33'],
        boxclr => '#FFFFCC',
    long_ticks => 1,
);
```

dclrs sets a list of colors to use for each data set, boxclr sets the color to use in the background of the plot, and setting long_ticks to a true value tells GD-Graph3d to draw a grid on the background (connecting all the ticks). See Figure 25-3 for the results.

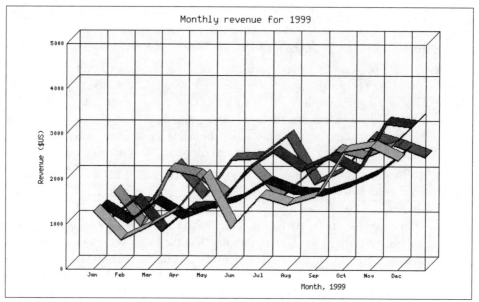

Figure 25-3. Choosing colors.

Now let's work on the fonts. GD-Graph3d uses GD's font mechanisms (through GD::Text). This means, that by default, you can choose one of five predefined fonts, defined in the GD::Font class (GD::Font->Small, GD::Font->Large, GD::Font-> MediumBold, GD::Font->Tiny, or GD::Font->Giant). If you built libgd with TrueType support (ActiveState's build includes this on Win32), then you can also use True-Type fonts (if you give the full pathname to the font). For this example, we'll use built-in fonts and insert these three lines after the $graph->set call to specify the fonts to use for the title above the graph and the labels on each axis:

```
$graph->set_title_font  ( GD::Font->Giant );
$graph->set_x_label_font( GD::Font->MediumBold );
$graph->set_y_label_font( GD::Font->MediumBold );
```

We'd also like to add a legend to the graph so that the people who see it know what each line refers to. First, we add these key/value pairs to the $graph->set statement:

```
legend_placement  => 'RC',
legend_spacing    => 10,
```

(RC means Right Center.) We also add these two new statements later to create the legend, by defining the labels associated with each data set and setting the font for the legend text.

```
# Define a legend
$graph->set_legend( 'Affiliate A', 'Affiliate B', 'Affiliate C',
                    'Affiliate D', 'Affiliate E' );
$graph->set_legend_font( GD::Font->MediumBold );
```

The result is shown in Figure 25-4.

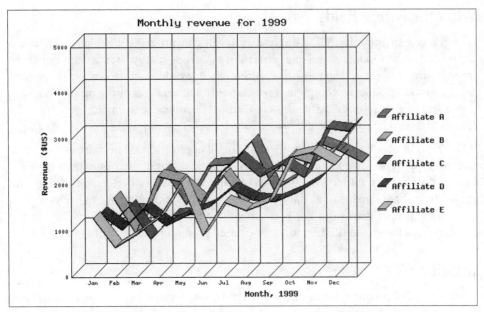

Figure 25-4. Specifying fonts and adding a legend

There's a lot more you can do with GD-Graph3d. For example, you could format the y-axis labels to include the "$" sign, or you could adjust the maximum y-value by hand to better fit the data, as shown in Figure 25-5. Read the documentation in GDGraph and GD-Graph3d for details on the options and settings available.

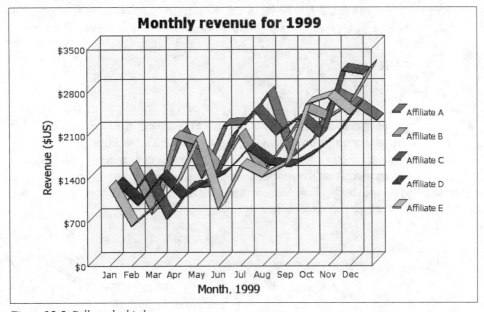

Figure 25-5. Bells and whistles

What the Future Holds

Like many Perl modules, GD-Graph3d is a work in progress. I'd like to include a drop-shadow option for the pie charts. The drop-shadow rendering could be improved to look more shadow-like, although it would slow down graph generation. I would also like to complete three-dimensional versions of the point, area, and point-and-line graphs available in GDGraph. Finally, the ultimate goal of GD-Graph3d would be to handle the projections for any viewing angle.

GD-Graph3d isn't meant to meet the needs of all applications. There are now a number of graphing modules available for Perl, mainly differentiated by which graphics library they require under the hood. GD-Graph3d also does not provide for graphing of true three-dimensional data—it merely graphs two-dimensional data with a three-dimensional extrusion. For real three-dimensional rendering, users should use the Perl Data Language (PDL) and its associated graphing and rendering modules.

Installing GD

To install GD on your system, you'll need to install some system libraries first. Here is a step-by-step guide to retrieving and installing them. Again, none of this is necessary if you're using Perl on Windows or a Mac.

zlib

> The zlib compression library can be obtained from one of the mirrors listed at *http://www.info-zip.org/pub/infozip/zlib/*. Download and extract the archive. On most systems (Solaris is an exception) you will *not* have to build the zlib library, because when you build libpng later, it incorporates the source files rather than the actual library. If you choose to build and install zlib, use the standard install procedure:
>
> ```
> % ./configure
> % make
> # make install (as root)
> ```

libpng

> Installing libpng is a little more complicated. You can get the latest version from a mirror listed at *http://www.libpng.org/pub/png/libpng.html*. Look for something like *libpng-x.y.z.tar.gz*, where *x.y.z* is the highest version number. Download and extract the archive. You'll need zlib on the same level as the libpng directory, and they should both be named without their versions. In other words, your directory structure should look like this:
>
> ```
> |
> +- zlib
> |
> +- libpng
> ```

Something like the following should do it. The actual commands may differ from system to system. You'll have to remove the archive before doing this (rm *.tar or rm *.tar.gz).

```
% mv zlib* zlib
% mv libpng* libpng
% cd libpng
% cp scripts/makefile.stf Makefile
% make
# make install (as root)
```

You should choose one of the makefiles in the *libpng/scripts* directory according to your system (such as *scripts/makefile.linux* for Linux or *scripts/makefile.sunos* for Solaris).

libfreetype *(optional)*

If you want support for TrueType fonts in your graphs (say, because you want your axis labels in Japanese), you can install the libfreetype library. You cannot build this if you don't have X Windows installed. You can download lttf from *http://freetype.sourceforge.net/download.html* and then build it as usual:

```
% ./configure
% make
# make install (as root)
```

jpeg-6b

You will need the jpeg-6a (or later) library on your system for GD.pm to compile. It is often already installed, so check */usr/lib* or */usr/local/lib* for libjpeg. If it's not installed, you can download it from *ftp://ftp.uu.net/graphics/jpeg/* and build it with the steps shown previously. Alternately, there may be a precompiled packaged version (RPM, DEB, etc.) available from your local package site.

libgd

Installing libgd should now be straightforward. Download the latest version from *http://www.boutell.com/gd/*. After extracting the archive, edit the Makefile so that it includes support for jpeg and ttf if you installed those packages. You may also have to add -I/usr/local/include/freetype to the INCLUDEDIRS= line to make it work with freetype-1.3.1. You can then build the library as follows:

```
% make
# make install (as root)
```

You will now be able to install GD and the rest of the Perl modules mentioned in this article.

CHAPTER 26
GD and L-Systems

Jason Reed

(Or, how to see plants on your computer without getting soil on the keyboard.)

In *GD-Graph3d*, you learned how Perl could create three-dimensional graphics. Naturally, Perl is quite comfortable with two-dimensional images as well. Lincoln Stein's GD module (based on Thomas Boutell's *gd* library and available from the CPAN) makes it possible to import, manipulate, and even generate GIFs from the comfort of your very own Perl. In this article, we'll use GD to create images of plants using mathematical constructs called *L-systems*.

GD

Using GD is straightforward: all that's necessary to create a GIF suitable for displaying on a web page is a GD::Image object, some colors, and a few drawing commands. It takes only six lines of code to produce a lone brown dot on a white background, a work surely worth millions to a sufficiently avant-garde patron of the arts:

```
#!/usr/bin/perl

use GD;

$im    = new GD::Image(100,100);
$white = $im->colorAllocate(255, 255, 255);
$brown = $im->colorAllocate(128,   0,   0);

$im->setPixel(42, 17, $brown);

open (OUT, ">masterpiece.gif") or die $!;
print OUT $im->gif();
```

Here we create an image 100 pixels square and allocate two colors. GIFs use color tables (in particular, a 256-color palette) so it's necessary to specify in advance which colors are to be used. The colors themselves are specified by their red, green, and blue components, which range from 0 to 255.

The dot is then drawn with setPixel, 42 pixels to the right of the edge and 17 pixels below the top left corner. Finally, the contents of the GIF itself, obtained through the GD::Image::gif method, is printed to the file *masterpiece.gif*.

GD provides other drawing commands, special brushes and patterns, and the ability to load existing GIFs from files. But we already have everything we need. The rest of this article is devoted to using GD to build and use code that implements L-systems, a task that proves quite comfortable in Perl, because it requires both graphical output and text manipulation.

L-Systems

For our purposes, an L-system is simply a very abstract way of modeling cell-scale growth within a plant. Bear in mind that the level of abstraction is quite high—an L-system won't tell you much about how real plants grow. Real plant growth depends on cytoplasm structure, cell membranes, mitosis rates, and plenty of other hard-to-model phenomena. However, L-systems are quite good at generating realistic images of plants.

Originally developed by Astrid Lindenmayer (hence the 'L') in the late 1960's, L-systems have undergone a number of generalizations and improvements in the decades since, including the addition of randomness, multiple transition tables, and non-discrete evolution. The core of the idea is quite simple: take a string, called the *axiom*, and apply a series of rules to each character of the string. For example, suppose your axiom (commonly designated ω) is A and you have two production rules:

1. Every A is translated to BA, and
2. Every B is translated to AB.

This system would be written in L-system notation as:

ω: A
p_1: A -> BA
p_2: B -> AB

These rules are applied simultaneously to the axiom, producing BA, since we start with A and change according to rule p_1. The rules are then applied to that result, yielding ABBA (no relation to the band). Then the rules are applied again, generating BAABABBA.

When does the process stop? It doesn't. In principle, the combination of axiom and rules describes an infinite sequence of words:

A
BA
ABBA
BAABABBA
ABBABAABBAABABBA
BAABABBAABBABAABABBABAABBAABABBA

and so on. This might seem to have little relevance to plant development. However, the output of an L-system can be interpreted as the shape of the plant at various ages. Finding the appropriate time to stop, then, is equivalent to deciding how big or old a tree (or fern, or flower, or blue-green algae colony) you want.

How could an L-system resemble a tree, then? To get branches we can use a *bracketed L-system*. That just means that we add [and] to our L-system's alphabet. Any string enclosed in brackets is interpreted as separate branch, protruding from the string it would otherwise be part of. Brackets can also be nested. For example, A[B][CD[E[F]G]H] can be loosely interpreted as Figure 26-1.

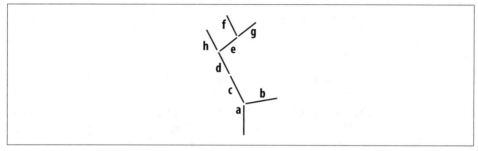

Figure 26-1. A[B][CD[E[F]G]H]

Turtles

Typically, objects modeled with L-systems are rendered with *turtle graphics*. Turtle graphics were invented for the LOGO programming language; they're used to give children a simple metaphor for expressing graphics algorithmically. Implementations of LOGO have virtual turtles that turn, move, and leave trails across the screen. Older versions sometimes had an actual robot controlled by the program. The robot moved a pen around on paper and was sometimes fashioned to look like a small, plastic-shelled turtle.

The Turtle class (in the Turtle.pm module on this book's web site) implements simple turtle graphics. The humble turtle can produce some striking graphics if controlled, but itself knows little more than its position, orientation, how to turn, and how to move forward at an angle. The most important method of the Turtle class is forward:

```
sub forward {
    my $self = shift;
    my ($r, $what) = @_;
    my ($newx, $newy) = ($self->{x} + $r *  sin($self->{theta}),
                         $self->{y} + $r * -cos($self->{theta}));
    if ($what) {
        # Do something related to motion according to
        # the coderef passed in
        &$what($self->{x}, $self->{y}, $newx, $newy);
    }
        #... and change the old coordinates
        ($self->{x}, $self->{y}) = ($newx, $newy);
    }
```

forward first uses a bit of trigonometry to calculate the (*x*, *y*) position given the distance *r* and angle Θ. (All angles are measured in radians, with zero being directly up and angles increasing as you move clockwise.). Then it does something with the old and new coordinates, but exactly what it does is up to $what. Whoever calls Turtle:: forward passes in a code reference; that coderef gets the turtle's old and new coordinates as parameters and can do whatever it wants with them. For now, all we want the turtle to do while moving forward is draw a line, but this flexibility will prove quite handy later. Another method worth examining is turn:

```
sub turn {
    my $self   = shift;
    my $dtheta = shift;
    $self->{theta} += $dtheta * $self->{mirror};
}
```

Our turtle will occasionally need to turn left into right and right into left; this is accomplished by calling the turtle's mirror method; that toggles the mirror attribute between 1 and –1 and has the effect of changing clockwise rotations into counter-clockwise rotations.

A Turtle Draws a Tree

A turtle can't do much by itself. Starting with a subroutine in lsys.pl, we'll make it more useful. To get an L-system rule to tell the turtle what to do, we create a turtle, an image, and a hash to translate characters into behavior:

```
sub lsys_init {
    # S => Step Forward
    # - => Turn Counter-clockwise
    # + => Turn Clockwise
    # M => Mirror
    # [ => Begin Branch
    # ] => End Branch
    %translate=(
                'S' => sub { $turtle->forward($changes->{"distance"},
                                              $changes->{"motionsub"}) },
                '-' => sub { $turtle->turn(-$changes->{"dtheta"}) },
                '+' => sub { $turtle->turn($changes->{"dtheta"}) },
                'M' => sub { $turtle->mirror() },
                '[' => sub { push(@statestack, [$turtle->state()]) },
                ']' => sub { $turtle->setstate(@{pop(@statestack)}) },
               );
    my ($imagesize) = @_;

    # Create the main image
    $im = new GD::Image($imagesize, $imagesize);

    # Allocate some colors for it
    $white       = $im->colorAllocate(255, 255,255);
    $dark_green  = $im->colorAllocate(  0, 128,  0);
    $light_green = $im->colorAllocate(  0, 255,  0);

    # Create the turtle, at the midpoint of the bottom
    # edge of the image, pointing up.
    $turtle = new Turtle($imagesize/2, $imagesize, 0, 1);
}
```

To have the turtle perform the action identified by the character $chr, we just say &{$translate{$chr}}, which calls the appropriate anonymous subroutine.

$changes, the hash reference inside %translate, holds information specific to a given L-system rule. It'll go in a separate file, tree.pl, whose beginning is shown below.

```
#!/usr/bin/perl

require "lsys.pl";

# Set some parameters
$changes = {   distance => 40,
                  dtheta => 0.2,
              motionsub => sub { $im->line(@_, $dark_green) } };
```

The first two keys of the hash referred to by $changes are straightforward: distance is how far the turtle moves every instance of S, and dtheta is how much the turtle's angle changes for every + or -. The last key, motionsub, identifies the anonymous subroutine passed to Turtle::forward. Recall that Turtle::forward passes the old position and the new position of the turtle. sub{ $im->line(@_, $dark_green); } merely takes that argument list, tacks on $dark_green, and hands everything off to GD::Image's line method. That draws the line.

Now we have a turtle that can turn, flip, go forward, and trace a line. Only the left and right bracket characters remain—they'll help the turtle remember a position and later recall where it was. The [character pushes the turtle's current state (x, y, q, and mirror) onto a stack, @statestack. The] character, conversely, pops an element off @statestack and forces the turtle back into that state.

Putting L-Systems to Work

To create an honest-to-goodness L-system inside all this mess, we just need one more hash table to describe the production rules and a scalar initialized with the axiom. Let's start with a small system:

ω: A

p_1: A -> S[-A][+A]

This system has every A go forward (S) and produce two branches, each with an A: one to the left ([-A]), and one to the right ([+A]). On every iteration, the tree will split in half, yielding a binary tree growing upward from the turtle's initial location. This L-system is expressed in Perl, as follows:

```
%rule  = ( A => 'S[-A][+A]' );
$axiom = "A";
```

%rule contains the single rule of our L-system; $axiom is our start string. The lsys_execute subroutine, in lsys.pl on the book web site, applies the rules to the axiom $repetitions times:

```
sub lsys_execute {
    my ($string, $repetitions, $filename, %rule) = @_;
    # Apply the %rule to $string, $repetitions times,
    # and print the result to $filename
    for (1..$repetitions) {
        $string =~ s/./defined ($rule{$&}) ? $rule{$&} : $&/eg;
    }
```

...and calls the appropriate subroutines held in %translate...

```
foreach $cmd (split(//, $string)) {
    if ($translate{$cmd}) {&{$translate{$cmd}}( );}
}
```

...and finally prints out the GIF itself:

```
open (OUT, ">tree.gif") or die $!;
print OUT $im->gif;
close(OUT);
}
```

This program creates the GIF shown in Figure 26-2.

```
#!/usr/bin/perl

require "lsys.pl";

%rule = ( 'A' => 'S[-A][+A]', );
$axiom = "A";

$changes = { distance => 40,
               dtheta => 0.2,
             motionsub => sub { $im->line(@_, $dark_green) } };

$repetitions = 8;
$imagesize   = 400;
$filename    = "tree1.gif";

lsys_init($imagesize);
lsys_execute($axiom, $repetitions, $filename, %rule);
```

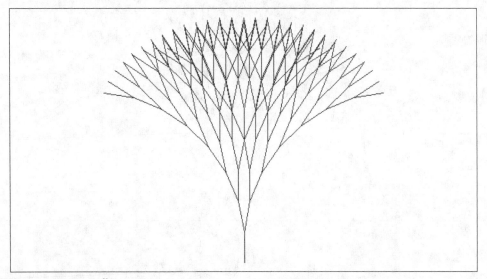

Figure 26-2. A small L-system

Not breathtaking, but moderately tree-like. Its most glaring flaw is that all the branches are the same length. Younger branches should be shorter, because they've had less time to grow. Changing the system makes every G produce an S at every step.

ω: A
p_1: A -> GS[-A][+A]
p_2: G -> GS

Here's the program to code the rule in Perl and shorten the distance a bit:

```perl
#!/usr/bin/perl

require "lsys.pl";

%rule  = ( 'A' => 'GS[-A][+A]', 'G' => 'GS' );
$axiom = "A";

$changes = { distance => 10,
               dtheta => .2,
             motionsub => sub { $im->line(@_, $dark_green) } };

$repetitions = 8;
$imagesize   = 400;
$filename    = "tree2.gif";

lsys_init($imagesize);
lsys_execute($axiom, $repetitions, $filename, %rule);
```

This produces the tree shown in Figure 26-3.

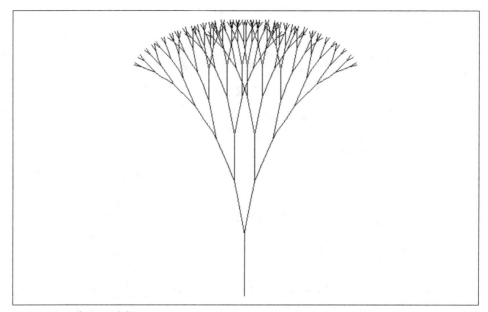

Figure 26-3. Shortened distances

A definite improvement. However, most plants aren't perfectly symmetrical. Let's try forcing the right branch to wait before splitting. Specifically, we'll use this L-system:

ω: A
p₁: A -> GS[-A][+B]
p₂: G -> GS
p₃: B -> C
p₄: C -> A

Now every right branch spends less time splitting and growing. Here's the program that implements this system:

```perl
#!/usr/bin/perl

require "lsys.pl";

%rule = ('A' => 'GS[-A][+B]',
         'G' => 'GS',
         'B' => 'C',
         'C' => 'A');

$axiom    = "A";
$changes  = { distance => 2.8,
                dtheta => .2,
             motionsub => sub { $im->line(@_, $dark_green) } };

$repetitions = 15;
$imagesize   = 400;
$filename    = "tree3.gif";

lsys_init($imagesize);
lsys_execute($axiom, $repetitions, $filename, %rule);
```

The result is shown in Figure 26-4.

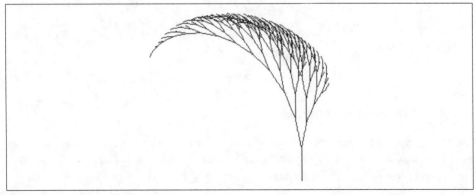

Figure 26-4. Right branches stunted

Interesting, but kind of lopsided. Remember Turtle's mirror method? Now's a good time to take advantage of it. Let's try changing the first rule of the L-system to

p₁: A -> GS[---A][++MB]

and decreasing dtheta a bit:

```perl
#!/usr/bin/perl

require "lsys.pl";

%rule = ('A' => 'GS[---A][++MB]',
         'G' => 'GS',
         'B' => 'C',
         'C' => 'A');

$axiom   = "A";
$changes = { distance => 2.8,
                dtheta => .06,
             motionsub => sub { $im->line(@_, $dark_green) } };

$repetitions = 15;
$imagesize   = 400;
$filename    = "tree4.gif";

lsys_init($imagesize);
lsys_execute($axiom, $repetitions, $filename, %rule);
```

The tree produced by this program is shown in Figure 26-5. Now the second branch of every subtree is flipped, and the tree looks less like the victim of gale-force winds.

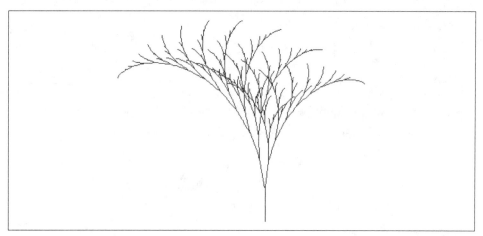

Figure 26-5. Every second branch flipped

Merely drawing branches may be good enough for trees in winter, but around this time of year, plants acquire things that are harder to draw: leaves and flowers. Fortunately, GD can draw and fill polygons and import other GIFs.

Leaves

Our leaves will be polygons oriented in some direction relative to the branch they're on. We'll use the already-existing turtle code and create a "polygon mode," using the traditional L-system notation of curly braces. The turtle will trace out the polygon and then fill it. Turtle::forward can perform any sort of movement as long as we pass it the appropriate coderef—we just need to construct one that tells GD to convert part of the turtle's path into polygon vertices.

It would be convenient to modify distance and dtheta in polygon mode independently of their values in "stem mode." Since these two values are stored in %$changes, we'll create two hashes: %stemchanges for stem mode, and %polychanges for polygon mode. $changes will always be current whatever the mode, so it'll initially refer to %stemchanges. The most important difference between them is their motionsub; %stemchanges has the familiar sub { $im->line(@_, $dark_green) }, but %polychanges has sub { $poly->addPt(@_[0..1]) }.

Skipping what that means for the moment, let's handle curly braces with two more entries to %translate:

```perl
%translate = (...
                '{' => sub {    $poly = new GD::Polygon;
                            $changes = \%polychanges;     },

                '}' => sub { $im->filledPolygon($poly, $light_green);
                            undef $poly;
                            $changes = \%stemchanges;     } );
```

What's going on? The GD module defines the GD::Polygon class, an instance of which $poly gets created whenever we encounter a {. Every time the turtle moves in polygon mode, $polychanges{motionsub} is called, so we call GD::Polygon::addPt to add a point to the list of vertices in $poly. Once the polygon is drawn, a } is processed, filling the polygon with $light_green. Then $poly is thrown away and stem mode is restored.

```perl
#!/usr/bin/perl

require "lsys.pl";

%rule  = ( 'A' => 'SLMA', 'L' => '[{S+S+S+S+S}]');
$axiom = "A";

%stemchanges = ( distance => 24,
                    dtheta => .15,
                 motionsub => sub{ $im->line(@_, $dark_green) } );

%polychanges = ( distance => 6,
                    dtheta => .4,
                 motionsub => sub{ $poly->addPt(@_[0..1]) } );

$changes     = \%stemchanges;
$repetitions = 15;
$imagesize   = 400;
$filename    = "tree5.gif";

lsys_init($imagesize);
lsys_execute($axiom, $repetitions, $filename, %rule);
```

The result (Figure 26-6) resembles a vine.

Figure 26-6. Single stem with leaves

This system is pretty easy to follow—it merely leaves commands for moving forward, drawing a leaf, and flipping the turtle, repeated an arbitrary number of times. The M character once again proves useful, this time allowing easy alternating placement of leaves. Also note that GD automatically closes polygons if they're not closed already.

Flowers

Let's use some GIFs of flowers: flower.gif, flower2.gif, and flower3.gif, all available on the book web site. Creating a GD::Image from an existing file is easy—the newFromGif method does exactly that. All you need to add to lsys_init is the following:

```
open(IN, "flower.gif") or die $!;
$flower = newFromGif GD::Image(IN);
close(IN);

open(IN, "flower2.gif") or die $!;
$flower2 = newFromGif GD::Image(IN);
close(IN);

open(IN, "flower3.gif") or die $!;
$flower3 = newFromGif GD::Image(IN);
close(IN);
```

Once all the flowers are loaded, we need to copy them onto the main image. We'll delegate that to a small subroutine in lsys.pl, which centers the image at the turtle's current coordinates. It uses GD::Image's getBounds method:

```
sub flower {
    my $flower=shift;
    my ($width, $height) = $flower->getBounds();
```

```
        my ($x, $y) = $turtle->state();
        $im->copy($flower, $x-$width/2, $y-$height/2, 0, 0, $width, $height);
}
```

GD::Image::copy does the dirty work here, even copying the flowers' color tables if necessary. We'll add a few more entries to %translate:

```
%translate = (...
               'f' => sub { flower($flower)  },
               'g' => sub { flower($flower2) },
               'h' => sub { flower($flower3) } );
```

We can test the new features with this program:

```
#!/usr/bin/perl

require "lsys.pl";

%rule  = ( 'A' => 'GS[-fA][+fA]', 'G' => 'GS');
$axiom = "A";

%stemchanges = ( distance => 9,
                    dtheta => .25,
                 motionsub => sub{ $im->line(@_, $dark_green) } );

%polychanges = ( distance => 6,
                    dtheta => .4,
                 motionsub => sub{ $poly->addPt(@_[0..1]) } );

$changes     = \%stemchanges;
$repetitions = 8;
$imagesize   = 400;
$filename    = "tree6.gif";

lsys_init($imagesize);
lsys_execute($axiom, $repetitions, $filename, %rule);
```

Now our tree has flowers, as shown in Figure 26-7.

It looks odd with flowers growing out of every branch. One way to avoid this is forcing flowers to die every step, leaving live flowers only at the very tips:

```
#!/usr/bin/perl

require "lsys.pl";

%rule  = ('A'=>'GS[-fA][+fA]', 'G'=>'GS', 'f'=>'');
$axiom = "A";

%stemchanges = ( distance => 9,
                    dtheta => .25,
                 motionsub => sub { $im->line(@_, $dark_green) } );

%polychanges = ( distance => 6,
                    dtheta => .4,
                 motionsub => sub { $poly->addPt(@_[0..1]) } );

$changes     = \%stemchanges;
$repetitions = 8;
```

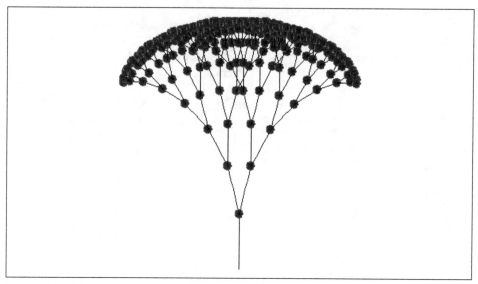

Figure 26-7. Flowers

```
$imagesize   = 400;
$filename    = "tree7.gif";

lsys_init($imagesize);
lsys_execute($axiom, $repetitions, $filename, %rule);
```

The result is shown in Figure 26-8.

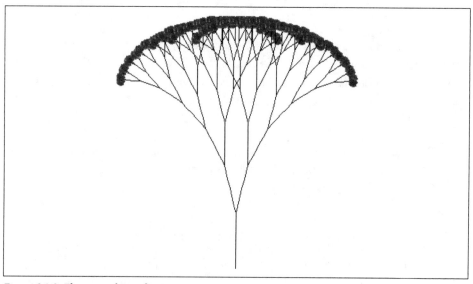

Figure 26-8. Flowers only on the tips

Alternately, you can have the flowers change before they die:

```
#!/usr/bin/perl
```

```
require "lsys.pl";

%rule  = ('A' => 'GS[-fA][+fA]', 'G' => 'GS', 'f' => 'g', 'g' => 'h', 'h' => '');
$axiom = "A";

%stemchanges = ( distance => 9,
                   dtheta => .25,
                motionsub => sub { $im->line(@_, $dark_green) } );

%polychanges = ( distance => 6,
                   dtheta => .4,
                motionsub => sub { $poly->addPt(@_[0..1]) } );

$changes     = \%stemchanges;
$repetitions = 8;
$imagesize   = 400;
$filename    = "tree8.gif";

lsys_init($imagesize);
lsys_execute($axiom, $repetitions, $filename, %rule);
```

Figure 26-9 shows the changed flowers.

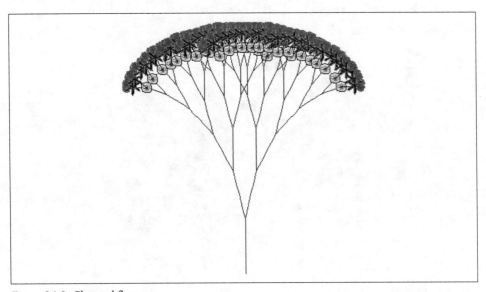

Figure 26-9. Changed flowers

Bringing It All Together

The L-system itself is an incredible source of variety; even the primitive system I've presented is still capable of making appealing pictures. For a few final examples, we'll experiment with some additional rules. Using just one type of flower:

```
#!/usr/bin/perl
require "lsys.pl";
%rule = ('A' => 'GS[---fMA][++++B]',
```

```
           'B' => 'C',
           'C' => 'GS[-fB][++A][++++A]',
           'f' => '',
           'G' => 'HS',
           'H' => 'HSS');

    $axiom = "A";

    %stemchanges = ( distance => 4,
                       dtheta => 0.12,
                    motionsub => sub { $im->line(@_, $dark_green) } );

    %polychanges = ( distance => 6,
                       dtheta => 0.4,
                    motionsub => sub { $poly->addPt(@_[0..1]) } );

    $changes     = \%stemchanges;
    $repetitions = 10;
    $imagesize   = 400;
    $filename    = "tree9.gif";

    lsys_init($imagesize);
    lsys_execute($axiom, $repetitions, $filename, %rule);
```

The result is illustrated in Figure 26-10.

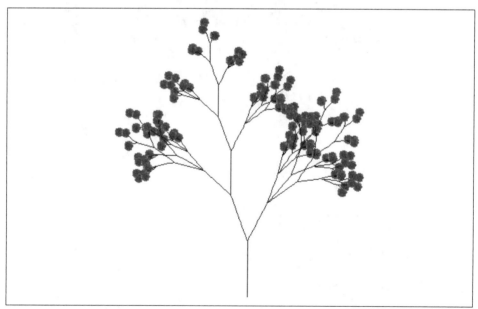

Figure 26-10. A single type of flower

With leaves and a different flower:

```
#!/usr/bin/perl
require "lsys.pl";
```

```
%rule = ( 'A' => 'S[---LMA][++++B]',
          'B' => 'S[++LBg][--Cg]',
          'C' => 'S[-----LB]GS[+MC]',
          'g' => '',
          'L' => '[{S+S+S+S+S+S}]' );

$axiom = "A";
%stemchanges = ( distance => 18.5, dtheta => 0.1,
                 motionsub => sub { $im->line(@_, $dark_green) } );

%polychanges = ( distance => 3, dtheta => 0.4,
                 motionsub => sub { $poly->addPt(@_[0..1]) } );

$changes     = \%stemchanges;
$repetitions = 10;
$imagesize   = 400;
$filename    = "tree10.gif";

lsys_init($imagesize);
lsys_execute($axiom, $repetitions, $filename, %rule);
```

This gives us a bush (Figure 26-11).

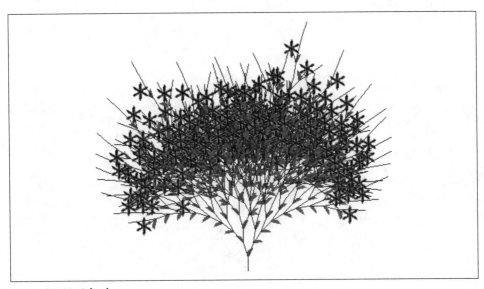

Figure 26-11. A bush

With all three flower types, leaves, and slightly weird axial growth, use this program:

```
#!/usr/bin/perl

require "lsys.pl";

%rule=( 'A' => 'GS[---fA][++MB]',
        'B' => 'C',
        'C' => 'A',
        'f' => 'g',
```

```
                'g' => 'h',
                'h' => '',
                'G' => 'HS',
                'H' => 'IS',
                'I' => 'GLMS',
                'L' => '[{S+S+S+S+S+S}]' );

    $axiom = "A";
    %stemchanges = ( distance => 2.8, dtheta => 0.06,
                     motionsub => sub { $im->line(@_, $dark_green) } );

    %polychanges = ( distance => 3, dtheta => 0.4,
                     motionsub => sub { $poly->addPt(@_[0..1]); } );

    $changes     = \%stemchanges;
    $repetitions = 17;
    $imagesize   = 400;
    $filename    = "tree11.gif";

    lsys_init($imagesize);
    lsys_execute($axiom, $repetitions, $filename, %rule);
```

Figure 26-12 depicts our final L-system-generated tree.

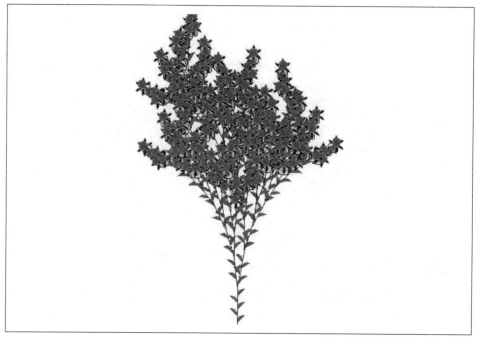

Figure 26-12. Three types of flowers and leaves

Resources

You can find several L-systems programs for Unix, Macs, and DOS platforms at *http://www.cpsc.ucalgary.ca/projects/bmv/software.html*. If you don't mind peeling your eyes off the monitor, the definitive text on L-systems is *The Algorithmic Beauty of Plants*, by Lindenmayer and Prusinkiewicz (Springer-Verlag, 1990).

CHAPTER 27
OpenGL

Alligator Descartes

With the plethora of emerging Doom clones and dancing web logos, we tend to take three-dimensional graphics for granted. This is due in part to the surging capabilities of computers to render scenes quickly. In recent years, Silicon Graphics Incorporated (SGI) has pioneered not only hardware tuned especially for 3D graphics, but software as well, notably OpenGL, an elegant and stable graphics API. OpenGL has proven a success, with implementations for all major platforms and the resulting portability advantages for applications. Add to the mix the plummeting costs of cheap 3D graphics cards and free OpenGL-like implementations, and you have a force to be reckoned with.

Enter Perl, stage left. Portable. Compilable. Powerful. Couple it with OpenGL and you have a match made in heaven for rapid 3D development.

Back to Basics

Before we delve into the soupy, steaming innards of 3D graphics and OpenGL, we ought to explain some of the concepts needed for 3D graphics programming.

The three-dimensional space we're used to can be navigated in any of three directions: up/down, left/right, and forward/backward. The premise of *Euclidean 3D space* is exactly the same, although it requires more precision than "up and left a bit," or "a few yards backward." Imagine being blindfolded in a large field with a tree near the middle and have a friend direct you to that tree. Difficult? Try it and see! Even the simple matter of "forward" becomes a relative concept with different meanings depending on the person's orientation. We need to establish some ground rules.

First, we need to define our *origin*, the central reference point in the 3D space. Everything we describe is relative to this point. The origin is usually dubbed (0, 0, 0) in coordinate systems.

So how do we agree which direction corresponds to which axis in our coordinate system? This requires the creation of another concept known as the *handedness* of a coordinate system. Coordinate systems can be either left-handed or right-handed.

Wrap your hand around the Z-axis, with your thumb pointing along the Z-axis and the X-axis running back along your arm. If you had to use your right hand, you're in a right-handed coordinate system. Illustrations of each are shown in Figure 27-1.

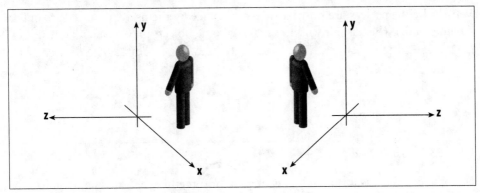

Figure 27-1. Left-handed and right-handed coordinate systems

Right-handed coordinate systems are more common in today's applications, yielding the directions shown in Table 27-1.

Table 27-1. Right-handed coordinate system directions

Axis	Direction
X-axis	Right
Y-axis	Up
Z-axis	Backward

For the programmer looking at the screen, the directions to use are shown in Table 27-2.

Table 27-2. Right-handed coordinate system directions

Axis	Direction
X-axis	Right
Y-axis	Up
Z-axis	Backward

Now that we've sorted out the framework of our space, we can look at how to fill it.

Graphical Primitives

Graphical primitives are the most basic components that can be used by a 3D graphics system. These range from the fairly obvious to the not-so-obvious. We shall deal with these in turn.

The Vertex

Any discrete point in 3D space is called a vertex. The origin is a vertex because it's a point at (0, 0, 0).

Vertices by themselves are only partly useful, since by themselves they create only a "point cloud," which is fairly useless for discerning objects in. Consider Figure 27-2.

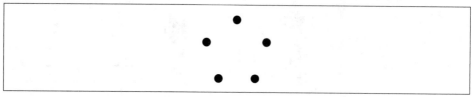

Figure 27-2. A point cloud

Do these five vertices form a star, a pentagon, or something else? It's impossible to be sure, since it all depends on how your perceive it. That's an inherent problem with point cloud rendering; it's nigh-impossible to construct any sort of coherent impression from points alone. They can be used to render *real* clouds, but that's about it.

The Line

Lines are the building blocks of wireframe models, a staple of 3D graphics. On a slow computer, they provide a quick way to render scenes. If you want to see through objects, they let you do that as well. They are of most use in CAD tools, where the designer needs to be able to manipulate any part of the design. If the models were solid, they wouldn't be able to see all of it at once.

Lines allow us to depict the edges of an object, which helps the viewer's brain assign meaning to the picture on the screen. But for rendering solid objects, polygons are preferable.

The Polygon

Polygons are 2D surfaces bounded by vertices. Triangles are polygons with three vertices; squares, rectangles, and other quadrilaterals are polygons with four vertices, and so on. Polygons must always be flat (or *planar*)—all the vertices must lie on the same plane. Polygons that are non-planar are usually automatically split up into smaller planar polygons by the rendering software. In many rendering libraries, including OpenGL, polygons with more than three vertices are split into triangles. This process of polygon-splitting is referred to as *tessellation*, where large complicated polygons become sets of smaller polygons that aren't necessarily triangles, or *triangulation* where larger polygons are split completely into triangles. (OpenGL doesn't actually perform automatic triangulation of polygons, but you can use its GLU routines to do that.) This is all quite a mouthful, so let's look at a diagram that illustrates the principles. Figure 27-3 shows a quadrilateral and how it might be triangulated.

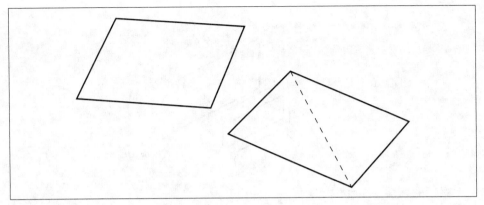

Figure 27-3. Triangulating a quadrilateral

Polygons are the most common tool for rendering 3D graphics, since they can be filled to produce solid-looking objects. Now that we're armed with the basic concepts of three-dimensionality, we can address how to render scenes on screens.

Drawing on the Screen

Drawing things on the screen is the whole point of graphics. But how do we get our collection of points and polygons onto the screen? And what will it look like? Will it look realistic? All simple questions with complicated answers.

To make any headway into this subject, we need to introduce a few more concepts: the *viewport*, the *view frustum*, and *perspective*.

The Viewport

The viewport is our window onto our 3D world. Imagine standing at the window of your house, looking out onto the world outside. That's your viewport. We'll only discuss rectangular viewports for the moment, which means we can assume that the viewport can be described by a width and a height. How do we work out what we're looking at in the world, and how do we translate that into the boundaries of this viewport? To accomplish this, we need to consider the view frustum.

The View Frustum

The view frustum enables our rendering engine to work out what the user can see through their viewport onto the world. To help envision this, consider Figure 27-4.

The view frustum is pyramid-shaped, with the apex positioned at the eyes of the viewer. To use our house window analogy, the eyepoint of the view frustum is right between our eyes as we look out the window. The other two planes we'll discuss in a later section, but the *far clipping plane* can be considered the base of the pyramid and constitutes the farthest distance at which we can see objects in the world. Anything farther is invisible.

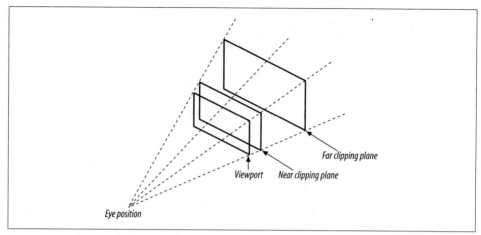

Figure 27-4. The view frustum

Hopefully you can orient this diagram in your mind's eye as if you were looking through the window outside. The edges of the pyramid depicted in dashed lines extend from your eyes through each corner of the viewport until they intersect with the far clipping plane. From knowing these points of intersection with the pyramid base, we could calculate the dimensions of the base if we desired.

Fine, so now we know *what* we can see in the world, but how do we translate that onto the viewport? How can we resolve those 3D objects into 2D objects for displaying on our screen? The answer is simple and one known by artists for centuries.

Perspective

Perspective is an optical effect that makes identically sized objects far away from us appear smaller than objects nearby. Therefore, with perspective, we can judge distance between two objects by the difference in apparent size.

We project perspective towards a *vanishing point* (Figure 27-5), a point on the horizon at which all objects converge. That's the opposite of our view frustum, which converges squarely between the user's eyes.

Do not despair. We can still tackle the vanishing point perspective—we just need to think of it back-to-front. We project the objects away from the horizon and toward the eyepoint. But what do we project? The vertices, of course. Once the vertices have been mapped onto the viewport, the polygons will automatically be projected too, since they're defined by their vertices. In OpenGL, a polygon has no knowledge of where it is—it only knows what it is constructed from. Therefore, if we can calculate the projection from a three-dimensional coordinate system onto a two-dimensional coordinate system, we can determine where our objects should lie on the viewport.

And, that, in a nutshell, is how we convert our three-dimensional world into something we can view on a two-dimensional screen!

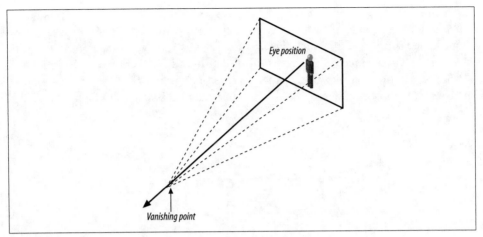

Figure 27-5. Perspective is projected toward a vanishing point

Now, on to the fun part: techniques for representing objects on the screen. These different drawing techniques are called *rendering pipelines* and constitute the gory innards of any graphics engine. They can be implemented in either software or hardware.

Rendering Pipelines

At this point, we have a good idea of what we want to draw and where on the screen we want to draw it. The big question is *how* do we draw it? Do we draw it as lines, filled polygons, or with some other funky technique? We'll now discuss the various rendering pipelines available to today's programmers.

Wireframes. The *wireframe* pipeline is the simplest by far; it draws only polygon outlines. As we discussed before, the outline of the polygon is essentially a set of lines that connect the vertices in the object. We're drawing a lot of lines, as seen in Figure 27-6.

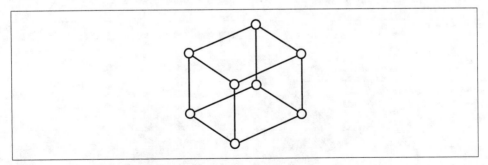

Figure 27-6. A wire-frame cube

Wire-frame pipelines are generally the fastest pipeline in graphics engines, since painting pixels is usually the slowest part of any rendering pipeline, and we're painting a lot less here than we would if our polygons were filled.

There are, however, a few additional things we can do to our wire-frame pipeline to make it more realistic, without slowing it down too much. We could use a technique called *depth-cueing*, which darkens the lines as they get further away from the viewport. This heightens the perception of depth and is a very useful technique. A second and more complex technique is *hidden-line removal*, which makes objects appear solid. A cube rendered with hidden-line removal is shown in Figure 27-7.

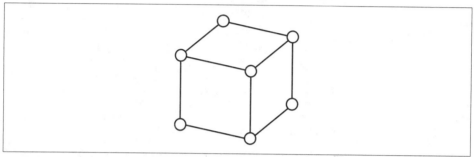

Figure 27-7. A wire-frame cube with hidden-line removal

Flat shading. Unlike the wireframe pipeline, the *flat-shaded* pipeline actually fills polygons. Each polygon is *rasterized*—converted into horizontal lines—and then drawn on the screen. The result: All the objects in the scene seem like solid 3D objects.

An important aspect of a filled pipeline is that each polygon can be given a different brightness, implying the orientation of that polygon to the source of light. For example, if we hold a toaster near a light bulb, the parts of the toaster facing the bulb will be brighter than those facing away from the light. Hidden-line removal can't simulate this, making "filled" pipelines a better choice. Figure 27-8 illustrates a flat-shaded Utah teapot. (Martin Newell's Utah teapot is widely used as a test object for rendering engines.) A light shines from the viewport towards the teapot, causing the polygons in the center to appear brighter than those on the sides.

Figure 27-8. A flat-shaded object.

Smooth shading. The *smooth-shaded* pipeline is an enhancement of the flat-shaded pipeline. Instead of uniformly coloring the polygons in the scene, we grade the colors across the polygons, dependent on the colors of the neighboring polygons. This algorithm is known as *Gouraud shading*, after its discoverer, Henri Gouraud.

This approach is slightly more time-consuming than the simple uniform color filling flat-shaded pipeline, but the effects are spectacular. Objects that previously looked blocky now have the appearance of being curved, as can be seen in Figure 27-9, which depicts a Gouraud-shaded Utah teapot.

Figure 27-9. A Gouraud-shaded object

Texture mapping. The fourth and final pipeline we'll consider is the *texture mapped* pipeline. This is probably the most realistic and can be generated in real-time by today's (but not yesterday's) rendering engines. Most of you will be acquainted with games like Doom, Quake, Half-Life, or Tomb Raider, all popular 3D games that make heavy use of texture mapping.

The basic purpose of texture mapping is to allow the artist to create realistic looking surfaces, such as a stone wall, with a minimum of computation. You *could* do without texture mapping, modeling each individual stone using points and polygons. Or you could simply map the texture of some stones onto a single flat polygon. That's texture mapping.

Anyway, you now know enough of the theory involved in 3D graphics to be dangerous, so let's take a look at the rendering engine we're going to be using: OpenGL.

Introduction to OpenGL

OpenGL is a powerful and elegant 3D graphics API developed by SGI. It provides platform-independent mechanisms to let you to manipulate the graphical primitives discussed earlier and has an unofficial extension library providing programmers with standard routines for platform-dependent tasks, such as the manipulation of windows and the handling of window events. Even though these libraries are not officially part of OpenGL, they're found with most OpenGL implementations.

The OpenGL architecture is basically a large state machine: you can pull levers at any point in the execution of the machine to alter any subsequent operations the machine may execute. For example, if we were rendering a cube comprised of six polygons and had already rendered three of these polygons with a flat-shaded pipeline, we could then make a single function call to pull a lever in the state machine and render the final three with a smooth-shaded pipeline instead.

OpenGL and Perl

Brian Paul's superb Mesa, an OpenGL-like library, makes possible OpenGL programming on lower-end PCs. Mesa provides an almost fully-featured OpenGL implementation (although not a licensed one, so it can't call itself OpenGL). Currently at Version 5.0, it's fast and stable.

Keeping pace with Mesa is Perl's OpenGL module, which provides access to most OpenGL functions. The module's speed is comparable to compiled C code but allows for the ease of use we have come to know and love from Perl!

Since the readership of this article are probably champing at the bit to get on with some groovy Perl hacking, let's discuss how to use the OpenGL module.

Creating a Viewport

The first thing we need to do is create our viewport. The OpenGL module provides glpOpenWindow, a useful method that pops up a GL canvas for us. It also handles some of the icky stuff like allocating colors. The following short example creates a default window for us.

```
1  #!/usr/bin/perl -w
2  #
3  # Creates a GL viewport
4
5  use OpenGL;
6
7  glpOpenWindow( );
8
9  print "Press return to exit\n";
10
11 while ( <> ) {
12     exit;
13 }
```

You'll notice that the window is empty. And if you move it around, it'll never redraw. Not so useful. What we need to do now is create the view frustum, so that OpenGL will at least have some clue about what it's going to be rendering.

Creating the View Frustum

The example code below provides OpenGL with an idea of where you want objects to be in the world and how it should project those objects onto your viewport.

```perl
1  #!/usr/bin/perl -w
2  #
3  # Creates a GL viewport and view frustum
4
5  use OpenGL;
6
7  sub glInit {
8      # Creates the OpenGL viewport to render into
9      glpOpenWindow( );
10
11     # Creates the view frustum, with near clipping
12     # plane at z = 1 and far clipping plane at z = 20
13     glMatrixMode( GL_PROJECTION );
14     glFrustum(-1.0, 1.0, -1.0, 1.0, 1.0, 20.0);
15 }
16
17 ### Main program body
18
19 # Initialize any GL stuff
20 glInit( );
21
22 print "Press return to exit\n";
23
24 while ( <> ) {
25     exit;
26 }
```

In the listing above, lines 13 and 14 are the most important. Line 13 pulls the lever in the OpenGL state machine that says "Any operations from now on alter my idea of the view frustum." These operations might be matrix arithmetic if we needed to scale or rotate our view frustum. Line 14 defines the frustum itself, by fixing the coordinates of the viewport corners and the near and far clipping planes.

However, after running the script, you'll see the same thing as before. A window containing nothing, and that won't redraw.

Drawing Objects

Drawing objects in OpenGL is relatively simple. We need a method that redraws the screen and all of the objects on it. This sounds quite intensive, but OpenGL is a state machine-based rendering engine, which means that a good majority of the work is already done for us.

To begin drawing, we change the MatrixMode from GL_PROJECTION to GL_MODELVIEW to calculate matrix operations from our viewpoint and define a display method that will be invoked when the screen needs to be redrawn.

```perl
 1  #!/usr/bin/perl -w
 2
 3
 4  use OpenGL;
 5
 6  ### Initialization function
 7  sub glInit {
 8
 9      # Create the viewport
10      glpOpenWindow( );
11
12      # Define the view frustum
13      glMatrixMode( GL_PROJECTION );
14      glFrustum(-1.0, 1.0, -1.0, 1.0, 1.0, 20);
15
16      # Prepare to specify objects!
17      glMatrixMode( GL_MODELVIEW );
18  }
19
20  ### Display callback
21  sub display {
22
23      # Make sure we're smooth-shading now, so
24      # we can to blend the colors of the
25      # background polygon.
26      glShadeModel( GL_SMOOTH );
27
28      # Draw graded black->blue polygon first
29      glBegin( GL_POLYGON );
30      glColor3f( 0, 0, 0 );
31      glVertex3f( -20, 20, -19 );
32      glVertex3f( 20, 20, -19 );
33      glColor3f( 0, 0, 1 );
34      glVertex3f( 20, -20, -19 );
35      glVertex3f( -20, -20, -19 );
36      glEnd( );
37
38      glFlush( );
39      glXSwapBuffers( );
40  }
41
42  ### Main body of program
43
44  glInit( );
45  display( );
46
47  print "Press return to exit\n";
48
49  while ( <> ) {
50      exit;
51  }
```

This program is a little more involved! The interesting chunk is the `display` method between lines 21 and 40, which has OpenGL set the graphics pipeline to be smooth-shading, and then draw a polygon.

After the polygon is begun with `glBegin(GL_POLYGON)`, the next step is to tell OpenGL "Anything I do from now on will be black," as specified by `glColor3f(0,0,0)`. We then create two vertices at the top left and top right of the far clipping plane. Then we switch to blue by calling `glColor3f` again with the new RGB value (0, 0, 1). Finally, we create another two vertices of the polygon at the bottom right and bottom left of the far clipping plane, and then tell OpenGL that we have finished specifying that polygon with `glEnd`.

Lines 38 and 39 contain two commands to flush the graphics pipeline, resulting in the viewport being filled with a smoothly-shaded polygon as shown in Figure 27-10.

Figure 27-10. A smoothly-shaded polygon

And that's how we draw objects in OpenGL.

Some Viewport Tricks

You may have noticed that the viewport filled in as shown in Figure 27-11.

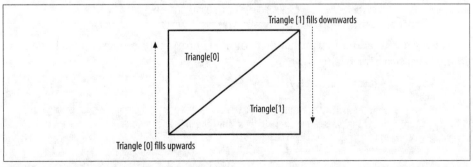

Figure 27-11. A smoothly-shaded polygon

This is quite a disturbing effect. Now, if you run the example program called planespin on the book web site, you can see the plane flickering and various visual artifacts appearing. This is horrible! What can we do?

Well, OpenGL supports *double buffering*, which means that instead of having only one buffer for your viewport, you have two. You render onto the off-screen buffer, and when rendering is complete, that buffer is swapped with the on-screen buffer. This completely eliminates the flickering, with very little overhead. If you alter the glpOpenWindow as follows, double-buffering will be enabled.

```
glpOpenWindow(attributes => [ GLX_RGBA, GLX_DOUBLEBUFFER ]);
```

We can also use other parameters with the glpOpenWindow call, such as the width and height of the viewport. For example, this creates a 200x200 double-buffered viewport for you.

```
glpOpenWindow(    width => 200, height => 200,
                attributes => [ GLX_RGBA, GLX_DOUBLEBUFFER ]);
```

Viewport Resize Issues

What happens if we resize the viewport in planespin? The actual window resizes, but the viewport doesn't. Yuck. We really ought to handle these events gracefully.

Stan's solution in the Perl OpenGL module is to add event handlers for certain events that we want to trap. We first need to add another parameter to glpOpenWindow informing the viewport which events to keep and which to discard. In the case of resizing the viewport, we wish to know only about StructureNotify requests, so the corresponding call is:

```
glpOpenWindow(    width => 300, height => 300,
                attributes => [ GLX_RGBA, GLX_DOUBLEBUFFER ],
                    mask => StructureNotifyMask );
```

The mask is a bit vector, so if we wished to trap keyboard events as well, we would bitwise OR StructureNotifyMask with KeyPressMask:

```
glpOpenWindow(    width => 300, height => 300,
                attributes => [ GLX_RGBA, GLX_DOUBLEBUFFER ],
                    mask => StructureNotifyMask | KeyPressMask );
```

We also want to add an event handler for ConfigureNotify requests, which we store in the %eventHandler hash:

```
$eventHandler{&ConfigureNotify} =
  sub {
    my ( $event, $width, $height ) = @_;
    print "Resizing viewport to $width x $height\n";
    glViewport( 0, 0, $width, $height );
  };
```

Now, all we need to do is process these events within the main while loop.

```
# While there are events in the X event queue
while ( $pendingEvent = XPending ) {
```

```
    # Fetch the next event in the queue
    my @event = &glpXNextEvent;

    # If we have a handler for this event type
    if ( $s = $eventHandler{$event[0]} ) {

        # Execute the handler
        &$s( @event );
    }
}
```

And that's all there is to it!

For your delectation and delight, there's a program called paperplane on this book's web site that whizzes some paperplane objects around inside the view frustum. It illustrates some of the more useful facets of Perl and OpenGL and is a good guide to help you navigate the murky waters of 3D programming.

Resources

To allow you to program OpenGL code from within Perl, you'll need the following:

- Perl.
- OpenGL. If you have a lot of money, there's a possibility that you may have a *real* OpenGL implementation on your machine already. This is quite likely on SGI platforms. If you don't have OpenGL, you can use Mesa instead; see *http://www.mesa3d.org/*.
- The Perl OpenGL module. You'll find this on CPAN.

References

Some literature that budding OpenGL gurus might find of interest:

- *Computer Graphics: Principles and Practice*, Second Edition, by Foley & Van Dam (Addison-Wesley). This weighty tome tells you *everything* you need to know about 3D graphics. If you're serious about graphics, this book is a must.
- *OpenGL Reference Manual: The Official Reference Document to OpenGL*, Version 1.1 (OpenGL ARB Architecture Review Board). This book has all you need to know to start programming with OpenGL, from basics such as creating polygons to complex lighting effects and texture mapping.
- The OpenGL web site: *http://www.opengl.org*.
- *Programming OpenGL for the X Window System*, by Kilgard (Addison-Wesley). This book details the use of OpenGL in the X Window System environment. It's filled with useful information and sample code, and discusses the interaction between OpenGL and X, which is of utmost importance in getting the best out of the Perl, OpenGL, and Tk threesome.

Acknowledgments

Thanks, in no particular order, go to: Mark Kilgard for graciously allowing permission to use parts of the paperplane code in this article; Stan Melax for writing the OpenGL module and reviewing this article; Andy Colebourne for reviewing this article and writing the splendid AC3D modeller which helped build many of the example code models. See *http://www.ac3d.org*.

## CHAPTER 28

Ray Tracing

Mark Jason Dominus

In this article, we'll look at one of the most flexible and versatile methods of rendering three-dimensional images with a computer: *ray tracing*. Suppose you have a model of a three-dimensional space, with some three-dimensional objects in it, and some light sources. Somewhere in that space is an observer, whom we'll call "you," and we'd like to render your view of the space and the objects in it. Ray tracing is a way to do it. This is serious stuff, used to render all kinds of computer graphics, including special effects in the movies *Terminator II* and *Toy Story*.

In order for an object to be visible to you, a ray of light must leave one of the light sources, bounce off the object, and reach your eye without bumping into anything opaque along the way. The idea behind ray tracing is simple: you can't see any light that doesn't enter your eye, so we can ignore all the other light. To understand what you see, all we need to do is follow the path of the light rays *backwards* from your eye and see if they eventually intersect a light source, perhaps after bouncing off of some objects along the way. If so, we render the objects appropriately. We'll see what "appropriately" means later on.

The important thing to notice here is all the zillions of light rays that we never had to consider at all. All sorts of light is bouncing around our space, and we ignored most of it, because we only followed the rays that came back to your eye.

I've written a small ray-tracing application called tracer. You can download it from the web page for this book and from *http://perl.plover.com/RayTracer/*. In the rest of this article, you'll see how it works.

Technique

We're going to be rendering your view into a rectangular "canvas" of pixels. Let's say for concreteness that this canvas is 200 pixels tall by 320 wide. The first thing we do is to imagine a *view plane* hanging in space in front of you. Figure 28-1 shows a rudimentary view plane, used by the artist Albrecht Dürer to help him study perspective and foreshortening effects.

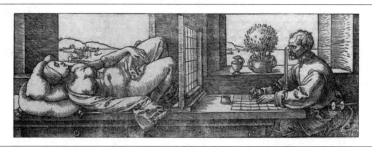

Figure 28-1. A rudimentary view plane

Dürer's view plane has only 36 divisions, because he could fill in all sorts of detail into each of his divisions; ours is going to have 64,000 divisions, one for each pixel. (We're crossing Dürer and Seurat here.)

For each pixel on the screen, we compute the ray that starts at your eye and passes through the pixel. We do some computations to see if it intersects any of the objects.

One tactic we can use to make things a lot simpler, at the expense of a little reality, is to just forget about the light sources. Instead, we'll just suppose that the entire space is uniformly lit from some invisible source. Each object will have a color, and if a ray strikes an object, we'll assume that we could have traced the reflected ray back to the omnipresent light source if we wanted to and render the appropriate pixel in that color without actually following the ray any farther.

How do we decide if the ray intersected an object or not? It depends on the object. For example, let's suppose that the object is a polyhedron. A polyhedron is made of faces, which are plane segments. To decide if the ray has intersected the polyhedron, we need to know if it has intersected any of the plane segments that contain its faces.

To do this, we first have to understand rays. The easiest way to represent a ray in the computer is with *parametric equations*. Imagine an insect flying along the ray; at each moment it has a particular x, y, and z position. Each of these depends on the current time, so there are three functions that depend on the time t: $x(t)$, $y(t)$, and $z(t)$>. These tell you the x, y, and z coordinates of the insect at any given moment. The path of the insect is completely determined by these three functions. t is the parameter that the parametric equations get their name from.

For straight lines such as light rays, the three equations are particularly simple. Suppose the ray starts at point (O_x, O_y, O_z) and also passes through the point (S_x, S_y, S_z). Then the three equations for the line are shown below.

$$x(t) = O_x + t \cdot (S_x - O_x)$$
$$y(t) = O_y + t \cdot (S_y - O_y)$$
$$z(t) = O_z + t \cdot (S_z - O_z)$$

Mathematicians get tired of writing everything three times, so they have a short-hand. They represent points by single boldface letters, so that each boldface letter stands for the three coordinates of some point.

For example, we'll write O instead of (O_x, O_y, O_z). For triples of functions like $(x(t), y(t), z(t))$, they use ordinary function notation with boldface, so they might write $\mathbf{P}(t)$ as an abbreviation for $(x(t), y(t), z(t))$, and the (t) in $\mathbf{P}(t)$ means the same as in $x(t)$: the whole thing still depends on t.

Then they play a trick; and call the boldface letters *vectors* and say that you can add and subtract them. You don't need to worry about what that really means; it's just a notational shorthand, so that we can write simply:

$$\mathbf{P}(t) = \mathbf{O} + t \cdot (\mathbf{S} - \mathbf{O})$$

instead of the three equations above. This one vector equation means exactly the same as the three earlier equations, no more and no less; the only difference is that the vector equation is quicker to write. The boldface tells you that it's standing for three equations instead of one; $\mathbf{S} - \mathbf{O}$ is shorthand for the three expressions that look like $(S_x - O_x)$, so $t \cdot (\mathbf{S} - \mathbf{O})$ is shorthand for the three expressions that look like $t \cdot (S_y - O_y)$. The t isn't in boldface; that tells you that the t is the same in all three equations instead of having x, y, and z versions. The whole thing is shorthand for the three equations shown earlier.

Now let's return to the polyhedron. Each face of the polyhedron is defined in terms of two parameters like this: $\mathbf{F}(u, v)$. We won't see a detailed example of this, because we won't need it. The ray intersects the face if there are some values for u and v and some number d that satisfy $\mathbf{P}(d) = \mathbf{F}(u, v)$.

Once we've found the point of intersection, $\mathbf{P}(d)$, we can figure out how far away from you it is. If there are two points of intersection, we just take the closer one, and render it; we can ignore the farther intersection because the closer one is in front of it, blocking your view of the farther one.

To handle a complete polyhedron, we do the same thing for each face. We compute whether or not the ray intersects each face, and if it does, we make a note of where; then we find the closest of all the intersection points and render it. We can ignore the intersection points that are farther away; you can't see them, because the faces with closer intersection points are in the way. I'm going to skip the mathematics again.

Make It Faster

To compute a low-resolution picture of 320×200 pixels, we need to send out 64,000 rays. If the space contains, say seven pyramids, nine cubes, and thirteen spheres, that makes $7 \times 5 + 9 \times 6 + 13 = 102$ objects altogether and that means we have to compute $64,000 \times 102 = 6,528,000$ intersections in all. You can see that ray tracing even simple images requires either a very fast computer or a lot of time—sometimes both.

(In computer graphics, "We took a lot of time with a very fast computer" is often the answer. In *Toy Story*, the character Andy had 12,384 hairs on his head, and Pixar had to render 114,240 frames of animation.)

Perl is not the best language for ray tracers, because Perl is pretty slow. For a good ray tracing demonstration that draws a reasonable picture before the seasons change, we have to cut some corners. We'll use a two-dimensional space instead of a three-dimensional space.

In two dimensions, we have to forget about fancy things like spheres and pyramids, and restrict ourselves to straight line segments. These can represent walls, so we'll be rendering pictures of mazes, as shown in Figure 28-2.

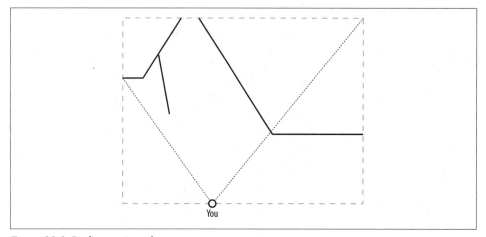

Figure 28-2. Bird's eye view of a maze

Why is this a win? Observers in two-dimensional spaces have two-dimensional eyeballs with one-dimensional retinas, and that means that the view plane, which was 320 × 200 pixels, becomes a view line 320 pixels long. Because there's no Y direction any more, instead of 64,000 rays, we only need to send out 320. That speeds things up about 200 times.

The picture that we draw should theoretically be 320 pixels wide by 1 pixel high, but unless you actually live in a two-dimensional universe, you probably haven't learned how to interpret such pictures. We'll cheat a little to fake an appearance of height without actually having to compute a lot. Walls look smaller when they're farther away, and the relationship between how far away they are and how big they look is very simple. Each time we trace a ray and find the wall that it intersects, instead of drawing one pixel, we'll draw a vertical line, and if we draw taller lines for nearer walls and shorter lines for farther walls, then the various parts of an oblique wall will appear to recede into the distance as the wall gets farther away from you. Figure 28-3 shows the output of tracer for the maze in Figure 28-2.

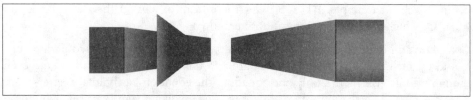

Figure 28-3. tracer output for the maze in graphics-ray-figure-2

This is an awful cheat but does make things faster. Don't be too quick to dismiss it, because when the folks at id Software wanted to put real-time ray-traced graphics into their game DOOM, this cheat is exactly what they used. DOOM takes place in a two-dimensional universe; consequently there are no stairwells or underpasses in DOOM. Sometimes things seem lower than other things, but that's because the id folks are faking height just the way we are. DOOM sold at least 250,000 copies, and you can't laugh at that kind of success. (DOOM also uses some other tricks that we'll see later.)

Mathematics

Let's suppose that our program knows where the walls are. A wall is just a line segment, and a line segment is completely determined by its two endpoints, let's say **G** and **H**. Remember that boldface letters represent entire points: three numbers in a three-dimensional space, or just an x and y coordinate in our flat space. The equation for a line segment is:

$$\mathbf{P}(t_1) = \mathbf{G} + t_1 \bullet (\mathbf{H} - \mathbf{G}) \quad (0 \leq t_1 \leq 1)$$

This is actually the equation of a line, not a line segment. When we find the intersection of our line of sight with $\mathbf{P}(t_1)$, we won't immediately know whether the ray actually intersected the wall. But this equation also has some other properties that make it easy to decide whether a given point is actually on the segment of interest:

- $\mathbf{P}(0) = \mathbf{G}$
- $\mathbf{P}(1) = \mathbf{H}$
- $\mathbf{P}(t_1)$ is on the line segment, between **G** and **H**, when $0 \leq t_1 \leq 1$
- If $t_1 < 0$ or $t_1 > 1$, then $\mathbf{P}(t_1)$ is not in the segment, although it is on the line that contains the segment.

The ray we want to follow starts at **O** (for "observer") and passes through the point **S** on the view plane that we're going to render. (View line, really.) Its equation:

$$\mathbf{I}(t_2) = \mathbf{O} + t_2 - (\mathbf{S} - \mathbf{O}) \ (t_2 \geq 0)$$

Again, this is the equation of a line, and that line passes through you. Since we'll be finding the intersection of this line with other lines, we'll need a way to decide if the intersection is in front of you or behind you. Happily, this equation has the property that if t_2 is positive, $\mathbf{I}(t_2)$ is in your line of sight, and if t_2 is negative, then $\mathbf{I}(t_2)$ is behind you. For example, $I(1) = S$, which is infront of you on the view plane, and $I(0) = O$, which is neither in front of nor behind you.

Computing an intersection between $P(t_1)$ and $I(t_2)$ requires finding two parameters, t_1 and t_2, such that $P(t_1) = I(t_2)$. There are two unknowns here, t_1 and t_2, and even though it looks like there's only one equation, the equation has boldface letters in it. That means it's shorthand for two equations, one involving x and one involving y, so finding the appropriate values for t_1 and t_2 is a simple exercise in high school algebra, which we'll omit because it's tedious (just like everything else in high school).

If you think you might enjoy the tedium, examine the program's Intersection subroutine. The best way to understand this is to solve the algebra problem on paper first, and then look at the code, because that's what I did to write it. This is an important general strategy for writing programs that need to do a lot of calculations: don't try to have the program actually do any mathematics, because mathematics is hard, and programming it is ten times as hard. Instead, do the mathematics yourself, until you get a totally canned solution that only requires that the numbers be plugged in, and then implement the canned solution.

The interesting part of the equations is the special cases. The equations for t_1 and t_2 turn out to be quotient of two complicated quantities, which I'll call A and B. B turns out to be zero exactly when the wall is parallel to your line of sight. In this case, the equations have no solution because they're going to say what part of the wall you see, and if your line of sight is parallel to the wall you can't see any of it. (In the code, B is stored in the variable $DEN.)

If t_2 turns out to be negative, the wall is actually behind you, and you can't see it, as Figure 28-4 shows.

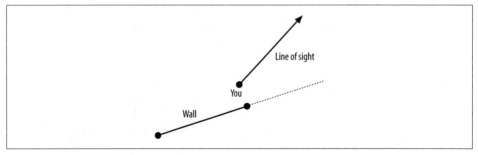

Figure 28-4. t_2 is negative, so the wall must be behind you

If $t_1 < 0$, or if $t_1 > 1$, then your line of sight misses the wall entirely, and you'll see past it to something else, as Figure 28-5 depicts.

In these cases, we shouldn't render part of the wall. But if $t_2 > 0$ and $t_1 \geq 0$ and $t_1 \leq 1$, then we have a real intersection, and your line of sight will intersect the wall if it hasn't intersected something else closer. TrueIntersection checks for these special cases.

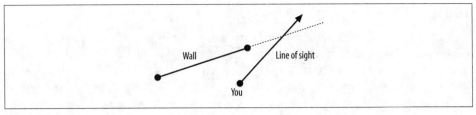

Figure 28-5. A missed ray

The Program

The main part of the program is structured like this:

```
for $p (0 .. 319) {
    Compute the appropriate point S on the view plane
    Compute the line of sight ray through S
    foreach wall ( all the walls ) {
        if ( the line of sight intersects the wall ) {
            find the intersection point X
            if ( X is nearer to you than N) {
                N = X;
                W = wall;
            }
        }
    }

    # W is now the nearest wall in the line of sight,
    # and N is the point on the wall that you see

    Figure out what color W is
    Figure out how far away N is
    Render this part of W appropriately
}
```

There's some code up front that reads a configuration file that says where the walls are and some code at the end to print out the rendered image in a suitable format, but the important part is right there.

The only interesting part of this that we haven't seen yet is "render appropriately." What that means is this: objects get smaller in proportion to how far away they are, so compute $h = 1/d$, where d is the distance that the wall is from the observer. Multiply h by an appropriate constant scaling factor, and the result is the apparent height of the wall, in pixels. In this program, the scaling factor we use arranges that a wall at distance 1 exactly fills the canvas; a wall at distance 2 fills half the canvas, and so on. Then "render appropriately" means to color a vertical line of pixels from $h/2$ to $200 - h/2$ in whatever color the wall is.

The Input

Input is simple. The file you provide contains descriptions of walls, one per line. Each line of data should have the x and y coordinates for each of the wall's two endpoints and a fifth number that says what color the wall is. These colors go from 0 to 360, with 0=red, 120=green, and 240=blue. Blank lines are ignored, and comments begin with a #, just like in Perl. You can find some sample files at my site and on the web page for this book.

The program understands a number of command-line options: -X and -Y set the size of the output picture in pixels and default to 320 and 200, respectively. Normally, the observer is at position (0,0), facing north; to change this, use -P X, Y, F, where X and Y are the x and y coordinates you want and F is the facing you want, with north=0 and east=90. For example, to position the observer at x=3, y=5, facing northwest, use -P 3,5,315.

Figure 28-6 illustrates the meaning of some other command-line parameters. You are at P, looking in the direction of the arrow. The view plane is the perpendicular segment from S_l to S_r. The -d command-line argument controls the distance between P (you) and the view plane; the default is 1. Object heights are computed relative to this distance, so if you make it too close, everything else will look really far away in relation. The -a option sets your range of vision. In the picture, that's the angle $\angle S_lPS_r$. The default is 90 degrees, so that you will be able to see 1/4 of the universe. You can set this parameter to any value larger than zero and less than 180°. Making it smaller will give you tunnel vision, and making it larger will turn you into a frog that can see on both sides of his head at once. Zero would mean that the view plane would have zero length, and 180° would give the view plane infinite length. Both are hard to divide into pixels, so tracer won't let you choose such extreme values.

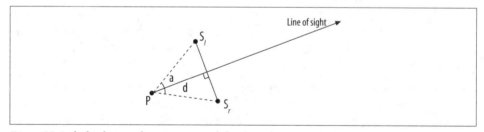

Figure 28-6. d, the distance between you and the view plane

The Output

I had a conundrum in designing the output routine. The ray tracer has to emit graphics in some format. GIF was an obvious choice, but GIF files are complicated, and I would have needed to use the GD library to write them. I didn't want to make everyone get GD just to run my ray tracer, so I made what might turn out to be a bad decision. I had tracer write its output as PPM.

PPM is an extremely simple 24-bit color graphics format; it was designed to be used as an interchange format, which means that if you need to convert from weird format *A* to weird format *B*, you probably don't have an appropriate converter program—but you might very well have a program for converting *A* to PPM and another from PPM to *B*. PPM is simple and fairly common; many popular image display programs can display it. For example, if you have the X Window System program xv, just say tracer | xv -. You probably have some PPM-capable conversion programs installed on your computer already; for example, the reference implementation of the JPEG standard comes with a program called cjpeg for converting PPM to JPEG. If you don't have any, the page *http://www.acme.com/software/pbmplus/* has links to programs that will convert PPM files to almost any format you care to name.

Internals

There are two important data structures in this program. One of these is the rendering canvas that the program draws on; the other is the collection of lines and vectors used to compute what you see.

The *rendering canvas* is a 320×200 array of pixels, where each pixel has three numbers from 0 to 255 representing the red, green, and blue intensities at that point. This is stored as an array of 200 strings, each with 320×3 = 960 characters. To set the color of the pixel in row $y and column $x, you just use a simple assignment:

```
substr($canvas[$y], $x*3, 3) = "j4K";
```

To make it black, you assign the string "\x0\x0\x0"; to make it bright green, assign "\x0\xff\x0". (ff is the hexadecimal code for 255, the maximum possible value.) Under some circumstances, assigning to substr is slow, because if the assigned-to string changes length, Perl has to copy the end part of it to a new position. In our program, we're always replacing exactly three bytes with exactly three new bytes, so the assignment is very quick.

It so happens that these 320 strings are already in PPM format (I told you it was simple); the output function (DisplayCanvas) is only two lines long. Another win for PPM.

Points and vectors in the program are represented as references to arrays with two elements: [$x, $y] is the point (*x*, *y*). There are a bunch of utility functions for adding vectors, scaling them, and so on; most of these are pretty simple. Here's an example: the Partway subroutine. It take three arguments: two points and a number *t*, and computes a third point partway between the two points, *t* of the way from the first to the second. If *t* = 0, you get the first point back; if *t* = 1/2 you get the point halfway between the two points; if *t* = 2/3 you get the point 2/3 of the way from the first point to the second.

```
sub Partway {
    my ($p1, $p2, $t) = @_;
    [($p1->[0] * (1-$t)) + ($p2->[0] * $t),
     ($p1->[1] * (1-$t)) + ($p2->[1] * $t)];
}
```

Lines, rays, and line segments are also references to arrays. Each array has three elements; the third is a string identifying the type: SEGMENT, RAY, or LINE. The first two items in each array are two points. For segments, they are the two endpoints; for rays, they're the endpoint and any other point; for lines, they're any two points on the line. All lines in this program are assumed to be parameterized in terms of the two points. That is, if the program needs a parametric equation for the line [$p1, $p2, WHATEVER], it just uses $P(t) = p_1 + t \cdot (p_2 - p_1)$, which, as we've seen, has convenient properties.

Other Directions

Ray tracing is such a useful and flexible technique that there are a lot of directions you can go. Here are just a few.

Sorting the objects

> If there are a lot of objects in the space, you can get a big performance win by sorting the objects into a list with the nearest objects first. Then when you're looking for intersections, you can try them in order from nearest to farthest. Near objects are likely to occlude farther objects, so doing this can save you from having to check a lot of far-away objects for intersections if you can decide that they'd be invisible anyway. Good-quality ray tracing software always does this.

Mirrors

> One fun and easy feature that this program omits is mirrors. Mirrors are awfully easy to handle in ray tracing software: when the line of sight intersects a mirror, you just change direction as appropriate and keep following it to its final destination. Ray tracing was invented in the early 1980's and caused an immediate outpouring of computer-generated pictures of stacks of ball bearings, Christmas tree ornaments, chrome teapots, and other shiny items. An excellent beginning project would be to add reflective walls to this ray tracer.

Light sources

> We made the simplifying assumption that there were no specific sources of light and that the whole space was uniformly lit from all directions. That was convenient, but not realistic. OMAR (Our Most Assiduous Reader) might like to try to add real light sources to this ray tracer. One complication: When the line of sight hits a wall, it scatters, and you have to follow every scattered ray to see how many of them make it back to the light source. You can tackle this head-on, if you have a big enough computer, or you can devise some clever ways to cheat.
>
> If you're going tackle the problem head-on, you end up following a lot of useless rays, and at some point, you're doing so much work that it makes more sense to just start at the light source and follow the rays forward instead. Rays start out with a certain intensity when they leave the source, and every time they reflect, you compute how far they've travelled and how much was absorbed in being reflected, and follow the new, dimmer rays, until you find the ones that reach the observer's eye. This is called *radiosity modeling*. It wasn't popular as long ago

as backwards ray tracing, because it requires so much more computer power. As computers have gotten better, radiosity methods have become more common.

Stereoscopic images

One nifty trick you can play for cheap is to render the same space from two slightly different positions, and then put them in a stereoscope. A stereoscope is a gadget that presents one picture to each eye at the same time; if the two pictures depict the same scene from slightly different positions, your brain will be fooled into seeing the scene in three dimensions. Details vary depending on what kind of stereoscopic equipment you have. If you have red-and-green 3-D glasses, then run the ray tracer in grayscale mode with the -G option, use image modification software to make the left one pink and the right one green, superimpose the pink and green images into one file, and print it on a color printer.

If you don't have a stereoscope or 3-D glasses, you can make a cheap stereoscope with a small pocket mirror. Reverse one of the images left-to-right, print out both images, and arrange the two pictures side by side on a table. Hold the mirror perpendicular to the table, between the pictures, silvered side facing left. With your right eye, look directly at the right image; with your left eye, look at reflection of the left image in the mirror. Adjust the mirror, the pictures, and your head until the left and right-eye images are superimposed.

Texture mapping

The walls drawn by tracer are single-colored. However, it's easy to render walls covered with arbitrarily complicated wallpaper. The intersection computation knows how far along the wall the intersection with the line of sight is (that's simply the t_1 parameter), and from that we can compute what part of the wallpaper you're looking at, and so what color to draw. This is quick and easy, and it's the second big trick that DOOM used to get good-looking pictures. This wallpapering technique is called *texture mapping*.

More interesting objects

In this program, everything is a wall, and all the walls are the same height. That makes it easy to draw the picture, because walls are simple, and if they're all the same height, you can't see over one to what's behind it. But the pictures are pretty dull. OMAR might like to modify this ray-tracer to support variable-height walls. With walls of uniform height, we just computed the intersection with the nearest wall, rendered that wall, and threw away the other intersection points. With variable-height walls, a tall wall farther away might be visible over a short nearby wall, so we must adopt a more complicated rendering strategy. We retain all the intersection points, and render all the visible walls, starting from the farthest and working toward the nearest, overwriting older walls with nearer ones as appropriate.

With this change, walls no longer need to start at the ground and go up; they could start in the air, or they could be very tall walls with horizontal windows in them, or whatever you like; you get all that for free. Doom does this, too.

## CHAPTER 29

Perl and the Gimp

Aaron Sherman

Once, early in my career, I needed a high resolution version of my company's logo. Any hand drawing of this logo would have been ugly, so I decided to write a small program in Tcl/Tk that drew the image and generated PostScript. This had the advantage of producing an infinitely scalable, mathematically perfect version of the company logo (which happened to be quite regular).

Well, times have changed, but I'm still doing company logos for projects that I'm working on. Now I have a new tool in my belt: the Gimp (*http://www.gimp.org*). The Gimp is a powerful, Photoshop-like image manipulation program with a plug-in interface. Unlike Photoshop, this plug-in interface is self-documenting and extensible. Also, the Gimp allows programmers complete control from their favorite language. Mine is Perl, of course, but APIs also exist for Scheme, C, and C++.

As an introduction to the Gimp and its Perl interface, I will go over what *you* might want to do with the Gimp. If you're familiar with the Gimp, you might want to skip this section. Then I'll discuss where you can get the tools you need, and finally I'll walk you through a simple Gimp/Perl script that generates the logo for my current company (nothing like a shameless plug). Figure 29-1 shows the beginning of this process. This is a very simple example, but it has the advantage of being small enough to analyze in depth.

Using the Gimp

The Gimp (which is an acronym for GNU Image Manipulation Program) was written by Spencer Kimball and Peter Mattis, two graduate students at UC Berkeley. They released the source code for an early version, and since then development has been a whirlwind of effort by hundreds of people writing everything from simple plug-ins to language interfaces to documentation. The graphics toolkit (Gtk+) that was written to handle the Gimp's display (buttons, scroll-bars, and so on) has even become the cornerstone of many other efforts, including the GNOME user interface.

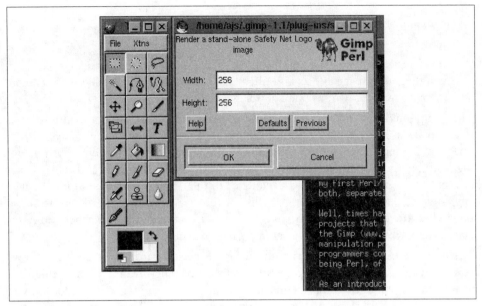

Figure 29-1. Creating a Gimp image using Gimp-Perl

So what does it do? The simple explanation is that the Gimp can be thought of as a paint program with several key features:

Layers

> *Layers* allow you to work on different parts of the image as though they were on separate sheets of transparent plastic. Anyone who has ever cut up a newspaper and pasted portions onto a single sheet of paper for photocopying is familiar with the process: you pull elements from different sources together and combine them.

Channels

> Your image is made up of pixels, and each pixel has several *channels*. For example, in a typical color image there is one red channel, one green channel, and one blue channel. In the Gimp, you can manipulate each of these channels separately. You can also add other channels, which might be useful for storing information which relates to the image, but is not visual (for instance, a selection shape). Such user-defined layers do not appear in the composite image, but can be saved in certain file formats. You can also break down an image into the alternate cyan, magenta, yellow, and black colorspace for pesky physical processes like printing.

Alpha channels

> In order for layers to have transparent or translucent parts, there needs to be a separate chunk of data associated with each pixel of a layer that describes how opaque or transparent it is. This is called the *alpha channel* and is stored along with the other channels used for holding color information.

Animation

Use Gimp's layers as as series of frames to edit animation, such as animated GIFs.

Scripting

Many programming languages can be used to write extensions for the Gimp, including new image effects and filters and scripts that use the Gimp to generate an image of their own (as our example will do).

The Gimp builds on and combines each of these concepts, creating a wealth of tools that can be used to do just about anything to an image, including analysis of an image in alternate colorspaces (for printing); photographic touch-up features including burning and dodging (techniques used in photo developing); and many other advanced features. For an excellent reference to the Gimp, I recommend *http://www. gimp.org/docs.html*, which has a good list of tutorials and manuals. There is also a book, *The Artists' Guide to the Gimp* by Michael J. Hammel (Frank Kasper and Associates, Inc.), which has a web page at *http://www.thegimp.com/*.

The Perl interface to the Gimp is built on top of the standard Gimp C API. It allows you to create new functions and menu entries called *plug-ins* that are indistinguishable from the standard Gimp menus and functions. When you write a plug-in, you are writing a stand alone program using Gimp libraries. The Gimp executes this program once during start-up to register the plug-in name and to add its menu entry. When that menu entry is selected (or the function is called from another plug-in), the Gimp runs the plug-in again. For example, if you select the Xtns (extensions) menu from the toolbox window and then select the Render sub-menu, you will see an SNS Logo entry if *and only if* you have installed the example code from below in your *.gimp/plug-ins* directory. It will appear as shown in Figure 29-2.

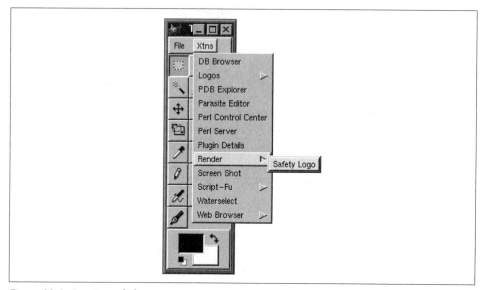

Figure 29-2. A registered plug-in

When the user runs a plug-in, they are presented with a dialog box that lists each of the plug-in's parameters. Fortunately, you don't have to write the code that displays the dialog box; that's all been taken care of for you. You just have to specify the parameter types so that the Gimp knows what sorts of things to ask the user.

To demonstrate plug-ins, you can run the many Script-Fu Logo plug-ins (under Xtns/Script-Fu/Logos), which all take a text string and render it using an effect (e.g., chrome, neon, or alien glow.) A demonstration of the Cool Metal plug-in is shown in Figure 29-3.

Figure 29-3. The Cool Metal plug-in

Perl opens up many areas to Gimp developers unavailable in other languages. For example, one of the recently contributed Perl plug-ins, image-tile, can render an image by tiling several thousand other images as the parts of the overall picture. This technique is so memory-intensive that the information stored about each image needs to be stored in a Berkeley DB database, which Perl knows how to map to a hash, transparently. This kind of convenience makes writing large, complex plug-ins for the Gimp quite simple and puts the focus of the programmer back on the effect.

Getting the Tools

Right now the Gimp works on both Unix and Windows, but the Windows version doesn't support Perl yet.

You can get a precompiled version of Gimp from *http://www.gimp.org/download.html* and Gtk+/Glib from *http://www.gtk.org/download.html*. The development series is available from the same places but usually only in source code form.

The Gimp and PDL Perl modules can be downloaded from CPAN. For access to the source, I highly recommend the article (by Zach Beane, the maintainer of the Gimp News site) at: *http://www.xach.com/gimp/tutorials/cvsgimp.html*.

If you want, you can get the Gimp straight from the source code repository. It will be more unstable (this is where new bugs first appear) but can be worth the extra effort in terms of getting access to the latest features. When reading Zach's article, add gnome-perl to the list of modules to download and install:

```
cd $PREFIX
cvs -z3 get gnome-perl
cd gnome-perl
perl Makefile.PL PREFIX=$PREFIX
make
make install
```

Do this after the steps described for downloading the source, compiling Glib and compiling gtk+, but before compiling Gimp.

The 5.004 Perl series may work for Gimp, but there are some features that will not be supported. For example, the Last Vals button will not work without Data::Dumper, which is bundled with 5.005.

For all versions, the Gimp module really wants to have both the Perl Data Language (the PDL module; see *http://pdl.perl.org*), which in turn likes to have Mesa (a 3D OpenGL library described in *OpenGL*) around. Mesa is supposedly optional for PDL, but I've had problems compiling without it. It's a very nice library to have around, especially in combination with the xscreensaver program, which can take advantage of it. PDL is quite large by itself, but the Gimp uses it to allow efficient manipulation of image data (which would be very slow in Perl if you had to do it pixel-by-pixel). Most of the time, you'll find that you don't need PDL, because many high-level functions already exist to generate the effects that you want. You can find Mesa at *http://www.mesa3d.org/*.

The order of installation should be:

1. Perl
2. Mesa (optional)
3. PDL (optional)
4. Glib
5. Gtk+ (C library)
6. Gtk (Perl module)
7. Gimp (program)
8. Gimp (Perl module)

Using the Gimp Module

A Gimp/Perl plug-in, as mentioned previously, is a Perl program. It is called by the Gimp and uses the Gimp API to perform some action. Some plug-ins affect the current image, such as the blur filter; others let you type a string and then render it with

---

a special effect, such as Cool Metal's chrome. The example in this article is like a logo plug-in, but generates a shape instead of text.

Plug-ins for the Gimp go into your *$HOME/.gimp/plug-ins* directory. (If you are using Gimp version 1.1, you will need to put things under *$HOME/.gimp-1.1/plug-ins*.) They need to be made executable, so chmod a+x the program from your Unix prompt. I recommend that you edit them elsewhere and copy them in, as things such as backup copies and auto-save files can confuse the Gimp.

Before getting into the example, let's discuss a few basic concepts. Your plug-in is either being provided with an image, or (as in this example) you'll be creating one. This image is represented by a Perl scalar variable, and most plug-ins call it $img or $image. When you want to modify an image, you will need a drawable. A *drawable* is an abstract term that can refer to a layer or any other part of an image that you can draw into. Your plug-in doesn't have to worry about this, it just needs to use the drawable that it was given. Or, if it's creating its own image, the layer that you create. To make this even more convenient, every Gimp/Perl plug-in that operates on an existing image takes the image and drawable as its first two parameters.

There are a few other types to know about when writing plug-ins, but the only one that we will work with here is a *color*. Colors are manipulated by reference in a three-element array (red, green, and blue), but most often, you simply tell Gimp/Perl that your plug-in needs the user to select a color, and it will be passed to your plug-in. Other types such as layers and channels are similar to the image type. They are opaque data-structures, which you manipulate by reference. (Actually, they're objects, but unless you want to use the object-oriented interface you don't have to worry about that.)

Now let's see the Gimp in action. Example 29-1 creates a new image and draws the logo for my company in it. The current foreground and background colors are used, as well as the currently selected paintbrush (check out the Brushes menu option under Dialogs, which is under File from the toolbox window for the available brush styles).

Example 29-1. A sample Gimp Perl script

```
#!/usr/bin/perl
#
# The Safety Net Solutions, Inc. Logo as a Gimp plug-in
#
# Written by Aaron Sherman, and distributed under the same terms
# as the Gimp itself. See http://www.gimp.org/ for details.
#
# This is an example script. For purposes of distribution of the logo
# which this program generates the Safety Net logo is a trademark of
# Safety Net Solutions, Inc. All rights reserved. (they made me say it ;)

# Initialize the Gimp library modules
use Gimp qw(:auto);  # The core Gimp API
```

Example 29-1. A sample Gimp Perl script (continued)

```perl
use Gimp::Fu;          # Gimp registration and data types
# use Gimp::Util;      # Gimp helper functions

use strict;

# Our plug-in function:
sub perl_fu_safety_logo {
  my $width  = shift;
  my $height = shift;
  my $img = gimp_image_new($width, $height, RGB); # Create the new image

  # Add a layer for us to work in:
  my $layer = gimp_layer_new($img, $width, $height, RGB_IMAGE,
                             "Safety Logo", 100, NORMAL_MODE);
  gimp_image_add_layer($img, $layer, 0);

  # Add background
  my $oldcolor = gimp_palette_get_foreground();
  gimp_palette_set_foreground(gimp_palette_get_background());
  gimp_selection_all($img);
  gimp_bucket_fill($layer, FG_BUCKET_FILL, NORMAL_MODE, 100, 0, 0, 0, 0);

  # Draw the vertical and horizontal axes:
  gimp_palette_set_foreground($oldcolor);
  gimp_selection_none($img);
  gimp_paintbrush($layer,0,
                  [$width/2, $height/18, $width/2, $height-$height/18]);
  gimp_paintbrush($layer,0,
                  [$width/18, $height/2, $width-$width/18, $height/2]);

  # Draw the diagonal axes:
  my $magic = ($width/18*7) / sqrt(2);
  gimp_paintbrush($layer,0,
                  [$width/2-$magic, $height/2-$magic,
                   $width/2+$magic, $height/2+$magic]);
  gimp_paintbrush($layer,0,
                  [$width/2-$magic, $height/2+$magic,
                   $width/2+$magic, $height/2-$magic]);

  # Draw the concentric ellipses:
  for (my $i = 0; $i < 4; $i++) {
      gimp_ellipse_select($img, $width/18*(2+$i),    $height/18*(5+$i),
                                $width/18*(14-$i*2), $height/18*(8-$i*2),
                          SELECTION_REPLACE, 1, 0, 0);
      gimp_edit_stroke($layer);
      gimp_ellipse_select($img, $width/18*(5+$i),    $height/18*(2+$i),
                                $width/18*(8-$i*2), $height/18*(14-$i*2),
                          SELECTION_REPLACE, 1, 0, 0);
      # gimp_edit_stroke will use current foreground color and brush
      gimp_edit_stroke($layer);
  }
```

Example 29-1. A sample Gimp Perl script (continued)

```
   # Finish up, and display:
   gimp_selection_none($img);
   gimp_displays_flush( );
   return $img;
}

# Register the plug-in:
register("safety_logo", "Render a stand-alone Safety Net Logo image",
         "Renders the Safety Net Solutions company logo in the " .
         "currently selected brush and fg/bg colors.",
         "Aaron Sherman", "(c) 1999, Aaron Sherman",
         "1999-03-29", "<Toolbox>/Xtns/Render/Safety Logo", "*",
         [
          [PF_INT32, "Width",  "Width",  256],
          [PF_INT32, "Height", "Height", 256]
         ],
         \&perl_fu_safety_logo);

# Call Gimp::Fu's main( ):
exit main( );
```

Let's look at what each step of this plug-in does. You need to include and initialize the Gimp modules:

```
use Gimp qw(:auto);
use Gimp::Fu;
```

These are the two basic libraries. (The :auto forces inclusion of the entire Gimp Procedural Database as auto-loaded functions.) Don't confuse the Gimp::Fu module, which implements things like the registration interface, with Script-Fu. Script-Fu is the Scheme scripting interface for the Gimp. (Scheme is a programming language derived from LISP.) Gimp::Fu and Script-Fu have nothing to do with each other.

```
# use Gimp::Util;
```

Gimp::Util is not strictly necessary, but if you include it, you can use a few extra goodies that it provides. For example, this module provides functions for adding text to an image (usually a multiple-step process) or finding a layer's position in an image. You can use perldoc Gimp::Util for more information. This script does not use these functions, so the line has been commented out.

Most of your plug-in will be a subroutine, whose name can be whatever you like. Since you can register the function under a different name with the Gimp, you *can* choose any name here. However, be careful to avoid any name which is currently in use in the Gimp's Procedural Database (PDB). Use the DB Browser under the Xtns menu to make sure that your function name is not already in use. If you choose the same name as a PDB function, you will hide the Gimp version of the function from your program.

```
sub perl_fu_safety_logo {
```

In this function, you need to receive any arguments that were passed to you, and (as you'll see below) you can tell the Gimp what types of parameters you expect. If your plug-in is for working on an existing image, the first two parameters will always be an image and a drawable. In this case, we are creating our own image, so we expect only the plug-in specific parameters:

```
sub perl_fu_safety_logo {
    my $width  = shift;
    my $height = shift;
```

Now, this is where we need to actually start talking to the Gimp. You do this through calls to the PDB. The Perl interface for doing this looks just like normal function calls. Use the DB Browser, as mentioned previously, to search the PDB for the function you're looking for. This browser allows you to look at all of the Gimp functions and plug-ins, their arguments and return values, and documentation for each one. In the following examples, I won't touch on *all* of the parameters for every function; you can use the PDB browser to look up anything from the example source code that I skip.

The first thing we want to do is create our new image with the given width and height:

```
my $img = gimp_image_new($width, $height, RGB);
```

That's it! You've now got a new image (of type RGB—full color). Of course, it has nothing in it. That's not quite the same as being blank, which would mean that it has a background and nothing else. This image really has *nothing* in it. In order to have actual image content in the Gimp, we must add a layer:

```
my $layer = gimp_layer_new($img, $width, $height,
                    RGB_IMAGE, "Safety Logo", 100, NORMAL_MODE);
gimp_image_add_layer($img, $layer, 0);
```

Notice that the type for this layer is RGB_IMAGE, and not RGB as we used for our image. Also, an *opacity* must be specified, which tells us how opaque or transparent this layer is (here, we give 100%). NORMAL_MODE refers to the layer combination mode, which is an advanced feature that can be used for some stunning effects.

The third parameter to gimp_image_add_layer specifies which layer this should be in the image's list of layers. The first layer, layer 0, is the closest to the observer. Each successive layer is farther away from the viewer and may thus be obscured by layers above it. Here, we'll use only the one layer, to keep things simple.

Now you have to clear out your new layer, because at first it might have random garbage in it. You can do this by using gimp_bucket_fill to put a background color in it or by using gimp_edit_clear. gimp_edit_clear will have different behavior, depending on whether the layer can have transparent areas (an alpha channel). Here we simply paint our background using gimp_bucket_fill, which could also be used to paint a pattern, if we wished. Note that gimp_drawable_fill is a new function that should be a little faster and easier but may not exist in your version of Gimp yet.

```
my $oldcolor = gimp_palette_get_foreground();
gimp_palette_set_foreground(gimp_palette_get_background());
gimp_selection_all($img);
gimp_bucket_fill($layer, FG_BUCKET_FILL, NORMAL_MODE,
        100,0,0,0,0);
gimp_palette_get_foreground() and
        gimp_palette_set_foreground()
```

`gimp_palette_get_foreground` and `gimp_palette_set_foreground` both work on the user-selected foreground and background colors. This is why we save the value: so that it can be restored later. We could have used the `BG_BUCKET_FILL` parameter, and then none of this would be necessary, but doing it this way lets us demonstrate more features.

`gimp_selection_all` selects the entire image, and `gimp_bucket_fill` fills up the entire selection with the current foreground color. As before, the `NORMAL_MODE` and 100 arguments are layer mode (paint mode, in this case) and opacity. The last four arguments only matter if there is no selection, and that is not the case, here. So, we've filled the entire layer with the background color, which is a good starting place.

An important thing to note: the second parameter to `gimp_bucket_fill` must be a drawable. In this case, we pass a layer, which is one kind of drawable. There are other drawables, and you will find them as you work with the Gimp. However, keep in mind that if you write a plug-in that works on an existing image (see the register function, below) you will be given a drawable, which you can use for calls like `gimp_bucket_fill`, but it may not actually be a layer. You should never assume that it is, which is what you're doing if you pass it to a a function such as `gimp_layer_resize`.

```
gimp_palette_set_foreground($oldcolor);
gimp_selection_none($img);
gimp_paintbrush($layer, 0, [$width/2, $height/18,
        $width/2, $height-$height/18]);
gimp_paintbrush($layer, 0, [$width/18, $height/2,
        $width-$width/18, $height/2]);
```

Here, we reset the user's foreground color, unset the selection, and draw our first two lines. It is possible to select a brush shape for the `gimp_paintbrush` function, but we leave this up to the user. Note that the third parameter to `gimp_paintbrush` is an anonymous array (the list inside brackets); more on this later.

```
my $magic = ($width/18*7) / sqrt(2);
gimp_paintbrush($layer, 0,
        [$width/2-$magic, $height/2-$magic,
        $width/2+$magic, $height/2+$magic] );
gimp_paintbrush($layer, 0,
        [$width/2-$magic, $height/2+$magic,
        $width/2+$magic, $height/2-$magic] );
```

Here, we draw the next lines, diagonally, using a little bit of geometry to figure out where the endpoints of the vertical or horizontal lines would be if we rotated them by 45 degrees:

```
for (my $i = 0; $i < 4; $i++) {
    gimp_ellipse_select($img, $width/18*(2+$i),
```

```
          $height/18*(5+$i), $width/18*(14-$i*2),
          $height/18*(8-$i*2), SELECTION_REPLACE,
          1, 0, 0);
     gimp_edit_stroke($layer);
     gimp_ellipse_select($img, $width/18*(5+$i),
          $height/18*(2+$i), $width/18*(8-$i*2),
          $height/18*(14-$i*2), SELECTION_REPLACE,
          1, 0, 0);
     gimp_edit_stroke($layer);
}
```

The gimp_ellipse_select function selects an elliptical region defined by the given x, y, width, and height. The SELECTION_REPLACE parameter tells it to replace any existing selection, and the next parameter tells it to use anti-aliasing for smoothing the "stair-stepping" on the edges. gimp_edit_stroke is like gimp_paintbrush but traces the current selection. So the two functions together draw an ellipse:

```
gimp_selection_none($img);
gimp_displays_flush();
return $img;
```

These are final steps that should be used to leave the user in a sane state. We unset the selection, flush any pending display draws, and return the image that we created. The Gimp module will display it for us.

Now, the most important part: registration. In order for the Gimp to use our plug-in, it must know what it is called and how to execute it. Here is the registration statement:

```
register("safety_logo", "Render a stand alone Safety Net Logo image",
     "Renders the Safety Net Solutions company logo in the " .
     "currently selected brush and fg/bg colors.",
     "Aaron Sherman", "(c) 1999, Aaron Sherman",
     "1999-03-29", "<Toolbox>/Xtns/Render/Safety Logo", "*",
     [
     [PF_INT32, "Width",  "Width",  256],
     [PF_INT32, "Height", "Height", 256]
     ],
     \&perl_fu_safety_logo);
```

The full documentation can be found in Gimp::Fu, but the basic idea is that the first seven parameters are just strings that set the name of the plug-in, the description, help text, author's name, copyright message, date of last modification, and the menu in which the plug-in appears. The menu path is the only interesting parameter. If it begins with <Image>, then it will be placed in the menu that comes up when the user right-clicks in an image. If it begins with <Toolbox>/Xtns, then it will show up under the Xtns menu in the main Gimp window. You can also use the menu <None> to tell the Gimp not to display your plug-in as a menu option. You might do this if you were writing a function meant to be used only by other plug-ins.

The eighth parameter describes the image types that this plug-in can work on. In our case, * makes sense because there is no input image, only an output.

The next parameter specifies the list of parameters to the plug-in. It is a list of lists, using anonymous arrays. Each of the inner anonymous arrays contains the description of a single expected parameter. The description is made up of at least four values: the type, name, description, and default value. As an example, let's say you added the following item to the end of the list of plug-in parameters:

```
[PF_COLOR, "Brush stroke color", "Color", [0, 0, 0]]
```

The Gimp module displays a dialog box like the one in Figure 29-4. Notice the black button [0, 0, 0] is black in RGB notation. If the user clicks on the button, they get a nice color selection dialog box for choosing a new brush color Figure 29-5. The parameter types are all defined in the PARAMETER TYPES section of the Gimp::Fu documentation. The only remaining argument to register is a reference to your new function.

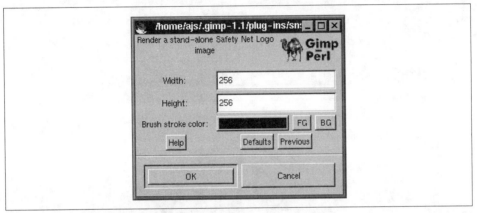

Figure 29-4. A Gimp dialog box

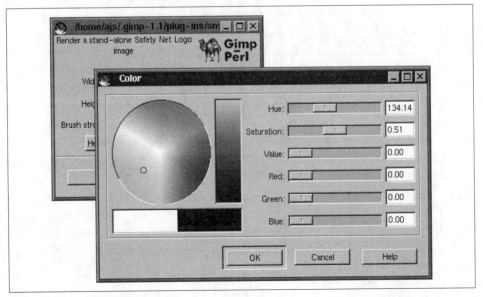

Figure 29-5. A color selection dialog

Plug-ins in the <Image> menu will be available under the pop-up menu that appears when you click the right mouse button in an image. They will automatically get the image and drawable to work on as their first two parameters, so don't list these parameters yourself. Plug-ins such as ours that live in the <Toolbox> menu aren't associated with any particular image, although you can declare one or more image parameters that allow the user to select from any currently open image. The last parameter to register is a reference to the function that actually implements the plug-in.

The last thing that your plug-in should do is exit with the status returned from the main function, like so:

```
exit main;
```

This closes the loop with the Perl::Fu interface, allowing it to take over. The Gimp can then tell it which of several ways it is being asked to behave. You don't have to worry about any of this; just call main. Be sure not to define a subroutine in your plug-in called main, or you'll be sorry. The finished product is shown in Figure 29-6.

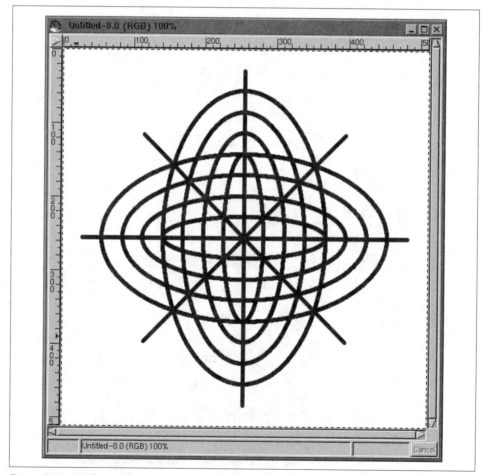

Figure 29-6. Our logo in progress

Moving On

Some notes to help you in your budding career as a plug-in author:

- There is a mailing list for discussion about Gimp-Perl. To subscribe, send mail with the single line `subscribe` to `gimp-perl-request@lists.netcentral.net`.

- You can be notified of new versions. Send mail with the single line `subscribe notify-gimp` to `majordomo@plan9.de`.

- Please upload anything you think would be useful to others to the Gimp Plug-In Registry: *http://registry.gimp.org/*.

- In the example above, `gimp_paintbrush` demonstrated a very useful feature of the Perl Gimp module. If you look in the PDB documentation for `gimp_paintbrush`, you will see that the third parameter is a number of stroke coordinates, and the fourth parameter is the array of stroke coordinates. In Perl, we only have to give an array reference, and the module will calculate its length for us. So wherever you see a function that needs a count followed by an array, just pass the array.

- Fonts are the most evil thing ever, because (like X) the Gimp failed to abstract them sufficiently. As a result, you have to force the user to select a font and size, even though the font selection box already includes a size parameter. This is because some font names (such as scalable fonts from a TrueType font server) don't include size information, and the Gimp only tracks fonts by their full XFont name. I've started using the convention that if the user enters a size of < 1, I use the font-provided size, but that's a kludge around a broken feature.

- You will really want to study other sources of Gimp user info (see *www.gimp.org*) and find out more about feathering, alpha layers, and channels.

- For the menu path, don't put your plug-ins under Script-Fu, and don't invent new menus if you can help it. Put them in with the other plug-ins that are written in C (e.g., `<Image>/Filters/section/plug-in` or `<Toolbox>/Xtns/section/plug-in`).

- Read the Gimp-Perl documentation. You can use your plug-in standalone, or talk across the network to a Gimp process. You can even debug plug-ins using the Perl debugger, which is almost impossible with some of the other plug-in interfaces.

- Gimp 1.0 and 1.1 differ in that some functions no longer take an image as their first parameter. Gimp-Perl gets around this by allowing you to leave out the image parameter in the older Gimps, but you may have to patch your 1.0 scripts to make them work with 1.1, or eventually 1.2.

- If you write two or more related plug-ins, they can go in the same file. You just need to have one `register` statement per plug-in.

- If you want to know what's going on inside your plug-in, try using `Gimp::set_trace(TRACE_ALL)`. This spews a *lot* of information, but lets you see everything that's going on.

When you look at the PDB documentation, you'll see that all of the functions have dashes in their names. So that you can call these as Perl functions, the Gimp module converts all PDB names to use underscores instead of dashes. It will also do the reverse to your plug-in's name (as declared in the `register` statement) so that other Gimp plug-ins can use the standard Gimp naming conventions. This means that you should name your plug-ins with underscores, not dashes (e.g., `my_plug_in`, not `my-plug-in`).

Good luck, and happy Gimping!

## CHAPTER 30

Glade

Ace Thompson

There once was a time when "Windows" meant Microsoft. Nowadays, if you don't precede the word with "Microsoft" or "X," you may unwittingly reveal yourself as out-of-the-know. There are very few Linux distributions that don't try to start an X session during the installation process, and the battle over desktop environments (Gnome versus KDE) and GUI toolkits (GTK+ versus Qt) puts the Cola Wars to shame.

The Unix desktop wars are clearly not limited to the various Linux distributions; the Gnome Project, for example, has gained the support of several large corporations. And it isn't too far-fetched to imagine stable ports of XFree86 and other Unix-y essentials coming to the Microsoft and Apple worlds (think Cygwin and Apple's OS X), opening up the possibility of even more widespread exposure for these desktop environments and the tools and applications that live in them.

How does this affect Perl developers? Perl has never lacked muscle in the world of back-end tool development and is often described as the duct-tape of the Internet. On the server side, Perl is considered by many to be the language of choice for web development (look at the hundreds of Apache:: modules), database tools (DBI), text processing, application prototyping, haiku generation, and more. But GUI development?

What does it mean when the ground Perl sits on most firmly (the Unix world) begins its move to the desktop? In a peek at an increasingly popular area, this article presents one of the options available for developers wishing to develop GUIs with Perl on Unix.

GTK+/Gnome

One of the major players in the Unix desktop game is the Gnome Project, which is now steered by the Gnome Foundation. A Gnome desktop consists of applications built using GTK+ (Graphical ToolKit). The Gnome framework also provides other important features, such as CORBA services, internationalization, and session management. GTK+ provides the widgets—buttons, windows, menus, detachable toolbars, and so on—which, when assembled properly, create the user experience.

There are also several Gnome widgets, many composed of multiple GTK+ widgets, which provide a common cross-application interface for basic tasks; there's a Gnome

Number Entry widget for entering numbers, a Gnome File Entry to let users select files, and a Gnome About Dialog that provides a standard format for About dialog boxes.

These widgets save time for developers, providing built-in functionality for basic tasks in addition to creating a common and convenient user experience across applications. For example, the Gnome Number Entry widget allows the user to enter a number manually or to bring up a calculator for complex calculations, without a single line of code by the programmer. Also, the Gnome File Entry dialog box lets users browse filesystems to choose a file. These types of widgets make life easier for developers, and shorten the learning curve as users move from one Gnome application to another.

Perl and GTK+/Gnome

There are several tools that bring Perl to the world of GUI development on the Gnome desktop. The most important are the Perl bindings to the GTK+ library. The Perl GTK+ bindings, known collectively as Gtk-Perl, are currently maintained by Paolo Molaro and available on CPAN or at the Gtk-Perl homepage (*http://www.gtkperl.org/*).

Gtk-Perl allows you to create widgets and respond to user input in a fashion similar to Perl/Tk and Perl-Qt. Using Gtk-Perl alone, however, forces you to manage the creation and arrangement of widgets in your code. Not only is this time-consuming and prone to error, it can also be an obstacle in creating medium- to large-sized applications, because the functionality of your application gets mixed up with the definition of the user interface, one of the first no-no's in good GUI design.

Glade

Luckily, we have Glade. Glade is a free user interface builder for GTK+ and Gnome, available at *http://glade.gnome.org/*. Glade doesn't force a language upon you; as of this writing, Glade applications can be designed with C, C++, Ada95, Python, or Perl.

Glade simply defines the arrangement of the graphical widgets making up your application and stores this definition as XML. Then special code in your language of choice reads this definition, and using the GTK+/Gnome bindings in that language, puts together the interface when your application launches. Your code, and the main GTK+ user event handler, do the rest. In the case of Perl, the "special code" gluing Glade and Perl together is creatively named Glade-Perl and was developed by Dermot Musgrove. It is available on CPAN or at *http://www.glade.perl.connectfree.co.uk/*. To summarize:

Gnome
　　A graphical user environment
GTK
　　GUI library used by Gnome
Glade
　　A graphical interface designer for GTK applications
Perl
　　A language that can implement a Glade-designed interface

Installation

Setting up the Glade-Perl development environment is fairly simple. First, you must have a Gnome desktop running. Most Linux distributions include an option to install Gnome. If you don't want to go through a fresh Linux installation, you can go to the Gnome Project web site (*http://www.gnome.org*) and find installation information there. Ximian (*http://www.ximian.com*) also provides an easy Gnome installation.

The latest stable version of Glade-Perl (0.57) requires gnome-libs 1.2.4 and GTK+ 1.2.7. You can discover your version of gnome-libs by typing `gnome-config --version` at a shell prompt, and you can find out which version of GTK+ you have by typing `gtk-config --version` at a shell prompt. Second, you must download and install the most recent version of Glade from *http://glade.gnome.org/*. Finally, you should install the most recent versions of Glade-Perl and XML::Parser from CPAN. You should get the latest version of Gtk-Perl from the Gtk-Perl homepage (*http://www.gtkperl.org*).

Designing an Interface

Putting together a user interface in Glade is easy. Start Glade, and look at the Palette window, shown in Figure 30-1. This window displays the various widgets you can use. The widgets are grouped into various categories (more categories and widgets can be added to the palette; for example, if you install gnome-db, the Gnome database connectivity package, you can include gnome-db widgets in your application).

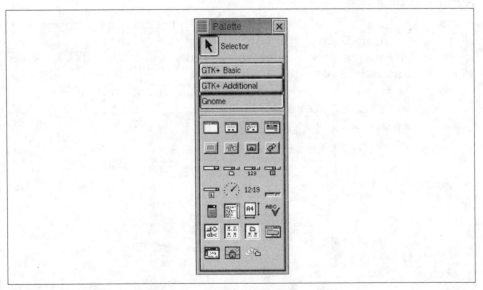

Figure 30-1. The Palette window

Gnome applications typically start with a Gnome application window. You can find this widget under the Gnome tab in the Palette window. When you create this widget, Glade gives it the name `app1`. We'll use this name later.

The Gnome application window contains a standard menu bar, toolbar, and status line; it's an effort to give Gnome applications a standard look and feel (Figure 30-2).

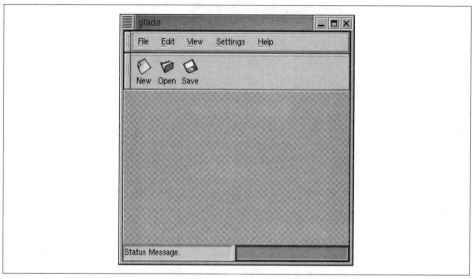

Figure 30-2. The Gnome application window

Adding Code

A standard look and feel doesn't do much good if the buttons don't do anything. To illustrate, we will attach some code to the New button. First, click on the New button in the Gnome application window you created. Then go to Glade's Properties window and select the Signals tab, shown in Figure 30-3. Signals connect your code to user interface events (button clicks, list selections, mouse movements, and so on).

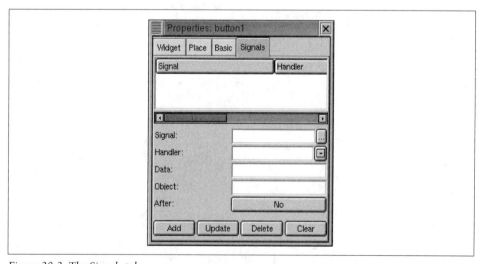

Figure 30-3. The Signals tab

Every widget has a set of signals which it emits if and when the user interacts with it. Clicking on the ellipsis (...) next to the Signal input box provides a list of the signals our New button can emit (Figure 30-4). Select clicked, press OK, and, returning to the Properties window, click the Add button (Figure 30-5).

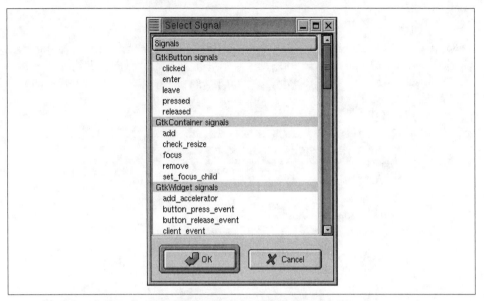

Figure 30-4. Signals from the New button

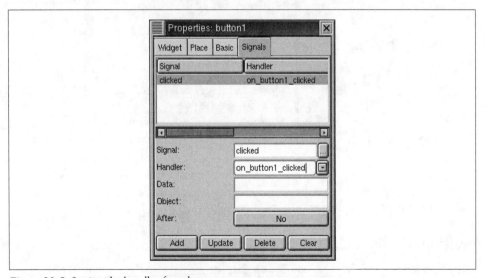

Figure 30-5. Setting the handler for a button

We want a Perl subroutine to be called when our button is clicked. This subroutine is called a *signal handler*, and Glade automatically gave ours a name: on_button1_clicked. But where do we put this subroutine? As always in Perl, There's More Than One Way To Do It. See "Writing the Signal Handler Code" below for our approach.

Saving and Building the Project

Now we will save and build our new project. First, click the Save button in the main Glade window. The first time you save a project, you are given a Project Options window where you can set the name of your project (it should say Project1) as well as the language you wish to have it built in (Figure 30-6). Select Perl as your language and click OK.

Figure 30-6. The Project Options window

Now click the Build button in the main Glade window. The source code for your application will be written to the directory specified in the Source Directory input on the Project Options window.

Writing the Signal Handler Code

There are several methods by which you can add signal handlers to your application. Remember that signal handlers are the Perl subroutines that respond to GUI events, such as mouse clicks or cursor movements. In our example application, we have specified that we wish to invoke a subroutine when a user clicks on the New button.

Glade writes several files to the source code directory. The names of the files are based on the project name specified in the Project Options window (Figure 30-6). *Project1UI.pm* is a module used by the other modules to build the user interface; you generally won't have to modify this code. *Project1SIGS.pm* contains stub routines for the application's signal handlers.

Most of the time you'll copy the stubs to another file and fill them in with your signal handler code. As a convenience, Glade-Perl creates such a file the first time you build your project. This file is *Project1.pm*. Open it and locate the signal handler stub that Glade created for the New button; remember that it is called on_button1_clicked. Modify that subroutine so that it looks like this:

```perl
sub on_button1_clicked {
    my ($class, $data, $object, $instance, $event) = @_;
    my $me = __PACKAGE__ . "->on_button1_clicked";

    # Get reference to a hash of all the widgets on our form
    my $form = $__PACKAGE__::all_forms->{$instance};

    # We will display a message box to the user.
    my $button_pressed = Gnome::MessageBox->new(
        "New What?",        # the message
        "question",         # the message type
        "New Car",          # the button labels...
        "New House",
        "Never Mind"
    )->run();

} # End of sub on_button1_clicked
```

Now we just need to run our application. In the project directory (see the Project Directory option in the Project Options window, shown in Figure 30-6), create a file called app.pl:

```perl
#!/usr/bin/perl
# app.pl

use lib qw(./src);
use Project1;

app_run app1;
```

Project1.pm is the module to which we just added our signal handler. We have to use lib, the recommended method of altering @INC, to tell Perl where to find this module. As explained previously, Glade writes this file to the Source Directory specified in the Project Options window (Figure 30-6). Since we are running app.pl in the parent directory of the Source Directory, we provide use lib with a relative directory reference (qw(./src)).

app1 is a package defined in *Project1.pm*. You will recall that our Gnome application window was given the name app1. The app1 package is thus a Perl class representing the Gnome application window we created.

`app_run` is a class method defined for the `app1` class, created by Glade-Perl. Running this class method initializes our Gnome application, creating a new instance of the `app1` class, showing it to the user and entering the main GTK+/Gnome event loop.

The GTK+ event loop handles user interactions, handing off processing to our signal handler subroutines if the user does anything to trigger one of those signals.

Execute the `app.pl` script from a shell prompt:

```
perl app.pl
```

Clicking the New button, we see the fruits of our signal-handling labors in Figure 30-7. What is remarkable is that we have written only four lines of code: one to fill in the stub of our signal handler and three to start up the application. Filling in a signal handler to make File → Exit quit the application is left as an exercise to the reader (hint: use the method `Gtk->main_quit`).

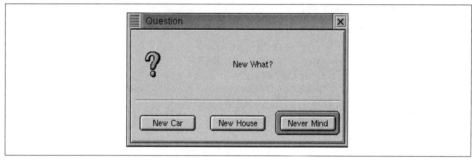

Figure 30-7. The dialog box shown after clicking the New button

Inheritance as a GUI Development Tool

Now we will see how class inheritance can make our life as a GUI developer easier. Using Glade's Palette window, create a Gnome Dialog Box and fill it in with widgets as demonstrated in Figure 30-8. Name the dialog box `dialog_details` and name the combo boxes `combo_model` and `combo_color`, respectively (hint: the Table widget greatly simplifies layout).

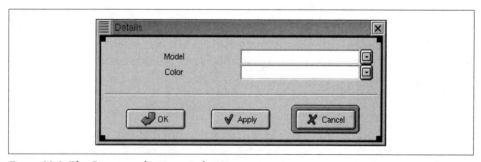

Figure 30-8. The Gnome application window

The problem is simple. If a user wants a new car, we'd like to ask the user for details on which new car they want. If the user wants a new house, on the other hand, we want to provide them with choices appropriate for a new house. But designing two different dialog boxes which differ only in their combo box options seems like overkill; in addition, what if we want the choices to come from a database or some other external data source? A better approach would be to separate the design of the interface from the specific options themselves.

To do this, we'll create two classes that inherit from the dialog_details class. Each will override the object constructor, filling in the combo boxes with options appropriate for its class. For simplicity, we'll put the class definitions in app.pl:

```perl
#!/usr/bin/perl
# app.pl

use lib qw(./src);
use Project1;

# Class definition for the "New Car Details" window
package Car_Details;

use vars qw(@ISA);
@ISA = qw(dialog_details);

my @models = qw(Audi Ford Honda Toyota);
my @colors = qw(Blue Green Red Watermelon);

sub new {
    my $class = shift;
    my $self = bless $class->SUPER::new(), $class;
    $self->TOPLEVEL->title('New Car Details');
    $self->FORM->{'combo_model'}->set_popdown_strings(@models);
    $self->FORM->{'combo_color'}->set_popdown_strings(@colors);
    return $self;
}

# Class definition for the "New House Details" window
package House_Details;

use vars qw(@ISA);
@ISA = qw(dialog_details);

my @models = qw(Mobile Ranch Suburban Victorian);
my @colors = qw(Brick Brown Red White);

sub new {
    my $class = shift;
    my $self = bless $class->SUPER::new(), $class;
    $self->TOPLEVEL->title('New House Details');
    $self->FORM->{'combo_model'}->set_popdown_strings(@models);
    $self->FORM->{'combo_color'}->set_popdown_strings(@colors);
    return $self;
```

```
    }
    package main;
    app_run app1;
```

We have created two new classes: Car_Details and House_Details. Each of these inherits from dialog_details, the class Glade-Perl created for us corresponding to the Details window (Figure 30-8). They override the new method (the constructor) inherited from dialog_details. The new first calls the inherited new, thus obtaining a valid object reference for the Details window being created. It then sets the appropriate window title and combo box options.

Now we must modify our New button signal handler to load up the appropriate Details window in response to the user input. Remember that this signal handler is in *Project1.pm*. Modify on_button1_clicked as follows:

```
sub on_button1_clicked {
    my ($class, $data, $object, $instance, $event) = @_;
    my $me = __PACKAGE__ . "->on_button1_clicked";
    # Get ref to hash of all widgets on our form
    my $form = $__PACKAGE__::all_forms->{$instance};

    # We will display a message box to the user.
    my $button_pressed = Gnome::MessageBox->new(
        "New What?",      # the message
        "question",       # the message type
        "New Car",        # the button labels...
        "New House",
        "Never Mind"
    )->run();

    # $button_pressed is the 0-based index of the button pressed.
    # 0 = "New Car", 1 = "New House", 2 = "Never Mind", and so on.

    # Stop if user pressed "Never Mind".
    return if $button_pressed == 2;

    # Create details window based on user response.
    my $details = undef;
    $details = Car_Details->new() if $button_pressed == 0;
    $details = House_Details->new() if $button_pressed == 1;

    # Display the details window, hiding it when the user is done choosing.
    $details->TOPLEVEL->run_and_close();
      Gnome::MessageBox->new(
                          "You are using free software! " .
                          "You obviously can't afford that model!",
                          "info", "Ok" )->run();

} # End of sub on_button1_clicked
```

By virtue of being an instance of one of our two inherited classes, the window referenced by $details has combo box options appropriate to the user response

(Figure 30-9). Since $details inherits from dialog_details, the TOPLEVEL method is available. This method returns the top-level widget corresponding to that class, in this case a Gnome::Dialog, widget which in turn implements the run_and_close method.

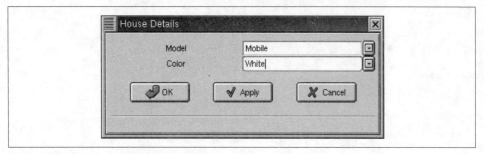

Figure 30-9. The Gnome application window

Further Exploration

With just a few clicks of the mouse and a little organization we have laid out an extensible framework for a new application. We even used Perl's OO features to provide the framework for clean GUI development. Perl is already known as a rapid development language; combining it with a tool like Glade enables lightning-fast GUI application development.

As is often mentioned on the perl5-porters mailing list, most every problem domain Perl is brought into quickly becomes a Simple Matter of Programming (SMOP). GUI development is no different, and Glade fulfills the exciting potential of bringing Perl and SMOP to the desktop.

More Information

For an introduction to using Gnome and Perl together, read Simon Cozens' excellent article at *http://www.perl.com/pub/a/2000/10/gnome.html*.

An invaluable resource in working with Gtk-Perl is the tutorial written by Stephen Wilhelm, available at *http://personal.riverusers.com/%7Eswilhelm/gtkperl-tutorial/*.

For information on object-oriented Perl, read the definitive book of the same name by Damian Conway.

CHAPTER 31

Gnome Panel Applets

Joe Nasal

Gnome is the desktop environment of choice on my home Linux system, because it's feature-packed and user friendly. Gnome is also flexible, and thanks to the Gtk-Perl module and associated desktop toolkit bindings, I can use my favorite programming language to further customize and extend my Gnome environment.

This article shows how a useful Gnome tool can be be built in an afternoon. It is also an example of some common techniques one employs when doing this sort of GUI programming, including widget creation, signal handling, timers, and event loops. It also reviews some Perl basics. Read on, and you may be inspired with notions of your own.

Gnome

On a Gnome desktop, the *panel* contains a variety of buttons and other widgets that launch applications, display menus, and so on. It's standard desktop fare, just like the Microsoft Windows Start menu.

An *applet* is a particular kind of Gnome application that resides within and operates on the panel itself. The Gnome distribution comes with several of these, such as a variety of clocks, the game of Life, and system resource utilization monitors. The Gtk-Perl module enables a Perl programmer to create custom Gnome panel applets.

The Gnome panel applet we'll build finds the local host's default TCP/IP gateway and affixes the gateway's status to the label of a button. When the button is in an off position, the gateway is not polled (Figure 31-1).

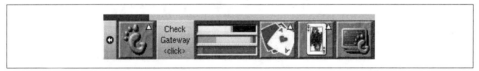

Figure 31-1. A Gnome panel applet

When the button is on, the gateway is polled at scheduled intervals and the button's label is updated with the result: response or non-response (Figure 31-2 and Figure 31-3).

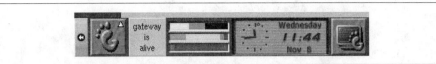

Figure 31-2. The gateway is up

Figure 31-3. The gateway is down

This diagnostic may be used to regularly and unobtrusively report the status of the local network relative to the machine's default gateway. Users can check the button's label to see how things are faring on the upstream network. The applet uses the netstat and ping commands familiar to Unix users.

Program Overview

The top-level code in the program (shown in Example 31-1) is contained in lines 1 through 21; lines 23 through 68 establish subroutines. One subroutine is called by our code (fetch_gateway), but two others are callbacks (check_gateway and reset_state). A *callback* is a subroutine that will be called by the Gnome code when something happens, such as a timer expiring or a button clicking. Now, let's learn how the application is set up.

Example 31-1. The ping_gateway.pl Gnome program

```
1  #!/usr/bin/perl -w
2
3  use Gnome;
4
5      init Gnome::Panel::AppletWidget 'ping_gateway.pl';
6  $a = new Gnome::Panel::AppletWidget 'ping_gateway.pl';
7
8  $off_label = "Check\nGateway\n<click>";
9
10 Gtk->timeout_add( 20000, \&check_gateway );
11 $b = new Gtk::ToggleButton("$off_label");
12 $b->signal_connect ( 'clicked', \&reset_state );
13
14 $b->set_usize(50, 50);
15 show $b;
16 $a->add($b);
17 show $a;
18
19 &fetch_gateway;
20
21 gtk_main Gnome::Panel::AppletWidget;
22
```

Example 31-1. The ping_gateway.pl Gnome program (continued)

```
23 sub fetch_gateway {
24
25     foreach $line (`netstat -r`) {
26
27         my ($dest, $gate, $other) = split(' ', $line, 3);
28         $hostname = $gate if $dest eq "default";
29         $hostname = lc($hostname);
30
31     }
32
33 }
34
35 sub reset_state {
36
37     $state = ( $b->get_active() );
38     if (!$state) { $b->child->set("$off_label") }
39     else         { $b->child->set("Wait...") }
40
41 }
42
43 sub check_gateway {
44
45     my $uphost;
46
47     if (length ($hostname) > 8) {
48         $uphost = "gateway";
49     } else {
50         $uphost = $hostname;
51     }
52
53
54     if ($state) {
55
56         my $result = system("/bin/ping -c 1 2>&1>/dev/null $hostname");
57
58         if ($result) {
59             $b->child->set( "$hostname:\nNo\nResponse" )
60         } else {
61             $b->child->set( "$uphost\nis\nalive" );
62         }
63
64     }
65
66     return 1;
67
68 }
```

Initialization

Line 3 indicates that we'll be using the Gnome module. Gnome.pm is distributed
with the Gtk-Perl package. As of this writing, the latest version of Gtk-Perl on CPAN

is 0.7008; it's also available at *http://projects.prosa.it/gtkperl/*. Gnome.pm has to be installed separately; after downloading, unpacking, and installing Gtk-Perl, change directories into the Gnome distribution and install that too. If you want to develop panel applets (as we're doing here), you'll need to append the build option `--with-panel` to the end of the usual `perl Makefile.PL` portion of the install process:

```
perl Makefile.PL --with-panel
```

Although Gnome.pm hasn't made it to Version 1.0 yet, I've found it to be stable. The biggest problem is the lack of documentation.

Lines 5 and 6 initialize a new AppletWidget object in $a. This object is the container for all the doodads that will be part of our applet. Line 8 creates a label for use when our button is in the off position.

Line 10 creates a timer. The prototype for the `Gtk->timeout_add` function is:

```
Gtk->timeout_add( $interval, \&function, @function_data );
```

Here our interval is 20,000 (this value is in milliseconds, so the timer will go off every 20 seconds), and the function to be called when the timer goes off is `check_gateway`. We could use the third parameter to pass some data into the `check_gateway` function if it were appropriate to do so. In this case it isn't.

Line 11 creates a new ToggleButton object in $b, and labels it off.

Line 12 registers the other callback in this application. This one, `signal_connect`, will be called when a particular signal occurs within Gnome. These aren't normal Unix signals like `SIGINT` and `SIGCHLD`, but specific GUI events. In this case, the event is a button click. The ToggleButton widget also has the signals "pressed", "released", "enter", and "leave", each of which is emitted in response to either mouse actions or direct function calls such as `$b->pressed`. In our application, Gnome will call `reset_state` whenever ToggleButton $b is clicked.

Line 14 sets the button's size to be a square with sides of 50 pixels, a good fit for the default Gnome panel. Gnome references theme and style information in shared libraries that specifies how the button is to be drawn: line, color, shadow, and so on. Line 15 calls the button's `show` method, indicating that we're finished setting its attributes and that it is ready for display. Line 16 adds the button to the applet. Technically, we've packed the ToggleButton widget into the AppletWidget container by invoking the AppletWidget's add method on the ToggleButton. The Toggle-Button is now a child of its container. In line 17, the applet is made visible by calling its `show` method as well. A widget's children are not displayed until the parent's `show` method is invoked.

Line 19 calls the `fetch_gateway` routine to gather the local host's default TCP/IP gateway. In that subroutine, `netstat -r` captures the local routing table. The comparison in line 28 forces a value into the scalar $hostname when the first field within the captured text matches the string `default`. Finally, we translate this value to lowercase, so it will look better when we finally display it on the button. Then `fetch_gateway` returns.

At line 21, we're ready to hand off to the gtk_main event loop, which is responsible for drawing the application on the screen and managing user interaction. At this point our only interface with the application will be through signal handling and callback functions. The Gnome Toolkit (GTK) is event driven: once we enter gtk_main, the application stays put until an event occurs (caught via a signal) and the associated callback function is invoked. Therefore, we'd better have completed all of our initialization beforehand.

The Callbacks

Now let's examine the two callback functions: reset_state on line 35, which catches a "clicked" signal on our button (line 12), and check_gateway on line 43, which catches timer expirations (line 10).

On line 37, we query the state of the toggle button by invoking its get_active method. This returns 0 if the button is off and 1 if it's on. By default, the ToggleButton widget has one child—its own label. So we label the button with the contents of $off_label if it is in the off position, or the string "Wait..." (Figure 31-4) if it is the on position, because we know that check_gateway is going to be called within the next 20 seconds. Part of check_gateway's job is to update the button with the status of our TCP/IP gateway, which after all is the whole point of this applet.

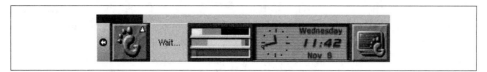

Figure 31-4. The gateway is down

Line 47–51 store in $uphost either the value in $hostname or the string gateway, depending upon whether $hostname is longer then eight characters. (Any longer than eight characters, and it won't fit comfortably within the button's label.)

If the button is in an on position (line 54), we go ahead and attempt to ping the gateway with a single ICMP packet. We only care about the return value of the ping command and not its output, so we execute the command with system. ping returns 0 upon success (the gateway is alive) and something else if it fails (probably because the gateway is dead), so we check the result and update the button's label appropriately in lines 58–62.

We want check_gateway to continue to be called, every 20 seconds, until the application terminates. So at line 66, the function returns a true value. That true return value keeps the timer alive.

Note that 20 seconds is enough time to allow the call to ping to timeout and return a value to the application. It is also an appropriate level of resolution for this kind of discovery activity; if information about the status of my gateway is less than 20 seconds old, I'm happy. Your mileage may vary.

Conclusion

It's easy to write Gnome applets in Perl. This simple example showed you the basic elements of Gnome programming, including the event model and callbacks. Go forth and hack your own applet!

Afterword

Author's note: since this article was written, I've been contacted by a number of people who have pointed out that the program is more portable if the interface to the system ping command is abstracted via Net::Ping. Something like:

```
use Net::Ping;
```

In the check_gateway function, call:

```
$p = Net::Ping->new("icmp");
```

Line 56 goes away, and the conditional at Lines 58 through 62 becomes:

```
if ($p->ping($hostname)) {
    $b->child->set( "$uphost\nis\nalive" )
} else {
    $b->child->set( "$hostname:\nNo\nResponse" );
}
```

Specifying icmp in construction of the ping object requires that the program run as root or setuid root to support ping( ) method calls. If you're running Gnome on something other than a Linux box, though, this might be easier than massaging a system call to your local ping binary.

CHAPTER 32
Capturing Video in Real Time

Marc Lehmann

Perl is not currently a common choice for real time applications. The dynamic nature of the language makes it difficult to predict run-time behavior (and speed) reliably. However, video capturing applications (for instance, digitizing a television signal and saving it to disk) have to be real time. If you miss a frame, it's gone forever, so the programs have unavoidable deadlines.

One of my principles for programming is to use the right language for the job. In recent years, this has mutated into "let's combine the strengths of various languages to solve a problem" or, more precisely, "write a Perl interface to the problem."

Video::Capture::V4l

The Video::Capture::V4l module was created to solve such a problem: I wanted to record a television show that was broadcast daily at different times, on a TV channel that didn't properly support the Video Programming Service (VPS) signal to switch on my VCR. What I will describe here will *not* work in the U.S.—but being able to capture fifty 704×528 fields per second with a 333 MHz dual Pentium II is worth attention anyway.

To do this, I had to get at the video data and compare it with some prerecorded sequence, trying to match the beginning of the show (which fortunately was always the same). I then used the Kermit serial protocol to transfer commands to my HP-48 calculator and switch on the VCR, but that's another story.

The Video::Capture::V4l module solves this problem in a generic way. With it, you can control the tuner, capture frames, compress them using the RTjpeg codec, and do whatever processing you like in the time allotted. Another interesting area is the Vertical Blanking Interval (VBI), which can contain interesting data like videotext, electronic program guides, intercast, and even MP3s.

Part I: Video Capturing

The V4l module follows the Video4linux standard (Version 1), so all the documentation for Video4linux applies to the module as well. Actually, the documentation for the V4l module (perldoc Video::Capture::V4l once you've installed it) is nothing more than an enumeration of the supported constants.

The simplest way to capture a single frame looks like this:

```
use Video::Capture::V4l;

# Open the video device (the default is /dev/video0)
my $grab = new Video::Capture::V4l or die "Unable to open video device: $!";

my $frame = $grab->capture(0, 640, 480);

$grab->sync(0);

# Now $frame contains 640x480x3 bytes of RGB (BGR) pixel data.
```

While this is short, it's not exactly intuitive. The call to new Video::Capture::V4l creates a new V4l object and opens the video device. The memory will be allocated as long as this object exists, so a script should not use it longer than necessary.

The next statement tells V4l that you want to capture a frame into the variable $frame. The first argument tells V4l the number of the frame you want to capture; most drivers can be told to capture up to two frames. Since we only want to capture a single frame, a zero (indicating the first buffer) suffices.

The second and third arguments are the width and height of the image. A standard PAL frame is 960 pixels wide and 625 lines high (of which only 768 x 576 contain usable image data), but most chipsets can scale the image in steps of 16 pixels, so other sizes are usually not a problem.

The capture method supports a fourth argument specifying the format of the video frame. The default (used in the previous example) is VIDEO_PALETTE_RGB24, where pixels are stored linearly as triplets of blue, green, and red bytes (BGRBGRBGRBGR...). Another useful format is VIDEO_PALETTE_GREY (each pixel is an intensity value between 0–255). Other formats are more hardware-oriented and less portable between chipsets.

The capture method returns a Perl scalar that will eventually contain the image data, which will be just large enough to hold all the pixels you requested. And it will be filled with garbage, since capture is just a request to fill it once a frame is complete. You will therefore need to wait until the actual image data has arrived before manipulating the data, and you do this by calling the sync method with the frame number you want to wait for.

In the above example, we just call sync(0) after the call to capture, to ensure that $frame contains the image.

There are a number of ways to display the image data. All of them require that the BGR data is reordered to the more conventional RGB format. Since this whole process needn't be time-sensitive, we can use a simple regex:

```
$frame =~ s/(.)(.)(.)/$3$2$1/gs; # Takes a second or so
```

You could also use PDL (the Perl Data Language; *pdl.perl.org*) and some dimension magic to get the same result much faster. But since you would usually only display images for debugging purposes, you could use this regex to view the BGR image in RGB mode by switching the red and blue channels.

To display the image, we could save it as a PPM file and use an image viewer like xv:

```
open PPM, ">frame.ppm" or die "frame.ppm: $!";
  print PPM "P6 640 480 255\n$frame";
  close PPM;
```

Or pipe it directly into an image viewer, such as ImageMagick's display:

```
open IM, "| display -size 640x480 RGB:-" or die;
  print IM $frame;
  close IM;
```

Or use the ImageMagick Perl module:

```
use Image::Magick;
my $img = new Image::Magick;
$img->set(magick => 'RGB', size => "640x480");
$img->BlobToImage($frame);
$img->Display;
```

Or even create a PDL and save, display, and modify it, in which case you don't even need the earlier regex substitution:

```
use PDL;
use PDL::IO::Pnm;

# Create an empty piddle. This should be done outside the loop, actually,
# but it doesn't hurt much this way.
my $img = zeroes byte, 3, 640, 480;

# Replace PDL's data storage with our frame data
${$img->get_dataref} = $fr; $img->upd_data();

# Reverse both the pixel order (BGR->RGB) and
# the top/bottom, since this is what PDL requires
$img = $img->slice("2:0,:,-1:0");

# Write a PNM file
wpnm $img, 'frame.ppm', 'PPM', 1;
```

Instead of simply writing the image unchanged, we could perform some transformations on it. For instance, this enhances the contrast:

```
$img -= $img->min;
$img = byte (ushort($img) * 255 / $img->max);
```

Or we could mask out parts of the image that are brighter than a given threshold. Figure 32-1 is a frame from the movie *Plan 9 from Outer Space*, captured with Perl and saved without any modifications. Figure 32-2 is another image, with part of the sky masked out (replaced by black) before saving, using PDL code.

Figure 32-1. A frame from Plan 9 from Outer Space

Figure 32-2. Using PDL to black out the sky

Capturing Frames in a Loop

When capturing multiple frames, we have a classic buffering problem. While we're in the middle of processing one frame, we have to begin processing the next to avoid missing it. All V4l drivers can therefore accept at least one call to capture in advance. To capture frames in a loop we have to start capturing the next frame and then sync on the previous one:

```
# It's always good to use variables for width and height.
my ($w, $h) = (640, 480);

my $buffer = 0; # the buffer to use next

# Start capturing the first frame
my $frame = $grab->capture($buffer, $w, $h);

# Enter an endless capturing loop
for (;;) {
    # Start capturing the next frame
    my $next_frame = $grab->capture (1-$buffer, $w, $h);

    # Sync the current frame
    $grab->sync($buffer) or die "unable to sync";

    # Now do something with the frame data in $frame
    dosomething $frame;

    # And now switch buffers
    $buffer = 1 - $buffer;
    $frame = $next_frame;
}
```

The variable $buffer contains the number of the buffer, 0 or 1, used to capture the current frame. 1-$buffer is thus the number of the other buffer.

So the loop simply starts by capturing the "next" frame (1-$buffer) and then syncs on the "current" frame. After that, the script has 0.02 seconds (for the PAL and SECAM television formats; about 0.0167 seconds for NTSC) to process the image data. After processing, the buffers are switched, and $next_frame becomes the current frame ($frame).

The example script examples/grab bundled with the V4l module prints some information about your capturing hardware and then jumps into exactly this loop, so it's a good starting point when you want to create your own capturing applications.

Channels, Tuners, and Audio and Picture Settings

If the above scripts show white noise *without* printing an error, then your hardware probably wasn't initialized or tuned to a channel. In that case, starting a program such as XawTV and selecting a TV channel before starting the Perl script should initialize your video card and tune it to a useful source.

Most of my applications let the user use his program of choice to select the video source. In contrast, the V4l module offers full control over the video hardware.

There are a number of building blocks in the V4l system, all of which are represented by some object on the Perl level. The most important of these objects is the "device" object, which represents a single video device in the system. It is returned by a call to Video::Capture::V4l->new (*PATH*) and can be used to query your hardware's name, type, and capabilities. The examples/grab script contains code that prints out all useful information about device (and other) objects:

```
print "Device: ";
print "name ",$grab->name;
print ", type";
for (qw(capture tuner teletext overlay chromakey clipping
        frameram scales monochrome subcapture)) {
    print " $_" if eval "\$grab->$_";
}

print ", channels ", $grab->channels;
print ", audios ", $grab->audios;
print ", sizes ", $grab->minwidth, "x", $grab->minheight,
      "-", $grab->maxwidth, "x", $grab->maxheight;
print "\n";
```

$grab->name returns the device name, $grab->capture returns a boolean specifying whether the hardware can do video capturing, and so on. Here's the result for my video card:

```
Device: name BT878(Hauppauge new),
        type capture tuner teletext overlay clipping
            frameram scales,
        channels 3,
        audios 1,
        sizes 32x32-924x576
```

The "channels" entry shows the number of video sources the card supports; my card supports television, composite, and S-video inputs. The "audios" entry shows the number of audio sources.

Each of the "channels" and "audios" is represented by another object, which is returned by a call to the channel and audios methods. To get information about the first video source, you would use my $channel = $grab->channel(0). The grab example script iterates through all channels and audio sources and prints some information about them:

```
Channel 0: name Television, tuners 1, flags tuner audio, type tv, norm 0
Channel 1: name Composite1, tuners 0, flags audio, type camera, norm 0
Channel 2: name S-Video, tuners 0, flags audio, type camera, norm 0

Audio Channel 0: volume 65535, bass 32768, treble 32768,
                 flags volume bass treble, name TV, mode 1,
                 balance 0, step 0
```

You can change the settings for specific objects by calling the same methods used for querying, followed by a call of the set method to inform the video driver of your change. For instance, to set the broadcast norm of the first channel to PAL:

```
my $channel = $grab->channel(0);

$channel->norm(MODE_PAL);
$channel->set;
```

To tune the bass setting to its maximum, you do this:

```
# Get the audio object
my $audio = $grab->audio(0);

# Set bass to the maximum
print "old setting: ", $audio->bass, "\n";

$audio->bass(65535);
$audio->set;

print "new setting: ", $audio->bass, "\n";
```

Another interesting attribute is the mode of the audio source. mode can be set to SOUND_MONO, SOUND_STEREO, SOUND_LANG1, or SOUND_LANG2. Most cards (or actually their drivers) automatically detect whether an audio source is mono, stereo, or dual-channel, so about the only time you need to change this setting is when you want to hear the second language in dual-channel mode (this is quite common in Europe).

In addition to being able to control audio parameters, most cards can control picture settings. Just as your TV can change contrast, hue, color, and brightness, so can V4l:

```
my $picture = $grab->picture;

# The range of all settings is 0-65535

# Set contrast to some medium level
$picture->contrast(27648);

# The same for brightness
$picture->brightness(32000)

# Better leave the hue setting alone -- for PAL, changing the hue angle
# starts to cancel the color.  This is only sensible for NTSC.

# We want a slightly color-intensive picture
$picture->colour(32900);

# Don't forget to call "set"!
$picture->set;
```

In general, both the audio and picture settings should only be changed by human interaction, as every card reacts differently to the values.

Going back to the channels, we can see that the composite and S-video inputs have the type camera, which means they are hardwired to some physical device (usually a camera). The television input is of type tv and has a tuner associated with it.

A tuner is used to select different channels multiplexed on the same medium. The tuner is what lets you tell your card which TV channel, out of all the channels you could possibly receive, is the one you want to receive now. Just like all other objects, you can access the tuner object by calling the tuner method of the V4l object:

```
my $tuner = $grab->tuner(0);
```

Check out the grab script to learn about your tuner's attributes. Mine has these:

```
Tuner 0: name Television, range 0-4294967295,
         flags pal ntsc secam, mode 0, signal 0
```

The most important setting is mode, which must be one of TUNER_AUTO, TUNER_NTSC, TUNER_PAL, or TUNER_SECAM. Since TUNER_AUTO doesn't work with most cards, you'll probably have to choose the mode yourself. The signal method returns the strength of the received video signal (0-65535) and can be used to decide whether there's video to be had on a particular frequency. Unfortunately, signal is not well defined. It can take a few seconds until the card has finished its measurement, and not all cards support it.

Interestingly, there is no method to set the frequency in the tuner object. The only way to set a frequency is using the freq method of the Video::Capture::V4l object itself. I am not sure why Video4linux supports many tuners when you cannot use them independently; hopefully the next version will be saner.

Many programs (and many example scripts) use something like the following to tune to some channel (all values are hardwired):

```
use Video::Capture::V4l;

# Initialize the card and tune it to a specific frequency

# "Arte" uses this frequency in my city
my $freq = 140250;

my $grab = new Video::Capture::V4l or die "unable to open video device";
my $channel = $grab->channel(0);
my $tuner    = $grab->tuner(0);

# Let's use PAL
$channel->norm(MODE_PAL); $channel->set;
$tuner->mode(TUNER_PAL); $tuner->set;

# Now tune.
$grab->freq($freq);

# ...and sleep for 400 milliseconds while letting the card lock to the channel
select undef, undef, undef, 0.4;
```

Magic Constants for Frequencies?

Note that the above code hardcodes a frequency for the particular city where I live. The frequencies used by TV stations vary from town to town, or cable network to cable network. (That's why a new TV has to scan for available channels before it can be used.) Later in this article, I'll describe a small program that can automate this task. But first, I'll explain some of the standards used to manage these frequencies.

To help poor programmers like us, there is a module called Video::Frequencies (part of the Video::Capture::V4l package), which does nothing more than export some useful tables. (Unlike its mother module V4l, it is fully documented.)

For example, it tells me that Germany, Kuwait, and Sudan use the PAL format, while Chile, Taiwan, and the U.S. use NTSC. It also exports (among others) the hashes %NTSC_BCAST (U.S. broadcast), %NTSC_CABLE_JP (Japan cable), and %PAL_EUROPE (Europe broadcast).

These hashes contain the official channel name to frequency mappings; for instance, %PAL_EUROPE defines channels 21-69, E2-E12, S01-S03, and SE1-SE20. What counts is not these historically-derived and senseless designations, but that you often get a table from your cable or broadcast provider that tells you that, in your area, channel "E2" corresponds to "Zweites Deutsches Fernsehen."

Instead of hardwiring the channel frequency, we could also hardwire the channel designation (which is slightly better than before):

```
use Video::Frequencies;
$freq = $PAL_EUROPE{E2};
```

Example: Image Sequence Detection

In addition to the examples/grab script, there are a few other examples that might give you interesting ideas. The two scripts indexer and finder together implement the "identify re-occurring image sequences" task I needed to recognize my favorite show.

indexer is used to record an image sequence by scaling a 128x128 color image down by a factor of 8 (to 16x16) and writing these into a file named db. More interesting is the script finder, which constantly captures video images, scales them down (just like indexer), and compares them to the images stored in the database.

While the first implementation of these scripts used PDL, I didn't want to waste more CPU power than necessary (finder might run in the background for many hours), so I implemented some functions inside the V4l module. While this is not very clean programming practice, it was easy to add a few functions to V4l/V4l.xs, written in C for speed. (My first prototype was written in PDL, of course.)

The inner loop of finder, for example, is just this:

```
# reduce2 reduces the image size by two in each dimension
Video::Capture::V4l::reduce2($fr, $w<<4);
```

```
Video::Capture::V4l::reduce2($fr, $w<<3);
Video::Capture::V4l::reduce2($fr, $w<<2);
Video::Capture::V4l::reduce2($fr, $w<<1);

# normalize() does some primitive contrast enhancement
Video::Capture::V4l::normalize($fr);

# findmin compares the frame $fr to all images
# in the database $db, by summing pixel differences
($fr, $diff) = Video::Capture::V4l::findmin($db, $fr, $expect_frame, $expect_count);

# Remember the frame number
push(@reg, $this_frame, $fr);

# linreg is a simple linear approximation
my ($a, $b, $r2) = Video::Capture::V4l::linreg(\@reg);

my $b1 = abs($b-1);
if ($r2 < 100 && $b1 < 0.01) {
    $found++;
    print "LOCKED\n";
    # do something
}
```

findmin simply compares the frame to all frames stored in the database by taking pixel differences and summing these together. The smaller the difference, the more similar the frames. While false hits are quite common, a linear regression afterwards filters them out. Since the images are sent in the same sequence as they were recorded, the detected frame numbers should increase monotonically by one when the script has synchronized the database to the video stream. The finder script tries to detect repeated sequences and filter out jitter.

Example: Real Time Video Capturing

The second capturing problem I had was to capture a full-length movie in high resolution (640 x 480 or even higher). A small calculation will show you why this is indeed a problem: 640 x 480 pixels, two bytes per pixel when digitized, and 25 frames per second makes for a data rate of 640 * 480 * 2 * 25 == 15 megabytes per second. And that's not even full resolution. Nor does it include audio. It is very difficult (read: impossible) to get a PC to handle this data rate steadily over extended periods. Remember that there must never be a pause longer than 20 milliseconds, or else the next frame will be lost.

I first experimented with a program named streamer, striping the movie data to different partitions. However, even with real time priority, Linux sometimes paused the program for too long.

The next thing to try was writing a new program, in Perl of course. The key idea was to compress the image data before writing it to the disk, since this not only saves space (one hour of uncompressed movie requires about 52 gigabytes!), but also cuts down on the required I/O bandwidth. I took the existing RTjpeg code by Justin Schoeman and wrote a Perl interface to it.

The compelling reason to use Perl, however, was that my machine (a dual P-II 333) was fast enough to compress the stream in real time when I used two CPUs, but a single CPU wasn't fast enough. Thus, my capturing program had to manage a process that captures and avoids other blocking syscalls, a process that captures the audio, and two or more processes that encode video images into a file. Splitting the encoding work into multiple processes (and files) also made it easier to surpass the two gigabyte filesize limit on Linux. Implementing all this logic and experimenting with different implementations in C would have been much more difficult.

This capturing script is named examples/capture in the Video::Capture::V4l distribution. I confess that I'm lousy at designing user interfaces; you have to edit it manually before you can use it.

The first thing the program does is to fork the audio capturing and video compression processes. It then goes into the standard capturing loop we already saw. It then writes the image data into a shared memory segment (using Perl's shmwrite builtin) and notifies an encoding process that a new frame has arrived, to avoid being paused by some slow subprocess (or heavy disk activity).

The encoding process sits in a tight loop reading frame data, compressing it and writing it to a file:

```
# Quality factor (255 is highest quality and corresponds to
# a setting of 75 in the IJG jpeg library)
my $Q = 255;

# $M is the motion suppression value. 0 is the highest quality
my $M = 0;

# Create the output file
open DATA, "datafile" or die "$!";

# Initialize the compressor (the RTjpeg codec is not
# thread safe, so we need one process per encoder!)
my $tables = Video::RTjpeg::init_compress(640, 480, $Q);

# Also initialize motion suppression.
Video::RTjpeg::init_mcompress();

# Save the compression parameters to the file
syswrite DATA, $tables;

for (;;) {
    ...wait for next frame...

    # Read the image data
    shmread $shm, $buf, $buffer * $fsize, $fsize;
```

```
# Motion compression. Since many movies are shown in letterbox format
# when broadcast on TV, you can specify the offset and size of the image
# part you want to compress. This saves a lot of time!
my $fr = Video::RTjpeg::mcompress($buf, $M, $M>1, $x, $y, $w, $h);

# Write the frame data
syswrite DATA, $fr;
}
```

The script examples/xsview is a very simple viewer (not real time, of course) that reads the stream files and uncompresses the images in order. examples/mp2enc is a similar script that uses mp2enc to encode the images into a standard MPEG-1 (layer II) stream.

The only remaining question I have is: "Why hasn't anybody else used the RTjpeg codec so far?" As far as I know, the V4l Perl module is the only place where that code is actually used.

Part II: The Vertical Blanking Interval

In the second part of this article, I will describe the vertical blanking interval (VBI) decoder included with the V4l module.

Not all of the 625 lines of a standard PAL frame are used for the image; some of them are empty, providing the TV set with some regeneration time so that the electron gun can move from the bottom of the screen back to the top. 32 of these empty lines can carry data—videotext, for example, or the VPS (Video Programming Service) signal used to tell my VCR when a specific program starts and stops.

Videotext is pretty boring, but I wanted to find out why the VPS signal didn't work for my favorite TV show. To give you an impression of what the VBI looks like, I made a few snapshots of the raw analog data. Figure 32-3 is a snapshot of the VBI area of *France 3*, which is quite boring and contains a line carrying the VPS signal (the first non-empty line), two test patterns, and a single line with videotext information. Since each PAL frame consists of two half-frames, the pattern is repeated for the other frame. Using only a single line for videotext means that you can receive about two videotext pages per second. The videotext line is a bit darker, because the frequency used to transmit videotext is slightly higher than most other protocols used in the VBI.

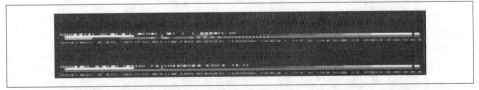

Figure 32-3. The vertical blanking interval of the France 3 channel

Figure 32-4 shows the VBI lines of *Premiere World*, featuring videotext (the first six lines), four lines of some encrypted data (it's pay TV), a single line carrying the VPS signal, three lines used to transmit test patterns and two additional videotext lines. The pattern is then repeated for the second half-frame.

Figure 32-4. The vertical blanking interval of the Premeire World channel

The last example (Figure 32-5) is from *NBC Europe*. Apart from the two bright test patterns, it consists of only videotext lines. The reason is that NBC Europe transmits MP3 data at 128 kilobits per second, which requires almost the full bandwidth that is available. This also causes its much more random-looking appearance—videotext is quite repetitive compared to MP3 data!

Figure 32-5. The vertical blanking interval of NBC Europe.

Of course, you don't need to understand all these patterns to use the VBI module. An easier way to detect the kinds of services available on a channel is to run the examples/vbi-info script (a video capturing program such as XawTV can run in parallel with a program using VBI, so that you can, for example, capture videotext in the background while viewing TV). Here is the output for some channels:

```
# France 3
alloc[.........000.T...........000.T..]
VT NI30/1[33f3=France 3]
# Premiere
alloc[TTT.TccccVO0OTT.TTT.Tcccc.O0OTT.]
3/31[f] VPS[fdac=Premiere|PREMIERE] VT NI30/1[0000=]
# Eurosport
alloc[TTTTTTTTTVO0TTTTTTTTTTTTTT.O.TTTT]
VT 2/31[0] NI30/1[fe01=Euronews] 0/31[0] 7/31[0]
2/31[ffffff] 3/31[7] EPG VPS[0000=|] 1/31[0]
```

alloc shows the allocation of VBI lines to services. A dot means that no signal was detected. T stands for videotext, V for VPS, c for encrypted video, and 0 for other signals. In addition to identifying the lines, vbi-info decodes the videotext and VPS lines a bit more. For instance, *France 3* transmits a so-called "Network Identification" code. You can import the hash %VT_NI from the Video::Capture::VBI module that maps NI-codes (like 33f3) to station names (like France 3).

Premiere additionally sends a VPS line (which contains another datum called the CNI (Country and Network Identification) code. %VPS_VNI maps CNI codes to names. *Eurosport* features videotext and an Electronic Program Guide (EPG). Some channels even send Intercast (IC), which is actually the Internet protocol over videotext!

Standards

Unfortunately, most of these protocols are based on videotext, which is a very old protocol. It was invented at a time where you had to be really careful not to waste a single bit and where data compression wasn't used at all. The main task of the Video::Capture::VBI module therefore is to analyze the VBI lines and do all the bit-shifting and unscrambling of the VBI data, returning some decoded representation.

To understand this, however, you still have to know what to expect. The best sources of information are the teletext (videotext) standards itself. The European Telecommunications Standards Institute (ETSI) publishes almost all of their standards on the web, and for free, which is very nice (and the exception for standards organizations). The "References" section at the end of this chapter mentions some of the more important standards and their purpose.

The ETSI standards apply only to PAL television and therefore mostly to western European countries only. If you look at the source (*VBI/VBI.xs*), you can see that the PAL and NTSC formats use different frequencies to encode videotext, so you'll need to change the source to make it work with NTSC (just look for FREQ_VT_NTSC and follow the comments). Unfortunately, just changing the frequency won't work, since the actual encoding is different.

This means that while PAL users can use the module out of the box, NTSC users will need to work at it—but, they can be sure that whatever they discover will be relatively new knowledge, since the millions of other V4l users all use PAL. If you find any standards on non-European teletext or other protocols I haven't found yet, I'd love to hear from you.

Decoding VPS

Capturing vertical blanking intervals is even easier than capturing image data:

```
use Video::Capture::V4l;
use Video::Capture::VBI;

my $vbi = new Video::Capture::V4l::VBI
  or die "unable to create VBI capturing object";

# The next line is optional
$vbi->backlog(25);              # Maximum 1 second backlog (~1600kb)

# We all love endless loops ;)
for (;;) {
    # Retrieve next vbi frame
    my $field = $vbi->field;

    # Decode the field and iterate over all lines
    for (decode_field $vbi, VBI_VPS) {
        # ... Do something ...
    }
}
```

Capturing and decoding the VBI are separate tasks and also separate modules. The idea is that Video::Capture::V4l captures VBI data using the V4l API (which is very system-specific), but the actual VBI processing is done in an OS-independent way (with Video::Capture::VBI). In the future, other API's besides V4l could be supported.

The program first creates a VBI capture object (of type Video::Capture::V4l::VBI). The next line of code creates a cache of 25 frames. This is implemented by launching a separate thread that captures VBI frames and queues them in memory, so your program can take as long as one second to process a frame without losing any intermediate data. Since each frame requires 64 kilobytes of memory, 25 frames require 1.6 megabytes. Not too much, but if your program is fast enough (or you can tolerate skipped frames), leave out this line to conserve memory. It then enters an endless capturing loop. If you want, you can use select (or the great Event module) to wait on the filehandle returned by the fileno method:

```
use Video::Capture::V4l;
use Event;

my $vbi = new Video::Capture::V4l::VBI
  or die "unable to create VBI capturing object";

Event->io(fd => $vbi->fileno, poll => "r",
          cb => sub {
                    my $field = $vbi->field;
                    # ... Decode and process the field ...
                  });
```

Inside our capture loop, we fetch the next VBI field and call decode_field, a function exported from the Video::Capture::V4l module. decode_field takes two arguments: the VBI data (a Perl scalar with a length that's a multiple of 2,048) and a bitmask that specifies which types of VBI lines you are interested in, OR'ed together. In this example, it's merely VBI_VPS, but if we were interested in VPS and videotext lines, we would use VBI_VPS | VBI_VT. decode_field decodes the lines you requested and returns an array reference for each line it could decode (it returns an array of array references). The content of these arrays depends on the line data and differs for each packet type.

All VPS lines follow the same pattern, including several time-related fields that specify the time of the *last* program that started. A VCR constantly compares the programmed date/time with the date/time sent via VPS and, if equal, starts recording. The reason this didn't work in my case—the problem that inspired the module in the first place—was that the VPS signal switch was performed manually. For instance, the change from 13:55 to 14:10 took a few seconds and went digit by digit: 13:55 => 14:55 => 14:15 => 14:10 and was often delayed or simply forgotten. Sigh.

The Autotune Script

Now we are ready to look at how the examples/autotune script works. If you use XawTV to watch television, you can automate the task of scanning channels. The basic idea of the autotune script is to scan through all channels, wait a bit, test whether a valid TV signal is being received, and try to identify the sender name. With the modules we know, this should be easy. First, we need control over the tuner and VBI device:

```
$v4l = new Video::Capture::V4l;
$tuner = $v4l->tuner(0);

$channel = $v4l->channel(0);
$tuner->mode(TUNER_PAL);      $tuner->set;
$channel->norm(MODE_PAL);     $channel->set;

$vbi = new Video::Capture::V4l::VBI or die;
```

The next step is to load an existing ~/.xawtv config file, which we can parse with the Video::XawTV module.

One of the useful things stored inside the .xawtv file is the frequency table that should be used (for example, pal-europe). The Video::Frequencies module provides a hash named %CHANLIST that maps these frequency-table-names into the actual frequency table. Iterating through all possible frequencies is thus quite easy:

```
# Create a new Video::XawTV-object and try to load an existing ~/.xawtv file
$rc = new Video::XawTV;
eval { $rc->load("$ENV{HOME}/.xawtv") };

# Use the frequency table specified in it
$ftab = $rc->opt('freqtab') || "pal-europe";
$freq = $CHANLIST{$ftab} or die "no such frequency table: $ftab";

# Channel information will be stored here
my @channels;

# Now iterate through all frequencies
for $chan (sort keys %$freq) {
    # tune to channel $chan and try to detect the sender
}

# Store the channel information int he XawTV-Object...
$rc->channels(@channels);

# ...and save it locally (don't overwrite the user's file!)
$rc->save("xawtvrc");
```

Inside the for loop, we first tune to the new frequency:

```
my $f = $freq->{$chan};
print "tuning to $chan ($f)...";
$vbi->backlog (0); # don't save frames from old channel
$v4l->freq($f);
select undef, undef, undef, 0.2;
```

Before tuning, we remove any saved VBI frames using backlog(0). Otherwise we might miss a new channel while analyzing frames from the previous one.

After setting the frequency, we have to wait a bit until the tuner stabilizes. While 200 milliseconds is good enough for my video card, it might be too long or too short for your card, so you might want to play around with that number if some channels can't be detected, because the tuner can't cope with our speed.

Once the tuner is stabilized we can measure the signal strength. If it is more than 30,000, we assume that a sender was received.

```
if ($tuner->signal > 30000) {
    # Capture 30 frames (at least one second)
    $vbi->backlog (30);
    # Wait some time so the buffer fills
    select undef, undef, undef, 1.6;
    # As long as frames are available...
    while ($vbi->queued) {
        # Decode frame and analyze...
        for (decode_field $vbi->field, VBI_VT|VBI_VPS) {
            #
            #   check VBI line data
            #
        }
    }
}
```

The autotune script jumps through hoops to do the actual sender name detection. It takes about a minute to scan all 106 frequencies in PAL-Europe (most are empty).

Decoding Videotext

The VPS signal is pretty lame. It always uses the same format, is well-specified, and is very consistent between stations. However, videotext and teletext are nothing like that. They use a wild assortment of different encodings for different lines, binary data (MP3, Intercast), VCR programming information, subtitles, navigational hints, program guide information, and occasionally just plain text.

This leads to the unsatisfactory situation where you have to first decode videotext pages, and then dissect some of those videotext pages into two or more datastreams, and finally decode these streams into EPG blocks, all just to get at the Electronic Program Guide. The Video::Capture::VBI module handles most of this.

Now to the basics of videotext. The three digits used to select a specific teletext page (000–799) are actually three hex digits. The rule is, "If it's decimal digits, it contains human-viewable teletext data. If it's hexadecimal data, it's probably something else." "Normal" (non-subtitled) teletext pages contain 24 lines. Each VBI line corresponds to one line of the page (pages used for subtitles usually contain a single line only) The first line (number zero) contains only the page number, the sender name, and the current time. The lines that follow contain the meat of the data.

In practice, there are oddities like *subpages* (pages consisting of more than one screen) and *interleaved pages* (since subtitles and other pages can interrupt other pages). This is handled by the Video::Capture::VBI::VT class. Using it is as simple as subclassing it:

```
package MyDecoder;

use Video::Capture::VBI;

# Derive from videotext-decoder
use base 'Video::Capture::VBI::VT';
```

```
# Enter_page gets called for each assembled page
sub enter_page {
    my($self, $page)=@_;
    my $sub = $page->{ctrl} & VTX_SUB;

    printf "Teletext page %03x / %04x\n",$page->{page},$sub;
    print "subtitle page\n"  if $page->{ctrl} & VTX_C5;
    print "newsflash page\n" if $page->{ctrl} & VTX_C6;

    # Now print the page
    for ($y=0; $y<25; $y++) {
        my $x = $page->{packet}[$y];
        print $x ? decode_ansi decode_vtpage $x : "", "\n";
    }
}

# Other (non-page-related) teletext packages end up here
sub enter_packet {
    my $packet = $_;
}
```

The Video::Capture::VBI::VT class implements a simple teletext decoder. The class itself does nothing with the decoded data unless you overwrite either enter_page or enter_packet, which are called when pages or packets are received. The VBI module defines two functions to convert the videotext data into a human-readable form: decode_vtpage, which returns text in a national language encoding, and decode_ansi, which takes that text and approximates the page using ANSI codes. These functions can be used to display the blocky graphics of the vertical blanking interval, as in Figure 32-6.

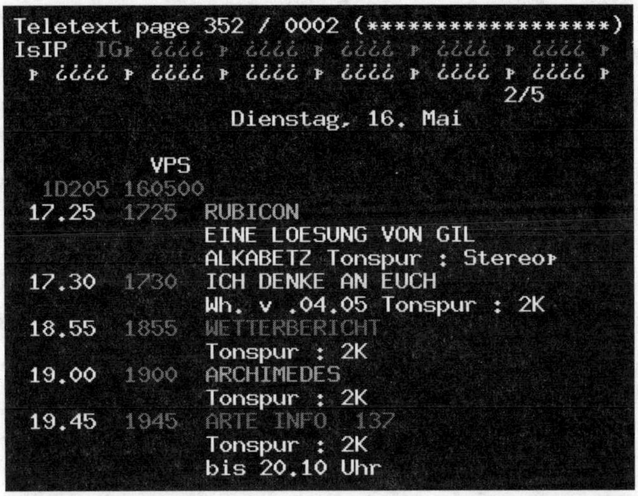

Figure 32-6. Text hidden in the vertical blanking interval

Figure 32-7 shows an index page using the *vtx* web interface (which is part of the PApp Perl module). Videotext suddenly becomes usable when it is hyperlinked!

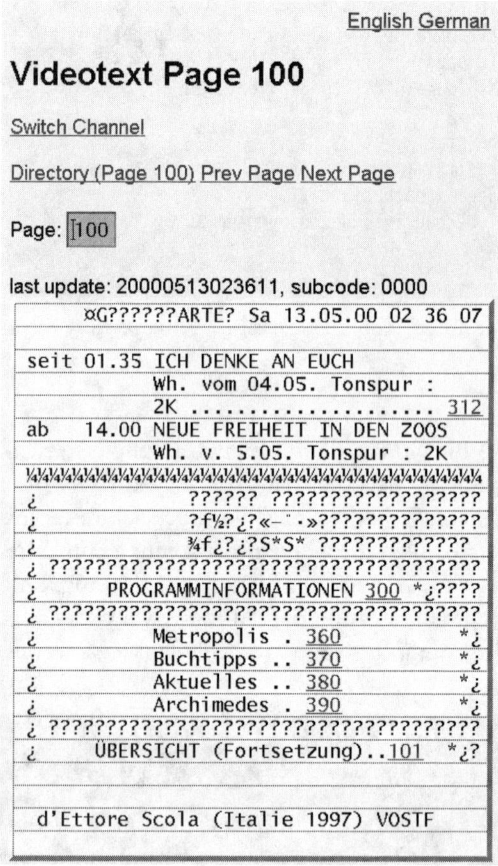

Figure 32-7. Hypertext derived from the vertical blanking interval.

To manipulate the Electronic Program Guide, the Video::Capture::VBI::VT module was subclassed to create the Video::Capture::VBI::EPG package. This can be used to present the user with a menu of choices (all movies marked with two stars, all documentaries, all drama movies currently running, and so on). Since EPG's can be quite large (up to a quarter megabyte) and the data rate is low (sometimes less than one kilobyte per second), it can take up to 20 minutes to gather the entire EPG database.

There are three programs in the V4l distribution that cope with EPG data: examples/getepg, which starts capturing EPG data as soon as it receives a valid data stream; examples/dumpepg, which simply dumps a database in text format; and examples/epgview, which is a curses-based (it requires the Curses module) interactive viewer. It continuously updates its display, so I often run it in a separate window for the whole

---

evening. That way I always have an up-to-date program listing, shown in Figure 32-8. The perfect toy for a TV addict.

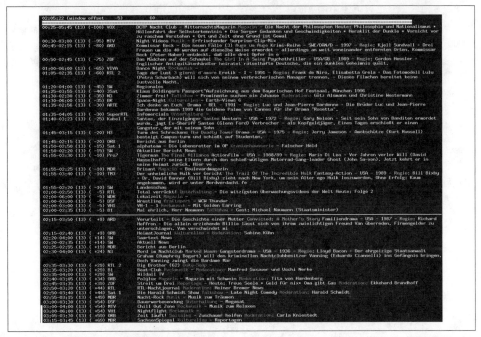

Figure 32-8. The Electronic Program Guide.

References

Some resources for your video hacking:

Video::Capture::V4l
> The module is available on CPAN and should build and install cleanly using the CPAN shell.

http://v4l.sourceforge.net/
> The V4l module is also a project on SourceForge. You can get the newest version via CVS.

http://www.imagemagick.org
> ImageMagick is a formidable image manipulation package that even has a nice Perl interface!

http://www.etsi.org/
> The European Telecommunications Standards Institute (ETSI) offers the following standards for download:
> - ETS 300 231, Programme Delivery Control (PDC)
> - ETS 300 706, Enhanced Teletext Specification

- ETS 300 707, Electronic Programme Guide
- ETS 300 708, Data transmission within Teletext
- TR 101 231, Country and Network Identification (CNI) codes
- TR 101 233, Code of practice for allocation of services in the Vertical Blanking Interval (VBI)
- TR 101 288, Code of practice for an Electronic Programme Guide (EPG)
- ETR 287, Code of practice for enhanced Teletext
- ETR 288, Code of practice for an Electronic Programme Guide (EPG)
- EN 300 294, 625-line television Wide Screen Signalling (WSS)

http://www.goof.com/pcg/marc/papp.html

PApp: multipage-state-preserving web applications. Includes a sample application named vtx that "webbifies" videotext.

PART III

Perl/Tk

The eight articles in this section provide an introduction to Perl/Tk, Perl's full-featured and popular toolkit for developing graphical applications. It works on both Unix/Linux and Windows, and most Perl/Tk applications will run without change in both environments.

Perl/Tk programming is different enough from regular Perl programming that it sometimes strikes newcomers as hard to learn. It doesn't have to be, though; there are really just three broad concepts that you have to keep in mind, and my *A Perl/Tk Roadmap* article describes them. Steve Lidie follows with an introduction to the basics of Perl/Tk programming in *Getting Started with Perl/Tk*, and I walk through the creation of a quick and dirty Perl/Tk application in *Scoreboard: A 15-Minute Perl/Tk Application*.

The rest of the section is all Steve. In *The Mouse Odometer*, he illustrates how you can add menus, timers, color selection, and widgets of your own devising to Perl/Tk applications. Next, in *Events*, he shows how your programs can respond to user actions such as keypresses, mouse clicks, or simply moving the mouse over an area of the application. The article also demonstrates the Photo widget and shows how to create animations, culminating in a crude implementation of a Breakout-style video game.

Geometry managers provide ways to organize spatial elements in your applications. *The Pack and Grid Geometry Managers* explores the two most common geometry managers in Perl/Tk: Pack and Grid. If you're just trying to draw as though you had a blank sheet of paper in front of you, you need the Canvas widget; *Drawing on a Canvas* shows how to use it.

Steve concludes the section with a brand-new article written specifically for this book, showing how you can manipulate and display databases via DBI and Perl/Tk's Tree widget. You can read more of Steve's writings in O'Reilly's *Mastering Perl/Tk*.

## CHAPTER 33

A Perl/Tk Roadmap

Jon Orwant

While editing TPJ, I often had trouble finding authors to write good beginner articles. I knew plenty of experts, but they usually preferred articles that displayed their expertise. Paradoxically, good articles on simple topics can be hard for experts to write, because it's been a long time since they were beginners and they may not remember all of the pitfalls they encountered when they started out.

Steve Lidie, the author of most of the articles in this section, doesn't have that problem: he's written for both beginners and experts. As I write this, he just finished *Mastering Perl/Tk* for O'Reilly (co-authored with Nancy Walsh), which adapted five of his ten TPJ articles that were originally planned for this section. We didn't feel right having similar Perl/Tk material appear in two of our books, so now you'll have to settle for me.

I'm an intermediate Perl/Tk programmer. Every so often I need to create an interactive graphical application, which I always find I can slap together quickly with Perl/Tk. But I do it infrequently enough that I forget the names of all the widgets and functions, and the order of their parameters. This makes me an unimpressive Perl/Tk programmer, but it has a hidden silver lining—the lack of familiarity with the material allows me to help novices learning Perl/Tk for the first time.

The goal of this article is modest: I'm going to give a nearly code-free roadmap to the Perl/Tk universe, explain what I think is important and what isn't, and then step out of the way so that Steve, the expert, can show you how it's done in subsequent articles.

Understand the Basics

Perl/Tk applications are Perl programs that use the Tk module. There are three basic concepts in Perl/Tk programming that distinguish it from regular Perl programming.

1. Perl/Tk is all about *widgets*. ("Widget" is a name used for something when you can't think of anything else to call it.) In Perl/Tk, widgets are graphical elements like buttons, scrollbars, and menus.

2. Perl/Tk is *event-driven*. Most of your programs will have a `MainLoop` statement in them; when Perl executes it, your application will go into stasis, taking action only in response to user-created events such as mouse clicks or key presses.

3. Perl/Tk makes extensive use of *callbacks*. For instance, when you create a button, you have to tell Perl/Tk what Perl code to execute when the user presses that button. The following expression creates a callback that prints `You pressed a button.`

```
$mw->Button(  -text => "Press me!",
              -command => sub { print "You pressed a button." }
           );
```

Ignore What You Don't Need

Perl/Tk is huge, and you shouldn't care. Chances are you only need a tiny subset to create your application. By my count, there are 39 basic widgets, and I almost always get by with just nine (Button, Canvas, Dialog, Frame, Label, MainWindow, Menu, Text, and TopLevel).

Some other Perl/Tk features I've never needed:

- The ability to create my own Perl/Tk widgets
- Perl/Tk's option database
- Tix widgets
- Interprocess communication
- Using C from Perl/Tk

If any of those topics interest you, or if you simply want the definitive Perl/Tk book, *Mastering Perl/Tk* is a natural next step.

If you're determined to create applications without understanding what you're doing, you can still get remarkably far by examining some of Steve's programs (on both *http:// www.oreilly.com/catalog/mastperltk/* and *http://www.oreilly.com/catalog/tpj2/*) and the example programs bundled with the Perl/Tk distribution, finding one that approximates the behavior you need, and chopping out the code for behaviors you don't.

To help you decide what *you* don't need, Table 33-1 lists all the basic widgets, what they do, and what options they accept.

Table 33-1. Perl/Tk widgets

Widget	Purpose	Options
Adjuster	Gives user control of widget size	Same as Frame plus -restore, -side, -delay, -widget
Balloon	Displays text when mouse is positioned over a widget	Same as MainWindow plus -font, -balloonposition, -statusmsg, -postcommand, -installcolormap, -initwait, -state, -cancelcommand, -balloonmsg, -motioncommand, -statusbar

Table 33-1. Perl/Tk widgets (continued)

Widget	Purpose	Options
Bitmap	Simple collection of pixels	-background, -data, -file, -foreground, -maskdata, -maskfile
BrowseEntry	Drop-down listbox that lets user type entries	Same as Entry plus -labelHighlightcolor, -labelHeight, -labelOffset, -arrowimage, -label, -labelWraplength, -labelRelief, -labelPadx, -labelPady, -labelTextvariable, -labelJustify, -command, -labelHighlightbackground, -options, -labelFont, -labelVariable, -labelBackground, -listcmd, -labelImage, -labelTile, -labelActivetile, -listwidth, -variable, -labelCursor, -browsecmd, -labelTakefocus, -labelDisabledtile, -labelAnchor, -labelHighlightthickness, -labelText, -labelWidth, -colorstate, -label-Pack, -labelForeground, -choices, -labelUnderline, -labelBitmap, -labelBorderwidth
Button	Something the user presses to trigger an action	Same as Label plus -default, -state, -command, -disabledforeground, -activeforeground, -activeimage, -activebackground
Canvas	A 2D area giving you pixel-by-pixel control	-activegroup, -background, -bd, -bg, -borderwidth, -closeenough, -confine, -cursor, -disabledtile, -height, -highlightbackground, -highlightcolor, -highlightthickness, -insertbackground, -insertborderwidth, -insertofftime, -insertontime, -insertwidth, -offset, -relief, -scrollregion, -selectbackground, -selectborderwidth, -selectforeground, -state, -takefocus, -tile, -width, -xscrollcommand, -xscrollincrement, -yscrollcommand, -yscrollincrement
Checkbutton	A Button that the user can select or deselect	Same as Label plus -onvalue, -selectcolor, -variable, -offvalue, -state, -command, -disabledforeground, -activeforeground, -indicatoron, -selectimage, -activebackground
ColorEditor	Lets user select colors	-background, -bd, -bg, -borderwidth, -class, -color, -color_space, -colormap, -command, -container, -cursor, -display_status, -fg, -foreground, -height, -highlight, -highlightbackground, -highlightcolor, -highlightthickness, -initialcolor, -offset, -overanchor, -popanchor, -popover, -relief, -takefocus, -tile, -title, -visual, -widgets, -width
Dialog	Pop-up window for immediate user action	Same as Label plus -title, -overanchor, -command, -popover, -popanchor
DirTree	HList tailored for showing directories	Same as HList plus -dircmd, -value, -image, -showhidden, -opencmd, -ignoreinvoke, -closecmd, -directory
Entry	Lets users enter a little text	-background, -bd, -bg, -borderwidth, -cursor, -disabledtile, -exportselection, -fg, -font, -foreground, -fgtile, -foregroundtile, -highlightbackground, -highlightcolor, -highlightthickness, -insertbackground, -insertborderwidth, -insertofftime, -insertontime, -insertwidth, -invalidcommand, -invcmd, -justify, -offset, -relief, -selectbackground, -selectborderwidth, -selectforeground, -show, -state, -takefocus, -textvariable, -tile, -validate, -validatecommand, -vcmd, -width, -xscrollcommand
ErrorDialog	Dialog for alerting user about application errors	-appendtraceback, -background, -bd, -bg, -borderwidth, -class, -cleanupcode, -colormap, -container, -cursor, -fg, -foreground, -height, -highlightbackground, -highlightcolor, -highlightthickness, -menu, -offset, -relief, -screen, -takefocus, -tile, -use, -visual, -width

Table 33-1. Perl/Tk widgets (continued)

Widget	Purpose	Options
FileSelect	Listbox tailored for files	Same as Listbox plus -labelHighlightcolor, -resetlabel, -labelHeight, -labelOffset, -scrollbars, -homelabel, -verify, -defaultextension, -label, -labelWraplength, -labelRelief, -labelPadx, -labelPady, -labelTextvariable, -labelJustify, -command, -labelHighlightbackground, -filelabel, -labelFont, -labelVariable, -initialdir, -labelBackground, -create, -title, -labelImage, -transient, -labelTile, -labelActivetile, -cancellabel, -filter, -labelCursor, -acceptlabel, -labelTakefocus, -overanchor, -labelDisabledtile, -dirlabel, -labelAnchor, -labelHighlightthickness, -labelText, -labelWidth, -regexp, -dirlistlabel, -labelPack, -initialfile, -accept, -directory, -labelForeground, -popover, -popanchor, -labelUnderline, -labelBitmap, -labelBorderwidth, -filelistlabel
Frame	Container for other widgets	-background, -bd, -bg, -borderwidth, -class, -colormap, -container, -cursor, -fg, -foreground, -height, -highlightbackground, -highlightcolor, -highlightthickness, -label, -labelPack, -labelVariable, -offset, -relief, -takefocus, -tile, -visual, -width
HList	Hierarchical list	-background, -bd, -bg, -borderwidth, -browsecmd, -columns, -command, -cursor, -dragcmd, -drawbranch, -dropcmd, -exportselection, -fg, -font, -foreground, -gap, -header, -height, -highlightbackground, -highlightcolor, -highlightthickness, -indent, -indicator, -indicatorcmd, -itemtype, -padx, -pady, -relief, -selectbackground, -selectborderwidth, -selectforeground, -selectmode, -separator, -sizecmd, -takefocus, -wideselection, -width, -xscrollcommand, -yscrollcommand
Label	Noninteractive widget displaying an image or text	-activetile, -anchor, -background, -bd, -bg, -bitmap, -borderwidth, -cursor, -disabledtile, -fg, -font, -foreground, -height, -highlightbackground, -highlightcolor, -highlightthickness, -image, -justify, -offset, -padx, -pady, -relief, -takefocus, -text, -textvariable, -tile, -underline, -width, -wraplength
LabEntry	An Entry with a Label	Same as Entry plus -label, -labelPack, -labelVariable
LabFrame	A Frame with a Label	Same as Frame, plus -labelside
Listbox	List of text strings	-background, -bd, -bg, -borderwidth, -cursor, -exportselection, -fg, -font, -foreground, -height, -highlightbackground, -highlightcolor, -highlightthickness, -offset, -relief, -selectbackground, -selectborderwidth, -selectforeground, -selectmode, -setgrid, -takefocus, -tile, -width, -xscrollcommand, -yscrollcommand
MainWindow	TopLevel widget displayed by MainLoop	-background, -bd, -bg, -borderwidth, -class, -colormap, -container, -cursor, -fg, -foreground, -height, -highlightbackground, -highlightcolor, -highlightthickness, -menu, -offset, -overanchor, -popanchor, -popover, -relief, -screen, -takefocus, -tile, -title, -use, -visual, -width
Menu	Emergent window displaying menu items	-activebackground, -activeborderwidth, -activeforeground, -activetile, -background, -bd, -bg, -borderwidth, -cursor, -disabledforeground, -disabledtile, -fg, -font, -foreground, -offset, -overanchor, -popanchor, -popover, -postcommand, -relief, -selectcolor, -takefocus, -tearoff, -tearoffcommand, -tile, -title, -type
Menubutton	Individual menu items	Same as Label plus -menu, -state, -disabledforeground, -direction, -activeforeground, -indicatoron, -activebackground
Message	Displays message for user	-anchor, -aspect, -background, -bd, -bg, -borderwidth, -cursor, -fg, -font, -foreground, -highlightbackground, -highlightcolor, -highlightthickness, -justify, -padx, -pady, -relief, -takefocus, -text, -textvariable, -tile, -width
NoteBook	Groups tabbed windows together	-background, -backpagecolor, -bd, -bg, -borderwidth, -cursor, -disabledforeground, -dynamicgeometry, -fg, -focuscolor, -font, -foreground, -inactivebackground, -ipadx, -ipady, -relief, -slave, -tabpadx, -tabpady, -takefocus, -width

Table 33-1. Perl/Tk widgets (continued)

Widget	Purpose	Options
Optionmenu	Menu offering the user many mutually exclusive options	Same as Menubutton plus -variable, -command, -options
Pane	A scrollable Frame	Same as Frame plus -sticky, -xscrollcommand, -gridded, -yscrollcommand
Photo	Holds an image	-data, -format, -file, -gamma, -height, -palette, -width
ProgressBar	Shows user the "percentage complete"	Same as Canvas plus -colors, -troughcolor, -value, -to, -blocks, -variable, -foreground, -from, -length, -resolution, -fg, -gap, -anchor, -padx, -pady
Radiobutton	A Button that, when selected, deselects the rest in the group	Same as Label plus -value, -selectcolor, -variable, -state, -command, -disabledforeground, -activeforeground, -indicatoron, -selectimage, -activebackground
ROText	Text widget, read-only	Same as Text
Scale	Slider for controlling a number	-activebackground, -activetile, -background, -bigincrement, -bd, -bg, -borderwidth, -command, -cursor, -digits, -fg, -disabledtile, -font, -foreground, -from, -highlightbackground, -highlightcolor, -highlightthickness, -label, -length, -offset, -orient, -relief, -repeatdelay, -repeatinterval, -resolution, -showvalue, -sliderlength, -sliderrelief, -state, -takefocus, -tickinterval, -tile, -to, -troughcolor, -troughtile, -variable, -width
Scrollbar	Slider for moving a widget horizontally or vertically	-activebackground, -activerelief, -activetile, -background, -bd, -bg, -borderwidth, -command, -cursor, -elementborderwidth, -highlightbackground, -highlightcolor, -highlightthickness, -jump, -orient, -relief, -repeatdelay, -repeatinterval, -takefocus, -tile, -offset, -troughcolor, -troughtile, -width
Table	Displays a table of items	Same as Frame plus -rows, -scrollbars, -fixedcolumns, -fixedrows, -columns
Text	Displays text, editable by user	-background, -bd, -bg, -borderwidth, -cursor, -disabledtile, -exportselection, -fg, -font, -foreground, -height, -highlightbackground, -highlightcolor, -highlightthickness, -insertbackground, -insertborderwidth, -insertofftime, -insertontime, -insertwidth, -offset, -padx, -pady, -relief, -selectbackground, -selectborderwidth, -selectforeground, -setgrid, -spacing1, -spacing2, -spacing3, -state, -tabs, -takefocus, -tile, -width, -wrap, -xscrollcommand, -yscrollcommand
TextUndo	Text widget suited for writing documents	Same as Text
Tiler	A Frame of matrix cells	Same as Frame plus -rows, -columns, -yscrollcommand
TList	Text list	-background, -bd, -bg, -highlightbackground, -borderwidth, -browsecmd, -command, -cursor, -fg, -font, -foreground, -height, -highlightcolor, -highlightthickness, -itemtype, -orient, -padx, -pady, -relief, -selectbackground, -selectborderwidth, -selectforeground, -selectmode, -state, -sizecmd, -takefocus, -width, -xscrollcommand, -yscrollcommand
Toplevel	Decorated container for other widgets	Same as MainWindow
Tree	HList that lets user open and close portions	Same as HList plus -opencmd, -ignoreinvoke, -closecmd

In the next article, *Getting Started with Perl/Tk*, Steve provides a gentle introduction to show you what some simple Perl/Tk programs look like.

CHAPTER 34

Getting Started with Perl/Tk

Steve Lidie

Perl/Tk is a marvelous object-oriented Perl extension that provides a comprehensive collection of widgets for spiffy graphical applications. Tk was developed by John K. Ousterhout and adapted and extended for Perl by Nick Ing-Simmons.

Perl/Tk runs on all variants of Unix, Linux, and Windows. The original version ran on X windows, which uses a client/server model. *Clients* (such as the one you'll see in this article) communicate with a *server* that manages the computer's display, keyboard, and mouse. For every display there is a *window manager* that provides a consistent "look and feel," at least at a high level, for all clients sharing the machine's display. There are many different window managers, but they all provide similar facilities, such as iconifying, moving, and resizing windows, and framing them in decorative borders. You'll see window manager commands in later columns.

This article contains a gentle introduction to the fundamentals of Perl/Tk, after which it develops a real application step-by-step. (All of the programs in this book are available at *http://www.oreilly.com/catalog/tpj2*.)

Perl/Tk is available on CPAN, and a FAQ dedicated to it is available at *http://phaseit.net/claird/comp.lang.perl.tk/ptkFAQ.html*, the repository of Almost Everything Ever Written About Perl/Tk, thoughtfully maintained by Cameron Laird.

Perl/Tk Programming

Perl/Tk programs are written using the object-oriented syntax $object->method, where $object refers to a Tk widget (such as a Button or Menu, or even an image), and method names an action to be performed. We'll learn more about objects and such in the next column, but now, without further ado, here is your prototypical "Hello, world" program written in Perl/Tk, swiped from the distribution:

```
#!/usr/bin/perl -w
# A simple Tk script that creates a button that prints "Hello, world".
# Clicking on the button terminates the program.
#
```

```
# The first statement imports the Tk objects into the application, the
# second statement creates the main window, the third statement creates the
# button and defines the code to be executed when the button is pressed,
# the fourth line asks the packer to shrink-wrap the application's main
# window around the button, and the fifth line starts the event loop.

use Tk;

$MW = MainWindow->new;

$hello = $MW->Button(  -text => 'Hello, world',
                       -command => sub {print STDOUT "Hello, world\n"; exit;});
$hello->pack;
MainLoop;
```

When the program is executed, the window shown in Figure 34-1 appears.

Figure 34-1. A sample Perl/Tk window

The main window, $MW, is the program's first *top-level* window—the primary "container" for most, if not all, descendant widgets, which form a hierarchy (each widget always has a parent and might have children as well).

This particular top-level widget has a single child object belonging to the Button class. All widgets are objects derived from some base class, inheriting its characteristics. You might have several instances of button objects that look quite different, but share the distinguishing characteristics of the Button class: they display a text label or bitmap, and "do something" when pressed. When the button in the example is pressed, the anonymous subroutine is executed, which prints "Hello, world" and exits. The subroutine is called because it is bound to the button click. Almost all widget classes have default button and keypress bindings established by Perl/Tk, and you can add, delete, or modify bindings on a class or per-widget basis as you see fit.

The statement $hello = $MW->Button(...); is a *widget creation* command: an object of class Button is constructed and configured with the specified options, which becomes a descendant of widget $MW, the main window. The variable $hello is initialized with an *object reference* to the newly created button widget. In Perl, an object reference is just an ordinary reference that points to something that has been "blessed" (using the Perl bless function) into a certain class. The "something" is typically a hash or a list, and the act of blessing an object ties it to that particular class. Perl/Tk widget objects are hashes, as you can see from this debugging session:

```
% perl -de 0

Loading DB routines from $RCSfile: ch34,v $$Revision: 1.11 $$Date:
92/08/07 18:24:07 $ Emacs support available.
```

```
    Enter h for help.

    main::(-e:1): 0

    D1 use Tk
    D2 $ref = {}
    D3 $MW = MainWindow->new
    D4 $oref = $MW->Button
    D5 print $ref
    HASH(0x200f78c8)
    D6 print $oref
    Tk::Button=HASH(0x2021c780)
```

The variable $ref is a plain reference to an anonymous hash, whereas $oref is an object reference to a hash of class Tk::Button. But from now on, I'll refer to variables like $hello and $oref simply as objects or widgets. (If you're not familiar with the Perl debugger, the idiom perl -de 0 starts an interactive instance of Perl where you can debug, or simply enter Perl commands—a great environment for testing out code.)

The statement $hello->pack; is a *method invocation*: the Tk geometry manager known as the *packer* is invoked to assign a size and position to the $hello object, and then to "map" it. A widget must be mapped (or realized) before it becomes visible on the display. By default widgets are always packed inside their parent, and if you don't specify otherwise, the packer aligns them in a column, from top to bottom.

Perl/Tk programs are *event driven*, meaning that you don't write a main loop, but rather delegate that job to Tk. Instead, you write small code sections, referred to as *callbacks*, a fancy name for a subroutine, to process those *events* and which Tk invokes as required. There are many Tk events that need to be processed in a timely fashion: timers, file input and output, and motion and button events generated by your mouse. You activate the Tk event loop with a MainLoop statement, which should be the last line called by your program.

Most Perl/Tk applications share these common features:

- A use Tk statement at the beginning of the program that imports the base Tk definitions.

- A primary MainWindow as the root of the widget hierarchy.

- A series of widget creation commands.

- Optional binding and callback creation and registration commands. (More about those soon.)

- A series of geometry commands to pack widgets in a pleasing and user friendly manner.

- A MainLoop command to begin program execution. (Actually, there are times when you must control event processing yourself; we'll see an example of this in a later column.)

Tk provides 15 standard widgets, listed below; Perl/Tk provides additional *derived* widgets, as well as *composite* widgets, such as ColorEditor, Dial, FileSelect, LabEntry, and Table. Composite widgets, also called *megawidgets*, are complex objects built from these standard widgets.

Button

These widgets execute a callback when invoked. They're derived from the Label widget.

Canvas

These widgets provide a drawing surface for text and graphics.

Checkbutton

These widgets select one or more items from a list. They're derived from the Label widget.

Entry

These widgets allow users to enter and edit a single text string.

Frame

These widgets are primarily used as containers to group other widgets; for instance, during packing. Frames might be arranged inside an application's main window, with other widgets inside them. Frames are also used as spacers and to add colored borders.

Label

These widgets display a text or image label. Button, Checkbutton, and Radiobutton widgets are derived from the Label widget.

Listbox

These widgets display a list of strings and allow the user to select one, a range, or a scattered set of the strings.

Menu

These widgets are special widgets that work in conjunction with MenuButtons. Invoking a Menubutton displays its associated menu. There are various kinds of menu items, like buttons, checkbuttons, radiobuttons, separators, and cascades.

Menubutton

These widgets display a label (just like Buttons) but when selected display a Menu.

Message

These widgets are similar to Labels, but they display multiline strings instead of just single lines.

Radiobutton

These widgets select an item from a list. They're derived from the Label widget.

Scale

These widgets consist of a slider which allow users to specify a value by moving the slider.

Scrollbar

> These widgets control the view of other widgets, such as Canvas, Entry, List-box, and Text. Users can scroll the widget by dragging the slider.

Text

> These widgets display lines of editable text. Characters in a text widget can be colored, given specific fonts, spacing, margins, and more.

Toplevel

> These widgets are essentially secondary MainWindows. They resemble Frames in that they act as container widgets, except they aren't "internal" widgets.

A Sample Perl/Tk Program: plop

The Perl/Tk application that I develop here is called "Plot Program," or plop for short, featuring Button, Canvas, Dialog, Frame, Label, LabEntry, Menu, Menubutton, Scroll-bar, and Text widgets. It plots a list of mathematical functions of the form y = f($x), where $x iterates from the graph's X-minimum to X-maximum. Each function is evaluated in turn for a particular value of $x; the y value is then computed and a point is painted on the canvas. Plop emphasizes the canvas widget because I've noticed that new Tk users, after watching around two thousand lines of canvas documentation roll by, tend to place "exploring the canvas widget" at the end of their to-do list!

A canvas widget can be thought of as an artist's canvas for freehand drawing of graphics and text organized as a classical Cartesian coordinate system. A key difference is that the canvas origin, position (0,0), is defined to be the top *left* corner of the canvas window, so canvas X coordinates increase when moving right (as you'd expect) and Y coordinates increase when moving down (as you wouldn't). Also, canvas coordinates can't have negative values. For these reasons, we'll use and equation to transform between canvas and Cartesian coordinates.

Here's the first version of plop:

```
#!/usr/bin/perl -w
use strict;
use Tk;

my ($o, $s) = (250, 20);
my ($pi, $x, $y) = (3.1415926, 0);
my $mw = MainWindow->new;
my $c = $mw->Canvas(-width => 500, -height => 500);

$c->pack;
$c->createLine(50, 250, 450, 250);
$c->createText(10, 250, -fill => 'blue', -text => 'X');
$c->createLine(250, 50, 250, 450);
$c->createText(250, 10, -fill => 'blue', -text => 'Y');

for ($x = -(3*$pi); $x <= +(3*$pi); $x += 0.1) {
    $y = sin($x);
```

```
        $c->createText($x*$s+$o, $y*$s+$o, -fill => 'red', -text => '.');
        $y = cos($x);
        $c->createText($x*$s+$o, $y*$s+$o, -fill => 'green', -text => '.');
    }

    MainLoop;
```

Granted, this is really ugly code, lacking in style, but it's a proof of concept. As you'll see, I'll whip this code into proper shape pronto! Before I explain it, you can see what it looks like in Figure 34-2.

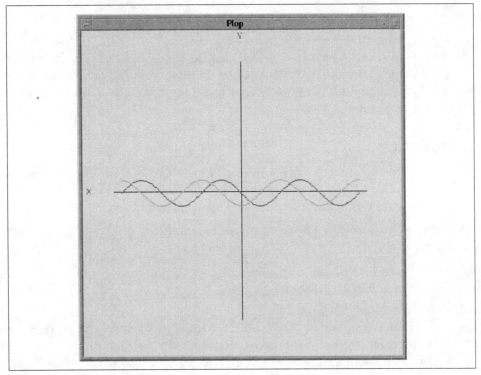

Figure 34-2. A "plop" graph of sine and cosine

Some global variables are initialized, the main window ($mw) and a canvas widget ($c) are created, and the canvas is realized. The next four statements create two canvas line items (for the graph axes) and two text items (for the axis labels). Other canvas item types are arcs, bitmaps, groups, images, ovals, polygons, rectangles, and windows.

These statements draw and annotate the X axis:

```
    $c->createLine(50, 250, 450, 250);
    $c->createText(10, 250, -fill => 'blue', -text => 'X');
```

Here, I'm creating one line item and one text item. Since the canvas is 500x500 pixels, I deliberately arranged for canvas coordinate position (250,250) to coincide with the Cartesian origin (0,0). I also wanted to have 50-pixel wide top/bottom and left/right margins. Given these constraints, the X axis line starts at (50,250) and extends horizontally to (450,250), with a blue letter "X" painted in the left margin at (10,250). Similarly, the Y axis is stroked vertically from top to bottom and labeled with a blue "Y". Now all that remains is to graph some functions.

The for statement varies from -3π to +3π radians, and even old biology-types like myself know that sine and cosine return values in the range [-1,1]. Such tiny values aren't especially useful unless you're looking for a graph one pixel high, so a transform is required:

```
$y = sin($x);
$c->createText($x*$s+$o, $y*$s+$o, -fill => 'red', -text => '.');
```

We want to scale our $y values, which is what the expression $y*$s+$o does: the Y value is enlarged 20 times and translated to the canvas origin. Then a red dot is deposited on the canvas. (There's actually a bug is the transform equation. Can you spot it? Hint: try graphing the exp function.)

Improving plop

So much for the ugly plop prototype; with a lot of work I can turn this code into a first-rate Perl/Tk application. For starters, I want to eliminate every single hard-coded value and use variables instead. Then I'll add these features:

- A menu across the top. Like all respectable applications, it'll have File and Help menubuttons.

- A title for the graph.

- Adjustable minimum and maximum X and Y values.

- An editable list of functions.

- The option to read in functions from a file. Heck, let's just do it: eval {require "plop.pl";}. Just store your private functions in the file plop.pl and they'll be available for plotting. For instance, plop.pl might contain these lines if you wanted to graph the hyperbolic arctangent:

```
sub atanh {
    return undef if ($_[0] < -1 or $_[0] > 1);
    return .5 * log( (1 + $_[0]) / (1-$_[0]) );
}

1;
```

Figure 34-3 illustrates a sample run of the new plop.

The main window is divided into three major regions: a top frame with menubuttons (containing the File and Help menus), the canvas in the middle (including the title and boundary values), and a bottom area containing a series of other widgets (including a scrollable text widget with the list of functions).

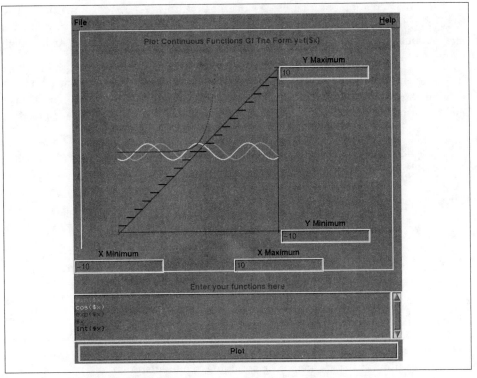

Figure 34-3. A sample Perl/Tk window

The Perl code has been modularized and looks something like this:

```
my $MW = MainWindow->new;
initialize_dialogs;
initialize_menus;
initialize_canvas;
initialize_functions;
```

Subroutine `initialize_dialogs` creates dialog widgets that aren't part of the main window proper—they pop up at certain times, wait for the user to respond, and then go away. Typically they persist for the lifetime of the application: thus, they are created once during program initialization and are then hidden until it's time to "Show" them; `Show` is a dialog method that deiconifies the widget, waits for the user to select a dialog button, and then returns the label of the selected button to the program. Here is how plop's "About" dialog widget is created:

```
$DIALOG_ABOUT = $MW->Dialog(
                    -title  => 'About',
                    -text   => "plot_program $VERSION\n\n" . ' 1995/12/04',
                    -bitmap => 'info',
                    -buttons => ['Dismiss'] );
```

Like all widget creation commands, $MW->Dialog returns a reference to an object. The buttons attribute is a list of strings that specify the button labels. In this case, there's only one button, "Dismiss," which hides the dialog after you've read the really informative "About" message!

To create the plop menus, initialize_menus reuses some old code that generates menubuttons from a data structure, mainly because I'm lazy and menus always take time to get just right. My next column goes into details on menus, cascades, and so on, but for now examine this code:

```
$MBF = $MW->Frame(-relief => 'raised', -borderwidth => 1);
$MBF->pack(-fill => 'x');

make_menubutton($MBF, 'File', 0, 'left', [['Quit', \&exit, 0]]);
make_menubutton($MBF, 'Help', 0, 'right',
                [ ['About', [$DIALOG_ABOUT => 'Show'], 0],
                  ['', undef, 0],
                  ['Usage', [$DIALOG_USAGE => 'Show'], 0] ] );
```

The first statement creates the container frame to hold the menubuttons, with a relief of "raised" and a borderwidth of one. The relief attribute specifies the widget's 3D look, but you need a non-zero borderwidth to see it. Notice that the frame is packed with its fill attribute set to "x", which makes the packer geometry manager expand the frame in the X direction to fill all available space. Otherwise, the File and Help menubuttons would be mapped side-by-side and centered in the frame. Creating the menubuttons and their corresponding menu items entails calls to make_menubutton with these five parameters:

1. The parent widget.

2. The menubutton label.

3. The shortcut character index. All our menubuttons have a shortcut character index of 0. For example, the 0th (first) character of "File" is 'f', which means that users can type *Alt-f* to activate the File menu.

4. The side of the menu frame to pack the menubutton.

5. A list of lists describing the menu items. Each inner list has three components: a label, a callback that is executed when the menu item is invoked, and a shortcut underline character. Null labels are treated as separators—do-nothing menu items that appear as lines.

Callbacks come in various flavors, and we'll see more of them in later columns. But in plop's case there are just two: an explicit reference to a subroutine (also called a code reference), and a reference to an array. An example of the first form is the Quit menu item, which calls exit. The Help menu items use the second form, where the first array element is an object (widget reference) and the second is the name of the method to invoke. Thus, when the user selects "About," the about dialog widget appears. Note that widgets used in callbacks must exist before they are referred to—that's precisely why we had to create the dialog widgets first.

The initialize_canvas subroutine generates the middle area of plop's main window but is slightly different than the first version, because it has a title, embedded widgets with editable X and Y values, and axes moved to the borders of the area to reduce visual clutter.

```
$CANV = $MW->Canvas( -width => $MAX_PXL + $MARGIN * 2,
                     -height => $MAX_PXL,
                     -relief => 'sunken');
$CANV->pack;
$CANV->CanvasBind('<Button-1>' => \&display_coordinates);
```

The above code creates the canvas but uses global "constants" rather than hard-coded values: $MAX_PXL is obviously the size of the canvas, in pixels. Here's our first *callback*, which binds the subroutine display_coordinates to mouse button 1.

```
$CANV->createText(325, 25,
    -text => 'Plot Continuous Functions Of The Form y=f($x)',
    -fill => 'blue');
```

Nothing new there, eh? But something new follows—the window canvas item type, demonstrated in the second and fourth statements below:

```
# Create the X axis and label it. Then label the minimum
# and maximum X values, and draw tick marks to
# indicate where they fall. The axis limits are LabEntry
# widgets embedded in Canvas windows.

$CANV->createLine($MIN_PXL + $MARGIN, $MAX_PXL - $MARGIN,
                  $MAX_PXL - $MARGIN, $MAX_PXL - $MARGIN);

$CANV->createWindow($MIN_PXL + $MARGIN, $MAX_PXL - $label_offset,
            -window => $MW->LabEntry( -textvariable => \$X_MIN,
                                      -label => 'X Minimum'));

$CANV->createLine($MIN_PXL + $MARGIN, $MAX_PXL - $MARGIN - $tick_length,
                  $MIN_PXL + $MARGIN, $MAX_PXL - $MARGIN + $tick_length);

$CANV->createWindow($MAX_PXL - $MARGIN, $MAX_PXL - $label_offset,
            -window => $MW->LabEntry( -textvariable => \$X_MAX,
                                      -label => 'X Maximum'));

$CANV->createLine($MAX_PXL - $MARGIN, $MAX_PXL - $MARGIN - $tick_length,
                  $MAX_PXL - $MARGIN, $MAX_PXL - $MARGIN + $tick_length);
```

The first canvas line item is simply the horizontal X axis, and the two remaining lines are the tick marks at each end. The two window items are containers where other objects can be stuffed, in this case two composite LabEntry widgets, which, as you might guess, combine the features of label and entry widgets. Their textvariable attributes are references to scalars $X_MIN and $X_MAX; when the program changes the variable's value, it's reflected on the display, and when the user edits a LabEntry, the associated textvariable is updated. The Y axis is handled in a similar manner.

Subroutine `initialize_functions` creates plop's remaining widgets, which are, in top-to-bottom packing order, a spacer frame, a label providing rudimentary instructions, a text widget with an attached scrollbar, and finally another container frame to hold a button or so.

```perl
$MW->Frame(-height => 20)->pack;
$MW->Label(      -text => 'Enter your functions here',
            -foreground => 'blue')->pack;

# Create a Frame with a scrollable Text widget that
# displays the function list, and a Button to
# initiate plot activities.

my $functions_frame = $MW->Frame;
$functions_frame->pack;
$TEXT = $functions_frame->Text(-height => 6);
$TEXT->pack;
$functions_frame->AddScrollbars($TEXT);
$functions_frame->configure(-scrollbars => 'e');
update_functions;

my $buttons_frame = $MW->Frame;
$buttons_frame->pack(-padx => 10, -pady => 5,
                      -expand => 1, -fill => 'x');
my @pack_attributes=qw(-side left -fill x -expand 1);
$buttons_frame->Button(   -text => 'Plot',
                       -command => \&plot_functions)->pack(@pack_attributes);
```

The above code creates a 20 pixel high frame (so much for the ban on hardcoded constants!) to occupy space, and some instructional text in blue. (Anywhere you can give a dimension as an integer pixel value, you can also append the characters i, c, m or p, to indicate inches, centimeters, millimeters, or points.)

Next we create the text widget, $TEXT, with a scrollbar anchored "east," and finally a large "Plot" button. Notice the convenient method `AddScrollbars` for attaching scrollbars to the text widget. The text widget contains the function list, which is particularly appropriate since each line can be tagged and assigned a different color. The function values are then plotted in that color.

The graphical interface in now complete, and when the user invokes the "Plot" button, the callback `plot_functions` is executed. Before plotting the function list, plop tidies up the text window and ensures that each function is assigned its proper color, providing for up to nine simultaneous functions before the colors cycle. Here's the code:

```perl
$TEXT->delete('0.0', 'end');
my $i = 0;
foreach (@FUNCTIONS) {
    $TEXT->insert('end', "$_\n", [$i]);
    $TEXT->tagConfigure($i, -foreground => $COLORS[$i % $NUM_COLORS],
                            -font => 'fixed');
    $i++;
}
$TEXT->yview('end');
```

First, everything is deleted, from line zero, character zero, to the end of the text widget. Then, each function from the @FUNCTIONS array is inserted and assigned a tag, which just happens to be its order in the text widget. A tag is simply an identifying string used for reference in other widget commands. In this case, the tagged text items are configured with their unique foreground color and assigned a fixed space font.

Now that the text widget is in sync with the function list, let's plot some functions:

```
$CANV->delete('plot');
$canv_x = $MIN_PXL + $MARGIN;      # X minimum
$DX = $X_MAX - $X_MIN;             # update delta X
$DY = $Y_MAX - $Y_MIN;             # update delta Y

ALL_X_VALUES:
for ($x = $X_MIN; $x <= $X_MAX; $x += ($X_MAX-$X_MIN) / $ALEN) {
  ALL_FUNCTIONS:
    foreach (0 .. $#FUNCTIONS) {
        $y = eval $FUNCTIONS[$_];
        $canv_y = (($Y_MAX - $y) / $DY) * $ALEN + $MARGIN;
        if ($canv_y > $MIN_PXL + $MARGIN and $canv_y < $MAX_PXL + $MARGIN) {
            $CANV->createText($canv_x, $canv_y,
                        -fill => $COLORS[$_ % $NUM_COLORS],
                        -tags => ['plot'], -text => '.', );
        }
    } # end of ALL_FUNCTIONS
    $canv_x++;                      # next X pixel
} # end of ALL_X_VALUES
```

After all this we're back to where we started, except that the code has been made more general and the transform equation has been fixed. $X_MIN and $X_MAX are dynamically assigned because they're part of the LabEntry widgets, and the X increment is calculated dynamically based on those values and the axis length. Y points painted on the canvas are automatically assigned their proper colors. And each point is tagged with the string "plot," so all current graphs can be easily deleted the next time the "Plot" button is pushed; that's what the $CANV->delete('plot') is for.

But there's one stone left unturned: the button binding established during canvas creation. Since we already know how to convert a Cartesian coordinate to a canvas coordinate, I thought it would be interesting to do the opposite: click anywhere on the canvas to display the Cartesian coordinates. The following code demonstrates how to handle an X event structure, in this case a button press:

```
sub display_coordinates {
    my ($canvas) = @_;
    my $e = $canvas->XEvent;
    my ($canv_x, $canv_y) = ($e->x, $e->y);
    my ($x, $y);
    $x = $X_MIN + $DX * (($canv_x - $MARGIN) / $ALEN);
    $y = $Y_MAX - $DY * (($canv_y - $MARGIN) / $ALEN);
    print "\nCanvas x = $canv_x, Canvas y = $canv_y.\n";
    print "Plot x = $x, Plot y = $y.\n";
}
```

When a binding callback is executed, the subroutine is implicitly passed a reference to its widget—here, the canvas. Using XEvent, the variable $e is now assigned a reference to the event structure. Two of $e's methods, x and y, return the relative position of the mouse when button 1 was pressed. Once the coordinates are known, it's a simple matter of using the existing transform equation, solving for X and Y, and printing the results.

In the next article, we'll look more into objects, build a composite widget, and examine menus in greater detail.

CHAPTER 35

Scoreboard: A 15-Minute Perl/Tk Application

Jon Orwant

In this article, I'll walk you through the scoreboard application I wrote for my Internet Quiz Show. (If you're interested in the show itself, the questions and answers will be available in the third Best of TPJ book, *Games, Diversions & Perl Culture*.) The application is a simple demonstration of Text, Button, and Frame widgets, as well as huge fonts.

The Need

As an undergraduate, I participated in College Bowl—a quiz competition for college students to test their trivia knowledge. Later, as a graduate student, I became a judge for College Bowl contests, during which I created an annual Perl Quiz Show for the O'Reilly Perl Conferences. As the conference grew in size and scope (becoming the Open Source Convention), my quiz show changed accordingly, and was rechristened the Internet Quiz Show.

In "real" College Bowl, there is a team of officials: the moderator, who reads the questions; the judge, who determines if player answers are correct; the recognizer, who calls out the name of the player who buzzed in first; and one or two scorekeepers who track the score on both paper and a chalkboard.

However, on stage at the O'Reilly conference, there's no team of officials—I have to do everything. Combining these roles isn't too hard, but I can't walk over to a chalkboard every time the score changes—it would take too much time, and people in the back of the 1,500-seat auditorium wouldn't be able to see. So I created a graphical application with Perl/Tk. (Perl/Tk runs under both Unix and Windows, so whatever operating system is running on the podium computer, chances are I'll be able to run scoreboard.)

The Design

As with all of my Perl/Tk programs, I began by envisioning what I wanted the finished product to look like. I wanted the score to be huge so that people in the back

353

of the auditorium could see it, and I wanted the buttons to be relatively large so that I'd be less likely to hit the wrong one. I needed to be sure that I could fix things in case I hit the wrong button. Figure 35-1 shows scoreboard in action.

Figure 35-1. The Internet Quiz Show scoreboard

Some of my desiderata for scoreboard:

- In addition to showing the score, I wanted a title showing the audience what round it was (e.g., "Semifinals Round 2") as well as titles of the teams.

- I wanted huge numbers for the score so that people in the back of the auditorium would be able to see.

- I wanted large buttons so that I didn't have to spend a lot of time positioning the mouse during the show. However, I wanted the large buttons to have small text so that it didn't steal attention away from the score.

The Implementation

The result was a 78-line program that creates two Frame widgets, five Text widgets, and 16 Button widgets. Example 35-1 shows the entire program; we'll walk through it line by line.

Example 35-1. The scoreboard application

```
01  #!/usr/bin/perl
02  #
03  # scoreboard.pl -- scoreboard appliation for the Internet Quiz Show
04
05  use Tk;
06
07  # Create the main window
08  $window = MainWindow->new;
09
10  # Create constants for the three fonts on the scoreboard
```

Example 35-1. The scoreboard application (continued)

```perl
11  use constant    bigfont => '-*-Helvetica-Bold-R-Normal--*-1920-*-*-*-*-*-*';
12  use constant   teamfont => '-*-Garamond-Bold-R-Normal--*-240-*-*-*-*-*-*';
13  use constant titlefont => '-*-Garamond-Bold-R-Normal--*-360-*-*-*-*-*-*';
14
15  # Create a text widget to display which round this is
16  $title = $window->Text(-width => 119, -height => 6, -bg => "light gray",
17                  -relief => "flat")->pack(-side => 'top', -expand => "no", -padx => 1);
18  $title->tag(configure => 'big', -font => titlefont);
19  $title->insert('end', "O'Reilly Internet Quiz Show\n" . $ARGV[0], 'big');
20
21  # Create two frames -- one for the left team, one for the right
22  $left  = $window->Frame->pack(-side => 'left', -expand => yes,
23                                  -padx => 1, -pady => 1);
24  $right = $window->Frame->pack(-side => 'right', -expand => yes,
25                                  -padx => 1, -pady => 1);
26
27  # Create a text widget to hold each team name
28  $teamleft = $left->Text(width => 45, height => 3, -relief => "flat",
29                          -bg => "light gray")->pack(-side => 'top');
30  $teamright = $right->Text(width => 45, height => 3, -relief => "flat",
31                          -bg => "light gray")->pack(-side => 'top');
32  $teamleft->tag(configure => 'team', -font => teamfont);
33  $teamright->tag(configure => 'team', -font => teamfont);
34  $teamleft->insert('end', $ARGV[1], 'team');
35  $teamright->insert('end', $ARGV[2], 'team');
36
37  # Create a text widget to hold each team score
38  $textleft = $left->Text(width => 45, height => 12)->pack(-side => 'top');
39  $textright = $right->Text(width => 45, height => 12)->pack(-side => 'top');
40  $textleft->tag(configure => 'verybig', -font => bigfont);
41  $textright->tag(configure => 'verybig', -font => bigfont);
42
43  # Set the initial scores to 0
44  $scoreleft = $scoreright = 0;
45  $textleft->insert('end', $scoreleft, 'verybig');
46  $textright->insert('end', $scoreright, 'verybig');
47
48  # Create the 16 buttons
49  for (my $score = -10; $score <= 30; $score += 5) {
50      next unless $score;   # (We don't want a button that adds zero points.)
51      $buttonleft[++$i] = $left->Button(-text => $score,
52                                  -command => scoreleftmaker($score));
53      $buttonleft[$i]->pack(-side => 'left', -padx => 10);
54      $buttonright[$i] = $right->Button(-text => $score,
55                                  -command => scorerightmaker($score));
56      $buttonright[$i]->pack(-side => 'left', -padx => 10);
57  }
58
59  # We're done creating widgets, so it's time to play.
60  MainLoop;
61
62  sub scoreleftmaker {
```

Example 35-1. The scoreboard application (continued)

```
63        my ($score) = shift;
64        return sub {
65          $scoreleft += $score;
66          $textleft->delete('1.0', 'end');
67          $textleft->insert('end', $scoreleft, 'verybig');
68        }
69  }
70
71  sub scorerightmaker {
72        my ($score) = shift;
73        return sub {
74          $scoreright += $score;
75          $textright->delete('1.0', 'end');
76          $textright->insert('end', $scoreright, 'verybig');
77        }
78  }
```

Lines 01–05 invoke the Perl interpreter and load the Tk module, and line 08 creates the application window. (Note that Figure 35-1 has a titlebar; the Scoreboard title appearing there was created automatically by Perl/Tk.)

Lines 11–13 create some font strings. They're just regular strings; there's no need to store them in variables (here, bigfont, teamfont, and titlefont), but the strings are so long that I prefer to give them shorter names. (The use constant pragma creates read-only variables, although for this application I could just as well have used regular Perl scalars.) These are X font strings, and Perl/Tk uses them even if it's not running under X (as is the case with the Windows laptop on which I developed scoreboard).

An X font string contains 14 attributes that collectively describe everything you might want to control about a font: the foundry, family, weight, slant, set width, style, pixel size, point sixe, horizontal and vertical resolution, spacing, average width, character set registry, and character set encoding. Typically, you'll just care about family, size, weight, slant, and set width. Whenever you don't care about a font attribute, you can defer the choice to Perl/Tk with an asterisk. So this font string means the Garamond family, with a Bold weight, Roman slant (i.e., no slant at all) and a size of 240:

```
'-*-Garamond-Bold-R-Normal--*-240-*-*-*-*-*-*'
```

Lines 16–19 create a Text widget to hold the title at the top of scoreboard; in Figure 35-1, it's the text reading "O'Reilly Internet Quiz Show, Semifinal Round 1." The "Semifinal Round 1" was passed in as the first argument to scoreboard (which I invoked as scoreboard "Semifinal Round 1" "Race Conditions" "Dining Philosophers". We use a plain Text widget, but we could also have used an ROText widget to make the title read-only. We create the widget by invoking the Text method of $window (lines 16–17), hardcoding the dimensions of the widget as well as the background color (chosen to match the application background) and a relief of flat so that the text appears painted on rather than raised or sunken. The widget is then packed—otherwise, the text wouldn't appear at all. Line 18 sets the font, and line 19 appends the text to the (currently blank) widget.

Lines 22–25 create two Frames: $left and $right. These are expandable spaces on the scoreboard application that are designed to hold other widgets. You can't point to anything in Figure 35-1 and say "That's the Frame," but these two Frames are what enable the buttons for the Race Conditions to be placed below the score for the Race Conditions. Likewise for the Dining Philosophers.

Lines 28–35 create two Text widgets for each team name: $teamleft and $teamright. Here's the first use of our two Frames: we invoke the Text method not from $window (as we did to create the title) but from $left and $right. We configure them with a smaller Garamond font and insert the team names (provided on the command line as the second and third arguments: $ARGV[1] and $ARGV[2]).

In lines 38–41, scoreboard creates one more Text widgets to display the score for each team. Lines 44–46 sets the initial score for each team to 0 and then displays it.

Lines 49–57 is the trickiest part of the program. Inside each Frame, just below the score, we want to display eight buttons for the different score changes (anywhere from subtracting 10 points to adding 30). We loop from –10 to 30 by increments of five, skipping over zero (since we don't need a button to add zero points). As we iterate through the loop, we build up an array of Button widgets. As you can see from the pack expressions, we give them a padx of 10—that's to ensure that the button is substantially bigger than the text on its label. (Remember, I wanted big buttons but small text.)

The -command => scoreleftmaker($score) expression in line 52 and its counterpart in line 55 are the keys to this application. scoreleftmaker and scorerightmaker are subroutines that themselves generate subroutines.. If you look at their definitions in lines 62–78, you'll see that they return anonymous subroutines. These anonymous subroutines are *closures*, because they bring their own lexical scope (the scope that remembers the $score) with them. scoreleftmaker and scorerightmaker are only invoked at the very beginning of the application, and not when the players are actually spouting off trivia. In contrast, the anonymous subroutines that they generate are invoked whenever I press one of the buttons. These are the *callbacks* for our buttons.

Another way to think about this process is that Perl/Tk evaluates whatever expression follows -command just once—when your application launches. So it's up to you to ensure that the expression yields a subroutine that can be executed. Usually, that will either look like an anonymous subroutine declaration:

```
-command => sub { print "Hello, world!" }
```

or a reference to a named subroutine:

```
-command => \&hello
```

but in `scoreboard`, we add a level of indirection by executing a subroutine that returns an anonymous subroutine:

```
-command => scoreleftmaker($score)
```

Finally, in line 60 we execute the usual last line of Perl/Tk programs: `MainLoop`, which signals that it's time to stop arranging widgets and start paying attention to the user's keyboard and mouse.

So there you have it! A 15-minute Perl/Tk application that uses the Text, Button, and Frame widgets. In the next article, *The Mouse Odometer*, Steve develops a more complicated application.

## CHAPTER 36

The Mouse Odometer

Steve Lidie

If you read *Getting Started with Perl/Tk* and *Scoreboard: A 15-Minute Perl/Tk Application*, you should be a seasoned Tk novice by now. Assuming so, let's move right along and examine the Perl/Tk implementation of the Mouse Odometer, named modo and pictured in Figure 36-1.

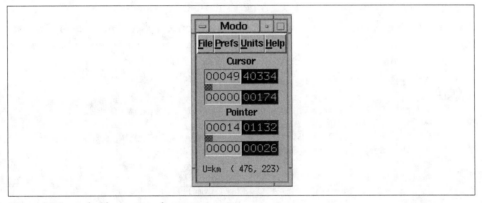

Figure 36-1. modo, the mouse odometer

modo has got to be one of the most pointless programs ever written. But it illustrates numerous Perl/Tk features, so it does have some value. I first saw similar code for the Mac, written by Sean P. Nolan, that simply tracked a machine's cursor. Currently I have logged well over 51 kilometers on my cursor, and my mouse has careened around its pad some 14 kilometers.

Measuring Distance

Most of this column is not about modo and how it works, but rather the Perl/Tk features it uses. This time we'll learn how to schedule asynchronous timer events, and look more closely at window manager commands, menus, menubuttons, and the ColorEditor. We'll also create and explain in detail an object-oriented Perl/Tk composite widget that we'll create called the Odometer. Like a car's odometer, we want our mouse odometer to record the *physical distance* traveled by the mouse, not the number of pixels. In a car, you want to know how many miles you've traveled, not merely the number of tire-lengths, which will vary from car to car. In the X window system you can use the xdpyinfo command to find out the number of millimeters-per-pixel of your display, and that, multiplied by a pixel count, gives the distance in millimeters. Unfortunately, pixels aren't always square, so there are actually two numbers to worry about: the horizontal and vertical millimeter per pixel ratios. Once we know those numbers, we can figure out the distance D given the number of pixels traversed in the X and Y directions, which we'll call dX and dY. In pseudocode:

$$D = sqrt((dX * (\$mmX/\$pixelsX)) ** 2 + (dY * (\$mmY/\$pixelsY)) ** 2);$$

How can we figure out dX and dY? Well, Tk provides the command pointerxy, which returns a two-element list: the cursor's absolute X and Y coordinates. (In deference to Einstein, who taught us that nothing is absolute, we'll say "relative to the root window of your display.") So if we call pointerxy twice, we can subtract the results, yielding our dX and dY. Then we can just apply the above formula. (Which is thankfully just the Pythagorean Theorem, since we're dealing with a non-curved two-space. Otherwise we might need Albert's ten-dimensional tensors.)

The major components are a row of menubuttons (often called a *menu bar*), two sets of odometers (one for the cursor and one for the pointer), and a status line showing the distance units and cursor coordinates. Here is modo's main loop, with a tiny amount of code dealing with pointing device distance removed for clarity:

```
sub modo {
    # Track the cursor forever, periodically updating the odometer file.
    my( $x, $y) = $MW->pointerxy;
    $W_MISC_TEXT = sprintf("U=%-3s (%4d,%4d)", $MODO_UNITS_HUMAN, $x, $y);
    my ($dx, $dy) = (abs($x - $LAST_X), abs($y - $LAST_Y));
    ($LAST_X, $LAST_Y) = ($x, $y);
    my ($dxmm,$dymm) = ($dx*$MM_PIXEL_X, $dy*$MM_PIXEL_Y);
    my $d = sqrt( ($dxmm * $dxmm) + ($dymm * $dymm) );
    $W_CODO->add($d,$MODO_UNITS) if $d > 0;
    if ($AUTOSAVE_COUNT-- <= 0) {
        $AUTOSAVE_COUNT = $AUTOSAVE_TICKS;
        eval {save_modo};
    }
    $MW->after($MILLISECOND_DELAY, \&modo);
}
```

Upon startup, modo is called once, and exactly once. The modo subroutine performs several tasks:

- It fetches the pointer's X/Y information and updates the variable $W_MISC_TEXT with the current display units and cursor's root window coordinates. This variable has been specified as the -textvariable option of the label widget packed at the bottom of modo's window. As you learned last time, changing a -textvariable updates the display immediately.

- It calculates the distance the cursor has moved, in millimeters.

- It adds a non-zero distance to the cursor Odometer widget $W_CODO. Note that add is a method of class Odometer. Later we'll see how the Odometer class was created and why it behaves like a standard Perl/Tk widget.

- It periodically saves the distance data to a file so that useless odometer data is not lost. The tick count is based on how often you want the state information saved and the time interval between invocations of modo.

- It reschedules itself via a call to after. There are several ways to invoke after, but in Tk-land the form shown above is the most common. The first parameter is the delay time in milliseconds after which the second parameter, a standard Tk callback, is executed. Since this event is asynchronous modo returns and "pops the stack." After the delay the callback is invoked and modo is called once again, does its thing, reschedules itself, and returns.

There are many aspects to designing and writing a robust application, and one of them is to give the user adequate real-time feedback so they know things are "working." Since modo takes some time to start up, we'll open a new top-level window that displays its current initialization state, along these lines:

```
$QUIT_COMMAND = sub {save_modo; exit};
$MW = MainWindow->new(-screen => $OPT{'display'});
$MW->withdraw;
$MW->title($OPT{'title'});
$MW->iconname('modo');
$MW->iconbitmap("\@$LIBDIR/icon.xbm");
$MW->minsize(50, 50);
$MW->protocol('WM_DELETE_WINDOW' => $QUIT_COMMAND);
unless ($OPT{'iconic'}) {
    # Realize a transient toplevel to display modo's initialization status.
    $STATUS = $MW->Toplevel;
    $STATUS->positionfrom('user');
    $STATUS->geometry('+100+100');
    $STATUS->title('Initializing modo');
    $STATUS_B = $STATUS->Label(-bitmap => "\@$LIBDIR/icon.xbm")->pack;
    $STATUS_L = $STATUS->Label( -text => 'Main Window ...',
                                -width => 25, )->pack;
    $MW->idletasks;
}
update_status 'Global Stuff';
```

What's that dangling anonymous subroutine doing there at the top? Well, it simply defines what needs to be done when terminating modo. There are at least two ways to exit: either by selecting Quit or by having the window manager close the main window, so it makes sense to define a subroutine. Thus, $QUIT_COMMAND is initialized with a code reference that can be used whenever necessary.

As always, we first open the main window on some display—the new method accepts an optional parameter specifying the particular display desired. (Be aware that modo uses a special hash, named %OPT, to hold argument name-value pairs, whether created by default or extracted from the command line.) Next there is a series of main window method calls known as *window manager commands*, because they are used to interact with the window manager.

We *withdraw* the main window to *unmap* it from the display, so only the status window will be visible (once it's created). The title method draws text at the top of the decorative border provided by the window manager, and the two "icon" methods specify a name and X bitmap for the application's icon. minsize restricts the user from resizing the window smaller than fifty pixels in either dimension (there is also a related maxsize method). Finally, note the idiom for registering a callback with the window manger to terminate an application: simply associate a standard Perl/Tk callback with the WM_DELETE_WINDOW protocol.

Assuming the user didn't fire up modo iconified, we next create the top-level status widget. The methods positionfrom and geometry are suggestions to the window manager on where to place the new top-level. Some window managers, fvwm for instance, normally require you to explicitly place top-level windows; positionfrom('user') overrides this behavior. Finally two label widgets are packed in the top-level, the first containing modo's X bitmap and the second containing the current initialization state. Since the X server tries to buffer events to improve performance, idletasks is used to flush idle callbacks and hence keep the display responsive. (We'll see more of event management in the next column.) A snapshot of the status window is shown in Figure 36-2.

Figure 36-2. modo's initialization window

Lastly note the first call to subroutine update_status, which simply uses configure to change the text in the status window via $STATUS_L; there are numerous calls to this subroutine sprinkled throughout modo's initialization code. Doing this keeps users happy.

Menus

Another key aspect in user-friendly GUI design is providing a reasonably consistent "look and feel." Whether an application is written for X, Windows, or the Mac, you find, and indeed *expect*, a row of menubuttons (the menu bar) at the top of the program's main window. And the leftmost button is a File menubutton, which at least allows you to exit the application. So to be conformant, modo also has a File menubutton, which we'll examine now.

A *menubutton* is a subclass of a button, meaning that it shares, or inherits, many of a button's characteristics. The big difference is that pushing a button executes a callback whereas pushing a menubutton posts a menu. A *menu* is simply a rectangular widget that contains one or more *menu items* that when pressed, might execute a callback, set a Perl variable, or invoke yet another menu (an action called *cascading*). Pressing the File menubutton displays the menu shown in Figure 36-3.

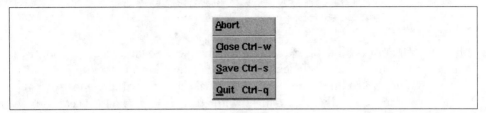

Figure 36-3. The File menu

The File menu itself is composed of simple button-like objects bound to callbacks. More precisely, we call these command menu items because they execute a command (callback) when pressed. Other types of menu items include cascade, checkbutton, radiobutton, and separator.

The File menu has three thin lines: separator menu items, whose sole purpose is to visually separate logically distinct portions of the menu.

The File menu also has a *tear-off*, which is the dashed line above Abort. Pressing a tear-off *reparents* the menu and puts it under control of the window manager. Thus, it gets its own decorative border, can be moved, iconifed, closed, and so on. By default all Perl/Tk menus have a tear-off.

Here are some other facts you need to know about menus:

- As a convenience, Perl/Tk automatically generates a menubutton's associated menu widget when the first menu item is created. Two common cases where you need to manually create a menu are to disable the tear-off and to create menu cascades.

- Menu items can be manipulated in several ways: added, configured, deleted, or invoked. To manipulate a menu item you refer to it either by its position in the menu (starting at zero) or by its text label. If there is a tear-off it is assigned index zero, making the first menu item have an index of one. Since a separator is a menu item, it too has a menu index. (I highly recommend referencing menu items by label name rather than index. You'll know why as soon as you insert a new menu item in the middle of a menu and then have to hunt through your code changing index values!)

In case that was all as clear as mud, maybe some code will clarify matters. Let's create the application's menubar using a frame, $mb, and pack our menubuttons in a row, from left to right:

```
# File menu.
my $mbf=$mb->Menubutton(-text => 'File', -underline => 0... );
$mbf->pack(qw(-side left));
```

```
$mbf->command(  -label => 'Abort', -underline => 0,
                -command => \&exit);
$mbf->separator;
my $close_command = [$MW => 'iconify'];
$mbf->command(  -label => 'Close',          -underline => 0,
                -command => $close_command, -accelerator => 'Ctrl-w');
$MW->bind('<Control-Key-w>' => $close_command);
```

When Perl/Tk finishes building the Abort menu item we know that a menu widget has been generated with a tear-off (index 0) and one command menu item (index 1, name Abort). (An often asked question is: "How do I make a menu without a tear-off?" The answer is you must explicitly create a menu with -tearoff => 0, and then configure the menubutton with -menu => $your_menu. Then you can proceed normally.)

The Close menu item (index 2) has an associated keyboard accelerator. However, this just adds more text to the menu item label; you still have to create the key binding. Since the close code is needed in two places, just create a code reference and use that.

Another common menu item is the cascade, illustrated in Figure 36-4.

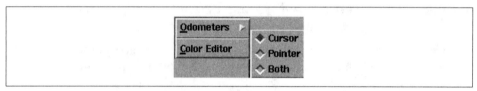

Figure 36-4. Cascading preferences for modo

Pressing the Prefs menubutton from the menubar displays the leftmost menu, containing a cascade and command menu item. Pressing the Odometers cascade displays the cascade's menu, containing three radiobutton menu items. (Of course, the cascade menu could contain another cascade, which could have another cascade, which... well, you get the picture.) Cascades are handled pretty much like menus without a tear-off, in that you create a menu widget manually and then configure the cascade to point to it, like this:

```
# Prefs menu.
my $mbp = $mb->Menubutton(-text => 'Prefs', ... );
$mbp->pack(qw(-side left));
my $odometers = 'Odometers';
$mbp->cascade(-label => $odometers, -underline => 0);
$mbp->separator;
$mbp->command(-label => 'Color Editor', -underline => 0,
              -state => $COLOR_STATE, ...);
```

So far, only -state might be unfamiliar. Many widgets have this option, which can have one of three possible values: normal, active, or disabled. Widgets start in the normal state, and when the cursor passes over them they become active. If you place a widget in the disabled state, it is dimmed and becomes unresponsive to button presses and other bindings. We'll see how $COLOR_STATE is initialized shortly.

```
my $mbpm  = $mbp->cget(-menu);
my $mbpmo = $mbpm->Menu;
$mbp->entryconfigure($odometers, -menu => $mbpmo);
$mbpmo->radiobutton(-label => 'Cursor', -variable => \$OPT{'odometer'},
                    -value => 'cursor');
$mbpmo->radiobutton(-label => 'Pointer', -variable => \$OPT{'odometer'},
                    -value => 'pointer');
$mbpmo->radiobutton(-label => 'Both', -variable => \$OPT{'odometer'},
                    -value => 'both');
```

Pay attention please: the Odometers cascade menu *must* be a child of the menu containing the Odometer cascade itself (here, the Prefs menu), hence the cget call to fetch the menu reference. Note that entryconfigure is to menus as configure is to other widgets, except you need to tell it which menu entry needs attention (which is analogous to itemconfigure for canvas items). Notice also that the menu entry is referenced by name rather than index.

Finally, three radiobutton menu items are added to the cascade menu. Just like ordinary radiobutton widgets, they allow you to select a single item from a list, and store its value in a variable. The actual value stored in the common variable depends on which radiobutton was pressed. (These widgets got their name because using them is similar to tuning an old fashioned car radio: selecting a station by pushing one button deselects all the other buttons by popping them out.)

If you'd like to see a complicated cascade created from a Perl list-of-list-of-list data structure, take a gander at the modo source code responsible for generating the Units cascades; that'll fry your eyes. The code is available at *http://www.oreilly.com/catalog/tpj2*.

The ColorEditor Widget

Let's add some colors and incorporate the ColorEditor widget into our application. ColorEditor lets you select a color attribute, say foreground, edit a color swatch and then apply the final color by calling a special ColorEditor subroutine (the colorizer) that descends through the application's widgets and configures each in turn.

A ColorEditor widget is created in the standard manner:

```
$COLOR_STATE = $MW->depth > 1 ? 'normal' : 'disabled';
if ($COLOR_STATE eq 'normal') {
    $CREF = $MW->ColorEditor(-title => 'modo');
}
```

But there's no need for one if your display can't support it, so first check the pixel depth of the display using the window information command depth. For monochrome displays we don't even bother creating the ColorEditor, and the menu item to invoke it, which we just discussed, is dimmed.

Once the ColorEditor is created and initialized, you can use it like a Dialog—just invoke its Show method. The most important thing to remember about the ColorEditor is that it maintains a *list* of widgets to colorize: *every* widget in the application present when the ColorEditor was created. Sometimes this is good, sometimes bad, and in modo's case it's bad. Bad because when $CREF is created, some of the applicable widgets aren't there yet, and there are some that *are* present that shouldn't be colorized in the first place. Of course, there are methods to deal with this, so as the last step of initialization:

```
$CREF->configure(-widgets => [$MW, $MW->Descendants]);
$CREF->delete_widgets(
        [$CREF,                 # ColorEditor...
         $CREF->Descendants,    # and all its descendant widgets.
         $W_CODO->Descendants,  # Odometer descendants because
         $W_PODO->Descendants,  # the class handles configuration changes.
        ]);
```

The first line ensures that the main window, $MW, and all of its descendants in the widget hierarchy are part of the color list. The second line then removes particular widgets that should not be colorized. As a rule of thumb, leave the ColorEditor alone in case you really mess things up, like setting the foreground and background to the same color! And the two composite odometers are excluded for the simple reason that the foreground and background colors of digits to the right of the "units" point are reversed, just like real odometers. How we deal with this is somewhat subtle, as you'll see in the next section.

Composite Widgets

At last it's time to discuss Perl/Tk composites featuring, of course, the odometer widget. The OO tables have turned and now you become a designer rather than a mere user! An odometer widget "ISA" frame. That is, it's a subclass of a frame widget: odometer objects are simply "mega-widgets" composed of standard Tk widgets packed inside a frame (we'll see what "ISA" is all about shortly). There are other kinds of extended widgets: a dialog widget ISA a top-level, while an axis widget is *derived* from, or "kind of," a canvas. A common attribute of all these extended widgets is that they behave just like standard Tk widgets, basically because Nick took great pains to ensure they do.

Since an odometer is contained in a frame you can create an instance and pack it inside your application just like, say, a button. Let's create a default odometer and add one millimeter to it:

```
$MW->Odometer->add(1, 1)->pack;
```

The result is shown in Figure 36-5.

Figure 36-5. A Tk::Odometer object

Notice how methods such as add and pack can be strung together, as long as they return an object reference for the next method to operate upon. The odometer is composed of six widgets: the odometer label, left and right labels indicating total distance, a trip reset button, and left and right labels indicating trip distance. Two labels are used for total and trip distances so that foreground and background colors can be reversed on either side of the "units" point. When modo creates its odometers it supplies some arguments in the Perl/Tk "key => value" style, including -odometerlabel, a keyword unique to class Odometer:

```
$W_CODO = $w->Odometer(-odometerlabel => 'Cursor',
                             -font => $OPT{'fontname'},
                       -foreground => $OPT{'foreground'},
                       -background => $OPT{'background'},
                           -cursor => $CURSOR);
```

In order to see the primary features of a frame-like composite, I need to gut Odometer.pm, which later I'll reconstruct piece by piece:

```
package Tk::Odometer;
require 5.002;
use Tk::Frame;
use base qw/Tk::Frame/;
Tk::Widget->Construct('Odometer');

sub Populate {
    my ($cw, $args) = @_;
    $cw->SUPER::Populate($args);
    # Create and pack frame subwidgets here.
    $cw->ConfigSpecs( ... );
    return $cw;
} # end Populate, Odometer constructor

1;
```

What we have is the definition of a new Perl/Tk widget class named "Tk::Odometer", with six salient features:

1. A unique class (package) name.

2. A use Tk::Frame that imports frame definitions and methods.

3. Declaration of the @ISA list, which is how Perl implements method inheritance. For instance, when you configure an odometer Perl first looks for that method in class Tk::Odometer. But as you'll see, there is no such method in this class, so Perl tries to locate that method by looking at any classes in the @ISA array. As it turns out, Tk::Frame has no configure method either, but a frame has its own @ISA list, so the search continues up the class hierarchy. Rest assured that Perl/Tk does indeed provide a configure method somewhere, but you don't have to know just where—OO at its best.

4. A call to Construct that dynamically creates the class constructor. Among other things, this magic arranges a call to the class method Populate when a new object is instantiated.

5. The actual code for `Populate`, written by the class implementor, which populates the incoming frame with the requisite component widgets, specifies the widget's configuration options, and returns a composite reference.

6. Any number of class-specific methods (not shown here) to manipulate objects of the new class. We already know of one for odometers: `add`.

`Tk::Odometer::Populate` is called with two arguments. `$cw` is a reference to the partially completed composite widget and `$args` is a reference to the argument *hash* (i.e., the keyword/value pairs from the widget creation command). By convention, `$args` is immediately passed to `SUPER::Populate`, where, sometimes, behind-the-scenes bookkeeping such as modifying configuration specifications is performed.

Now, in standard Perl/Tk fashion, we create and arrange the component widgets of the composite, using `$cw` as their parent (the list `@PACK` holds common pack attributes):

```
# Odometer label.
my $l = $cw->Label->pack(@PACK);

# Odometer total distance, left and right labels.
$cw->make_odo('total')->pack(@PACK);

# Odometer trip reset button. It's placed inside a container frame so
# there is a background to color, since trying to configure the
# composite containing frame results in nasty recursion problems. The
# button is anchored southwest so it stays "attached to" the trip odometer.

my $rbf = $cw->Frame(-relief => 'flat')->pack(@PACK);
my $rb = $rbf->Button(  -height => 2,
                         -width => 5,
                        -bitmap => 'gray50',
                        -relief => 'flat',
                       -command => [$cw => 'reset_trip'],
              -highlightthickness => 0)->pack(-anchor => 'sw', -expand => 1);

# Odometer trip distance, left and right labels.
$cw->make_odo('trip')->pack(@PACK);

# Maintain instance variables in the composite widget hash. Instance
# variables hold data particular to one instance of an Odometer object.
#
# reset            = widget reference to trip reset button for bind
# total_mm         = total distance in millimeters
# total_left       = total distance left label for add
# total_right      = total distance right label for add
# total_right_label = widget reference for colorizing
# (ditto for trip_mm, trip_left, trip_right, and trip_right label.)

$cw->{'reset'} = $rb;
$cw->{'total_mm'} = 0;
($cw->{'total_left'}, $cw->{'total_right'}) = ($Z, $Z);
$cw->reset_trip;
```

Once again there are several items worthy of note:

- The -text attribute of the odometer label $1 is not specified. So, just when does this happen and who does it? The answer follows shortly.

- The -command attribute of the reset button $rb invokes the class method reset_trip, emulating the reset button on a real odometer.

- make_odo packs the left and right labels side by side in a frame and creates the -textvariable references pointing to the above instance variables.

I hinted at this, but one job Populate should not do, generally, is directly configure its components; instead it makes a call to ConfigSpecs to specify configuration options and default values. Then, when Populate returns, Perl/Tk auto-configures the composite, supplying ConfigSpec values or perhaps values from the X options database:

```
# Now establish configuration specs so that the composite behaves like
# a standard Perl/Tk widget. Each entry is a list of 4 items
# describing the option: how to process a configure request, its
# name in the resource database, its class name, and its default value.
#
# The Tk::Configure->new specification renames -odometerlabel to
# -text, which is what Labels want, because -odometerlabel IS a Label.
#
# The DESCENDANTS specification applies configure recursively to all
# descendant widgets.
#
# The METHOD specification invokes a method by the same name as the
# option (without the dash), e.g.:
#
# $cw->background($bg);
#
# Normally you don't need configurators just for background and
# foreground attributes, but an Odometer is special since the colors
# are reversed for the right half of the odometers.
#
# The -cursor specification says to configure only the indicated list
# of widgets (in this case there is but one, $rb, the trip reset button.)

$cw->ConfigSpecs(
  -odometerlabel => [[Tk::Configure->new($1 => '-text')],
                    'odometerlabel', 'odometerLabel', 'Odometer'],
          -font => ['DESCENDANTS', 'font', 'Font', 'fixed'],
    -background => ['METHOD', 'background', 'Background', '#d9d9d9'],
    -foreground => ['METHOD', 'foreground', 'Foreground', 'black'],
        -cursor => [[$rb], 'cursor', 'Cursor',['left_ptr']]);

return $cw;
```

There's still more work left, however. So far, we've created a class constructor, but no methods to manipulate the objects it creates. So let's look at a few, starting with the simplest, `$W_CODO->get_total_distance`. Our program uses this method to save its state information:

```
sub get_total_distance { shift->{'total_mm'} }
```

This method just returns the value from an odometer's `total_mm` instance variable. The `shift` idiom is a shortcut for Perl's builtin `shift` function, returning the odometer reference. Here `bind` is overridden by providing a version specific to our class:

```
# Override bind to select trip reset button, the only sensible widget.
# Build an argument list to bind so that the call behaves normally.
sub bind {
    my ($odo, $event, $code) = @_;
    my @args = ();
    push @args, $event if defined $event;
    push @args, $code if defined $code;
    $odo->{'reset'}->bind(@args);
    return $odo;
}
```

Finally, here's `add`, which displays the millimeter count (modulus 100,000) in the user's units. The only thing new is the use of `BackTrace`, the Perl/Tk way of including traceback information:

```
sub add {
    my ($odo, $d, $u) = @_;
    $odo->BackTrace('Usage: $odo->add($distance, $units)') if @_ != 3;
    $odo->{'total_mm'} += $d;
    $odo->{'trip_mm' } += $d;
    my ($n1, $f1, $n2, $f2, $s);
    $n1 = $odo->{'total_mm'} * $u;
    $f1 = $n1 - int($n1);
    $n2 = $odo->{'trip_mm' } * $u;
    $f2 = $n2 - int($n2);
    $s = sprintf("%011.5f%011.5f", ($n1 % 100000) + $f1, ($n2 % 100000) + $f2);
    $odo->{'total_left'}  = substr($s, 0,  5);
    $odo->{'total_right'} = substr($s, 6,  5);
    $odo->{'trip_left'}   = substr($s, 11, 5);
    $odo->{'trip_right'}  = substr($s, 17, 5);
    return $odo;
}
```

The Odometer class has several private methods too. Unlike C++, in Perl a private method is only private because the class designer doesn't document the interface. Be polite and only use documented public methods. Here, I need to show you three private methods to complete the ColorEditor discussion.

Now, `Populate` used `ConfigSpecs` for foreground and background `configure` options, specifying the `METHOD` action, so when either of these odometer attributes are configured, one of the following subroutines is called with two parameters: an odometer widget reference and a color value.

```
# Odometer background/foreground color subroutines.
sub background {
```

```
    shift->bf(shift, '-foreground', '-background')
}

sub foreground {
    shift->bf(shift, '-background', '-foreground')
}
```

These immediately call the following subroutine, bf. Remembering that an odometer's component widgets have been removed from ColorEditor's color list, it's up to the class to colorize them. So bf simply walks the composite widget hierarchy, configuring each component in turn, but swapping foreground for background (or vice-versa) upon encountering any right-side label:

```
# Reverse background/foreground colors on right odometer labels.
sub bf {
    my ($odo, $color, $bf1, $bf2) = @_;
    my $total_right = $odo->{'total_right_label'};
    my $trip_right = $odo->{'trip_right_label'};
    $odo->Walk( sub {
                    my ($widget) = @_;
                    if ($widget == $total_right or
                        $widget == $trip_right) {
                        $widget->configure($bf1 => $color);
                    } else {
                        $widget->configure($bf2 => $color);
                    }
                });
}
```

So, we're finished implementing, right? Wrong. Gee, all the code's there, it's tested and it works...what could be missing? How about *user* documentation! The Perl Way is to include a pod (Plain Old Documentation) in your class module. Check out Odometer.pm for an example.

In the next article, we'll look at ways to handle events (like mouse clicks) in Perl/Tk.

CHAPTER 37

Events

Steve Lidie

event *(î-vênt'): something that happens: a noteworthy*
occurrence or happening: something worthy of
remark: an unusual or significant development.
(Paraphrased from Webster's Third.)

Events are what drive Perl/Tk programs. In the past I've described these events superficially, sweeping lots of detail under the MainLoop rug, all for the sake of simplicity. MainLoop is our friend, since it's all that is needed for nearly every Perl/Tk program. But sometimes it's not enough.

Today's featured program is a simple Pong-like game sporting a new widget derived from the Canvas class, which we'll compare to the Odometer composite widget described in *The Mouse Odometer*. Instead of using MainLoop, our Pong game handles events itself with DoOneEvent.

Before discussing Pong, we'll examine some other programs, including a simple animation called neko, demonstrating the Photo widget and some other Tk commands.

Tk defines four broad event categories: X, timer, input/output, and idle. *X events* are generated in response to mouse motion, button and keyboard actions, and window changes. You already know that many of these events have built-in Tk bindings, and that you can create your own bindings, so all you need to do is define the callback to handle the event. (There are lots of other X events, which we'll examine in detail in subsequent articles.) *Timer events* are used for periodic occurrences, from blinking items to animating images. *Input/output events* help prevent your application from freezing when reading and writing to terminals, pipes, or sockets. Finally, *idle events* are low priority callbacks invoked only when all events from the previous three event queues have been processed. Tk uses the idle events queue to redraw widgets, since it's generally a bad idea to redisplay a widget after every change of state. By deferring redraws until there is nothing left to do, widgets presumably reach their steady state. The result is improved performance and a flicker-free screen.

Timer Events

In *The Mouse Odometer* we saw a useful idiom for scheduling asynchronous tasks:

```
modo( );

...

sub modo {              # Do stuff, then reschedule myself.
    $MW->after->($MILLISECOND_DELAY, \&modo);
}
```

Before modo returns, it uses `after` to schedule a timer event and define the handler (callback). This idiom is so common that Perl/Tk provides `repeat` as a shortcut, so the above code can be condensed like so:

```
$MW->repeat->($MILLISECOND_DELAY, \&modo);
```

A working example named rpt is available at *http://www.oreilly.com/catalog/tpj2*.

Tk uses timer events to flash the insertion cursor for entry widgets. After the widget gets the keyboard focus, it displays the cursor and queues a timer callback. Then the callback erases the cursor and the cycle repeats, several times per second. This technique is often used to flash alert messages or special buttons. You can use repeat, but this is the idiom you'll almost always see:

```
my $b = $MW->Button(-text => 'Hello World!', -command => \&exit)->pack;
flash_widget($b, -background, qw(blue yellow), 500);

MainLoop;

sub flash_widget {      # Flash a widget attribute periodically.
    my ($w, $opt, $val1, $val2, $interval) = @_;
    $w->configure($opt => $val1);
    $MW->after($interval, [\&flash_widget, $w, $opt, $val2, $val1, $interval]);
}
```

As you see, the code is quite simple. On the first call to flash_widget, the button's background is configured blue. A timer event is then scheduled, reversing the background colors, so next time the widget is configured yellow. The periodic change in background color every 500 milliseconds yields the desired flashing effect. A working example, named flash, is on the book's web site.

You can also perform crude animations with nothing more than standard Tk timer events. To demonstrate, I created a basic neko program, using frames borrowed from Masayuki Koba's well known xneko. In case you're unfamiliar with xneko, a cat chases the cursor around the window. When you stop moving the cursor, the cat yawns and settles down to take a nap. When the cursor moves again, Neko wakes up and resumes the chase. My rendition of neko doesn't follow the cursor and moves solely in one dimension.

In the U.S., television creates the illusion of motion by flashing 30 full images per second. Movies show 24 images per second, but flash each image three times to lessen the flicker. Psychophysicists have determined that 10 images per second is, on average, the minimum number needed to perceive motion, so that's what we'll use for neko. I don't actually have ten images to show, just two: one of Neko with his feet together, and one with his feet apart.

When you run neko, Figure 37-1, depicting the six frames used by the application, is momentarily displayed.

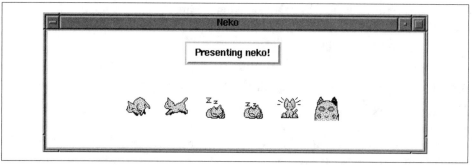

Figure 37-1. The Neko initialization screen

To make use of these frames we need to create Tk images. In Tk parlance, an *image* is just another Tk object with special methods for image manipulations. Once created, images are then imported into other widgets, such as a button, canvas or label. For example, this code creates a button with Neko's icon on it instead of text:

```
my $i = $MW->Photo(-file => 'images/icon.ppm');
my $b = $MW->Button( -image => $i, -command => sub {print "Meow\n"})->pack;
```

Images come in two flavors: *bitmaps*, which have only two colors, and *photos*, which have many colors or shades of grey. The six neko frames were originally plain X bitmaps, but have since been converted to colorized PPM files, a format (such as GIF) suitable for input to the Photo command.

The canvas widget provides an ideal backdrop for the animation, since images can be drawn on it and moved using standard canvas methods. Here's the code that created much of Figure 37-1:

```
# Create the six Photo images from the color PPM files and display
# them in a row. The canvas image IDs are stored in the global array
# @IDS for use by the rest of the Neko code. For instance, to perform
# a canvas operation on the Neko icon, simply fetch its item ID from
# $IDS[5]. Sorry for using hardcoded values, but this is just "proof
# of concept" code!

my $x = 125;

foreach ( qw(left1 left2 sleep1 sleep2 awake icon) ) {
```

```
    push @IDS, $C->createImage($x, $SCAMPER_Y,
                            -image => $MW->Photo(-file => "images/$_.ppm"));
    $x += 50;
}

# Wait for the main window to appear before hiding the Neko
# frames. (Otherwise you might never get to see them.)

$MW->waitVisibility($MW);
$MW->after(2000, \&hide_nekos);

MainLoop;
```

An immediate problem arises: the animation demands that only one frame be visible at any point in time, so we need to hide arbitrary frames (including the six frames currently on the canvas). One way might be to create and delete the images continually, but that's messy. Instead, neko uses a trick based on the canvas *display list*.

Tk uses the display list to control the order in which canvas items are displayed, so that items created later are displayed after items created earlier. If two items are positioned at the same (or overlapping) coordinates, the item earliest in the display list is obscured because the other item is displayed on top of it. Thus, the rightmost item in Figure 37-1, the neko icon, is on top of the display list. We'll move the icon off to the side, hide all inactive images under it, and no one will be the wiser!

```
my($i, $done, $rptid, $cb) = ($#IDS, 0, 0, 0);

$cb = sub {
        my($ir) = @_;
        hide_frame $IDS[$$ir--];
        $done++ if $$ir < 0;
    };

my $rptid = $MW->repeat(1000 => [$cb, \$i]);

$MW->waitVariable(\$done);
$MW->afterCancel($rptid);
```

There's more to these five statements than meets the eye, so let's examine them one by one. We want to move the icon image first, so set $i to its index in the @IDS array. Even though the icon is the first image moved, it will nevertheless obscure the remaining images because it's at the end of the display list.

The second statement defines a timer callback, $cb, whose sole purpose is to hide one neko frame, decrement the index $i and set the $done flag after the last image has been moved. Here's where it gets tricky: the parameter passed to the anonymous subroutine is not the value of $i itself, but $$i, a *reference* to $i. Passing $i directly would only postdecrement the copy local to the subroutine, $ir, and not the "real" $i. Thus, only the icon frame would be moved, and the callback would never set the $done flag.

The repeat queues a timer event that, until canceled, repeats once a second, forever. However, the callback has been designed to modify the $done variable after the last image has been hidden. Notice that repeat, like all asynchronous timer event scheduling methods, returns a *timer ID*, used to subsequently remove the event from the timer queue.

The waitVariable waits until the value of $done changes. Although the application's flow is logically suspended, it still responds to external events, and so is not frozen.

The afterCancel cancels the repeat event. The end result is that the images shown previously in Figure 37-1 are hidden, one at a time, once a second, from right to left. Figure 37-2 shows what the window looks like after all the neko images have been moved off to the side.

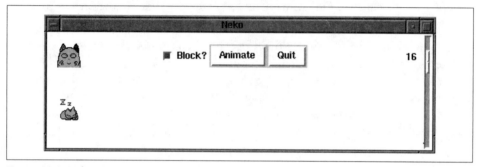

Figure 37-2. Neko in action

Note the neko icon, sitting in the upper left corner, hiding most of the other images. The snoozing Neko has subsequently been unhidden and animated for your viewing pleasure. So, how do we make Neko scamper across the canvas? This code snippet does just that:

```
# Move neko right to left by exposing successive
# frames for 0.1 second.

my $cb = sub {$done++};
my ($i, $k) = (0, -1);
$delay = 100;

for ($i = 460; $i >= 40; $i -= $DELTA_X) {
    $id = $IDS[++$k % 2];
    move_frame($id, $i, $SCAMPER_Y);
    if ($BLOCK) { $MW->after($delay) }
    else {
        $MW->after($delay => $cb);
        $MW->waitVariable(\$done);
    }
    hide_frame $id;
}

snooze;
```

Take one last look at Figure 37-1 and note the two leftmost images. Essentially, all we need to do is periodically display those images, one after another, at slightly different positions on the canvas. The scampering code shown above does just that: move one image from underneath the neko icon, wait for 0.1 second, hide it, unhide the second image and display it slightly to the left of the previous, wait for 0.1 second, and repeat until Neko reaches the left edge of the canvas. The exhausted Neko then takes a well-deserved nap.

It's possible to animate Neko using a blocking or non-blocking technique, depending on the state of the Block? checkbutton. Try each alternative and note how the buttons respond as you pass the cursor over them. $DELTA_X controls how "fast" Neko runs, and is tied to the slender scale widget to the right of the window. Varying its value by moving the slider makes Neko either moonwalk or travel at relativistic speeds!

Before we move on, here is how neko images are actually translated (moved) across the canvas (or "hidden" and "unhidden"):

```
# Move a neko frame to an absolute canvas position.
sub move_frame {
    my($id, $absx, $absy) = @_;
    my ($x, $y) = $C->coords($id);
    $C->move($id, $absx-$x, $absy-$y);
    $MW->idletasks;
}
```

The canvas move method moves an item to a new position on the canvas *relative* to its current position. Here we don't even know the *absolute* coordinates, so we use coords to get Neko's current position and perform a subtraction to determine the X and Y differences needed. When a neko image is hidden it's simply moved to the "hide" coordinates occupied by the Neko icon. The idletasks statement flushes the idle events queue, ensuring that the display is updated immediately.

I/O Events

If you think about it, a Tk application is somewhat analogous to a multi-tasking operating system: event callbacks must be mutually cooperative and only execute for a reasonable amount of time before relinquishing control to other handlers; otherwise, the application might freeze. This is an important consideration if your Tk application performs terminal, pipe, or socket I/O, since these operations might very well block, taking control away from the user.

Suppose you want to write a small program where you can interactively enter Perl/Tk commands, perhaps to prototype small code snippets of a larger application. The code might look like this:

```
use Tk;

while (<>) {
    eval $_;
}
```

When prompted for input you could then enter commands like this:

```
my $MW = MainWindow->new;
my $b = $MW->Button(-text => 'Hello world!')->pack;
```

However, this doesn't display the button as you might expect. No MainLoop statement has been executed, so no events are processed. Therefore the display isn't updated, and users won't be able to see the new button.

Realizing what's happening, you then enter a MainLoop statement, and lo and behold, something appears! But now you're stuck, because MainLoop never returns until the main window is destroyed,* so once again you're blocked and prevented from entering new Tk commands!

One solution is to rewrite your Perl/Tk shell using fileevent, the I/O event handler:

```
$MW->fileevent('STDIN', 'readable' => \&user_input);
MainLoop;

sub user_input {            # Called when input is available on STDIN.
    $_ = <>;
    eval $_;
}
```

The key difference is that the read from STDIN is now a non-blocking event, which is invoked by MainLoop whenever input data is available.

The fileevent command expects three arguments: a file handle, an I/O operation (readable or writable), and a callback to be invoked when the designated file handle is ready for input or output.

Although not necessary here, it's good practice to delete all file event handlers, in the same spirit as closing files and canceling timer events:

```
$MW->fileevent('STDIN', 'readable' => '');
```

The entire ptksh1 program is on this book's web site. Another program, tktail, demonstrating a pipe I/O event handler, is available from the Perl/Tk FAQ.

Idle Events

The idle event queue isn't restricted to redisplaying. You can use it for low priority callbacks of your own. This silly example uses afterIdle to ring the bell after 5 seconds:

```
#!/usr/bin/perl -w
#
# Demonstrate use of afterIdle() to queue a
# low priority callback.
```

---

* You can have more than one main window, so strictly speaking this should be "until *all* the main windows have been destroyed."

```
require 5.002;
use Tk;
use strict;

my $MW = MainWindow->new;
$MW->Button(   -text => 'afterIdle',
               -command => \&queue_afterIdle)->pack;
MainLoop;

sub queue_afterIdle {
    $MW->afterIdle(sub {$MW->bell});
    print "afterIdle event queued, block for 5 seconds...\n";
    $MW->after(5000);
    print "5 seconds have passed; call idletasks() to activate the handler.\n";

  $MW->idletasks;
  print "The bell should have sounded ...\n";
  $MW->destroy;
}
```

To recap, we are responsible for three event-related activities: registering events, creating event handlers, and *dispatching* events. Until now MainLoop has dispatched events for us, running in an endless loop, handing off events to handlers as they arise, and putting the application to sleep if no events are pending. When the application's last main window is destroyed, MainLoop returns and the program terminates.

Perl/Tk allows low-level access to Tk events via DoOneEvent. This event dispatcher is passed a single argument: a bit pattern describing which events to process. As you might guess, the event categories are those we've just explored. Direct access to the DoOneEvent bit patterns is via a use Tk qw/:eventtypes/ statement, here are the symbol names:

```
DONT_WAIT
WINDOW_EVENTS
FILE_EVENTS
TIMER_EVENTS
IDLE_EVENTS
ALL_EVENTS = WINDOW_EVENTS | FILE_EVENTS | TIMER_EVENTS | IDLE_EVENTS;
```

These symbols can be inclusively OR'd to fine-tune the list of events we want to respond too.

As it turns out, MainLoop is implemented using DoOneEvent, similar to this meta-code:

```
MainLoop {
  while (NumMainWindows > 0) {
      DoOneEvent(ALL_EVENTS)
  }
}
```

When passed ALL_EVENTS, DoOneEvent processes events as they arise and puts the application to sleep when no further events are outstanding. DoOneEvent first looks for an X or I/O event and, if found, calls the handler and returns. If there is no X or I/O event, it looks for a single timer event, invokes the callback, and returns. If no X, I/O, or timer event is ready, all pending idle callbacks are executed. In all cases DoOneEvent returns 1.

When passed DONT_WAIT, the DoOneEvent function works as above, except that if there are no events to process, it returns immediately with a value of 0, indicating it didn't find any work to do.

With this new knowledge, here is another implementation of our Perl/Tk shell that doesn't need fileevent:

```
#!/usr/bin/perl -w
#
# ptksh2 - another Perl/Tk shell using DoOneEvent( )
# rather than fileevent( ).

require 5.002;
use Tk;
use Tk qw/:eventtypes/;
use strict;

my $MW = MainWindow->new;
$MW->title('ptksh2');
$MW->iconname('ptksh2');

while (1) {
    while (1) {
        last unless DoOneEvent(DONT_WAIT);
    }
    print "ptksh> ";
    { no strict; eval <>; }
    print $@ if $@;
}
```

The outer while loop accepts terminal input, and the inner while loop cycles as long as Tk events arise as a result of that input.

Pong

I confess. This implementation of pong isn't the real thing. You won't see multiple game levels of ever increasing difficulty or even a database of high scores. All you get is the basic paddle and ball shown in Figure 37-3, and the chance to bounce the ball around until you grow bored, which took less than a minute for me.

The idea in this game is to keep the ball confined within the playing field; you get a point every time you hit the ball with the paddle, but lose a point every time the ball hits the floor or ceiling. This means that the paddle is tied to your mouse and follows its every motion. If at game's end the score is positive you win, else you lose. pong is derived in large part from bounce, the widget bouncing ball simulation written by Gurusamy Sarathy.

Figure 37-3. A pong prototype

Of course pong isn't meant to be fun, but to showcase Perl/Tk features: events, canvas commands, and the Pong derived widget.

pong really wants to be a CPU resource hog in order to keep the ball and paddle lively, but at the same time it needs to allow Tk events safe passage, so it has its own version of MainLoop:

```
while (1) {
    exit if $QUIT;
    DoOneEvent($RUNNING ? DONT_WAIT : ALL_EVENTS);
    $pong->move_balls($SPEED->get / 100.0) if $RUNNING;
}
```

The variable $RUNNING is a boolean indicating whether the game is in progress or has been paused. If the game has been paused ($RUNNING = 0), DoOneEvent is called with ALL_EVENTS, and sleeps until Tk events arise, but the ball and paddle aren't moved. Otherwise, DoOneEvent is called with DONT_WAIT, which may process one or more events (but certainly won't block), and then the game's ball and paddle are moved.

If this is the entire pong MainLoop, obviously the $PONG widget must be handling a lot behind the scenes. Indeed, the heart of the game is this single widget, which maintains the entire game state: paddle and ball position and movement, and game score. $PONG is a widget *derived* from a canvas, meaning that it automatically assumes all methods inherent in a canvas (and may provide more of its own, like move_balls).

A properly defined derived widget like Pong follows standard Perl/Tk conventions:

```
$PONG = $drawarea->Pong(-relief => 'ridge',
                    -height => 400,
                    -width => 600,
                    -bd => 2,
                    -balls => [{-color => 'yellow',
                             -size => 40,
                             -position => [90, 250]}]);
```

This command creates a 400x600 pixel *canvas*, with one paddle and one ball, and is placed at canvas coordinates (90,250). Because the Pong widget ISA canvas, anything you can do with a canvas you can do with a Pong widget. Defining a derived widget class is similar to defining a composite class (like Odometer from last issue).

```
package Tk::Pong;
require 5.002;
use Tk::Canvas;

use base qw/Tk::Derived Tk::Canvas/;
Tk::Widget->Construct('Pong');

sub Populate {                    # the Pong constructor
    my ($dw, $args) = @_;
    $dw->SUPER::Populate($args);
    $dw->ConfigSpecs( ... );      # Create needed canvas items here.
    return $dw;
}

1;
```

These statements:

- Define the new Tk::Pong class.

- Import canvas definitions and methods.

- Declare the @ISA list, which specifies how Perl looks up object methods. One difference between a derived widget and a composite widget is inclusion of Tk:: Derived, first, in the @ISA list.

- Create the Pong class constructor.

- Provide a Populate method (the class constructor) that customizes the canvas whenever a Pong widget is created,

pong's Populate procedure is really quite simple because it relies on existing canvas methods to create the game interface. This code automatically creates the paddle and one or more balls:

```
my $paddle = $dw->createRectangle(@paddle_shape, -fill => 'orange',
                                                 -outline => 'orange');

$dw->{paddle_ID} = $paddle;
$dw->CanvasBind('<Motion>' => \&move_paddle);

$dw->ConfigSpecs( -balls => ['METHOD', undef, undef, [{}]],
                  -cursor => ['SELF', undef, undef,
                             ['images/canv_cur.xbm',
                              'images/canv_cur.mask',
                              ($dw->configure(-background))[4], 'orange']]);
```

The createRectangle statement makes an orange paddle, whose shape is defined by the canvas coordinates of diagonally opposed rectangle corners. The paddle's canvas ID is saved in the object as an instance variable so that move_paddle can move the paddle around the canvas—this private class method is bound to pointer motion events.

Once again, in general, Populate should not directly configure its widget. That's why there's no code to create the ball. Instead, ConfigSpecs is used to define the widget's valid configuration options (-balls is one) and how to handle them. When Populate returns, Perl/Tk then examines the configuration specifications and auto-configures the derived widget.

A call to ConfigSpecs consists of a series of keyword => value pairs, where the widget's keyword value is a list of four items: a string specifying exactly how to configure the keyword, its name in the X resource database, its class name, and its default value.

We've seen the ConfigSpecs METHOD option before: when Perl/Tk sees a -balls attribute, it invokes a method of the same name, minus the dash: balls. And if you examine the source code on this book's web page, you'll see that all the balls sub-routine really does is execute a $PONG->createOval command.

The -cursor option to ConfigSpecs option is moderately interesting. The SELF means that the cursor change applies to the derived widget itself. But why do we want to change the canvas' cursor? Well, just waggle your mouse around and watch the cursor closely. Sometimes it's shaped like an arrow, and sometimes an underscore, rect-angle, I-beam, or X. But in a Pong game, when you move the mouse you only want to see the paddle move, not the paddle and a tag-along cursor. So pong defines a cursor consisting of a single orange pixel and associates it with the Pong widget, neatly camouflaging the cursor.

Like neko, the Pong widget uses the canvas move method to move the paddle around, but is driven by X motion events rather than timer events. An X motion event invokes move_paddle:

```
sub move_paddle {
    my ($canvas) = @_;
    my $e = $canvas->XEvent;
    my ($x, $y) = ($e->x, $e->y);

    $canvas->move($canvas->{paddle_ID},
                  $x - $canvas->{last_paddle_x},
                  $y - $canvas->{last_paddle_y});

    $canvas->{last_paddle_x}, $canvas->{last_paddle_y}) = ($x, $y);
}
```

This subroutine extracts the cursor's current position from the X event structure, executes move using instance data from the Pong widget, and saves the paddle's position for next time.

That takes care of paddle motion, but ball motion we handle ourselves, via the class method move_balls, which has its own DoOneEvent mini MainLoop. Ball movement boils down to yet another call to the move canvas method, with extra behaviors such as checking for collisions with walls or the paddle. Here's the code:

```
# Move all the balls one "tick." We call DoOneEvent() in case there are
# many balls; with only one it's not strictly necessary.

sub move_balls {
    my ($canvas, $speed) = @_;
    my $ball;
    foreach $ball (@{$canvas->{balls}}) {
        $canvas->move_one_ball($ball, $speed);
        # be kind and process XEvents as they arise
        DoOneEvent(DONT_WAIT);
    }
}
```

Although the details of reflecting a ball and detecting collisions are interesting, they're not relevant to our discussion, so feel free to examine move_one_ball yourself.

Miscellaneous Event Commands

There are three other event commands that merit a little more explanation: update, waitWindow, and waitVisibility.

The update method is useful for CPU-intensive programs in which you still want the application to respond to user interactions. If you occasionally call update, all pending Tk events will be processed and all windows updated.

The waitWindow method waits for a widget, supplied as its argument, to be destroyed. For instance, you might use this command to wait for a user to finish interacting with a dialog box before using the result of that interaction. However, doing this requires creating and destroying the dialog each time. If you're concerned about efficiency, try withdrawing the window instead. Then use waitVisibility to wait for a change in the dialog's visibility state.

We've now covered most everything you need to know about event handling in Perl/Tk. In the next article, we'll explore how to lay out widgets on the screen with the grid geometry manager.

## CHAPTER 38

The Pack and Grid Geometry Managers

Steve Lidie

We know that every Perl/Tk graphical application consists of a number of widgets arranged in a particular manner on a display. Although we may suggest the size and location of the widgets, the final say in the matter is up to a *geometry manager*, the software responsible for computing the actual layout of the widgets.

In essence, a geometry manager's job is to stuff what are known as, in X parlance, *slave widgets* inside a *master widget*. The topmost master widget in a Perl/Tk application is of course the MainWindow. In the simplest case it's the only master, but usually we need to employ one or more frames within which more slaves are packed. Once the slaves in these frames have been arranged, the frames themselves are laid out within the MainWindow.

This means that in order to calculate the final look of an application, geometry information propagates outwards from the innermost masters to the MainWindow. We'll see why and how to override this behavior later.

Before any widget can appear on the display, it must be managed by a geometry manager. There can actually be multiple geometry managers controlling an application, although this is unusual, and a widget can only be managed by one geometry manager at a time.

The Perl/Tk distribution contains various geometry managers, including place, pack, and grid, and in this article we'll discuss the "packer" and the "gridder." As its name suggests, the grid geometry manager places widgets in rows and columns inside a master. But why include the packer in a gridder discussion? The answer to that question begins innocently enough, with a simple pack problem posted to the Perl/Tk mailing list.* After comparing equivalent pack and grid programs, we'll see that the gridder provides a simpler solution for this problem.

---

* The Perl/Tk mailing list, "ptk," is archived at *http://www.rosat.mpe-garching.mpg.de/mailing-lists/ptk/*; you can subscribe by sending mail to `majordomo@lists.stanford.edu`.

A Brief Look at the Packer

Here's the question that stimulated this article:

> I'm having a problem understanding how 'anchor' is working. My current problem is:
> I want to display a list of names in one column and a list of numbers in a second col-
> umn. I want the names to be left justified and the numbers to be right justified. I have
> tried playing with the 'anchor' and 'width' mechanisms, but with no success.

This code sample (prob1 on the web site for this book: *http://www.oreilly.com/
catalog/tpj2*) represents the questioner's valiant attempt:

```
#!/usr/bin/perl -w

use Tk;
use strict;

my $MW = MainWindow->new;
my $f1 = $MW->Frame->pack;
my $f2 = $MW->Frame->pack;

$f1->Label( -text => 'This is a very long label',
            -width => 30) ->pack(-side => 'left', -anchor => 'w');
$f1->Label(-text => 123)->pack(-side => 'left');

$f2->Label( -text => 'A short one',
            -width => 30)->pack(-side => 'left', -anchor => 'w');
$f2->Label(-text => 456)->pack(-side => 'left');

$MW->Button(   -text => 'Quit',
            -command => ['destroy', $MW])->pack(-side => 'bottom');

MainLoop;
```

The names are packed left and anchored west, which seems reasonable. Packing the
numbers left as well looks dubious, however. Figure 38-1 shows what happens when
the code is run.

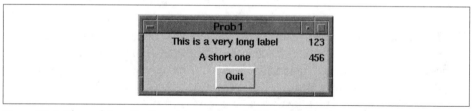

Figure 38-1. The prob1 application: the names aren't left-justified

Surprisingly, the names are *not* left justified but appear to be centered, and the numbers, which we thought might be left justified, seem to be right justified!

Something must be amiss. To figure out what's going on, consider these tips:

- When dealing with columnar data, use a fixed-width font rather than a proportional font.
- Use strings of varying lengths to expose boundary conditions, so that you know whether your data is justified properly.
- Use different background colors for your widgets to illuminate the allocation and placement decisions made by the geometry manager.

Here is a slightly modified version of the first program (program prob2).

```perl
#!/usr/bin/perl -w

use Tk;
use strict;

my $MW = MainWindow->new;

$MW->configure(-bg => 'white');
$MW->optionAdd('*font' => 'fixed');

my $f1 = $MW->Frame->pack;
my $f2 = $MW->Frame->pack;

$f1->Label(-text => 'This is a very long label', -width => 30,
           -bg => 'gray')->pack(-side => 'left', -anchor => 'w');
$f1->Label(-text => 1234567890, -bg => 'yellow')->pack(-side => 'left');

$f2->Label(-text => 'A short one', -width => 30,
           -bg => 'gray')->pack(-side => 'left', -anchor => 'w');
$f2->Label(-text => 456, -bg => 'yellow')->pack(-side => 'left');

$MW->Button(-text => 'Quit', -command => ['destroy', $MW])->pack;

MainLoop;
```

The changes just implement my three tips, with the exception of the last one: by default, the packer arranges a master's slave widgets from top to bottom, so -side => 'bottom' is superfluous. Because I'm lazy, I used optionAdd to change the X11 resource database so that all widgets use the default font fixed. Our newly instrumented program is illustrated in Figure 38-2.

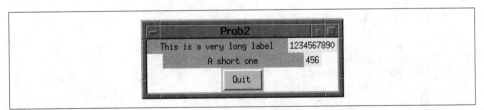

Figure 38-2. The prob2 application: background colors illuminate the widgets

First, note that the numbers are allocated an area just large enough to contain them. This is the default pack action and is sometimes called *shrink-wrapping*. Next, note that the names are allocated a space 30 characters wide (because that's what we requested) and the label text is centered—again, the default pack action. Remember, the packer likes to shrink-wrap and center widgets unless you specify otherwise. So, the two container frames are assigned the minimum required space and centered inside their master widget, the MainWindow. That's why unused space is equally apportioned on either side of the bottom frame.

Some observations about prob2:

- Packing the names with -anchor => 'w' is useless.
- But creating the label widgets with -anchor => 'w' *would* make a difference. It doesn't solve the problem, but it does left-justify the names in their 30 character allocated space.
- Packing the second frame with -fill => 'x' tells the packer to fill the frame east-west instead of shrink-wrapping. Once you do this, the frames will be the same length, and the names will be left-justified. But the numbers are also left-justified—after all, that's what we told the packer to do. The numbered should be packed right with -side => 'right'.

Our solution is called pack:

```perl
#!/usr/bin/perl -w
#
# Create two columns of data: left-adjusted text labels and right-adjusted
# numbers. Each row consists of a frame with two labels packed on opposite
# sides. The packer fills unused space in the X-dimension so that all
# frames are the same length (that of the widest frame).

use Tk;
use strict;

my $MW = MainWindow->new;
my @text = ('This is a long label', 'Then a short',
            'Frogs lacking lipophores are blue');

my ($i, $w, $f) = (0, undef, undef);

foreach (@text) {
    $f = $MW->Frame->pack(-fill => 'x');
    $w = $f->Label(-text => $_);
    $w->pack(-side => 'left');
    $w = $f->Label(-text => $i . '0' x $i);
    $w->pack(-side => 'right');
    $i++;
}

MainLoop;
```

The output of pack is shown in Figure 38-3.

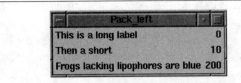

Figure 38-3. *The pack application: all frames are now the same length and left justified*

The Gridder

The corresponding code using the grid geometry manager, named grid, produces an identical display. Unlike the rest of Tk, grid elements are referenced by row (Y coordinate) and column (X coordinate), starting from 0 at the top left corner of the master widget.

```
#!/usr/bin/perl -w
#
# Create two columns of data: left-adjusted text labels and right-adjusted
# numbers. Each row consists of two labels managed by the gridder, which
# are "stuck" to opposite sides of their respective column. The gridder
# fills unused space in the east-west direction so that all rows are the
# same length -- that of the widest row.

use Tk;
use strict;

my $MW = MainWindow->new;
my @text = ('This is a long label', 'Then a short',
            'Frogs lacking lipophores are blue');

my ($i, $w) = (0, undef);

foreach (@text) {
    $w = $MW->Label(-text => $_);
    $w->grid(-row => $i, -column => 0, -sticky => 'w');
    $w = $MW->Label(-text => $i . '0' x $i);
    $w->grid(-row => $i, -column => 1, -sticky => 'e');
    $i++;
}

MainLoop;
```

The obvious difference is that here we define a grid, with three rows and two columns. -sticky replaces pack's -anchor and -fill attributes, so it's easy to west-align names in column zero and east-align numbers in column one. Also, we've dispensed with all the row frames required with the pack model.

As a more exhaustive test drive of the gridder, let's look at an implementation of the old chestnut *15-puzzle*, a game where you try to arrange 15 numbered tiles in numerical order. If you don't know what I'm talking about, try out the demo in the Tk widget program bundled with the Perl/Tk distribution.

This version of *15-puzzle* is called npuz because it's not limited to a 4×4 square; you can choose *n*, the length of a side, from the set (3, 4, 6, 8). To make the puzzle more difficult, the numbered squares have been replaced with segments of an image: the official Perl/Tk icon, which we all know as *Camelus bactrianus*. See Figure 38-4.

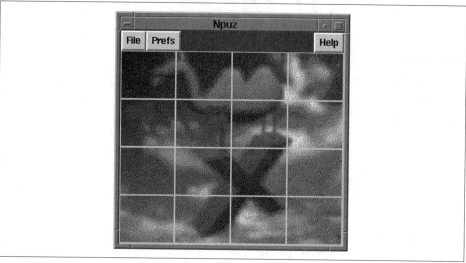

Figure 38-4. The npuz application

The grid geometry manager is well suited for this problem, not only for the initial layout of the puzzle, but also for moving the pieces. When a new game starts, the pieces are randomized. Then each is assigned an image and gridded, with one piece becoming the "space piece." Moving a piece simply involves exchanging it with the space, which entails a call to grid to swap the row and column coordinates.

Here's simp, a tiny program that gives you a feel for what npuz does:

```
#!/usr/bin/perl -w
#
# simp (simple_puz) - randomly grid 15 buttons and a space in a 4x4
# rectangle.

use Tk;
use strict;
use subs qw(create_puz xy);

my $MW = MainWindow->new;
my $PIECES = 16;
my $SIDE = sqrt $PIECES;
my @ORDER = (3, 1, 6, 2, 5, 7, 15, 13, 0, 4, 11, 8, 9, 14, 10, 12);

create_puz;

MainLoop;
```

```
sub create_puz {
    my ($i, $text, $num, $but, $c, $r);
    for ($i = 0; $i <= $PIECES-1; $i++) {
        $num = $ORDER[$i];
        $text = ($num == 0) ? 'Space' : $num;
        $but = $MW->Button(-text => $text, -command => [$MW => 'bell']);
        ($c, $r) = xy $i;
        $but->grid(-column => $c, -row => $r, -sticky => 'nsew');
    } # forend all puzzle pieces
}

sub xy {                         # ordinal to X/Y
    my ($n) = @_;
    return ($n % $SIDE, int $n / $SIDE)
}
```

For simplicity, think of the puzzle pieces as a linear list rather than a two dimensional array. So for *n = 4*, the pieces are numbered from 0 to 15, with piece 0 as the space. To position a piece we just need to convert a puzzle ordinal to a row/column pair—that's what subroutine xy does—and then grid it. The @ORDER list in effect shuffles the pieces so the game doesn't start already solved. (Perhaps @ORDER isn't an appropriate variable name, since the end result is to increase the game's entropy, or add disorder to it.) Running simp creates Figure 38-5.

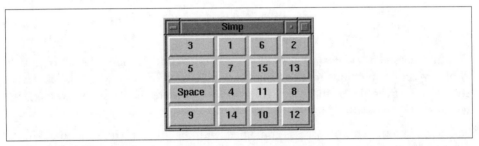

Figure 38-5. The simp application

The -sticky => 'nsew' attribute is analogous to the packer's -fill => 'both', and ensures that all buttons completely fill their allocated space. Notice that grid column zero is wider than the other columns. This is because the gridder assigns the column a width equal to that of the widest button—the button labeled "Space." Rerun this program without -sticky and you'll see the difference. But this won't be a problem for npuz, since all the buttons have images of identical size.

Three changes to *simp* will give us *npuz*:

1. Create a Photo image of *Camelus bactrianus* and replace button numbers with a portion of the image.

2. Keep track of every button widget and its grid position so we know when it's adjacent to the space piece.

3. Devise a button callback to re-grid a piece when it's eligible to move.

Since we think of the puzzle pieces as a list, we'll store the widget references in an array: @PUZ. The grid geometry manager obviously knows the location of all its slave widgets so npuz can simply ask the gridder for this data.

This npuz code is analogous to simp. A few lines have been excerpted from other areas of the program and included here for completeness.

```
$CAMEL = $MW->Photo>(-file => 'images/Xcamel.npuz');
$PF    = $MW->Frame->grid;               # create puzzle frame grid master

my ($i, $o, $c, $r, $w, $h, $x, $y, $but, $gif);

for ($i = 0; $i <= $#PUZ; $i++) {
    $o = $ORDER[$i]->[0];
    ($c, $r) = xy $o;                    # puzzle ordinal to column/row
    $w = $CAMEL->image('width')  / $SIDE;
    $h = $CAMEL->image('height') / $SIDE;
    $x = $c * $w;                        # x/column pixel offset
    $y = $r * $h;                        # y/row pixel offset
    $gif = $PF->Photo;                   # new, empty, GIF image
    $gif->copy($CAMEL, -from => $x, $y, $x+$w, $y+$h);
    $but = $PF->Button(-image => $gif, -relief => 'flat',
                    -borderwidth => 0, -highlightthickness => 0);
    $PUZ[$o] = $but;
    ($c, $r) = xy $i;
    $but->grid(-column => $c, -row => $r, -sticky => 'nsew');
    $but->configure(-command => [\&move_piece, $but]);
} # forend all puzzle pieces
```

The first statement creates a Photo object of our friendly camel. Like Tk objects, a Photo object has methods to manipulate it, which we'll use to create smaller rectangular photos from the main image. These new photos are then assigned to the game buttons.

Notice that frames are still used as containers with the gridder. Here the puzzle frame $PF, a slave of the MainWindow, is the grid master for the puzzle. (There's another MainWindow slave frame that holds the *npuz* menu bar, but I'll talk about that later.)

Once a puzzle ordinal is selected, we can use its row and column position, along with the width and height of a puzzle piece, to compute a bounding box that defines a sub-region of the main camel image. Then an empty photo is created and populated with the image sub-region using the copy method, which copies from the source image $CAMEL to the new image $gif.

It's important to note that when you're finished with an image you must explicitly delete it. Images don't magically go away just because a widget that happens to use it is destroyed. After all, several widgets might be sharing the same image. To prevent a memory leak when a new game is started and all previous buttons are deleted, we first delete all their images:

```
foreach (@PUZ) { $_->cget(-image)->delete }
```

After updating @PUZ with the new button, the piece is gridded and a callback to move_
piece is created, passing $piece, a reference to the button. Pushing a button invokes
the callback.

```perl
sub move_piece {
    my ($piece) = @_;
    my (%info, $c, $r, $sc, $sr);
    %info = $piece->gridInfo;
    ($c, $r) = @info{-column, -row};
    %info = $SPACE->gridInfo;
    ($sc, $sr) = @info{-column,-row};
    if (($sr == $r and ($sc == $c-1 or $sc == $c+1)) or
        ($sc == $c and ($sr == $r-1 or $sr == $r+1))) {
        $SPACE->grid(-column => $c, -row => $r);
        $piece->grid(-column => $sc, -row => $sr);
    }
}
```

A call to gridinfo returns a hash of grid configuration information. The hash keys
are the same as the attributes you can give to a grid (or gridConfigure) command,
such as -column and -row. It's a simple matter to take a slice of this hash, check to see
if the puzzle piece is directly north, south, east, or west of the space, and if so, swap
their grid locations.

As you can see, choosing the grid geometry manager for this problem greatly simpli-
fied the programming. pack could be used, with a lot of bookkeeping and
packForgeting, but the experience would not be pleasant. place is the second best
choice, but you'd have to maintain button coordinates manually, so @PUZ would be a
list of list of three:

```perl
$PUZ[$ordinal] = [$column, $row, $but];
```

You can grid menu bars easily as well. Here's an example that *doesn't* work:

```perl
#!/usr/bin/perl -w
#
# menu1 - first attempt at gridding a menubar.

use Tk;
use strict;

my $MW = MainWindow->new;
my $mf = $MW->Frame->grid;
my $PF = $MW->Frame(-width => 300)->grid;

my $mbf = $mf->Menubutton(-text => 'File', -relief => 'raised');
my $mbp = $mf->Menubutton(-text => 'Prefs', -relief => 'raised');
my $mbq = $mf->Menubutton(-text => 'Help', -relief => 'raised');

$mbf->grid(-row => 0, -column => 0, -sticky => 'w');
$mbp->grid(-row => 0, -column => 1, -sticky => 'w');
$mbq->grid(-row => 0, -column => 2, -sticky => 'e');

MainLoop;
```

The frame $PF represents the puzzle frame and artificially fixes the width of the application's display to 300 pixels. I did this so there's unused space for the menu buttons to move about in to help illustrate gridder mechanics. The goal in this example is to grid the File and Prefs menu buttons side by side west, the Help menu button east, with unused space in the center of the frame. Instead, Figure 38-6 is the result.

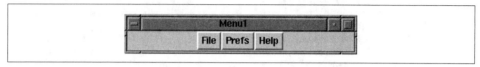

Figure 38-6. Improperly gridded buttons

Like the packer, the default grid action is to shrink-wrap the menu bar frame around the three menu buttons and center it in the 300 pixel allocated space. We'll need two small changes to achieve the effect shown in Figure 38-7.

Figure 38-7. Properly gridded buttons

First, the menu bar row needs to be east-west sticky:

```
my $mf = $MW->Frame->grid(-sticky => 'ew');
```

By itself, this change doesn't make any difference in the geometry arrangement, because the three grid columns containing the menu buttons have no *weight*. Without weight, a grid column (or row) can't be apportioned unallocated space. We can arrange for menubar column 1 (the Prefs menu button) to get all the unused space in the frame like this:

```
$mf->gridColumnconfigure(1, -weight => 1);
```

The -weight attribute is a relative value, and because the other columns are weightless, the Prefs column gets 100% of the unallocated space. It's important that Prefs be west sticky, but the other two columns don't need to be sticky at all, since they get no unused space. Although the current version of grid accepts floating point weight values, the next one will not, so always use integers.

Sometimes you'll want to disable the outward propagation of geometry configuration information. For instance, suppose you want to manage a frame of a particular size, and within the frame pack or grid other widgets. This example grids a frame with an embedded button but prevents the gridder from shrink-wrapping the frame around the button:

```
#!/usr/bin/perl -w
#
# Remove the gridPropagate() statement to shrink-wrap the display.
```

```
use Tk;
use strict;

my $MW = MainWindow->new;
my $f = $MW->Frame(-width => 200, -height => 100);

$f->gridPropagate(0);

$f->Button(-text => 'To shrink or not to shrink', -command => \&exit)->grid;

MainLoop;
```

There's an analogous function for the packer as well: packPropagate.

That wraps up my grid introduction. Be sure to read the grid documentation in the Perl/Tk distribution for further details.

## CHAPTER 39

Drawing on a Canvas

Steve Lidie

Last year, I mowed my lawn on a warm and wonderful late summer day. As I followed my usual mowing pattern. I wondered if there was a better way to do it. In this article, we'll use Perl/Tk to visualize some different mowing patterns and see how well they represent reality—and along the way demonstrate drawing on a Perl/Tk canvas.

Our Mower Is Programmable!

For this exercise we have at our disposal a programmable robotic mower. Our job is to write a software simulation of lawnmowing. It's exceedingly difficult to model the complexities of the physical world with a computer, so we'll make some simplifying assumptions. First, we'll define the lawn as a rectangular area without trees, gardens, rocks, ponds, or cats.* The lawn is also a perfect mowing surface without bumps or undulations, and the grass has uniform thickness; this way we know that the mower can be steered accurately. Finally, we'll assume the mower has a turning radius of zero: that is, it can pivot. (Automatic mowers that are always going forward have a nonzero turning radius.)

A Canvas Widget Is the Lawn

To represent the mowing area, we'll use a Perl/Tk canvas widget, colored chlorophyll green of course. Let's assume that to program the mower all we need is to write Perl/Tk code that overlays various items that display the mower's path (lines, arcs, ovals, and such) on the canvas, making sure that no green remains.

Our first program starts by mowing (drawing a line) 100 feet in a straight line and turning right. It repeats three times until it's mowed the periphery of the lawn. Then the mower shifts right by the width of one cut (I mow clockwise) and repeats the process until there's nothing left to mow.

---

* I once saw a solar-powered robot that mowed in a random direction until it bumped into something, at which time it took off in a new, random direction. Given enough time, it would mow any area completely. I hear these mowers use color/luminance to detect edges, so I guess my cats are safe as long as they don't turn green.

Defining the Perl Mowing Module

We'll be creating several variants of the mowing program, so we'll program for reusability by including constants in a module, Mow.pm. This module simply exports a list of variables. It's not object-oriented, although it does inherit some methods from Exporter. Here it is:

```perl
# Mow.pm - mowing module.

package Mow;

use 5.004;
use Exporter;
@ISA = qw(Exporter);
@EXPORT = qw/$CHLOROPHYLL $COLOR $CUT $D2R $PPF $SIDE $TURN/;

$CHLOROPHYLL = '#8395ffff0000';      # Rye-grass-green, maybe
$COLOR       = 0xffff;               # Initial line color
$CUT         = (38 / 12);            # Cut width in feet
$D2R         = 3.14159265 / 180.0;   # Map degrees to radians
$PPF         = 2;                    # Pixels/foot
$SIDE        = 100;                  # Size of square mow area
$TURN        = (27 / 12);            # Turn radius in feet

1;
```

When Perl sees a use Mow statement it populates the program with the variables from the @EXPORT list. With the definitions $CHLOROPHYLL, $CUT, and $SIDE in place (more on "color numbers" like $CHLOROPHYLL shortly) we can write a simple zero turning radius mowing program.

Zero Turning Radius, Take One

```perl
use Mow;
use Tk;
my $mw = MainWindow->new;
my $canvas = $mw->Canvas(     -width => $SIDE, -height => $SIDE,
                        -background => $CHLOROPHYLL)->grid;

$mw->waitVisibility;
```

A chlorophyll green, 100-pixel-square canvas is created and gridded. The waitVisibility statement forces Tk to display the canvas before the program can proceed, so we can watch the mowing process in real time. Otherwise, the simulation might complete before we could see it. All we need to do now is define a recursive subroutine and call it once:

```perl
mow $canvas, 0, 0, $SIDE, $SIDE;

sub mow { # Recursively mow until done.
    my ($canvas, $x1, $y1, $x2, $y2) = @_;
    return if $x1 >= $x2 or $y1 >= $y2;
```

```
    $canvas->createLine($x1, $y1, $x2, $y1, $x2, $y2, $x1, $y2, $x1, $y1);
    $canvas->idletasks;
    $canvas->after(250);

    mow $canvas, $x1+$CUT, $y1+$CUT, $x2-$CUT, $y2-$CUT;
}
```

Besides the reference to the canvas, the arguments to mow are simply coordinates of the top left and bottom right corners of a square. mow invokes createLine to paint four line segments—one across the top, right, bottom, and left of the canvas, in that order. Then mow updates the display and waits a quarter of a second ($canvas->after(250)) before invoking itself again, to mow a smaller square. Figure 39-1 shows the not-so-satisfying result.

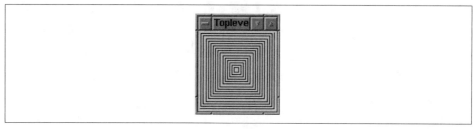

Figure 39-1. Using createLine to animate lawnmowing

The main problem is that the width of the cut is pencil thin, so the robot leaves lots of green behind. Luckily, createLine has some options that help.

The Canvas Line Item Type

createLine draws a line between two points. If you provide more than two points, it draws a series of joined line segments. The line segments can even be smoothed using a Bezier spline with the smooth parameter, as this code demonstrates:

```
my $mw = MainWindow->new;
my $canvas = $mw->Canvas(qw/-width 90 -height 100/)->grid;

$canvas->createLine(qw/10 25 20 55 48 15 80 95 -fill blue/);
$canvas->createLine(qw/10 25 20 55 48 15 80 95 -fill red -smooth yes/);
```

Figure 39-2 shows the smoothing effect of splines.

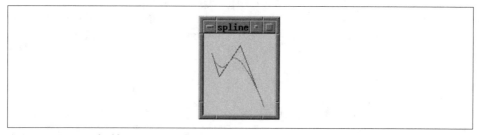

Figure 39-2. Smoothed lines

The ends of a single line segment can be adorned in several ways—with arrowheads (the widget demo, which Tk installs in the same directory as Perl, shows you the arrowheads to choose from), or one of these shapes, called a *capstyle* (Figure 39-3):

Figure 39-3. Perl/Tk's three capstyles

Capstyles become important as the width of the line increases. In the previous picture the fat lines with capstyles were each 25 pixels long and 20 pixels wide. The skinny white lines connect the same canvas points, but have a width of 1 and no capstyle. Notice that the width of the fat items is equally apportioned on each side of the connecting line.

But our mowing program cuts with multiple, fat, and connected line segments, so we need to use another attribute called the *joinstyle* (Figure 39-4).

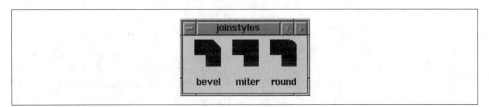

Figure 39-4. Perl/Tk's three joinstyles

The miter's right angle looks ideal. Finally, fat lines can be filled with a solid color or a stipple. The next version of mow uses graduated fill colors to highlight the mower's path.

Zero Turning Radius, Take Two

Putting everything together gives us the program below, called zero-tr2 on the web site for this book (*http://www.oreilly.com/catalog/tpj2*).

```
my $canvas = init;
mow $canvas, (0, 0), ($SIDE, $SIDE);
MainLoop;

sub init {
    my $mw = MainWindow->new;
    my $mow_side = $SIDE * $PPF;
    my $canvas = $mw->Canvas(      -width => $mow_side, -height => $mow_side,
                             -background => $CHLOROPHYLL)->grid;
    $mw->waitVisibility;
```

```
    $mw->after(1000);
    return $canvas;
}

sub mow {                              # Recursively mow until done.
    my ($canvas, $x1, $y1, $x2, $y2) = @_;
    return if $x1 >= $x2 or $y1 >= $y2;
    my $color = sprintf("#ffff%04x%04x", $COLOR, $COLOR);
    $COLOR -= 0x0800;
    $canvas->createLine($x1 * $PPF, $y1 * $PPF, $x2 * $PPF, $y1 * $PPF,
                        $x2 * $PPF, $y2 * $PPF, $x1 * $PPF, $y2 * $PPF,
                        $x1 * $PPF, $y1 * $PPF, -width => $CUT * $PPF + 0.5,
                        -fill => $color, -joinstyle => 'miter');
    $canvas->idletasks;
    $canvas->after(250);
    mow $canvas, $x1+$CUT, $y1+$CUT, $x2-$CUT, $y2-$CUT;
}
```

Four comments about zero-tr2:

- The variable $PPF is the scaling factor, in pixels per foot, which enlarges the canvas for better viewing.

- Anywhere a color name like CadetBlue or MediumOrchid4 is specified, a hexadecimal RGB number can be substituted. The program starts by drawing lines with a fully saturated color and darkens it slightly each time mow is called.

- The mowing width is a floating point number that must be rounded after scaling, otherwise we miss mowing parts of the lawn. Try running zero-tr2 without the 0.5 rounding term and see what happens. For a great primer on floating point gotchas, read the article "Unreal Numbers" in *Computer Science & Perl Programming: Best of the Perl Journal* (O'Reilly).

- All line segments are joined with a miter cut.

Figure 39-5 shows the result of zero-tr2.

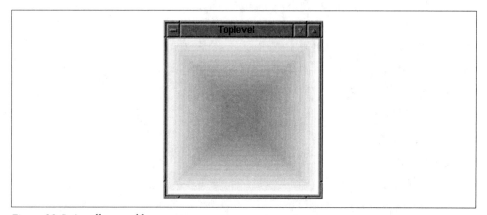

Figure 39-5. A well-mowed lawn

Rotating Simple Objects in Canvas Space

Let's complicate matters and assume our robot is in the shop for repairs. We have an older model with a nonzero turning radius; that is, it turns with an arc, leaving a small swath of green behind. To simulate this, the mowing program could draw connected lines and arcs for each side of the mowing area. While these eight items are still manageable, it might be easier to define one line and one arc, and have mow rotate them as required.

Rotating a line in a Cartesian coordinate space is simple if one of the endpoints is at (0, 0). Then the rotation reduces to rotating the other endpoint. Given such a point (x, y), we can rotate it through the angle Θ using these equations:

$x' = x \cos \Theta - y \sin \Theta$
$y' = x \sin \Theta + y \cos \Theta$
(x', y') is the new location of the point.

Rotating a line about an arbitrary point requires that the line be translated to the origin, rotated, and then translated back to its original location. The following code rotates (clockwise) the line whose endpoints are (0,0) and (20,40) about the center point of the canvas, (65,65). It draws a line and then creates an invisible *bounding rectangle*. We'll employ one of those shortly to define an oval for the turning radius arc.

```
my $mw = MainWindow->new;
my $canvas = $mw->Canvas(-width => 130, -height => 130)->grid;
$mw->waitVisibility;

my $origin = 65;                    # Origin of canvas
my($x2, $y2) = (20, 40);            # Endpoint of line segment

rotate $canvas, 0, $x2, $y2, 'black';
rotate $canvas, 90, $x2, $y2, 'red';
rotate $canvas, 180, $x2, $y2, 'green';
rotate $canvas, 270, $x2, $y2, 'blue';

MainLoop;

sub rotate {
    my ($canvas, $theta, $x2, $y2, $color) = @_;

    $theta *= $D2R;                 # Degrees to radians
    my $nx2 = $x2 * cos($theta) - $y2 * sin($theta);
    my $ny2 = $x2 * sin($theta) + $y2 * cos($theta);

    $canvas->createLine(0+$origin, 0+$origin, $nx2+$origin, $ny2+$origin,
                        -fill => $color);
    $canvas->createRectangle(0+$origin, 0+$origin, $nx2+$origin, $ny2+$origin,
                             -outline => $color);

    my $coords = sprintf("(%d,%d)", int($nx2), int($ny2));
    $canvas->createText ($nx2+$origin, $ny2+$origin,
                         -text => $coords, -font => 'fixed');
```

```
        $canvas->idletasks;
        $canvas->after(250);
    }
```

Figure 39-6 shows four rotations of a line.

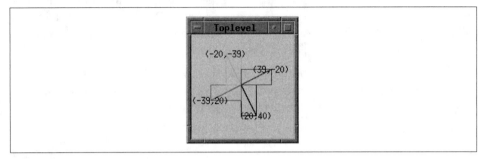

Figure 39-6. Line rotations

The Canvas Rectangle and Text Item Types

The previous code introduced two new canvas items: rectangle and text. Like the mowing area, two diagonally opposed corners define a rectangle (here, the end-points of the rotating line segment). You can't do much else with a rectangle other than specify the width and color of its outline, or fill it with a color or stipple.

The canvas text item annotates the business end of a line with its coordinates (the other endpoint is always (0,0)). These floating point values are truncated without rounding, which is why some of the numbers are a bit off. Text items can be anchored, justified and filled, as you'd expect. There are methods to insert and delete characters, too.

The Canvas Arc Item Type

The tools for the next mowing program are now at hand. We can take a line and rotate it through an arbitrary angle and draw it anywhere on the canvas. We can also use the two points that define a line and draw a rectangle instead, at any angle, any-where on the canvas. And since an arc is defined by an oval which is defined by a bounding rectangle, we can rotate and draw an arc anywhere on the canvas. Figure 39-7 shows three arc styles: pieslice, chord, and arc.

The three arc styles were created with the following statements. The first four elements represent the bounding boxes:

```
$canvas->createArc(qw/10 10 50 50 -start 0 -extent 270
                    -style pieslice -fill black -stipple error/);

$canvas->createArc(qw/70 10 110 50 -start 45 -extent -135 -style chord/);

$canvas->createArc(qw/130 10 170 50 -start -90 -extent -180 -style arc/);
```

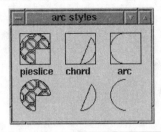

Figure 39-7. Three arc styles

Each arc has a starting angle and an extent, both in degrees, with zero degrees along the x-axis. Positive angles rotate counterclockwise and negative angles clockwise. The pie slice arc is stipple filled with a built-in bitmap.

Nonzero Turning Radius, Take One

The new controller code starts by defining two points: an endpoint of a line, and one corner of the arc's bounding box. The point (0,0) doubles as the line's other endpoint, as well as the opposite corner of the arc's bounding box. The bounding box is square, because the mower's circular turning radius must fit inside.

```
@LINE = ($SIDE, 0);    # Initial straight line mowing path
@ARC  = ($TURN, $TURN); # Generic turning radius arc
```

The change to mow: it now rotates the line and arc, computes three points, and then draws the two items (the full program is called nz-tr1). Points one and two are the line's endpoints; points two and three are the arc's bounding box. Thus, the end of the line and the start of the arc coincide. Here's an excerpt:

```
$canvas->createLine($start[0], $start[1], $end[0], $end[1],
                -fill => $color, -width => $CUT,
                -capstyle => 'round', -tags => 'path');

($x2, $y2) = @ARC[0,1];

$nx2 = $x2 * cos($theta) - $y2 * sin($theta);
$ny2 = $x2 * sin($theta) + $y2 * cos($theta);

$canvas->createArc($end[0], $end[1], $end[0]+$nx2, $end[1]+$ny2,
                -start => 270-20-$angle, -extent => 180+40,
                -style => 'arc', -outline => $color,
                -width => $CUT, -tags => 'path');
```

This simulation produces the same visible results as the zero turning radius code.

Canvas Tags

The previous snippet demonstrates *tags*, a powerful canvas concept. Tags are simply strings used to identify canvas items, which you add or delete as needed. A canvas item can have any number of tags, and the same tag can be applied to any number of items. The mowing program uses the path tag to group all the lines and arcs that define the mowing path. (Every canvas item has at least one tag, the string all.)

Tags are supplied to canvas methods to select which items to operate upon; for example, this binding turns all fat lines and arcs into skinny lines and arcs. This allows the green canvas background to show through:

```
$canvas->CanvasBind('<Double-1>' =>
                    sub { $canvas->itemconfigure('path', -width => 1) });
```

Figure 39-8 shows the output of nz-tr1.

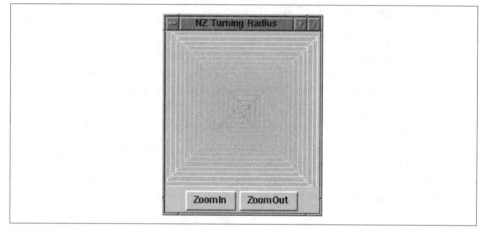

Figure 39-8. Non-zero turning radius lawnmowing

Scaling Canvas Items

A canvas can also be scaled to implement a primitive zoom function. Scaling adjusts each of the points defining an item by changing the points' distance from an origin by the scale factor. For example, this code uses the middle of the canvas as the origin and doubles the *x* and *y* coordinates of all items tagged with the string path. Scaling doesn't affect the line width, however.

```
my $origin = $SIDE / 2;

my $zi = $zf->Button(qw/-text ZoomIn -command/ =>
                    [$canvas => 'scale', 'path', $origin, $origin, 2.0, 2.0]);
```

After a few presses of the ZoomIn button we see the detail shown in Figure 39-9.

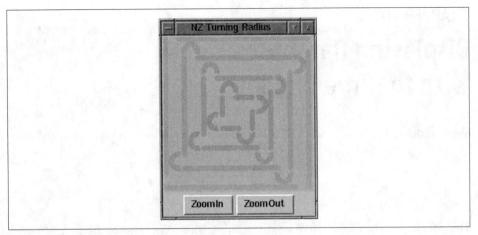

Figure 39-9. Zooming in on our lawnmowing

The Real World Is Uncertain

I can't mow as nicely as the robot. As I turn my tractor it continues to move forward, so the turning arc is almost teardrop in shape. My mowing surface is sloping and bumpy, and I don't always start and finish turns at the same time. No two turns are identical. My sloppiness often leads to uncut grass, as illustrated in Figure 39-10.

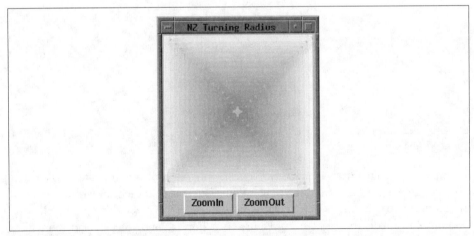

Figure 39-10. A little grass left uncut

I realized this was more like reality, and the global view of the situation gave me an idea. Modifying the program, I used two lines to paint a large X on the canvas, and a few trials later found that this code sufficed to cut the remaining grass:

```
$canvas->createLine(0, 0, $SIDE, $SIDE, -width => (2 * $CUT)+0.5, -fill => 'yellow');
$canvas->createLine($SIDE, 0, 0, $SIDE, -width => (2 * $CUT)+0.5, -fill => 'yellow');
```

The magic number was two mower widths, a trip up and back each diagonal. Last year I went out and performed the experiment, and the results agreed nicely with theory.

CHAPTER 40

Displaying Databases with the Tree Widget

Steve Lidie

This article discusses Perl/Tk's Tk::Tree widget, which displays hierarchical data in a tree format. In computer science, a tree is a data structure that starts at a *root node* and branches to other nodes, which can be *internal* nodes or *leaf* nodes at the bottom of the tree. An internal node has one or more *child* nodes; it's called the *parent* of those nodes. (Any child node at the end of a branch is a leaf node, since it has no children.) Nodes sharing the same parent are *siblings*. Unlike a physical tree, the root node is usually shown at the top, and leaves at the bottom of the structure. See Figure 40-1.

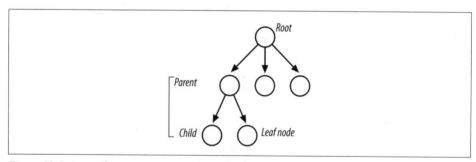

Figure 40-1. A sample tree

In contrast, Tk::Tree draws "sideways" trees, with the root node at the top left and branches growing down and to the right. While Tk::Tree is in the standard Perl/Tk distribution, there's another tree widget on CPAN: Tk::TreeGraph, by Dominique Dumont. I won't describe it here, but Figure 40-2 shows it, and you can read about it on the Perl/Tk modules page *http://www.Lehigh.EDU/~sol0/ddumont/ptk_module_list.html*.

Tk::Tree is derived from Tk::HList, the hierarchical list widget. From a programming point of view, Tree is *much* simpler to use because it masks the complexity of HList and automatically adds open and close buttons, thus exposing a much simpler interface. Figure 40-3 (interestingly enough, created using an HList widget), shows us the widget hierarchy of a Tree graphically. You can see that Tk::HList is a base class of Tk::Tree. For a detailed explanation of the Perl/Tk widget hierarchy, see Chapter 14, *Creating Custom Widgets in Pure Perl/Tk*, in O'Reilly's *Mastering Perl/Tk*.

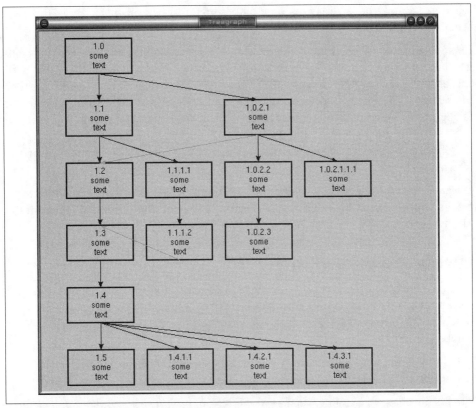

Figure 40-2. The Tk::TreeGraph widget in action.

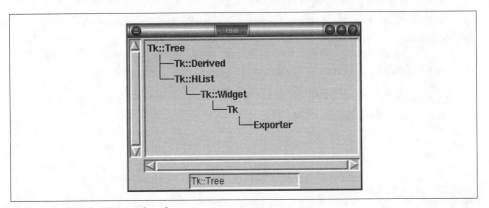

Figure 40-3. Widget hierarchy of a tree

The structure of a Tree is specified with an *entry path* when a node is created, consisting of one or more *entry names* separated by a character of your choosing, often a dot. This is analogous to a Unix or Windows file path name, in which the separator is a slash or reverse slash. Entry paths are simply the internal names used by Tk::Tree when generating the Tree layout. The names aren't drawn on the screen—there's a separate -text option for that.

As an example, suppose I have a database with several tables, and I'd like to visualize that structure. I might start by adding the root node and with the entry path tables. Let's say the first table is called video_catalog, because that's where I record interesting data about my video collection of DVDs, VHS tapes, and 8mm tapes. Giving it the entry path of tables.video_catalog would create a child node of the root. Now, for each DVD I could use entry paths of the form tables.video_catalog. dvd1, tables.video_catalog.dvd2, and so on, creating a series of siblings under the internal node tables.video_catalog.

If I had a second table of Tk widget information, I'd use an entry path of the form tables.widgets, and for each widget, entry paths of the form tables.widgets. widget1, and so on.

Using Databases from Perl

Since we are already talking of viewing a database, let's broaden the concept and write a simple database browser in Perl/Tk. I'll use MySQL, a popular and fast database that is freely available and relatively simple to use. Naturally I'll use DBI, Perl's database interface.

DBI allows you to manipulate every popular database engine from within Perl. If you haven't been using databases already, you need to do three things to get started:

1. Install a database engine, such as MySQL from *http://www.mysql.org/downloads*.
2. Install DBI from CPAN or *dbi.perl.org*.
3. Install the appropriate database driver; this is the database-dependent layer that mediates communiation between DBI and the database engine. If you chose MySQL, you'd install DBD::mysql; if you chose Oracle, you'd install DBD::Oracle. All database drivers are available on CPAN and at *dbi.perl.org*.

Fortunately, DBI and DBD utilize the standard Perl sequence for installing modules:

```
% perl Makefile.PL
% make
% make test
% make install
```

Ensure that the database is running before the DBD install—otherwise, the make test phase will fail.

Overview of the tkdb Application

Figure 40-4 shows us what the application looks like; you can find all of the code on the web page for this book: *http://www.oreilly.com/catalog/tpj2*. There's a Label widget at the top of the application displaying help instructions; please read them to learn what tkdb can do. Below the instructions is an Optionmenu that selects the database of interest, here tpj. Once that happens, the database tables are displayed in the Tree widget to the left. To the right of the Tree widget is an ROText widget that displays the results (and errors) of our activities. Next is a SQL Entry widget where the user can enter SQL select statements. And lastly, the Quit button that disconnects from the database server and exits the application.

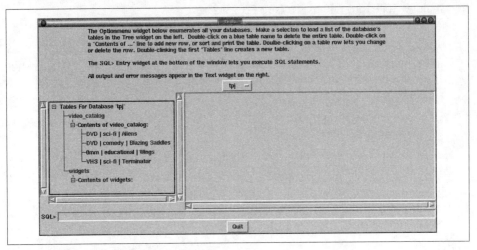

Figure 40-4. The tkdb application

We'll walk through the code in chunks.

```perl
#!/usr/local/bin/perl -w

use DBI;
use Tk;
use Tk::widgets qw/ItemStyle LabEntry ROText Tree/;
use subs qw/create_db_tree do_insert do_query get_input
            ins new_table update_db/;

use strict;

our ($DBH,              # The DBI database handle
     $GET_IN,           # Get user input window reference
     $MW,               # The Perl/Tk main window
     $RNUM,             # Unique row number
     $TNUM,             # Unique table number
     $ROTEXT,           # ROText widget reference
     $STYLE,            # Item style
     $TREE);            # Reference to the Tree widget

$RNUM = 1;              # Table row number
$TNUM = 1;              # DB table number
*ins = \&Tk::Error;     # Alias ins() to Tk::Error()

$MW = MainWindow->new;  # Our main window
```

I first import the DBI and Tk modules, as well as a number of Tk widgets, and I then predeclare some of the subroutines I'll be defining later. As always, my program uses the strict pragma.

The our declaration lists the program's global variables:

$DBH

> Database handle. The primary object for manipulating the database. To make an analogy, $DBH is to DBI as $MW is to Perl/Tk.

$GET_IN

> Widget reference to a Toplevel widget containing a single Entry widget I use to gather user input. The Toplevel widget is created once, and remains in a withdrawn state until needed.

$MW

> Main window of the application.

$RNUM and $TNUM

> Used to generate node entry paths; these variables are incremented after every row or table to keep entry paths unique. They are immediately initialized to 1 after the our declaration.

$ROTEXT

> Widget reference to the read-only text widget.

$STYLE

> Reference to a Tk::ItemStyle object. Item styles are used to configure Tree options like colors and fonts; with it, I can highlight tables names in blue.

$TREE

> Widget reference to the Tree widget.

Later, you'll learn more about the *ins glob in the second-to-last line, but for now it's sufficient to know that calling ins is just like calling Tk::Error. Soon, you'll also learn what Tk::Error does.

Building the Graphical Interface

Here is the help Label, simply a long string with double newlines wherever I want a paragraph break. As you can infer from the last two options, it's justified left in a window nine inches ("9i") wide.

```
$MW->Label(-text =>
    "The Optionmenu widget below enumerates all your databases.  Make " .
    "a selecton to load a list of the database's tables in the Tree " .
    "widget on the left.  Double-click on a blue table name to " .
    "delete the entire table. Double-click on a \"Contents of ...\" " .
    "line to add new row, or sort and print the table. Double-clicking " .
    "on a table row lets you change or delete the row. Double-clinking " .
    "the first \"Tables\" line creates a new table." .

    "\n\nThe SQL> Entry widget at the bottom of the window lets you " .
    "execute SQL statements." .
```

```
          "\n\nAll output and error messages appear in the Text widget on " .
          "the right.",
          -wraplength => '9i',
          -justify    => 'left',
    )->pack;
```

After the help Label, I create the Optionmenu containing the list of database tables:

```
my $db;
my (@dbs) = DBI->data_sources('mysql');
@dbs = map {m/.*:(.*)/} @dbs;

my $om = $MW->Optionmenu(-options => [reverse @dbs], -textvariable => \$db);
$om->pack;
$om->configure(
    -command => sub {create_db_tree($_[0], qw/db_user db_pw/)}
);
```

The DBI call to data_sources returns a list of databases of the form "DBI:mysql:db_ name", so the regular expression discards all but the database name. I add the database names to the Optionmenu in reverse order, since MySQL has two built-in databases and I want mine at the head of the list. The -command option is configured separately to inhibit an automatic invocation—it seems that during widget creation the -textvariable changes and the callback is triggered! But when the callback is legally invoked, create_db_tree is called with the database name, user name, and password. This subroutine actually builds the tree structure, as I'll explain shortly.

Now I create the container Frame that holds the scrolled Tree on the left and the scrolled ROText widget for collecting output and errors on the right:

```
my $frame = $MW->Frame->pack;

$TREE = $frame->Scrolled('Tree',
    -width => 40, -height => 20, -separator => '.',
    -itemtype => 'text', -relief => 'solid', -borderwidth => 2,
    -selectmode => 'single', -command => \&update_db,
);
$TREE->pack(qw/-side left/);

$STYLE = $TREE->ItemStyle('text');
$STYLE->configure(-foreground => 'blue');

$ROTEXT = $frame->Scrolled('ROText')->pack(qw/-side right/);
```

I chose the period as my entry path separator, set single select mode because I only want to process one Tree node at a time, and established a callback that's invoked when the user double clicks on a Tree entry. Finally, I make a text item style to colorize selected text entries. For complete details on item styles read the documentation on Tk::DItem (perldoc Tk::DItem).

Below, I create a LabEntry to accept and execute user select commands:

```
my $query;
my $le = $MW->LabEntry(
```

```
        -label       => 'SQL>',
        -labelPack   => [qw/-side left/],
        -textvariable => \$query,
    );
    $le->pack(qw/-fill x -expand 1/);
    $le->bind('<Return>' => sub {
        my ($fc, $rc, @rows) = do_query $_[0]->get;
        foreach my $row (@rows) {
            ins @$row;
        }
    });
```

The <Return> binding calls do_query, passing the SQL statement from the Entry widget and saving the results in the ROText widget. I'll explain do_query shortly, but,
briefly, it returns a list of lists: a list of table rows, each of which is a list of row fields.
The ins subroutine simply inserts a row into the ROText widget and positions the
widget so the last line is visible. As I mentioned earlier, you'll learn more about ins
and its relation to the Perl/Tk subroutine Tk::Error later.

To complete the interface, I build a Quit button that disconnects from the database
and exits the application. I also ensure that the callback is invoked even if the user
closes the window. Finally, MainLoop takes control:

```
    my $quit = sub {
        $DBH->disconnect if defined $DBH;
        exit;
    };
    $MW->protocol('WM_DESTROY_WINDOW' => $quit);
    $MW->Button(-text => 'Quit', -command => $quit)->pack;

    MainLoop;
```

Creating a Tree View of a Database

If you look back to Figure 40-4, you'll see that the database tpj is open and that its
two tables, video_catalog and widgets, are depicted in the Tree widget. The widgets
table is empty (it has no row data), but video_catalog has four rows. (tkdb caches
row data in individual node entries using the -data option.) The idea is to manipulate the row data locally and only update the database when the table is closed
(although I didn't implement this feature in the actual application).

The create_db_tree subroutine is responsible for opening a database and building a
tree structure of all the tables and the contents of their rows. With those thoughts in
mind, let's examine the code in detail:

```
    sub create_db_tree {
        my ($db, $user, $pw) = @_;
        $DBH = DBI->connect("dbi:mysql:$db", $user, $pw,
                            {PrintError => 0, RaiseError => 1});
        $TREE->deleteAll;

        my ($fc, $rc, @tables) = do_query 'show tables';
```

```
my $path = 'tables';
$TREE->add($path, -text => "Tables For Database '$db'");
$TREE->Activate($path, 'open');

foreach my $table (@tables) {

    my $tname = $table->[0];
    $path = new_table $path, $tname;

    my ($fc, $rc, @rows) = do_query "select * from $tname;";

    foreach my $row (@rows) {
        $TREE->add("$path.$RNUM",
                    -text => join(' | ', @$row),
                    -data => join(' | ', @$row),
                  );
        $RNUM++;
    }

    $path = 'tables';

} # forend

} # end create_db_tree
```

First, tkdb connects to the database and creates the database handle, $DBH. The PrintError and RaiseError attributes are important. Setting PrintError to a false value means that DBI will not call warn to display errors. Setting RaiseError to a true value, however, tells the DBI to call die. Normally this would terminate the program, but Perl/TK has a die handler to catch these errors, named Tk::Error. I've supplied my own Tk::Error so that it intercepts die calls and inserts the error message into the ROText widget. We'll see the connection between Tk::Error and ins eventually, I promise.

$TREE->deleteAll deletes all Tree nodes, in case there were any lying around from a previous call.

The do_query subroutine is called to fetch all the database table names, which are then stored in the array @tables. $fc is the field count (one in this case) and $rc is the row count (the number of tables).

Next, we add the root node of the Tree and open it. (The Activate method also draws the plus and minus boxes.)

Finally, we iterate over all the table names, calling new_table to actually add the node entry. Remember that @tables is really a list of lists, but the second list has only one field—the table name. For each table, we fetch all the rows and add them as sibling nodes, saving the row data in the -data option, and displaying it with the -text option. For simplicity, fields in a row are delimited by a vertical bar. $RNUM ensures that every row of every table has a unique entry path.

Here is a listing of new_table, which adds a special node with a blue foreground color, followed by the Contents node, which it activates. $TNUM ensures that every table has a unique entry path.

```
sub new_table {
    my ($path, $tname) = @_;

    $TREE->add("$path.$tname", -text => $tname, -style => $STYLE);
    $path = "tables.$tname.$TNUM";
    $TNUM++;
    $TREE->add($path, -text => "Contents of $tname:");
    $TREE->Activate($path, 'open');

    $path;

}
```

The do_query subroutine prepares and executes an SQL select statement, returning the number of fields per row, the number of rows, and the contents of all the rows as a list of lists.

```
sub do_query {
    my $query = shift;

    my $sth = $DBH->prepare($query);
    $sth->execute;

    my @rows;
    while ( my @row = $sth->fetchrow_array ) { push @rows, [@row] }

    ($sth->{'NUM_OF_FIELDS'}, scalar @rows, @rows);

}
```

Making Changes to a Database

As the user double clicks on different tree nodes, various actions take place. For instance, he or she can click on a Contents node to add a new row, and clicking on the name of a row allows it to be modified or deleted. When user input is required, I popup an Entry box, let the user type their input, hide the Entry and return the data. This is all done with the get_input subroutine:

```
sub get_input {
    my ($data, $msg) = @_;

    unless (Exists $GET_IN) {
        $GET_IN = $MW->Toplevel;
        $GET_IN->geometry("400x100");
        $GET_IN->{m} = $GET_IN->Message->pack;
        $GET_IN->{e} = $GET_IN->Entry->pack;
        $GET_IN->{b} = $GET_IN->Button(-text => 'Done')->pack;
    }

    my $done = 0;
```

```
$GET_IN->{m}->configure(-text          => $msg);
$GET_IN->{e}->configure(-textvariable => \$data);
$GET_IN->{b}->configure(-command       => sub {$done++});
$GET_IN->deiconify;

$GET_IN->waitVariable(\$done);
$GET_IN->withdraw;

return $data;
    }
```

Rather than creating the input window over and over, I use Exists to see whether it already exists. If not, I create the window, consisting of a Message widget with instructions, the Entry widget, and a Button to withdraw the window. Subsequent calls to get_input realize that the window already exists and simply reconfigure the widgets and deiconify the window.

But there is a trick here: the Message, Entry, and Button widgets need to be reconfigured every time this subroutine is called, since \$msg, \$data, and \$done change each time. This is because the variables are lexically scoped, and Perl/Tk only remembers the last reference. That's why I store the widget references as Toplevel instance variables for easy access.

Double clicking on a node invokes update_db, the master subroutine (not shown in its entirety due to its length) that figures out how to handle such events. By examining the node's entry path and -data option, update_db can differentiate between the various nodes and call the appropriate handler. If a node's -data option is defined, then the user wants to modify or delete a row. Otherwise, I pattern match on the entry path and perform other tasks, like deleting any tables.

For instance, when the user wants to modify or delete a row, update_db gets the user's input, and if the input is defined the Tree and database are updated. If it's not defined, the user must want to delete the row, so update_db removes the data from the Tree and database. In both cases, the ins subroutine appends useful information to the ROText widet, as this portion of the update_db subroutine shows:

```
$data = get_input $data, 'Make changes or clear to delete.';
if ($data) {
    ins $data;
    $TREE->entryconfigure($path, -data => $data, -text => $data);
    # update DB table here
} else {
    ins 'row deleted';
    $TREE->deleteEntry($path);
    # update DB table here
}
```

Similarly, to add a new row to a table I first add a new node to the Tree and then insert the row into the table:

```
$data = get_input $data, 'Enter new row or clear to ignore.';
return unless $data;
```

```
$TREE->add("$path.$RNUM",
            -text => $data,
            -data => $data);
$RNUM++;
do_insert $tname, split /\|/, $data;
ins $data;
```

Here's do_insert, which expects a table name and a list of row fields. The field values are quoted before insertion into the database.

```
sub do_insert {
    my $table = shift;

    my $query = "insert into $table values(" .
        join(',', map {$DBH->quote($_)} @_ ) . ");";
    my $sth = $DBH->prepare($query);
    $sth->execute;

}
```

To delete a table, users can simply click on its node, which invokes this code:

```
my $answer = $MW->messageBox(
    -message => "OK to delete table '$tname'?",
    -type    => 'okcancel',
    -default => 'cancel',
);
return if $answer =~ /cancel/i;

$TREE->deleteEntry($path);
$DBH->do("drop table $tname;");
ins "table '$tname' deleted";
```

The Tk::Error Subroutine

As I mentioned at the top of this article, the following glob statement:

```
*ins = \&Tk::Error;          # Alias ins() to Tk::Error
```

makes ins a synonym for Tk::Error, so that calling either ins or Tk::Error does the same thing. Tk::Error is Perl/Tk's die handler, called with a widget reference and an error message string as arguments. I've hijacked Tk::Error, and instead of messages going to STDERR (or a Dialog if a use Tk::ErrorDialog is in effect), I append them to the ROText widget instead.

```
sub Tk::Error {
    $ROTEXT->insert('end', "@_\n");
    $ROTEXT->yview('end');
}
```

Since I update the ROText widget in many places, the Perl virtue of laziness compelled me to use a short subroutine name like ins—and then to avoid writing ins by piggybacking on Tk::Error.

Index

We'd like to hear your suggestions for improving our indexes. Send email to *index@oreilly.com*.

About the Authors

Dan Brian (Chapter 23, *Wireless Surfing with WAP and WML*) is a composer, linguist, mentalist, gamer, and father of two. By day he masquerades as a software engineer at Verio, Inc., working on the next-generation of globalized hosting and messaging products.

Sean M. Burke (Chapter 14, *Scanning HTML*) is a columnist for *The Perl Journal*, a language technologist for Native American language preservation projects, and an all-around freelance roustabout and jackanapes. He is also the author of the popular O'Reilly book, *Perl & LWP*. His professional interests include markup languages and computational linguistics. He is one of the most prolific CPAN authors. Among his best-known modules are MIDI-Perl, for composing and processing MIDI music files; the current generation of HTML::TreeBuilder, for building parse trees of HTML documents; and Class::Classless, a framework for classless OOP. He lives in Juneau, Alaska, and in his spare time, he sleeps, reads the *Guardian*, and obeys his feline overlord, Fang Dynasty. He can be reached at *sburke@cpan.org*.

Alligator Descartes (Chapter 27, *OpenGL*) has been an itinerant fiddler with computers from a very early age, which was ruined only by obtaining a BSc in computer science from the University of Strathclyde, Glasgow. His computing credits include several years of Oracle DBA work, multi-user Virtual Reality servers, high-performance 3D graphics programming, and several Perl modules. He spends his spare time trudging around Scotland looking for stone circles and Pictish symbol stones to photograph. Alligator Descartes is not his real name.

Mark Jason Dominus (Chapter 28, *Ray Tracing*) is an itinerant freelance Perl trainer. He is the author of the Text::Template, Algorithm::Diff, Interpolation, and Memoize modules, and his work on the Rx regular expression debugger won the 2001 Larry Wall Award for Practical utility. He was for a time the managing editor of *www.perl.com*, is the author of the perlreftut man page, and is a moderator of the comp.lang.perl.moderated newsgroup. His book, tentatively titled *Perl Advanced Techniques Handbook*, will be published in 2003 by Morgan Kaufmann, unless he dies of it first.

When he is not teaching Perl, he lives in Philadelphia with his wife and a large number of toy octopuses.

Mike Fletcher (Chapter 6, *Creating mod_perl Applications*) is Network Operations Manager for StayOnline.net, where he currently plays with POE more than mod_ perl. Fletch once wrote several chapters about Java for several editions of *Java Unleashed* (ISBN 1-57521-298-6; look for it in fine remainder bins everywhere). He lives in Atlanta, Georgia, with his wife Cathy, kids Stuart and Carissa, and two dogs Phydeaux and Reauxvur. He can be found at *http://phydeaux.org/* and *fletch+botpj@phydeaux.org*.

Daniel Gruhl (Chapter 11, *Five Quick Hacks: Downloading Web Pages*) is a Research Staff Member at IBM's Almaden Research Center, where he works on local area distributed computation systems for text analytics. His other professional interests include steganography and privacy-preserving data mining. He lives in San Jose, CA and in his spare time, he mountain bikes and climbs. He can be reached at *druid@alum.mit.edu*.

Ed Hill (Chapter 16, *webpluck*) is the author of Webpluck.

Joe Johnston (Chapter 19, *Building Web Sites with Mason*) is an independent contractor, co-author of O'Reilly's *Programming Web Services with XML-RPC*, and a contributor to IBM's developerWorks web site. For contact information, please see *http://taskboy.com*.

Marc Lehmann (Chapter 32, *Capturing Video in Real Time*) studies Informatics at the University of Karlsruhe, but too often he hacks on things like gcc, Gimp, and a lot of Perl.

Steve Lidie (Chapter 34, *Getting Started with Perl/Tk*, Chapter 36, *The Mouse Odometer*, Chapter 37, *Events*, Chapter 38, *The Pack and Grid Geometry Managers*, Chapter 39, *Drawing on a Canvas*, and Chapter 40, *Displaying Databases with the Tree Widget*) is co-author of *Mastering Perl/Tk* and author of the *Perl/Tk Pocket Reference*, both published by O'Reilly. He works at Lehigh University, where he programs Perl as much as possible and manages the University's large-scale computing environment.

Doug MacEachern (Chapter 5, *mod_perl*) is the creator of mod_perl and co-author of O'Reilly's *Writing Apache Modules with Perl and C*.

Ken MacFarlane (Chapter 13, *HTML::Parser*) recently relocated to Columbus, OH, where his new job allows him to cook some occasional Perl while concentrating on enterprise systems management. Ken also wrote the Image::DeAnim module as a way to prevent image animation in web browsers, before it became an option in some modern browers. When not working or doing other Perlish things, Ken spends most of his time trying to keep up with his two sons, Timothy and Christopher. Ken can be reached at *kenmacf@cpan.org*.

Joe Nasal (Chapter 31, *Gnome Panel Applets*) does Software, Systems, and Data Network Engineering and Design. In his spare time, he's heavily into PalmOS development and playing chess. He's proud to be both a graduate of Temple University and father of Ben and Owen. He can be reached at *jnasal@yahoo.com*.

Jon Orwant (Chapter 33, *A Perl/Tk Roadmap*, and Chapter 35, *Scoreboard: A 15-Minute Perl/Tk Application*) founded *The Perl Journal* and served all editorial and production roles through TPJ #13, and remained editor-in-chief until TPJ #20. He is a co-author of *Programming Perl* and *Mastering Algorithms with Perl*, was CTO of O'Reilly, and now creates AI-laced communication systems for French Telecom and teaches game design at MIT. He can be reached at *orwant@media.mit.edu*.

Michael Parker (Chapter 8, *Authentication with mod_perl*) is a Software Developer who developed the Apache::AuthenSmb module, which does NT user authentication for the Apache web server. His primary interests are solving Web/Internet-related problems. He lives in Austin, Texas, and enjoys scuba diving in his spare time. He can be reached at *parkerm@pobox.com*.

Jason Reed (Chapter 26, *GD and L-Systems*) lives in Pittsburgh, Pennsylvania, where he is finishing up his undergrad at Carnegie Mellon University. He is the author of ptkfonted, a Perl/Tk editor for X11 bitmap fonts. Even after becoming a card-carrying academic programming-language weenie, he still uses Perl for lots of things, from lowly system administration to computer music. In his spare time, he spreads the gospel of category theory. He can be contacted at *jcreed@andrew.cmu.edu*.

Tony Rose (Chapter 22, *Summarizing Web Pages with HTML::Summary*) has a background in natural language processing and has published widely in the area of speech and language technology. His research interests include natural language interfaces and information retrieval.

Aaron Sherman (Chapter 29, *Perl and the Gimp*) has been programming in Perl since Version 3 and using the Gimp since the 0.99's. He is the author of the Gimp image-tile plug-in and the File::Copy module that comes with Perl.

Lincoln D. Stein (Chapter 2, *CGI Programming*, Chapter 3, *Saving CGI State*, Chapter 4, *Cookies*, Chapter 5, *mod_perl*, Chapter 7, *Proxying with mod_perl*, Chapter 9, *Navigation Bars with mod_perl*, Chapter 10, *Scripting the Web with LWP*, Chapter 17, *Torture-Testing Web Servers and CGI Scripts*, Chapter 18, *Securing Your CGI Scripts*, Chapter 20, *Surreal HTML*, Chapter 21, *Web Page Tastefulness*, and Chapter 24, *Web Plots with Gnuplot*) is a researcher at the Cold Spring Harbor Laboratory and is the co-author of *Writing Apache Modules with Perl and C* (O'Reilly), *Networking Programming with Perl* and *How to Set Up and Maintain a Web Site* (Addison-Wesley), and *Official Guide to Programming with CGI.pm* (Wiley). He is the author of the Perl CGI module and the World Wide Web Security FAQ.

Rob Svirskas (Chapter 12, *Downloading Web Pages Through a Proxy Server*) plays with computers for a living. After escaping from school with a degree in computer science, he went to work for Motorola's Paging Division in Computer Integrated Manufacturing (or, as the people on the factory floor call it, Computer Interrupted Manufacturing). In 1997, he shifted gears to work in bioinformatics and hasn't looked back since. He is currently a bioinformatician with Amersham Biosciences. He also continues to participate in the Berkeley Drosophila Genome Project as a guest bioinformatician. As eclectic as Rob thinks his career has been, he's put to shame by his wife (field geologist, accountant, and mother). Rob and his wife spend much of their time trying to keep up with their two children, and unsuccessfully attempting to convince their cat that he is their pet (and not the other way around).

Ace Thompson's (Chapter 30, *Glade*) main professional interests are in simulation and computational software. He works for Boeing creating simulation software and simulation software tools. Born and raised in the Sonoran desert, he appreciates long runs in the rain. You can almost reach him at *acethompson@yahoo.com*.

Tkil (Chapter 15, *A Web Spider in One Line*) can be reached at *tkil@scrye.com*.

Jeremy Wadsack (Chapter 25, *GD-Graph3d*) tries to eat five meals a day (and six on Sundays!). When he's not trying to coerce other programming languages to be more like Perl, he rock climbs, mountain bikes, and hikes. He's growing bored of permanent residences but can often be reached at *jwadsack@wadsack-allen.com*.

Ave Wrigley (Chapter 22, *Summarizing Web Pages with HTML::Summary*) heads up the New Media Development team at ITN, and has developed several Perl modules, mostly to do with the Web (e.g., HTML::Index, HTML::Summary, WWW::(Simple)?Robot, Net::SMS::Genie). He lives in London, plays squash and soccer badly, and is learning to paint.

Colophon

Our look is the result of reader comments, our own experimentation, and feedback from distribution channels. Distinctive covers complement our distinctive approach to technical topics, breathing personality and life into potentially dry subjects.

The animal on the cover of *Web, Graphics, and Perl/Tk: Best of the Perl Journal* is an emu (*Dromaius novaehollandiae*). This large, flightless bird is found throughout the Australian bush steppes. The emu is one of the largest birds in existence, second only to its cousin, the ostrich. Adult emus stand about 5 feet high and weigh up to 120 pounds. The grayish-brown emu's small wings contain only six or seven feathers. They are hidden by the long, hairlike rump plumage. Emus have extremely long legs, which they use as defensive and offensive weapons when fighting. A human limb can be broken by a kick from an emu. Their powerful legs make emus strong swimmers and fast runners; they can reach speeds of up to 50 kilometers per hour.

Male emus, which are slightly smaller than females, tend to the incubation of eggs and the raising of the young. An emu nest contains as many as fifteen to twenty-five deep green eggs, laid by several hens. Incubation of the eggs takes from twenty-five to sixty days. The large discrepancy in incubation time occurs because the male needs to leave the nest periodically to find food and drink. The length of time he is away affects the time for incubation. Newly hatched emus weigh about 15 ounces. They are fully grown at two to three years.

The relationship between emus and Australian farmers has always been adversarial; three coastal subspecies of emu have been exterminated. Because emus can jump over high fences, it is difficult to keep them out of fields, where they eat and trample crops. In the arid Australian bush, emus also compete with cattle and sheep for grass and water. On the other hand, emus eat many insects that would otherwise eat crops. In 1932, Australian farmers declared war on the emus, making an all-out effort to eradicate them. Fortunately, the effort failed. The battle between emus and farmers continues to this day.

Colleen Gorman was the production editor and the copyeditor for *Web, Graphics, and Perl/Tk: Best of the Perl Journal*. Claire Cloutier, Genevieve d'Entremont, and Jane Ellin provided quality control. Tom Dinse wrote the index.

Hanna Dyer and Ellie Volckhausen designed the cover of this book, based on a series design by Edie Freedman. The cover image is a 19th-century engraving from *Johnson's Natural History II*. Emma Colby produced the cover layout with Quark-XPress 4.1 using Adobe's ITC Garamond font.

David Futato designed the interior layout. Erik Ray, Mike Sierra, and Neil Walls converted the files from pod to FrameMaker 5.5.6. The text font is Linotype Birka; the heading font is Adobe Myriad Condensed; and the code font is LucasFont's TheSans Mono Condensed. The illustrations that appear in the book were produced by Robert Romano and Jessamyn Read using Macromedia FreeHand 9 and Adobe

Photoshop 6. The tip and warning icons were drawn by Christopher Bing. This colophon was written by Clairemarie Fisher O'Leary.